DE CRISTOFORO'S COMPLETE BOOK OF
POWER TOOLS
Both Stationary and Portable

DE CRISTOFORO'S COM

POWE

Both

A Popular Science Book

POPULAR SCIENCE PUBLISHING COMPANY, INC. □ HARPER & ROW

PLETE BOOK OF

R TOOLS

Stationary and Portable

by R. J. De Cristoforo

New York, Evanston, San Francisco, London

Library of Congress Catalog Card Number: 72-90935
SBN: 60-010999-8

Third Printing, 1975

Designed by Jeff Fitschen

Manufactured in the United States of America

to Mary

FOREWORD

R. J. De Cristoforo, Master of Tools

In 1951 a tall, dark-haired young man appeared in my New York editorial office, announced that he was moving to California, and said he hoped *Popular Science* would have lots of writing jobs for him.

I knew the man then only as the contributor of occasional brief articles from a New York address. But during the intervening two decades the name of R. J. De Cristoforo became familiar to all of us at *Popular Science* and De Cris himself has returned to visit on many enjoyable occasions.

For me, the arrival of a new article from De Cris was always a welcome event, and I shoved other work aside to see what new and surprising ideas his manuscript and perfectly executed photos contained. I was rarely disappointed. His assignments from us were always faultlessly executed. But it was in the articles that De Cris developed on his own initiative that his imagination and ingenuity in the use of power tools came into fullest flower. The jigs and shopmade accessories that he designed and made extend the usefulness of various tools far beyond what even the manufacturers claim for them. In the *use* of tools, R. J. De Cristoforo has been a true pioneer. To those of us who have watched him develop, De Cris has, without doubt, become the outstanding tool authority in the world. This book contains most of his best work.

Universities often reward achievement with honorary degrees. I believe De Cris is worthy of one—and I hereby offer the idea to any institution that wishes to honor both itself and a leader in the world of tools. Make it, officially, R. J. De Cristoforo, *Master of Tools*.

For that's what the man is!

Robert P. Stevenson

Formerly, Home and Shop Editor,
now Director of Plans and Projects,
Popular Science

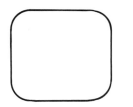

CONTENTS

PREFACE

Over the past twenty years or so there has been one author in the home shop and tool field whose work has shone out like a beacon in the night. That author is R. J. De Cristoforo. He has helped many thousands of home craftsmen to do better and more imaginative work with power tools through his articles in *Popular Science*, other magazines, and his books. His clear, crisp writing style and brilliantly demonstrated techniques are universally admired. His inventiveness and versatility with jigs, guides, and other innovations to extend the uses of power tools are unsurpassed.

Now the great fruitage of his life's work is presented in these pages, freshly rewritten and coordinated to give the reader a veritable treasury of instructions and imaginative techniques for use with every kind of power tool.

The reader interested in the big stationary tools will find all of the information he wants in Section I, while the reader who prefers the portable power tools will find what he needs in Section II. It is all here for each home tool enthusiast to study and to emulate, or to merely page through and enjoy the wizardry of a true craftsman.

WILLIAM B. SILL, Publisher
Book Division
Popular Science Publishing Company

INTRODUCTION

Nothing irritates me more than the comment that individual craftsmanship is dead. The people I know, and many who have sent me snapshots of their projects, are not from another world. They live in every state—in apartments, private homes, and on farms. They live in countries I may never see, and some of them still use foot power to run a lathe.

Some are affluent, some are poor; some make bread-and-butter money working behind a desk, or turning screws on an assembly line, or by safeguarding a forest, or by mixing cement. They all have one thing in common: the desire to originate.

The urge to make something has not been destroyed by technology or mechanization, and more and more young people today are turning to craftsmanship as a means of self-expression.

I'm convinced that more creative talent goes unrecognized than is ever honored with a ribbon or museum acceptance. There is a universal beehive of creativity with cells in some highly unlikely places—a closet in an apartment, a carport, a mobile home, a corner in an attic, a basement, garage, tool shed; any place the worker can set up his tools.

Anyone can learn to use tools. If you start today, you will not be an expert by tomorrow, but the time will come more quickly than you might expect.

This book takes the reader's point of view throughout. If you are a beginner, start from page one in each chapter. If you've made a table or two, you can probably skip some basic information but you *should* scan it, at least, since you may find a hint, a jig or two that will suggest a change in some technique you have adhered to.

If you are very knowledgeable about power tools, you can be selective but do be aware of everything that's here. This book really took about thirty years to produce and it is done in depth.

I'd like to stress the importance of safety in the shop. I've always been a little afraid of power tools; hence I still have all my fingers and no scars. That slight fear is healthy. If you allow yourself to become overconfident (as some craftsmen will attest) you will become vulnerable. You *are* the master of the tool so have no qualms there, but at the same time, remember that the tool is disinterested in what you put there for it to cut.

Follow all procedures as they are outlined. Don't be embarrassed to try a dry run before you flick the switch.

A lot of people deserve thanks for their help in producing this book: readers who have written to me through the years; editors, some gone, some still badgering me about deadlines and grammar; power tool manufacturers too numerous to list; photographers. At the start of my career in New York City, the Santerella brothers photographed the first story I every sold, posed for pictures, stole the props. Later, in California, Gene Smith did a lot of work on my first books. Then came William (Chuck) Eymann, who always kidded me about not shooting my own pictures and then got mad at me when I did. The bulk of the illustrations in this book are Chuck's or mine, and if you can't tell the difference it's because I learned by watching one of the best photographers in the country.

R. J. De Cristoforo
September, 1972

PART I

STATIONARY TOOLS

TABLE SAWS

The magic in a table saw is there for all to use. Anyone who has used a handsaw and then accomplished similar chores under power knows the value of this basic machine. The increase in production and the decrease in expended energy by no means cover its total usefulness. The gain in accuracy because the machine is organized to minimize the possibility of human error is more impressive.

Straight, square, and smooth cuts become automatic, allowing you to concentrate on the creative end. Anyone can flick the switch, and the tool will respond uninfluenced by whether the operator is an amateur or professional. The span between the novice and the expert is bridged by knowledge of the tool and its myriad practical applications and making fullest use of them.

GENERAL CHARACTERISTICS

Types. All table saws have the same general characteristics. A saw blade is mounted on an arbor that is turned by a motor; the blade projects through a table on which the work is rested. The table is slotted to receive a miter gauge and is organized to accommodate a laterally adjustable rip fence. Blade projection, miter-gauge head and blade angularity are controllable.

The question of selecting a table saw on the basis of whether it has a tilting arbor or a tilting table seems a moot point since it's rather difficult to find a tool today that provides only for tilting the table rather than the blade. It is true that there are plenty of ShopSmith model table saws around, and this multi-purpose tool does employ a tilting table. However, since the tilting

BASIC PARTS OF THE TABLE SAW

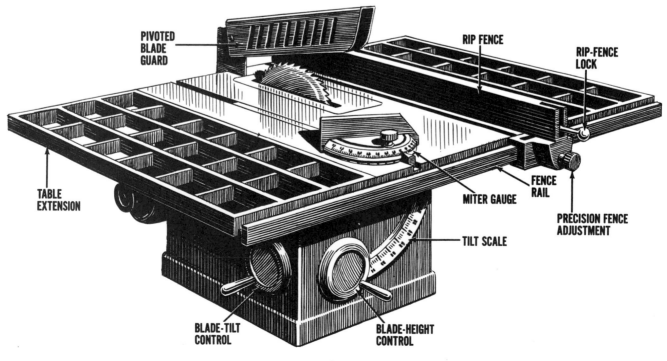

arbor is the predominant feature of most table saws these days, it would waste space to argue the subject. Furthermore, even if you choose to buy a ShopSmith, you shouldn't judge it on the basis of this one factor.

More important with individual tools are capacity, power, and physical machine size. All the table saws available will accomplish all the necessary operations. For more power and bigger tables with larger blades, you naturally spend more money, and there is no doubt that the bigger units are nice to have. But, fortunately, it is the guy behind the tool who is important: the painstaking craftsman with an 8″ saw can turn out better work than the less dedicated 10″ saw owner.

Safety. To talk about safety in relation to the table saw would be to fill this book with "do's" and "don't's," and this approach would not reduce the responsibility of the operator. It's simply wise to accept the fact that any machine designed to cut wood can hurt you. Therefore, a constant respect for the machine is necessary to operate it safely. Become professional but never so confident that you become nonchalant. Use the guards and when they can't be used, know that you are exposed to a more dangerous situation and behave accordingly.

Correctly aligned tools, clean tools, sharp tools, and a clean shop are all important safety factors. Carefully follow the safety procedures outlined in your owner's manual and, most importantly, always keep your hands away from the cutting area. Proper hand positions, feed speeds, use of push sticks, alignment of components, work supports, etc. are as vital as accomplishing the job in good fashion.

Adjustments. A table saw consists of parts bolted and screwed together. If any part slips, even just a bit, you lose the precision that was built into the machine. Therefore, any table saw should be checked thoroughly when it is new and regularly thereafter.

While methods of adjustment can vary from saw to saw, the correct relationship of components is the same. Doing the job is just a question of carefully following the instructions that are in the owner's manual that comes with the tool. Again, the beginner is on a par with the pro. There is no reason why a novice can't set up his machine just as accurately as anyone. However, his first problem may be an inability to analyze the reasons for getting poor results with his work.

There are checks you can employ as you work, and these will feed you a constant stream of information on how accurate the tool is. One of the most basic checks is to frequently apply a square to a ripped edge or a crosscut end. If the square tells you the cut isn't right, you know you must check to find out why.

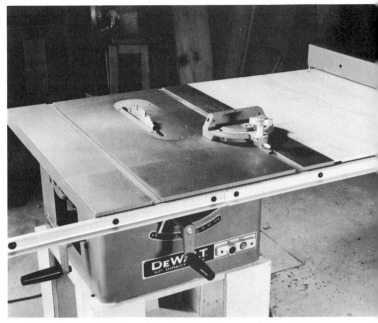

9″ saw is more in line with what the homecraftsman thinks about. 9″ or 10″ saw has very good capacity for all the work you are likely to do and in such sizes, prices are more reasonable. Here, long rails permit using a panel as a table extension.

12″ table saw is a large capacity unit that has a maximum depth of cut of $3\frac{9}{16}$″ and, with the extensions, can cut in the center of a panel 76″ wide. It takes a lot of "oomph"—3 to 4 *hp*—to run a saw like this efficiently.

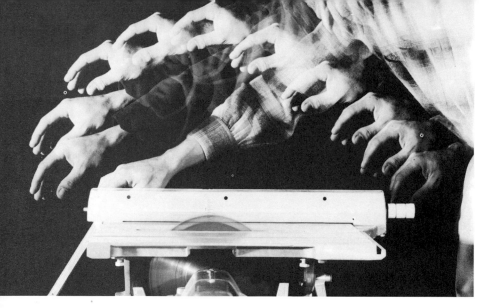

The table saw "arc of safety". The whole point is to keep your hands away from the saw blade especially after a pass. Make it a habit to exaggerate the height at which you bring your hand back to the front-table position.

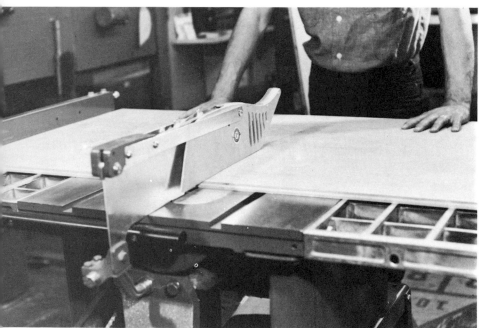

Some saws come equipped with a guard. On others you buy the guard as an accessory. Having one, *using one* makes sense. As you can see here, for most jobs, the guard will cover the saw blade. We don't always show it simply because it would interfere with the illustrations.

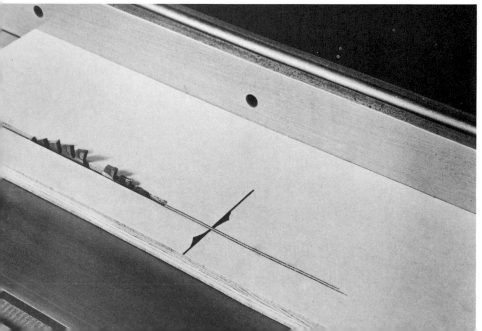

The "kerf" is that slot normally formed by the saw blade (arrows). Its width will differ depending on the style, the gauge and the amount of "set" on teeth of the saw blade.

Another simple as-you-go check is to use a square to draw a crosscut line. If the blade doesn't stay on that line as you cut, the miter gauge requires attention.

Three important alignment rules apply to any table saw. (1) The table slots, the rip fence and the saw blade must all be parallel. (2) The rip fence, the saw blade and the miter-gauge head must all be perpendicular to the table surface. (3) When the miter gauge is in the normal crosscut position, it must be at right angles to the blade and the rip fence.

Since the blade mounting, which is seated on the arbor, is the one thing over which you have no control, it's wise to start all alignment checks by determining whether the table slots are parallel to the saw blade. All other checks are made on the basis of this important relationship.

Since eliminating human error is an important factor in doing accurate work, it's wise to equip yourself with gauge tools. These tools you can make yourself, but you must be most careful with the construction. The idea is to make them to perfection and to care for them so they will remain precise checking tools. While the previous rules call for parallelism between the rip fence and the saw blade, it's not bad practice to be a bit generous at the rear of the blade so the "rear" teeth of the blade will not scrape the wood after the "front" teeth have cut. This offset kind of adjustment can reduce roughness in the cut and minimize feathering.

While blade projection is not an alignment factor, it's still a good idea to equip yourself with gauges that lead to accuracy, not so much for routine cutting where the blade projects through the work but for work like rabbeting, blind kerfing, and dadoing.

Saw blades. The blade that comes with the machine will be a combination type, designed to do both crosscutting and ripping. It will be an efficient blade but not the very best blade you can get for either type of cut.

It would be nice if one blade could do all kinds of jobs, but considering the nature of wood and the variety of materials the home craftsman works with, the results he seeks are so varied that it really isn't possible. On some jobs you may want a cut edge so smooth it looks sanded. On some particularly rough, extensive work, you might want to use an inexpensive blade that you can throw away rather than sharpen. On some jobs you may seek a blade that is less likely to feather or tear out wood at the end of the cut, or a blade that keeps kerf loss to a minimum for fine decorative work.

It would be expensive, and probably uncalled for, to equip yourself immediately with blades to meet all eventualities. It makes more sense to gradually increase

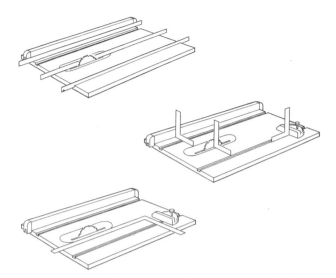

The three basic alignment rules for any table saw. Unless you are aware of these and check periodically to see that they are maintained, you will not function efficiently.

After you are sure that the table slots are parallel to the saw blade, check with a carpenter's square of the "0" setting of the miter-gauge head. No point being careless with this kind of thing. It has to be right.

You can make an L-shaped block to check miter-gauge settings or use it whenever a cross-angular cut is required. Be sure of accuracy by using a protractor to lay out the cut lines. Precision is a must here.

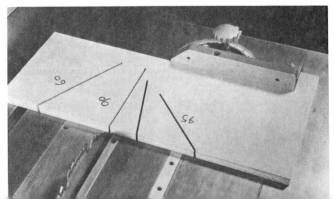

Making special gauges to check miter gauge and saw blade positions for most commonly used angular settings is good practice. You can't always trust the calibrations on tools.

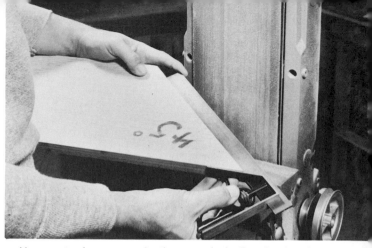

You must, of course, make them precisely. Best bet is to lay them out with a protractor, make a rough cut close to the line, and then finish *exactly* by sanding.

This kind of gauge can be used to set blade tilt more precisely than you might be able to do merely by using the scales on the machine. Again, place a protractor on the board and mark the lines carefully.

This is a more sophisticated cutter projection gauge. It is more accurate than holding a scale up next to the blade. Use this gauge with a saw blade, dado, or molding head.

Distance between rip fence and blade at "A" and "B" should be equal unless you offset a fraction at "B" so "rear" teeth won't be rubbing the wood after the "front" teeth have made the cut, (see text).

The post is made of two pieces, glued together after the groove is formed. Graduations are laid out on paper which is then glued to the side of the post.

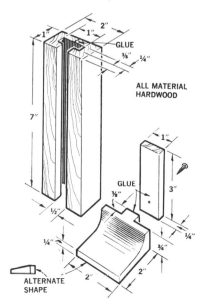

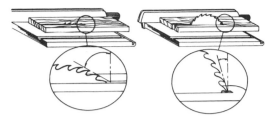

Little blade projection (left) gives long cutting angle. High projection is more efficient but also more dangerous. For most cuts, safer practice is achieved by limiting projection to not more than the deepest gullet on the blade.

your assortment of blades as you do more and more work and become more familiar with the table saw.

If you do a lot of work with plywood as most craftsmen do, you'll want to think immediately about getting a special plywood-cutting blade. This blade is designed to stand up under the abrasive action of the material while producing smooth cuts with minimum feathering. Without this special blade, you should work with a crosscut blade when cutting plywood. Its many small teeth will do a better job than the fewer, larger teeth of a combination blade.

Blade teeth tend to become clogged with sawdust and resin, which cause dragging during the cut. Clean frequently, using a resin solvent when necessary, and apply light coating of oil to prevent rusting.

Most blades have set teeth to produce a kerf that is wider than the blade gauge and so provide clearance. The hollow-ground blade, which is very nice for miters and similar cuts, does not have set teeth. Kerf width at the points of the teeth is the same as the blade gauge. It gets clearance because the area of the blade buried in the work during the cut is ground thinner. That's why such a blade should get more projection. If it doesn't, it will burn itself and/or the work. Too little projection will most certainly dull it faster.

A 55 tooth carbide blade is often very popular. It's expensive, but it stays on the machine through countless hours of cutting materials that include hardwoods, hardboards, plywood, laminates, plastics, and even nonferrous metals. Cut results are fine, and with good care it should last for as long as you care to use it.

No matter what blade you use, some attention to how fast you feed the work can result in better cuts. A slow feed is always better. You can prove this simply by making two crosscuts on the same piece of stock, one very quickly, the other very slowly. The slow feed will allow more teeth to pass over a given area of the wood, and the result will be smoother. The slow feed is especially important at the end of the cut when the blade breaks through. It will minimize splintering and feathering.

CUTTING PROCEDURES

Crosscutting. A simple crosscut is made by placing the good edge of the stock against the miter gauge and moving both the gauge and work past the saw blade. Most times, the miter gauge is used in the left-hand slot; the right hand moves the miter gauge, the left hand snugs the work. Your position should be almost directly behind the miter gauge so you will be out of line with the saw

A gauge for setting saw blade (or dado) height can be made by laminating stepped back pieces of ⅛" plywood.

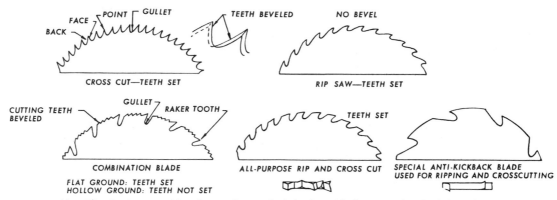

Use this chart as a guide when trying to find the best blade to use for the job on hand.

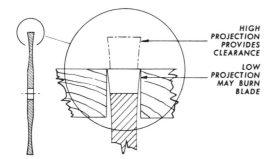

The hollow-ground blade must have more projection above the work than other blade styles. Otherwise the tips of the teeth will rub in the kerf and the wood or the blade, or both, will burn. Certainly, the blade will dull faster.

Blade sharpening in the home workshop hardly pays because the pros do a super job at reasonable prices. Cleaning the teeth, however, is a job you can, and should, do frequently. Use a stiff brush and resin solvent.

blade. Feed the work slowly, without pausing, until the cut is complete; then return both work and gauge to the starting position.

There will be variations of this basic procedure because of work size and types of cuts, but the important factors such as slow feed, good hand position for safety and proper support of the work should not change drastically. The size of the table and whether you have a table extension on one side of the blade or the other can influence in what slot you use the miter gauge. Your judgment should be based on what position provides the most support for the work.

When work width is such that the starting position places the miter-gauge head off the table, the job can be done better by using the miter gauge backwards. This means that one hand will be pulling the miter gauge against the forward edge of the work while the other hand is pushing against the opposite edge. On all such oversize jobs, pay extra attention to work support and positioning yourself safely.

Miter-gauge extensions make sense even if you only consider the additional support they provide for the work. Most miter gauges are designed to accept extensions. The means of attachment may be wood screws or nuts and bolts through a set of holes or slots in the gauge head. The extension can be a simple, straight piece of wood or a more elaborate jig. Often, a special design can be used to facilitate certain kinds of cutting. Don't plan to make all the jigs shown immediately. The simple, straight extension you should get to pretty quickly and the others as the need for them arises.

Many times an extension is used when the work is long and calls for extra support. In such cases, don't use a hand to push against the free end of the work. This can close the kerf, bind the blade, and result in a kickback that can be dangerous. If you have a hand on the free end of the work, use it only as a guide or for additional support.

This is my pet table saw blade. A multi-tooth carbide that holds up under long cutting sessions with all sorts of material. Expensive to begin with, but in the long run, may be more economical than an assortment of more conventional blades.

There are saw blades that are especially good for particular jobs, like this metal-cutting design. Its purchase is justified if you plan a considerable amount of such work.

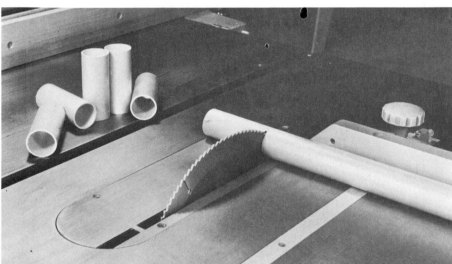

Cuts like this can result even with very good blades when you break through too fast. Some of this feathering is inevitable but you can certainly minimize it simply by slowing up.

TYPES OF TABLE SAW CUTS

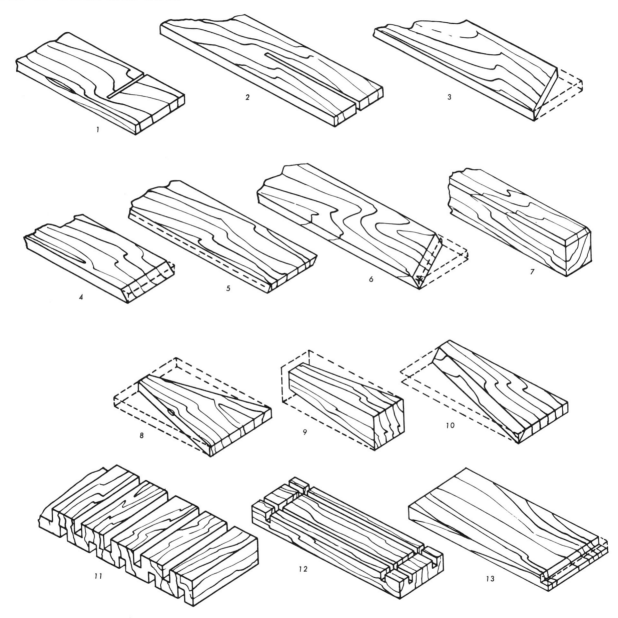

Types of table saw cuts you can accomplish with a regular saw blade

1 crosscut
2 rip
3 miter
4 cross bevel
5 rip bevel
6 compound miter
7 chamfer

8 two-side taper
9 four-side taper
10 compound rip bevel
11 kerfing (decorative & wood bending)
12 kerfing (for inlay)
13 rabbet (two-pass)

TYPES OF CUTS

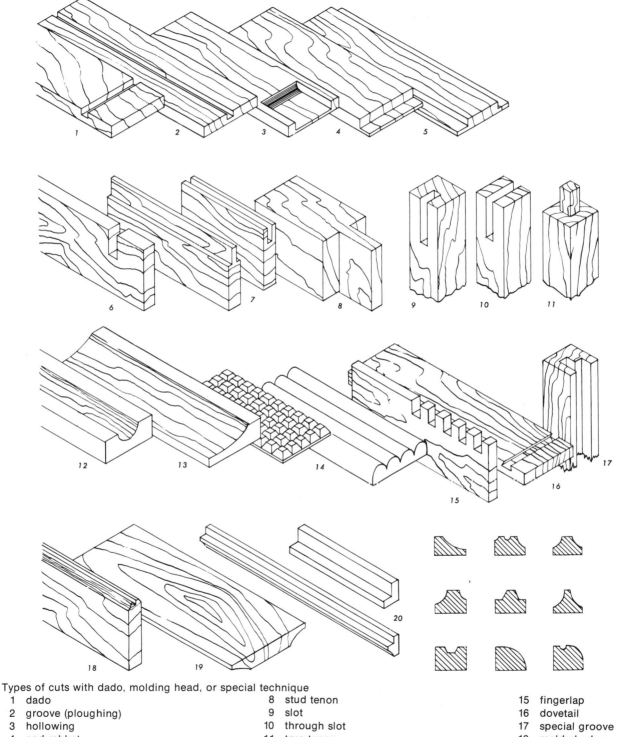

Types of cuts with dado, molding head, or special technique

1 dado	8 stud tenon	15 fingerlap
2 groove (ploughing)	9 slot	16 dovetail
3 hollowing	10 through slot	17 special groove
4 end rabbet	11 true tenon	18 molded edge
5 edge rabbet	12 cove	19 coved edge
6 notching	13 edge cove	20 moldings
7 tongue and groove	14 surface cuts	

Cuts on pieces of plywood reveal the difference between slow and fast feeds. The ragged piece on the left was pushed through as fast as the blade could handle it. The very slow pass result on the right speaks for itself.

When work is too wide to be handled conveniently in the normal miter gauge position, you can often use it backwards like this. Note use of the extension for more support.

Simple crosscut is accomplished by holding the work flat on the table and snug against the miter-gauge head. Position yourself to be out of line with the saw blade. (Blade is shown here far too high above work.)

Most operators habitually work in the left hand table slot, but on occasion the right side provides better support for long work. Either side can be used successfully.

The extension, a straight piece of wood, is counterbored for attaching with bolts or screws to the miter gauge. Kerf cut through it helps lining up with crosscut mark on work. A facing of fine sandpaper provides friction to keep the work from creeping.

A more elaborate extension provides for a stop block that can be set to gauge cut-off length when you require a number of similar pieces.

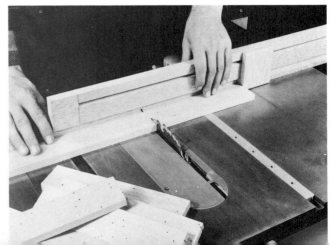

Extensions can be made as production tools for special jobs. This dadoed one provides for cutting off specific lengths. The stop block is a tight fit in any of the dadoes.

L-shaped extension with a nail stop is very good for cutting off dowels and similar pieces— and can also be used for cutting diametrical slots.

The rip fence is set so the block of wood is the gauge that determines the thickness of the pieces being cut. Notice that it is positioned well forward of the saw blade.

Never pick the cutoff from the table while the blade is still running. Avoid this dangerous situation by waiting a few seconds for the blade to stop.

It's also a good idea—and this applies to all power-tool work—to avoid wearing loose sleeves and free-hanging ties. Sleeves should be tight at the wrists or rolled above the elbows.

Crosscutting to length. Unless you are squaring off the end of a board, crosscutting is usually done to size a board to a certain length. Other times it's done to get duplicate pieces. In such cases, it's always wise to create some sort of mechanical setup so the length of the pieces will be gauged automatically. This can be done with commercial miter-gauge stop rods or with some of the extensions shown.

Never use the rip fence as a stop to gauge the cutoff length. The work will certainly be captured and twisted between the rip fence and the blade, and it can be tossed up or back to knock you about a bit. The rip fence can be used only if you also employ a stop block. The stop block doesn't have to be any more than a block of wood that you place against the fence at the forward edge of the table. The distance from the edge of the block to the saw blade equals the cutoff length. What the block does is provide room in excess of the cutoff length so the piece can not bind between the rip fence and the blade.

If you don't use a piece of wood for a stop block, you can make a special one (as shown in the accompanying drawing) for use whenever required.

Using two miter gauges. As you learn more woodworking techniques, the addition of an extra gauge is something to consider. In crosscutting, for example, you could make an extension longer than the width of the saw table and back it up with a gauge in each slot. This can take care of two work extremes, the overly long piece that can use a great deal of support and the very small piece that can't be held safely without special consideration.

The two-gauge idea is also good for other work. Making miter cuts, when the job calls for frequent readjustment of a single miter gauge to make mating cuts, is an excellent example. This will occur when the stock is so shaped that it can't be flipped over.

Extra long work. Good work support is important for both accuracy and safety. For very long work you must think in terms of more support than the table can provide. Rather than getting someone to hold up the free end, use a floor stand. Such stands are good for both crosscutting and ripping. In addition to providing support for extra long lumber work, you will find them use-

ful for initial sizing cuts on all sorts of panel materials.

Ripping. A rip cut is made by passing the work between the rip fence and the saw blade. When the blade has set teeth, be sure to measure from a tooth that slants toward the fence. If you are using the offset fence alignment, measure from the front of the blade.

A simple rip cut is done by placing the work at the front edge of the table, snugly against the fence and flat down. Use your left hand to hold the work in position and your right hand, with fingers hooked over the fence, to feed the work forward. Keep your left hand in its original position, snugging the work throughout the pass. Feed with your right hand until the work is well past the saw blade. There is no return on a rip cut. Feed until the overhang at the rear of the table causes the

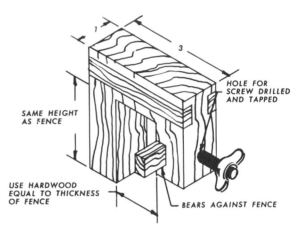

This stop block is made so it can be secured any place along the rip fence. It can be used to stop *lengths* of cuts, or to gauge lengths of cutoffs.

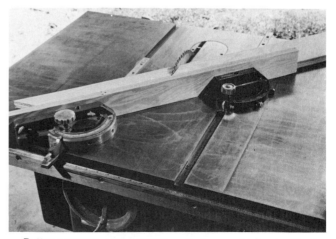

Better support, and greater control, are obtained with the use of two miter gauges to feed stock for angle cut.

Outboard supports are wise when you are cutting over-large stock. Most times they are better and safer to use than a friend who may not work in harmony with the cut.

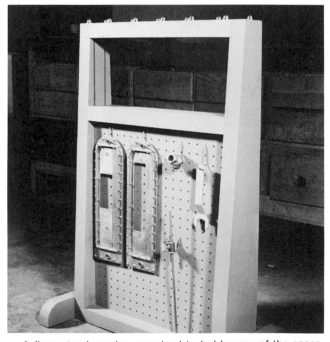

A floor stand can be organized to hold many of the accessories you would like to have close by. Perforated hardboard and standard hangers were used here.

The "roller" top is achieved by using ball roller glides. Even flat, furniture glides would do.

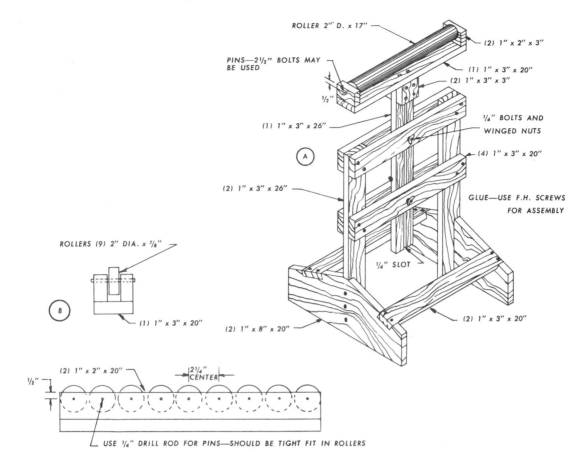

ROLLER 2″ D. x 17″

PINS—2½″ BOLTS MAY BE USED

½″

(1) 1″ x 3″ x 26″

Ⓐ

(2) 1″ x 3″ x 26″

ROLLERS (9) 2″ DIA. x ⅞″

Ⓑ

(1) 1″ x 3″ x 20″

(2) 1″ x 8″ x 20″

(2) 1″ x 2″ x 3″

(1) 1″ x 3″ x 20″

(2) 1″ x 3″ x 3″

¼″ BOLTS AND WINGED NUTS

(4) 1″ x 3″ x 20″

GLUE—USE F.H. SCREWS FOR ASSEMBLY

¼″ SLOT

(2) 1″ x 3″ x 20″

(2) 1″ x 2″ x 20″

2¼″ CENTER

½″

USE ¼″ DRILL ROD FOR PINS—SHOULD BE TIGHT FIT IN ROLLERS

Here are construction details for an adjustable extension floor stand. The long roller is used for ripping operations. The roller-cluster is good for crosscutting.

back end of the work to tilt up into the palm of your hand. Then grip tightly and lift it completely clear of the saw blade.

This process is standard as long as you have ample room between the fence and blade. On narrow cuts, when your hand gets about 6″ from the blade, substitute a push stick for your fingers.

Too often, a push stick is nothing more than a narrow strip of wood salvaged from the scrap heap. That's certainly better than fingers, but it's wiser to make a special one that you can use whenever necessary. It's also true that in some situations a tool that combines a hold-down and a pusher action is wise to have.

In some cases, when you are cutting multiple pieces that might be too narrow to be handled conventionally, a miter-gauge extension can be used. This must be sized so it butts against the rip fence which has already been set for the rip cut required. When using a jig like this, always advance the extension enough so the work is well past the saw blade before you return to the starting position.

Often, multiple pieces can be produced by pre-shaping a wide board and then ripping off pieces. This is better than ripping the pieces first and then shaping them.

If you have a number of similar pieces that you want to rip in half, rather than handle them as routine rip cuts, it would be better to make a jig that you could clamp to the rip fence. The jig would have a U-shaped opening centered over the saw blade. The work would be fed into the front end of the "U" and emerge in two pieces at the back.

On extremely long material, it might be wise to change your position about the middle of the cut. Start in the usual fashion, but approximately midway, move to the back of the saw and finish the cut by pulling the work through.

Squaring board. There are times when a piece of stock doesn't have an edge straight enough to ride the rip fence. Maybe it's left over from a jigsaw or band-saw job. The squaring board lets you mount it for cutting.

MAKING RIP CUTS

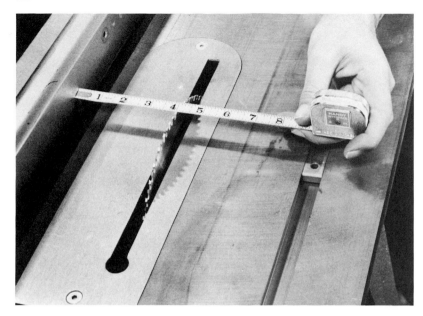

Rip fence is set by measuring from it to the blade. When blade has set teeth be sure to check against one that points toward the fence.

For routine cuts, keep the left hand at the front of the table as the right hand continues to move the work past the blade. Keep the fingers hooked over the fence.

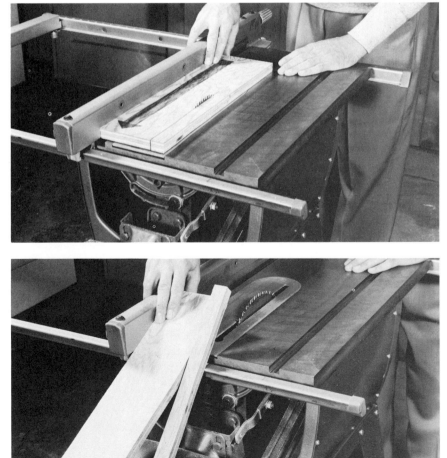

Feed until the overhang at the rear of the table tilts the work up into the palm of your hand. Then lift the work well clear of the saw blade.

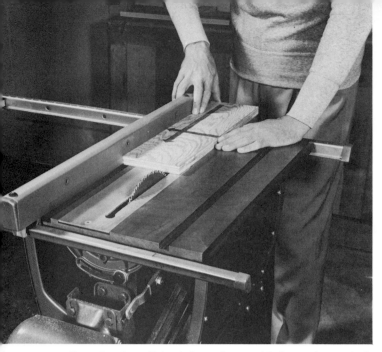

Keep hands well back from the saw blade as shown. Left hand snugs work against the rip fence, while right hand, with fingers hooked over fence, feeds the work forward.

The jig is just a platform with a saw-table-slot guide fastened to its underside. The cleat, secured to the forward edge of the platform, is at right angles to the saw blade. You butt the work against the cleat and push the whole assembly past the saw blade. Of course, there is a size limit to work that can be handled on the jig.

Very large pieces can be done by tack-nailing a straight, narrow piece of wood to the underside of the work. This is to be used as a guide along the edge of the saw table. Where you place the guide strip determines how much of the rough edge will be cut off. Another technique is to nail the guide to the top edge of the work along the rough edge. Then, the guide rides the rip fence as you make the cut to remove the bad edge.

Mitering. Few jobs in woodworking can be as frustrating as cutting a good miter joint. You can be a bit off in making the cut and the two parts will mate perfectly, but the angle formed by the two parts will not be 90°. This is discouraging on jobs that run from simple picture frames to the facing on case goods. The only solution to this problem is accuracy.

Make it a rule to mark the cut line on the work. You'll know immediately whether you are getting the accuracy you want. Be aware that the blade, cutting in a forward direction, tends to pull the work so that it "creeps" along the miter gauge. Also, there is a pivoting action where the work and the forward edge of the miter gauge meet. Positive holding action of the work against the miter-gauge head throughout the pass is absolutely necessary.

You can get help in holding the work against the gauge head by using a miter-gauge extension; even more help-

PUSHSTICKS AND HOLD DOWNS

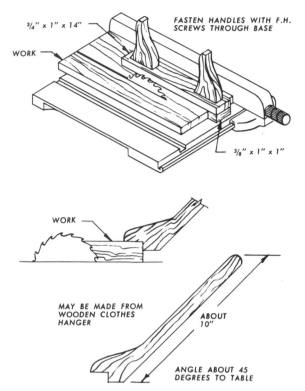

Simple pusher sticks or a combination pusher-hold down are easy to make and are a "must" if you plan on doing all jobs safely. The pusher-hold down may also be used for safety and convenience on the jointer.

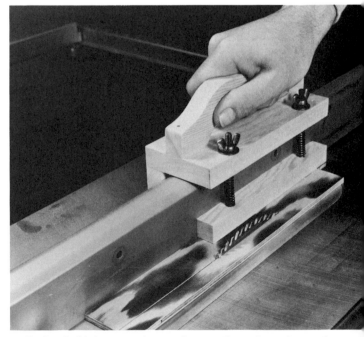

Pusher-hold down employs springs so the unit can be used on various stock thicknesses.

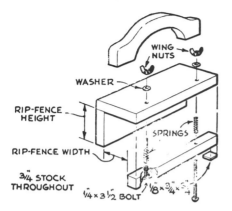

Construction details of spring-powered hold down.

STOP JIGS

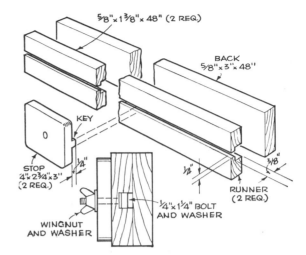

Construction details of the rip-fence stop jig.

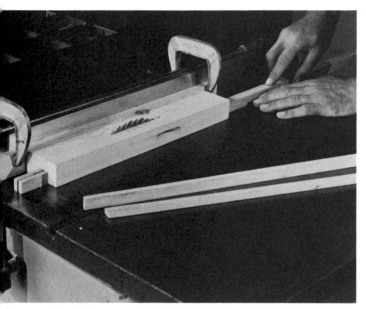

Special setups are helpful on many jobs. Here, a large number of square pieces had to be cut in half. The jig, grooved to receive the stock, acts as a guide and a hold down.

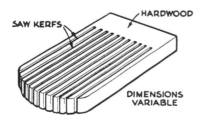

The "spring stick" is a horizontal hold down that will hold work firmly against the fence as you make the pass. The fingers are the result of parallel saw-blade cuts. In use, it is clamped to the table so the fingers bear against the work.

Stop jig attached to the rip fence has slot its full length so the hardwood stop blocks can be positioned easily for controlling length of cut. The blocks are secured with wing nuts. Start of chamfering is determined by the block nearest operator, cut is completed when the work advances to the forward block. Work carefully when the wood makes initial contact with the cutter.

ful is facing the extension with sandpaper. Make the pass even more slowly than you do normally. Needless to say, machine alignment has to be perfectly accurate.

A good way to work, even though it does waste some wood, is to cut frame parts to overall size to begin with and then miter the ends by using a stop block on the rip fence to gauge the cutoff. Another way is to work with one of the miter-gauge extensions that has been shown, employing a stop block on the extension to gauge the length of the work.

Simple miter jigs. Part of the problem of cutting true miters is the difficulty of matching left and right-hand cuts. This is most critical when the work is shaped so that it can't be flipped because it means having to work on both sides of the blade. To do that, you also have to

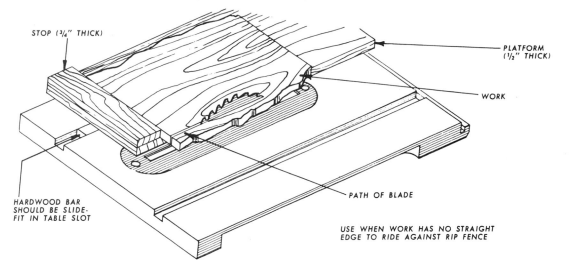

STOP (¾" THICK)

PLATFORM (½" THICK)

WORK

PATH OF BLADE

HARDWOOD BAR SHOULD BE SLIDE-FIT IN TABLE SLOT

USE WHEN WORK HAS NO STRAIGHT EDGE TO RIDE AGAINST RIP FENCE

The squaring board makes it possible to cut material lacking a straight edge for use against the rip fence. This can be the result of pieces left over from jigsaw or bandsaw operations.

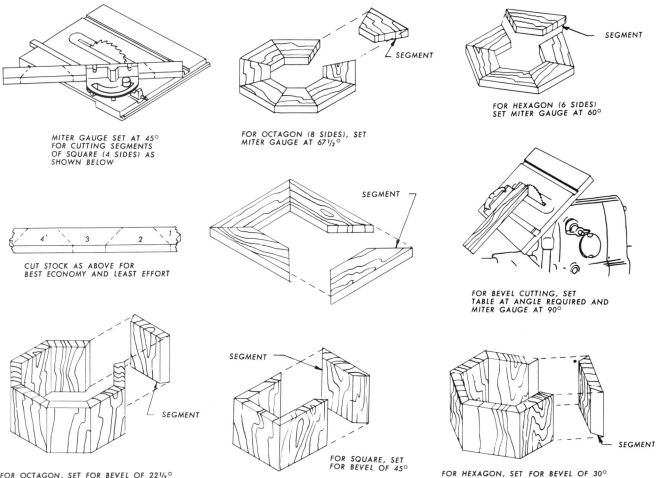

MITER GAUGE SET AT 45° FOR CUTTING SEGMENTS OF SQUARE (4 SIDES) AS SHOWN BELOW

SEGMENT

FOR OCTAGON (8 SIDES), SET MITER GAUGE AT 67½°

SEGMENT

FOR HEXAGON (6 SIDES) SET MITER GAUGE AT 60°

CUT STOCK AS ABOVE FOR BEST ECONOMY AND LEAST EFFORT

SEGMENT

FOR BEVEL CUTTING, SET TABLE AT ANGLE REQUIRED AND MITER GAUGE AT 90°

SEGMENT

FOR OCTAGON, SET FOR BEVEL OF 22½°

SEGMENT

FOR SQUARE, SET FOR BEVEL OF 45°

SEGMENT

FOR HEXAGON, SET FOR BEVEL OF 30°

How to set up for various types of common angular cuts. One sketch shows a table tilt (on a ShopSmith). On most tools the blade is tilted, not the table. On all these cuts, accuracy is a must.

Accuracy on miters can be spoiled simply because of the cut action. The work tends to pivot about the front edge of the miter gauge. It will also "creep." Firm work support is essential.

Safe way to work is to cut frame pieces to overall size and then set up as shown here to do the miters. Arrow points to line that should be perpendicular between stop block and diagonal of the square.

Easy safeguard when doing angle cuts is to mark the cut-line on the work. Thus you will know right off if the job is right. Mark cut lines with a square or protractor.

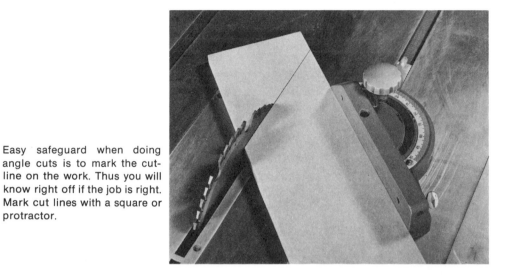

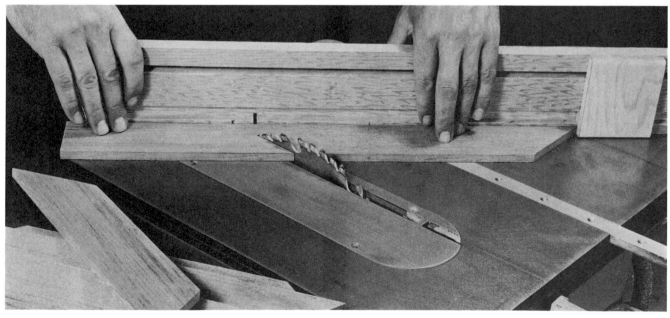

Extension with stop block may also be used to gauge the length of mitered pieces. When stock is flat, pieces may be cut in sequence by flipping the work after each pass.

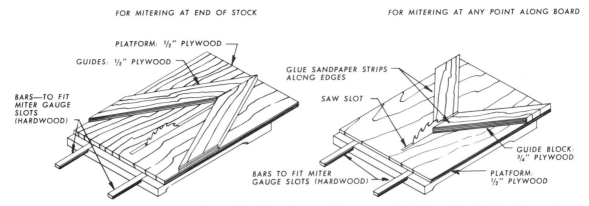

FOR MITERING AT END OF STOCK   FOR MITERING AT ANY POINT ALONG BOARD

PLATFORM: ½" PLYWOOD
GUIDES: ½" PLYWOOD
GLUE SANDPAPER STRIPS ALONG EDGES
BARS—TO FIT MITER GAUGE SLOTS (HARDWOOD)
SAW SLOT
GUIDE BLOCK: ¾" PLYWOOD
BARS TO FIT MITER GAUGE SLOTS (HARDWOOD)
PLATFORM: ½" PLYWOOD

Construction details of two types of sliding tables for miter cuts. The one on the left requires that the frame pieces be cut to length to begin with. The one on the right provides for cutting consecutively from a single piece. This is essential when the stock can't be flipped.

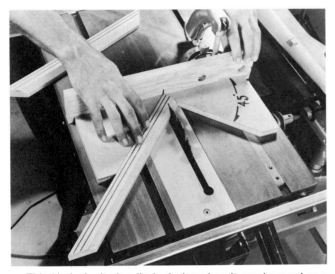

This kind of mitering jig is designed so it can be used as a miter-gauge attachment. Here, frame pieces must be cut to overall length before they can be mitered. Such a procedure does waste some wood but the gain in accuracy justifies it.

change the miter-gauge setting for mating cuts. You can avoid most of these problems by making some sliding tables.

These sliding tables are no more than platforms guided by twin bars that ride the slots in the saw table. Attached to the platforms are guides that position the work for the cut. If these sliding tables are made accurately and cared for, they will function in good style for as long as you care to use them.

In constructing the sliding tables, cut the platforms first, sizing them to suit your table. Then cut the bars so they will ride smoothly in the slots. Put the bars in the slots, and after lowering the blade, set the platform so it lines up with one edge of the saw table. Tack-nail through the platform into the bars, and while holding

down the platform, raise the saw blade so it cuts its own slot. The position of the guides on the platform should be made by layout from this slot.

Beveling. A bevel is made like a rip cut except that the blade is tilted to the angle required. When two such cuts are mated, the joint is called a miter. For the sake of clarity, blade-tilt cuts will be called bevels from here on.

There is more of a tendency on this type of cut for the work to move away from the fence, so use extra care to keep it snug throughout the pass. A chamfer (beveled edge) is done like a bevel, but you don't cut away as much stock. In either case, should you require the cut on all four edges or two adjacent edges, do the cross-grain cuts first. It's more likely that feathering will occur at the end of these cuts, so you rely on the final with-the-grain pass to remove the imperfection.

You can do bevel cutting on a number of pieces so that after assembly they will turn a corner. A circle is formed when the total included angles of all the pieces equal 360°. Determining the correct angle is simple. Divide 360° by the number of pieces you want in your circle to find the total angle that each piece will have. Then divide this in half to get the angle at which each side of the pieces should be cut.

Accuracy is very important. Part of a degree doesn't seem like much of an error, but multiply it by 20 and then picture the gap when you fit in the last piece. The same idea applies to flat work; the difference is that you use the miter gauge to do the cutting.

Tapering. A taper-cutting jig is a good tool for you to make. It provides a straight side that can ride the rip fence and an adjustable side so you can set for the amount of taper you want. Keep the legs clamped together when you attach the hinge. The crosspiece that you use to lock the setting can be made of sheet metal or hardwood.

Beveling done with the stock on its edge, riding against the rip fence. Hold the work snug against the fence throughout the cut and make the pass slowly, to counter the tendency for the work to shift away. When doing four edges, make the crossgrain cuts first.

A true bevel removes the entire edge of the stock. When the blade setting is figured mathematically in relation to the number of segments being cut, the assembled pieces will form a circle.

Mark a line on both legs 12″ in from the hinged end. By opening the jig and measuring between these two marks, you can determine how much taper per foot you are setting for.

To use the jig, set the straight side against the fence and place the work against the opposite leg. Advance both jig and work past the saw blade. If you require the same taper on both edges of the stock, open the jig up to twice the original setting before making the second cut.

There will be a tendency here for the work to move away from the jig as you cut, so be sure to set the work correctly at the beginning and keep it in place throughout the pass.

It's also possible to use notched jigs to accomplish taper cuts. These are no more than pieces of wood with parallel sides. What you do is recess one side to match the shape and size of what you wish to remove from the work. You nestle the work in the notch and do the job like a rip cut. Notched jigs are good to use when the job

calls for a setting that might be too extreme for the variable jig and for very small pieces. Notched jigs are also good for production runs since they eliminate resetting and thus reduce the possibility of error.

Compound angles. Some cuts require a miter-gauge setting, others a blade tilt. The compound angle requires both at the same time. Accuracy is essential. Settings must be done carefully and checked out on scrap before the good stock is cut. This type of cutting will often require alternating the miter gauge in the table slots. Of course, this means changing the miter-gauge setting, which offers another opportunity for error. There really is no reason why you can't cut a good compound miter in the basic fashion; it's just important to impress you with the need for precision.

The purist can work from the accompanying chart that supplies the settings for the most often used compound angle joints, but there is a much overlooked factor in this area of woodworking. The slope angle, as far as the appearance of the work is concerned, is very seldom critical. Any person who judges your shadowbox picture-frame project on the basis of whether the slope angle should have been a couple of degrees more or less is being needlessly critical.

If you use something to hold the work at the slope angle you want instead of keeping the work flat on the table, the job is done like a simple miter cut, but you produce a compound angle. This will occur regardless of the slope angle. Naturally it has limitations that are imposed mostly by work size and the capacities of your machine. But if the accompanying illustrations and the jigs shown can't solve the immediate problem, you can always use the chart.

In any event, use a blade that will produce a smooth cut, and be sure that it is sharp. Make all passes very slowly, and keep a firm grip on the work throughout.

Dadoing. If you set a regular saw blade to less than the stock thickness and make repeat passes to widen the normal kerf, you get a U-shaped cut that is a dado when done across the grain, a groove when done with the grain. You may even hear the word "ploughing," but this is the same as grooving.

The saw-blade, repeat-pass technique is fine for an occasional groove or dado, but if such cuts are needed often enough, the purchase of a dado tool accessory is justified. Also, this accessory can be used for a wider range of jobs than the two cuts just described.

Dadoing tools. The dado assembly is a set of outside blades with a number of chippers. Cut width is determined by how many chippers you use. Most can be used for cuts that run from $\frac{1}{4}$″ to better than $\frac{3}{4}$″ wide. Some

TAPER CUTTING

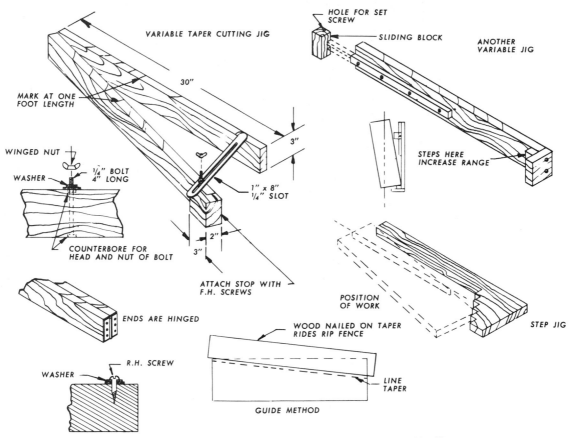

Construction details of various types of taper jigs. You'll find the variable one at the top left the most useful for general work. At the lower right is a technique for cutting pieces too large to be handled any other way.

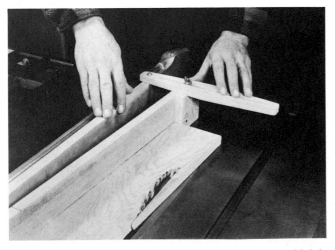

Taper jig is moved forward together with the work, which is pushed by a block on the jig. Adjustment for taper angle is determined by a mark across both arms of the jig, 12" from the hinged end. The gap between the jig arms at that mark gives the taper in inches, per foot of length.

Compound taper and bevel cut involves tilting the blade to correct angle. When the cut is repeated on the opposite edge, the jig is opened to twice the original angle to compensate for the first taper cut.

A notched jig is a solution to taper-cutting when you lack other means, and it is the best way to make accurate cuts with maximum safety.

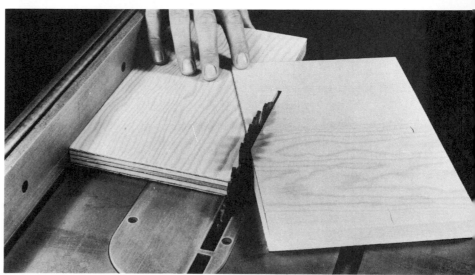

It is especially worthwhile to make a notched jig if you have a number of similar tapered pieces to cut.

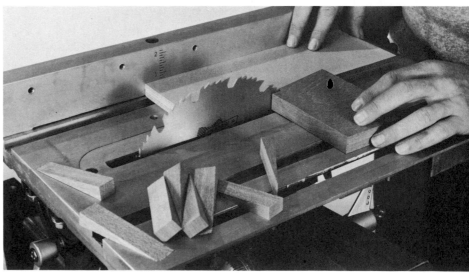

A notched jig is often the smart way to go when you require tapered pieces too small to be cut safely using conventional cutting techniques.

CUTTING COMPOUND ANGLES

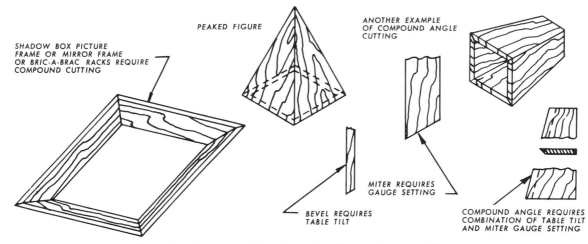

Examples of compound angle construction, and nomenclature.

WORK ANGLE	FOUR-SIDED FIGURE		SIX-SIDED FIGURE	
	tilt	miter-gauge setting	tilt	miter-gauge setting
15°	43¼	75½	29	81¾
30°	37¾	63½	26	74
45°	30	54¾	21	67¾
60°	49	49	14½	63½

This chart supplies the blade tilt and the miter-gauge setting for most commonly used work angles on four-sided and six-sided figures.

Slope angle jig used with the miter gauge makes compound angle cut without tilting the blade. A strip tacked along the top of the base holds the work at the correct angle. Various slope angles are obtained depending on thickness and location of the strip.

Adjustable tilt jig works with the miter gauge so you can secure work at the slope angle you want. With this kind of jig you *do not* have to pre-bevel the workpiece edge even though we show it done here.

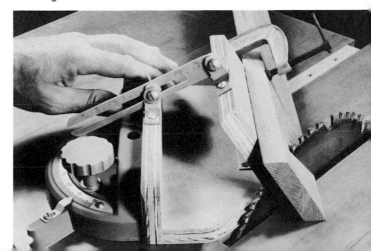

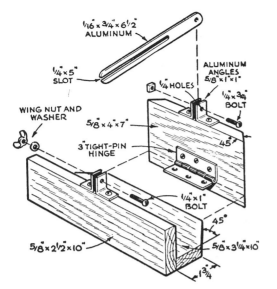

Construction details of the miter-gauge tilt jig.

sets come with hollow-ground outside blades, some with flat-ground. The hollow-ground ones are better but cost more.

"Wobblers" can be self-contained units or merely a set of washers that you use with a regular saw blade. In essence the blade is set slightly off vertically to the saw arbor. As the blade spins, the teeth move from side to side, so they cut a wide slot instead of a narrow kerf. The offset of the blade is adjustable. Since the lateral movement of the blade forms an arc at the tips of the teeth, the bottom of the dado will be slightly rounded instead of dead flat.

The "Quick-set" and "Tru-Cut" dadoes may look like wobbler types, but they work differently. Basically, they consist of a flat core that is studded with cutting knives and sandwiched between matched, tapered, outside plates. At minimum setting the blades cut in the same plane. As you tilt the core disc between the tapered

Sliding table fixture eliminates even the miter-gauge setting and lets you work on either side of the blade. Once it is set up accurately, there are no outside factors to mar fit of joints.

Slope angle is determined by distance between slides and miter guide. Make this setting exactly the same on both sides and your compound angle cuts will produce close-fitting joints.

Limitations on work width become negligible as slope angle decreases. Table will handle 80 to 90 percent of compound angle cuts that you're ever likely to encounter.

You can cut similar pieces from one length of stock simply by flipping it over for each pass. For molded shapes that can't be flipped, make alternate cuts on the other side of the blade.

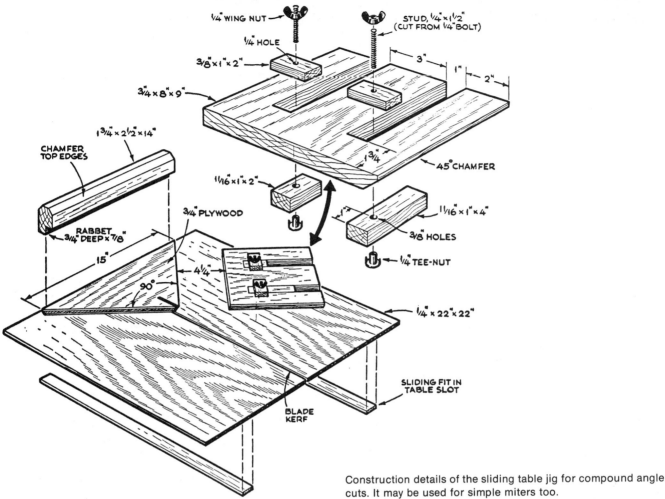

Construction details of the sliding table jig for compound angle cuts. It may be used for simple miters too.

plates, you in effect spread the knives apart so they cut a progressively wider slot. Both this type of dado assembly and the wobblers have the advantage of being infinitely adjustable between minimum and maximum settings.

All dado cuts remove much more material than a simple saw cut, so slow up on the feed to avoid choking the tool. On very deep cuts, especially on those wider than $\frac{3}{8}''$, set the projection for less than you need on the first pass and raise it for the second pass to complete the cut. Tool power will also affect this cutting process; if the work chatters or if the tool slows up, you'll know you are cutting too deeply.

Dadoing tools require special inserts simply because they make wider cuts. On some jobs, this can result in too much of an opening around the cutter. When this seems like an unsafe situation, make a special insert using plywood or hardboard. Use the regular insert as a pattern. Put the new insert in place with the dado at zero projection. Then, holding down the insert with a block of wood, slowly raise the dado so it will form its own slot. In this manner, you will have no opening whatever around the cutting tool.

Another good idea is to make a wooden facing for the rip fence. This facing is no more than a straight piece of stock attached with screws through the rip fence. After it is in place, you can situate it over the cut area and slowly raise the cutter to form a semi-circular clearance area.

Tenoning jig. It is not good practice to do dado work across the end of narrow stock without taking precautions to make the job accurate and safe. The tenoning jig shown is basically a U-shaped affair, so it can straddle the rip fence and hold the work in relation to the cutter. The work can be clamped, or it can be hand held against the guide as the jig is moved forward to make the cut. Clamping or handholding can be judged on the basis of work size and cut size.

Slots. To form slots, you must lower the work over

DADO CUTS

A dado is a U-shaped cut made across the grain. Its depth is controlled by cutter projection, while its width is controlled by the dado-tool setting.

A dado tool can do quickly what would require many repeat passes to accomplish with a saw blade. Grooves, rabbets, and tenons are just a few of the many examples.

By making repeat passes you can do hollowing jobs; extra-wide grooves. A well-jointed dado will leave a nice flat bottom on a job like this.

At the top left is a high-quality dado assembly with hollow-ground outside blades. Beside it is a self-contained wobbler. Two at the lower left rely on beveled or set teeth for clearance. The molding head can be used for dado work with blank knives doing the cutting.

the turning dado and, of course, this calls for extra care. Whenever possible, use a stop block or a clamp on the rip fence to act as a gauge as well as to provide a brace point to help you do the job. To determine slot length, use two stop blocks. This kind of work can be done through stock surfaces or in edges, should you wish to use splines to join pieces edge-to-edge.

Extensions. Miter-gauge extensions are useful for dado work, especially when you wish to automatically gauge the distance between cuts. In most cases, this can be accomplished by attaching a guide strip to the bottom edge of the extension. The strip is sized to suit the cut and positioned to gauge the spacing. Each cut made is placed over the strip to position the work for the next cut.

Round tenons. You can form tenons on round stock. Use the rip fence as a stop and the miter gauge to keep the work square. Keep the cutter projection to a minimum and use a hand position that pays maximum atten-

tion to safety. Advance the work and miter gauge to the depth of cut required, and then slowly turn the work against the direction of rotation of the cutter. For repeat cuts, mark the miter-gauge position. If the miter gauge is too loose in the table slot, it might be a good idea to clamp it in place as you make the cut.

Molding heads. Adding a molding head to your table-saw equipment and building up to a nice assortment of knives will enable you to create many standard or original molding designs. You can also form edge joints and cabinet-door lips as well as accomplish many other operations normally requiring a shaper.

There are many kinds of molding heads on the market, but they all work the same way on a table saw. The knives, usually in sets of three, are locked into slots around the edge of the head. The head is mounted on the saw's arbor between washers in the same way as a blade or a dado tool.

You can start your collection of knives with a few basic types; then add new ones as you need them. Knives

Dado assembly used as a planer to smooth or reduce thickness of a board. The secret of success in this operation is to leave enough stock at each side to maintain level of the work.

Tenoning jig rides the rip fence, holds the work safely and securely for grooving, tenoning, rabbeting across the end of narrow stock, without rocking. Duplication of cuts on opposite ends of the stock is done accurately, without further adjustments, by merely swapping ends and cutting again.

A wood facing for the rip fence is a good idea because it permits more flexible work positions. Length of this workpiece is too small to be fed safely over open table insert.

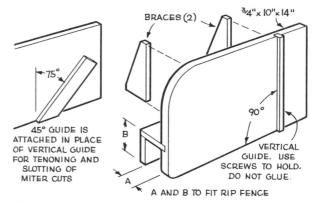

BRACES (2)   ¾" x 10" x 14"

75°

45° GUIDE IS ATTACHED IN PLACE OF VERTICAL GUIDE FOR TENONING AND SLOTTING OF MITER CUTS

B

A

90°

VERTICAL GUIDE. USE SCREWS TO HOLD. DO NOT GLUE.

A AND B TO FIT RIP FENCE

Construction details of a simple tenoning jig. Be sure that the vertical guide is exactly 90° to the saw table.

Cuts made across narrow pieces should always be fed with the miter gauge. It would be difficult to avoid "rocking" should you attempt such work freehand.

Slot is cut by lowering the work slowly over the turning cutter. Clamp provides a brace for starting the cut. Second method is to hold work flat on the table and *then* raise cutter until it projects through.

A guide strip, nailed into a notch that is cut in a miter-gauge extension, automatically positions the work for equally-spaced dadoes.

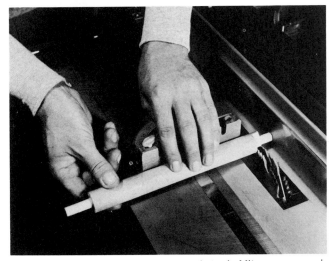

This is how to do a tenon on round stock. Miter-gauge position must be firm even if you must use a clamp. It's okay to use the rip fence as a stop. Turn work very slowly—keep hands clear.

can be combination types that permit different cuts, depending on which part of the contour you use. Standard cutters are each designed to do a specific job and usually require using the full profile of the blade. In this category fall such items as window sash, glue joints, and panel door inserts.

Much of what has been said about dado use applies to the molding head. Unlike a saw blade, which removes a minimum amount of material, the molding cutter takes a big bite. Never force the work or try to cut too deeply. On very deep cuts, make several passes, adjusting the height of the knife after each one to attain the full depth of cut required. If the machine slows up drastically, vibrates, makes it hard to hold the work steady, throws out chunks of wood instead of fine shavings, or stalls, chances are you are feeding too fast or cutting too deeply.

Immediately after using them, clean the knives of gum and dirt and coat them with a light oil to prevent rust. Store them so the cutting edges will be protected.

The head should also be cleaned, especially the slots in which the knives fit. Never leave knives locked in the head.

No matter how good your equipment is, you won't get optimum cuts unless the setups that you make are accurate. So spend a few extra seconds to check such things as knife height and rip-fence settings. It's wise to make trial cuts in scrap wood before cutting actual parts. This practice is especially important when you are using matched sets of cutters. For example, one set of knives will cut the tongue; another set will cut the groove for a tongue-and-groove joint. Forms shaped by the mating cutters must line up perfectly or the joints will be spoiled.

It's a good idea to cut the full profile shape of each knife as you acquire it. The cut can then be "filled" for reference. By doing this, you can easily tell, without a trial cut, what knife or what part of the knife you need to do the job.

In truth, as far as handling is concerned, molding head operations don't differ too much from dado work.

USING MOLDING CUTTERS

Different types of molding heads. Some of them are designed so sleeves can be used for mounting them on $\frac{1}{2}''$, $\frac{5}{8}''$ or $\frac{3}{4}''$ table-saw arbors.

Examples of surface cuts you can do easily with a molding head and various knives. For such work, knives may be blank or shaped, depending on the pattern you want.

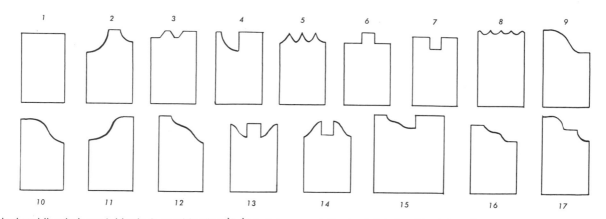

Typical molding knives: 1. blank; 2. combination $\frac{1}{4}''$, $\frac{1}{2}''$ quarter round; 3. glue joint; 4. cabinet-door lip; 5. V-flute; 6 & 7. tongue and groove set; 8. four-bead molding; 9. ogee; 10. ogee; 11. ogee; 12. reverse ogee; 13. panel-insert; 14. panel insert (cope); 15. sash; 16. sash cope; 17. bead-and-cove.

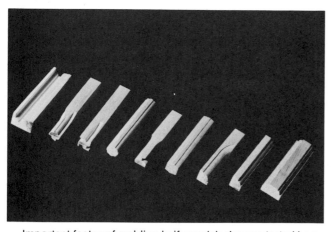

Important factor of molding knife work is demonstrated here. All these shapes were made with a single knife design. Changes were made in work position, cutter projection, etc.

Cut-out in wood facing of the rip fence is essential for clearance of dado blades or molding head. Make the cut-out by raising the arbor slowly after you have positioned and locked the fence, but making certain that blade does not come in contact with the metal fence.

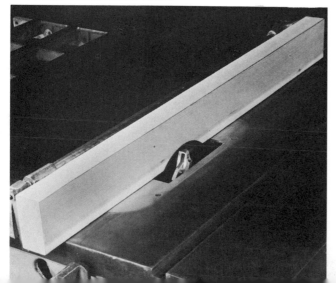

The results are completely different, of course, but such things as a rip-fence facing, special inserts when required, and the advisability of a tenoning jig apply to each.

Coving. Oblique sawing is what makes it possible to get arched shapes with a regular saw blade. The basic procedure is to clamp a guide strip to the table at some angle to the saw blade. The blade is set at minimum projection, and the work is moved along the guide strip. Many passes are needed with the blade projected an additional $\frac{1}{16}''$ to $\frac{1}{8}''$ for each. How much you add to the blade projection for each pass will depend on the nature of the wood and the angle of the guide. If you find it's difficult to make the cut without forcing the work piece, or if the work moves away from the guide, you probably are trying to cut too much in one pass.

A parallel rule (see accompanying drawing) can be made, so you can pretty much predetermine the cove cut you will get. To use it, spread the legs so the inside measurement equals the diameter of the cove you want. Set the saw blade height to equal the radius of the cove. Set the parallel rule over the saw blade so the opposite inside edges of the legs just touch the front and rear teeth of the saw blade. This establishes the correct angle for the guide strip.

In all situations, no matter how much material you can remove by the repeat shaping passes, the final pass should be just a light shaving cut, so the end result will be as smooth as possible.

The coving cut is seldom a true arc, but it comes close enough so that if perfection is essential, the job can be finished easily with a drum sander.

Notching jigs. There are times when a part can't be sawed accurately or safely using the rip fence or the miter gauge only. The part may be too small to be held

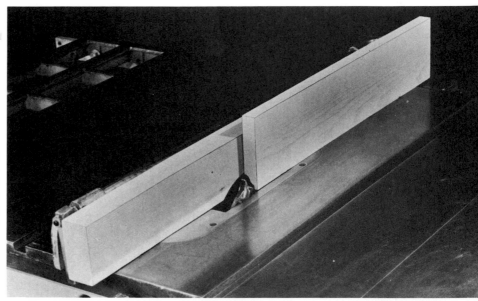

Work can be held on edge and fed across the cutter. Depth-of-cut depends on power, type of wood, etc. If you must force the work or if it chatters, chances are you are trying to cut too deeply in one pass.

The tenoning jig, like the type made for dado work, is essential for safe, accurate cuts across the edge of narrow stock.

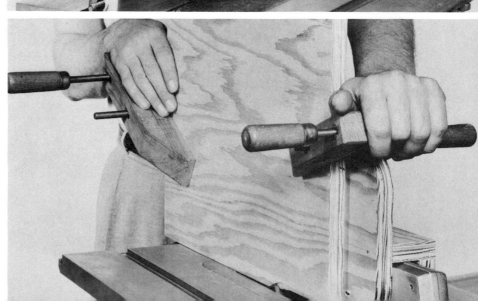

Such a jig can also be used to secure large pieces being edge-shaped when the form you want doesn't permit doing the job with the stock held flat.

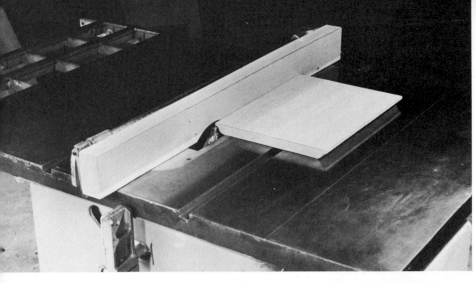

Never work stock that is too small to be held in complete safety. Many times, it's wise to shape the edge of a large piece and then rip off the part you want to use.

Use the miter gauge whenever possible. When you have to shape all four edges, do the cross-grain cuts first.

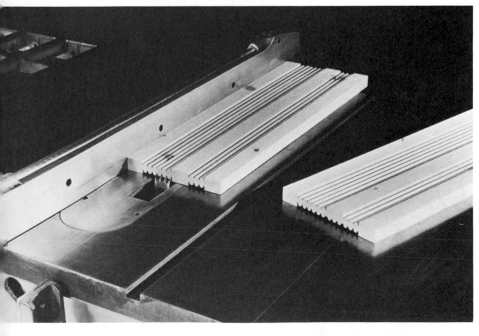

Surface cuts can produce many decorative effects. Accurate spacing of cuts is required when doing this kind of repeat-pass operation.

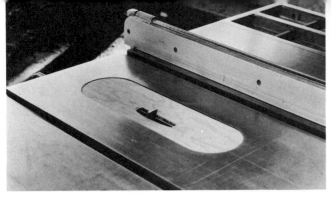

Don't neglect to make special inserts when the operation calls for minimizing the opening around the cutter. That's a good general rule but much more critical on small work.

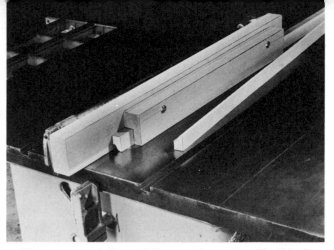

When you need slim moldings, make a setup like this. Pre-sized pieces are fed into one end of the fixture, pulled out the other, safely and surely.

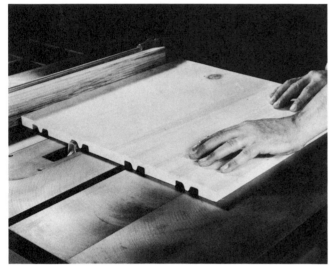

Results will always be smoother when you cut *with* the grain of the wood. Often, to produce many similar pieces, it pays to on wide stock and then rip up into widths you need.

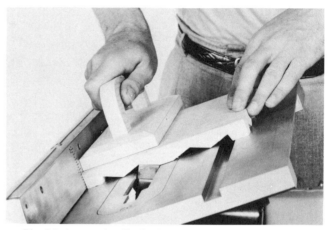

Blank knives and a tilted table or cutter can produce faceted surfaces. Good alignment of cuts is required.

You can shape the edge of circular stock by working with V-blocks as shown here. Work is moved into the cutter and rotated slowly against the direction of rotation of the tool.

Its also possible to do shaping cuts on assembled pieces like this square-to-begin-with picture frame. Slow up drastically as you approach the end of each cut.

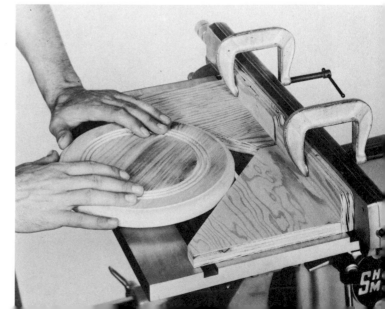

A V-block trough makes it possible to do longitudinal cuts on cylinders. The cutter pokes through the base of the jig which is secured to the rip fence. You must be very careful not to turn the work as you feed it.

A dado tool can be used to form cove cuts. How close you can come to a true right-angle feed direction depends on the type of cutter you have mounted.

COVING TECHNIQUES

CUTTING AWAY WASTE BY KERFING

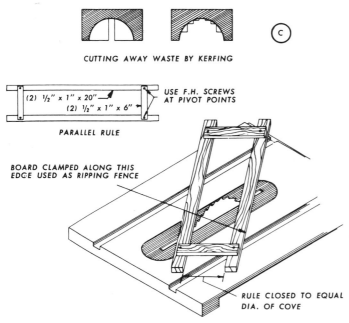

(2) ½" x 1" x 20"

USE F.H. SCREWS AT PIVOT POINTS

(2) ½" x 1" x 6"

PARALLEL RULE

BOARD CLAMPED ALONG THIS EDGE USED AS RIPPING FENCE

RULE CLOSED TO EQUAL DIA. OF COVE

How to make a parallel rule to be used to gauge cove cuts. Note that a good deal of stock may be removed by saw cuts before you do the coving.

Coving is done by making oblique, repeat passes over the saw blade. Depth of cut for each pass should not exceed $\frac{1}{8}$". $\frac{1}{16}$" is better. The very last pass should barely scrape.

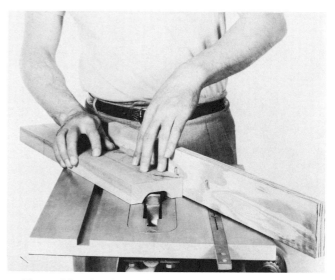

The molding head may also be employed. Note, with a blank cutter, the shape has a flat bottom. Angle of feed across the cutter can be varied to get different shapes.

Twin coves are formed by turning the stock end-for-end after each pass. Coving cuts are not true arcs but can be made so by drum sanding after the table-saw work.

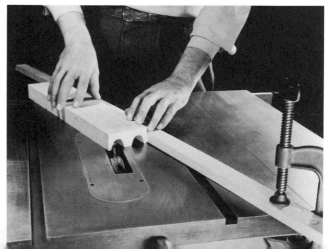

USING NOTCHED JIGS

A simple jig facilitates cutting duplicate discs from a wood rod. Depth of notch determines width of disc. Return the jig to starting position before removing the disc.

Jobs like tenon cheek-cuts can also be accomplished with notched jigs. Thus you can work safely with stock too narrow to be held on edge.

The cut in the jig may be the shape of the part you want or the waste that must be removed.

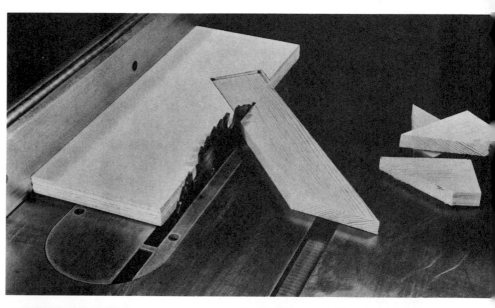

Small wedges are easily cut in this fashion. In all cases, cut the jig to width first. Then make the notch at the appropriate point.

safely or too oddly shaped to be done conventionally. A notched jig is often the solution.

This jig is a piece of wood with parallel sides. The notch can be the shape of the part you wish to keep, or it can be the shape of the waste piece. Usually, the jig will ride the rip fence and act as both carrier and gauge. It allows you to position the work precisely, even when unusual shapes are involved.

Making generalizations about the use of notched jigs is difficult because, in most cases, they are employed for very special jobs. In a few general situations, however, notched jigs can be very helpful. Think about using them when the part is so small or so oddly shaped that it can't be hand held safely, the cut is such that the piece can't be held in the normal manner with the rip fence or the miter gauge, or you need many identical parts so that making a special setup is justified.

Of course, the jigs must be made accurately. This may be too much trouble when you need only a piece or two. At such times, if accuracy is really critical, it may be better to lay out the workpiece, cut just outside the line, and then finish the job on a belt or disc sander.

Multi-blade work. Two, or even more, saw blades turning on a single shaft speed the production on thousands of industrial duplicating jobs. In limited fashion, the same method can be employed by homecraftsmen. All you need are extra saw blades and some suitable washers.

The basic idea is to mount the extra saw blades on the arbor and use the washers to hold them the desired distance apart. With one pass of the stock through the blades, you have two or three accurately spaced cuts. With this setup you can double or triple your output on all sorts of repetitive sawing chores that call for parallel cutting. As will be shown, the idea can be carried even

Notch on underside of this jig permits safe, easy cutting of thin strips. This is a good way to produce splines and similar pieces that you might need.

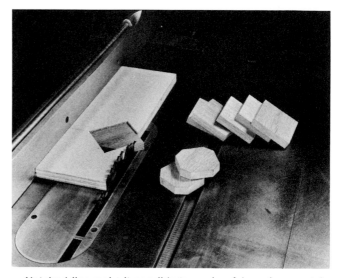

Notched jigs make it possible to work safely and accurately on parts that are too small to be done by pushing the work through in conventional fashion.

Wide slots cut with double blades by "piercing" method, in which the panel is eased down on the projecting blades. Clamps or markers help control start and completion of cut, to be sure of obtaining uniformity.

Cutting in double time, with a two-blade setup, to produce a number of similar parts. Washers or bushings determine spacing of blades. Feed the stock as for any rip cut.

further when you combine a saw blade with parts of a dado assembly.

The limitations of this setup should also be mentioned. The spacing of the multiple cuts is restricted by the length of the saw's arbor and the width of the saw slot in the table. Fortunately, most circular saws have a fairly long shaft and a removable table insert. This prompts a word of caution. It's usually not possible to use the regular insert when you mount more than one blade. Maybe you can substitute a dado or a molding head insert, but it's important to always provide maximum support around the cutting area even if you have to make special inserts.

There is not much cause to be concerned about power. If the saw will drive a dado assembly or a molding head, it will drive more than one saw blade. If you do experience some drag on any of the operations, simply slow down the rate of feed.

Running off a large number of identical strips or slats is an obvious situation where extra blades mounted on the arbor can be very useful. With the rip fence spacing the first part, you'll get as many strips in one pass as there are saw blades on the arbor. Similarly, you can make repetitive kerfs or grooves on the undersides of strips or panels that are to be curved (see the following section on wood bending).

When you mount blades of different diameters, you can saw through a board for an end cut and at the same time make a shallow cut for the side of a rabbet.

Two saw blades can be employed to make both cheek cuts for a tenon at the same time. Decoratively, multiple cutting can be used to saw parallel grooves or slots in panels or screens or to make multiple spiral grooves in doweling or spindles. All sorts of repetitive designs will occur to you once you become familiar with the basic setups for using multiple saw blades.

Wood bending. Bending wood with jigs and the use of steam is often impractical for the homecraftsman, especially when it is required on oversize pieces. For these, and any other wood-bending job where the full strength of the stock isn't needed, there is another and easier way. It's called "kerf curving."

The trick is to make a number of deep side-by-side cuts in the face of the stock. These cuts form the underside of the bend. In effect, the cuts give the opposite face flexibility. At the same time the material between each pair of kerfs becomes a reinforcing rib. It's possible, also, to bend the wood so the good face is inside the curve. Here, the kerfs will open up instead of close.

The closer you space the kerfs, the more sharply you can bend the wood. However, making too many kerfs

Three-blade setup can triple production of similar parts. Washers between blades on the arbor determine spacing between blades.

Tongue is produced in board with a single pass. This is accomplished by spacing two dado cutters with washers to obtain the necessary gap.

A substitute table insert, made of plywood or hardboard, is needed for multiple blade sawing. The insert can be placed flush with the table surface by applying blobs of thick putty on the table flanges and pressing in the insert. Use the fence to hold down the insert while the blade arbor is raised for cutting through—a shim under the fence may be necessary. Adhesion of the putty helps hold the insert in place.

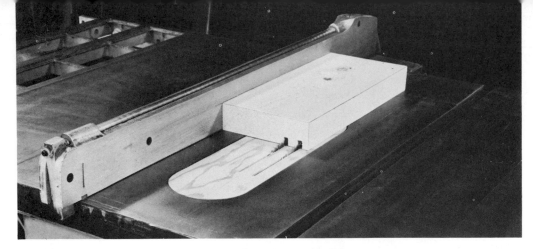

By making repeat passes and adjusting the fence position after each, you can form twin grooves. A nice production idea for sliding doors.

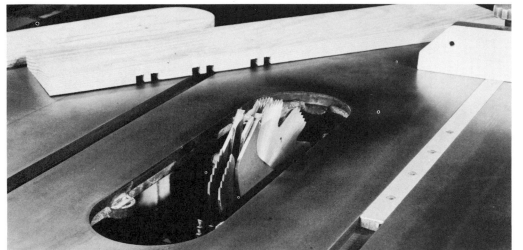

Dado assembly parts, too, can be organized to speed up jobs.

Here, such a setup produces a pair of matching dadoes with just one pass.

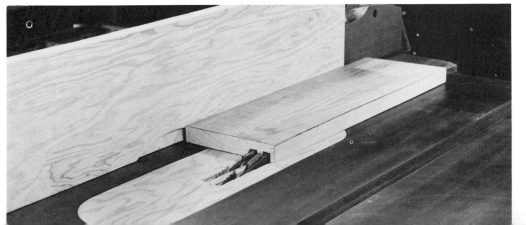

Or use them to do in one pass what would require repeat passes with a regular saw blade.

Combination of dado cutters and a saw blade speeds production of drawers. Shown here is drawer front being cut to length while two edges are being rabbeted, all in one operation. Not all blade arbors are long enough to receive the multiple cutters.

You must work carefully, but it is possible to use combination setups in tilt positions. Here, a double dado setup is cutting a tongue in a mitered edge for a lock miter joint.

With substitute insert in place, double-blade setup makes both cheek cuts for a tenon in a single pass.

wastes time and weakens the stock needlessly. To discover how to space the kerfs for any given radius, make a sample kerf in a scrap of wood of the same type and thickness as the piece you plan to bend. Depth of kerf is a factor, but it's good policy to leave at least $\frac{1}{8}''$ of solid stock above it. Next, clamp the stock to your workbench top, and on the free side of the kerf, measure out the distance of the desired curve radius. Then, lift the board until the kerf closes. The height from the bench top to the underside of the board at the radius mark is the correct kerf spacing.

It's a good idea to saw kerfs at right angles to the grain. This makes bending harder, but there will be less danger of the thinned stock fracturing.

When you are ready to bend, do it slowly. On stubborn woods you can wet the unkerfed side. When it's necessary to hide the kerfs, you can do it by gluing on some veneer. Kerfs that show on board edges can be filled with a thick mixture of wood putty. Most times, however, the kerfing is hidden by other project components.

When parts are to turn an outside corner and there is room to back them with glue blocks, you may find it easier to reduce the entire bend area to veneer thickness. When stock size permits, the job is done best on a jigsaw or band saw. Otherwise, you can work by making repeat passes with a dado head or even a molder with blank knives. The thinned section should be a couple of inches longer than the true length of the bend. This extra length will provide for a smooth and stress-free transition from a straight to a curved wood strip.

Cutting circles. Perfect circles can be cut on a table saw if you use a pivot-cutting technique. The trick is to remove the bulk of the waste stock by making tangent cuts first. This would be tedious with a miter gauge and unsafe to do freehand. But it can be done quickly and safely with a platform on which the work can ride.

The platform is a sheet of $\frac{1}{4}''$ or $\frac{3}{8}''$ plywood fitted along one edge with a hardwood strip that rides the table slot like a miter-gauge bar. You use the platform for both the tangent cuts and for the final pivot pass that produces the true circle. Throughout the operation, the work is mounted on the platform by a nail pivot through the center of the work and into the platform.

For the tangent cuts, just hold the work securely and make repeat, straight cuts. After the waste is removed, clamp the platform to the table so the center line of the work is near the front edge of the saw blade. Then, rotate the work slowly against the direction in which the blade is rotating. Your first impression may be that the cut is coved. There will be some resemblance, but you will discover that this occurs on the waste side only. The

BENDING WOOD

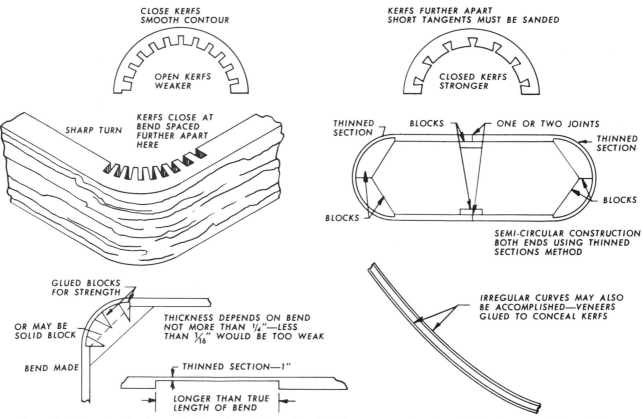

These sketches show kerfing and other ideas that can be utilized so you can bend wood in the home workshop without having to resort to steaming or laminating.

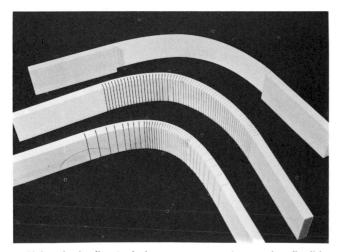

Using the kerfing technique, you can make wood so flexible it can be bent back on itself. Kerf spacing must be in relation to radius of the bend. The closer the kerfs, the tighter the bend can be. Kerfing, in effect, leaves a flexible veneer.

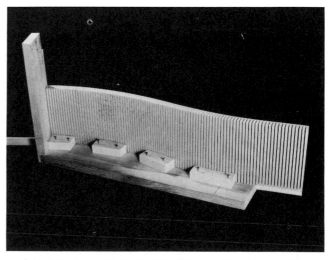

A kerfed piece can be bent in different directions as demonstrated by this cut-away view of a chair seat. Glue blocks support the piece in required shape, provide extra strength.

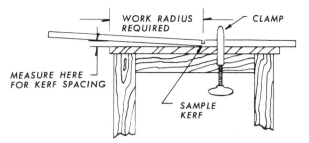

Guide to figuring kerf spacing. Type of wood, even variations in wood of the same species, requires consideration. It's wise to test in scrap stock first.

A miter-gauge extension jig is nice to have so you can position work for automatic, equal spacing of the kerfs. A multiple-blade setup would speed such operations.

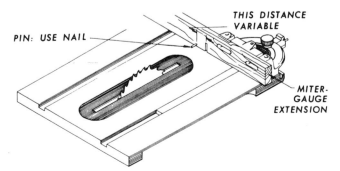

A miter-gauge extension jig you can make for kerf spacing.

good edge of the stock will be square.

Smoothest cuts will result when you do enough tangent cutting to leave a minimum of material for removal by the final rotation pass.

Although this idea was devised specifically for forming circles, it can also be used for forming bevels and coves on circular edges as well as for accurately cutting multi-sided pieces.

Spirals. The table-saw technique that will be discussed is used mostly to lay out a spiral pattern and to remove much of the waste stock that is ordinarily filed away. Of course, if square-shouldered spirals are acceptable, then the same technique can be used for a full job. A dado is shown doing the job, but a regular saw blade may be used instead.

The angle at which the miter-gauge head is set determines the "lead" of the spiral, so you can determine beforehand whether the grooves will be close or far apart. Determine the depth of cut by the position of the miter gauge and the projection of the cutter. A low projection is safer.

To start the cut, hold the stock firmly against the miter-gauge head (or use an extension) and lower it slowly over the turning cutter. When the stock rests solidly on the table, turn it slowly toward the cutter. If you turn slowly and hold firmly, the work will automatically lead to the correct pitch. There are no limitations to the length or the diameter of the work you can handle in this fashion.

Pattern sawing. The rip-fence jig shown permits cutting any number of odd-shaped pieces exactly alike. First, cut one of the parts you want to exact shape and size. Cut all other pieces to approximate this shape and size. Drive two nails through the pattern just far enough so they project slightly. Then, press the pattern down on each workpiece as you go. The pattern rides the guide that is clamped to the rip fence so the saw blade slices off the workpiece to match.

The forward edge of the rip-fence guide must be in line with the outside edge of the saw blade. Jobs like this are best done with a hollow-ground blade. When you work carefully, all the pieces you produce will be exactly alike.

SPECIAL JOINT TECHNIQUES

The finger lap. Finger-lap joints are often found on old works of enduring excellence. These joints are exposed in some areas to denote a good degree of craftsmanship and are used in some hidden areas because of their strength. Structurally, the appeal of a finger-lap joint lies in the unusual amount of gluing surface it

CIRCLE CUTTING

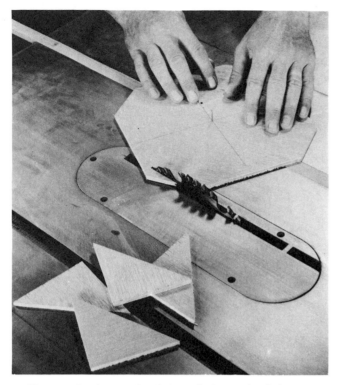

First step in pivot cutting is to make tangent cuts to remove most of the waste stock. The pivot is a nail that goes through the work into a hardwood bar that rides the table slot. Make repeat passes, turning the work a bit after each.

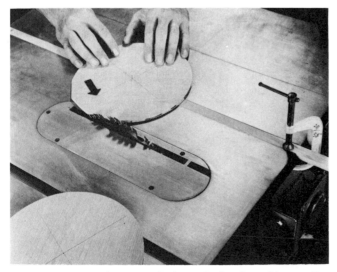

After the waste is removed, clamp the hardwood bar so the work centerline is near the front of the blade. Use a blade projection that is adequate for the stock thickness. Rotate in direction indicated by the arrow.

Large circles are cut by repeated passes over the blade, which is raised $\frac{1}{16}''$ after each full rotation. The work turns on a nail through its center into a plywood platform, which is attached to a hardwood bar fitted into the table slot and clamped in position. Turn into the blade, as shown by arrow.

Bevels are possible if you tilt the saw blade, *after* you have formed the circle with the saw blade straight. The bevel will be flat if you do the final pass with the work centerline on the blade centerline. Other positions can also be used.

You can even cove circular edges if you work with the blade tilted and the work positioned almost in front of the blade. Repeat passes are required with the blade raised after each. Changes occur when you change work position or blade tilt.

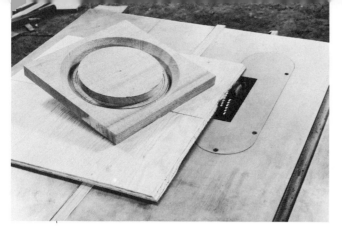

Pivot cutting with a dado assembly results in this kind of shape if the cut is not quite through the wood. Note that the waste side of the wood is beveled while the good side is square. Repeat passes are required.

A molding head may also be used but make experimental cuts in scrap first. The shape you get with a circular pass will not match the cut made with the same knife when the pass is straight.

You can cut a rabbet on a circular piece using the pivot technique and a dado assembly. Since the dado tool is free on the waste side of the work, fewer passes will accomplish the job, but see how the work behaves as you proceed.

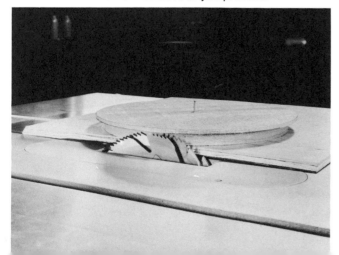

Circular stock is rabbeted with the aid of a vertical support, clamped or screwed to the rip fence. The pivot is a nail driven through the center of the material. Start by raising cutter as you hold the work. Turn the work very slowly and *grip it firmly* to counter the considerable thrust.

provides. The resulting strength is recommendation enough for using the joint on moving components like drawers and on frequently handled items like boxes. If it were done by hand, it would be a tiresome chore, but with a table saw and the jigs shown, you can turn out finger-lap joints precisely and quickly.

The generalization that the cut width should equal the stock thickness is not always a good rule to follow in making these joints. Being more flexible can lead to better looking joints on many projects. Consider the following ideas.

A $\frac{3}{8}''$ finger looks quite good on stock that ranges from $\frac{3}{8}''$ to $\frac{3}{4}''$ thick. A $\frac{1}{4}''$ finger is effective on stock that ranges from $\frac{1}{4}''$ to $\frac{1}{2}''$ thick. If you ever work on material that is less than $\frac{1}{4}''$ thick, match the cut to the thickness of the material or just a bit less.

Four types of jigs for making finger-lap joints are shown in the accompanying photos. The independent jig is good to use because its double miter-gauge bars provide firm support on both sides of the cutter. It might be especially appealing to owners of small saws. The second type of jig is just an extension, screw-attached to the miter gauge. The adjustable jig is designed primarily for those who anticipate frequent reliance on this type of joint and wish to be flexible in finger-size selection.

To make the guides in the jigs, saw the extension to size and then replace the saw blade with a dado. Set the dado for the cut thickness you want and its projection

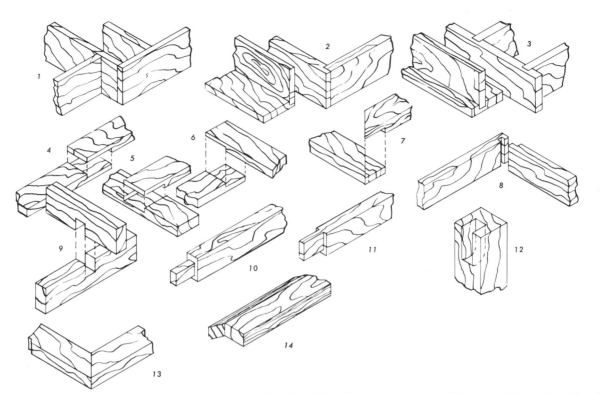

Here are some of the more common woodworking joints that you can accomplish on a table saw by using just a regular saw blade or a dado.

Spirals may be formed by limiting the depth of cut and rotating the stock as you hold it against a slanted guide. If you feed slowly, the cutting action will automatically hold the "pitch" established by the angle of the guide.

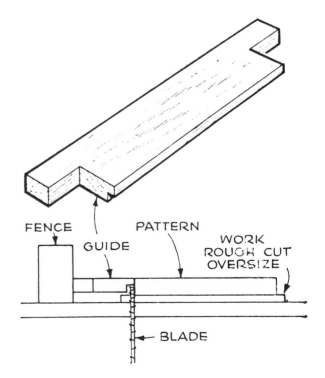

The how-to of pattern sawing. This is a good technique to use when you require similar, odd-shaped pieces.

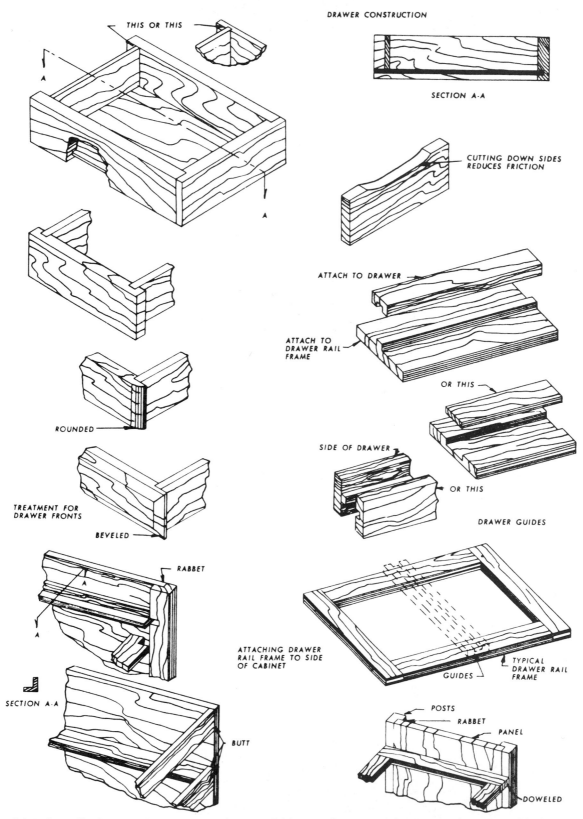

THIS OR THIS

DRAWER CONSTRUCTION

SECTION A-A

CUTTING DOWN SIDES
REDUCES FRICTION

ATTACH TO DRAWER

ATTACH TO
DRAWER RAIL
FRAME

OR THIS

ROUNDED

SIDE OF DRAWER

OR THIS

TREATMENT FOR
DRAWER FRONTS

BEVELED

DRAWER GUIDES

RABBET

ATTACHING DRAWER
RAIL FRAME TO SIDE
OF CABINET

TYPICAL
DRAWER RAIL
FRAME

GUIDES

SECTION A-A

BUTT

POSTS

RABBET

PANEL

DOWELED

Joints that will take you a long way toward accomplishing good cases and the drawers that are used in them.

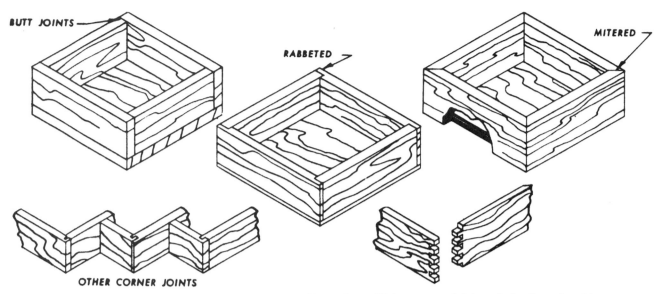

Joints that are often used on drawers, boxes and similar projects. Of these corner joints, only the finger lap at lower right requires a notching cut.

The finger-lap joint has a lot of strength simply because of the large amount of gluing area. It is tedious to do by hand, but easy to achieve on a table saw.

The finger lap doesn't lock like a dovetail so loosening can occur should the glue fail. To avoid this, you can drill a hole through the assembled joint and insert a dowel. Thus, the joint will hold even if the glue gives up.

The finger lap can be used to design swivel joints. Ends of the fingers must be dressed to permit the turning action.

The independent jig is a miter-gauge substitute with twin bars to ride both table slots. Back up the "head" with braces nailed to both the jig and the bars.

to equal the stock thickness. Screw the extension to the miter gauge so you can make a pass close to the center of the extension. Make this cut and then a duplicate cut spaced a groove width away. The guide block is glued and nailed in the second cut.

Follow the accompanying photos for the sequence of the cuts. Precision is fine, but don't work toward making the tongue and groove so snug that you must mate them with a mallet. A slip fit is more practical.

The simplest method of using the jig provides for a full-size groove at one edge of the assembly. Make the first cut in one piece, spacing it from the guide block with a strip of wood sized to match the groove width. Remove the strip of wood and butt the first piece against the guide block. Put the second piece in place, also butting it against the guide block. Proceed with the cutting, placing each formed groove over the guide block to position the work for the next pass.

A second method provides for equalizing partial cuts at each edge of the assembly. Make a vertical line midway between the facing edges of the guide block and groove. Make a second vertical line on the center line of the groove. Place one part in line with the first mark, the mating part in line with the second mark. Cut the two pieces together and butt them against the guide block for the following cut.

Rabbet-miter joints. Aside from picture-frame moldings and those few other cases where it is the only suitable connection, the classic miter is still a popular joint for one reason: it enables you to join pieces along an edge or an end without exposing unsightly, hard-to-conceal edge or end grain. It really doesn't have any advantages as far as strength is concerned. The diagonal cut increases glue area little more than you have in a simple butt, and it's not the easiest joint to assemble in the woodworker's book.

To greatly improve the miter joint, you can incorporate a rabbet in the miter so you will end up with the good looks of the miter joint as well as considerable additional strength. The design also makes for more convenient assembly.

Three designs, the "simple," the "locked," and the housed," are shown in step-by-step sequence of construction. They are not difficult to make, but accuracy is very important. Work with a sharp blade that will produce smooth cuts, and be sure your table-saw components are in correct alignment.

Splines and feathers. Splines are reinforcing, slim strips of wood set into grooves that are cut in the edges of mating pieces. One good rule is to cut the strips so the grain of the wood runs across the narrow dimension; then they can't be broken easily. It's often possible to

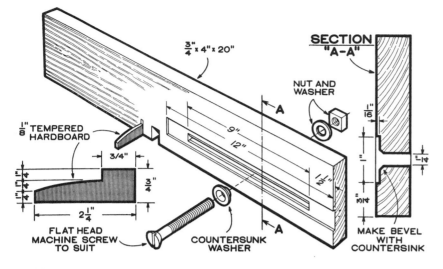

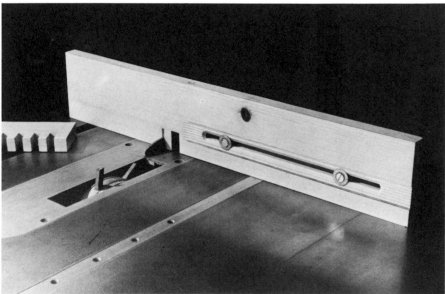

Adjustable jig provides greater flexibility with finger-lap jointing. Sketch shows details for making this jig.

The jig is essentially a piece of 1″ stock with cutouts as shown and a piece of ⅛″ tempered hardboard as a stop.

cut splines from thin plywood if the thickness of what you have available is suitable for the job.

The "feather" is also a spline, but it's used most often across the edge of miter joints in picture frames, for example. This calls for a triangular shape. In most cases, they are cut oversize and then sanded flush to the assembly after the glue has dried.

The spline grooves may be cut with a regular saw blade, using a single or repeat passes, or with a dado. It all depends on how many you have to do and the thickness of the spline you are going to use.

The dovetail. Making dovetails is not really a table-saw operation, but the need for the application could arise for some special purpose such as a dovetail slot

too large to be handled by more conventional means.

The idea is to make outline cuts with the saw blade slanted to the angle needed. Then, with the blade vertical, clean out the stock between. Blade slant, accuracy of cut, good depth-of-cut settings are all very important.

DECORATIVE WORK

Three ways are shown to do ornamental work on the table saw. The methods are practical, and the results can be rewarding when you desire something different for items such as a door, room divider or screen.

The "woven" technique calls for making multiple, stopped rip cuts inside a panel. When the material is flexible enough (and almost any material can be made flexible if you do enough cutting), it's easy to interweave

First cut in making the finger lap joint is made by butting one piece against the guide block as you make the first pass.

Place the first cut *over* the guide block and butt the second piece *against* it. Advance everything to make the second cut.

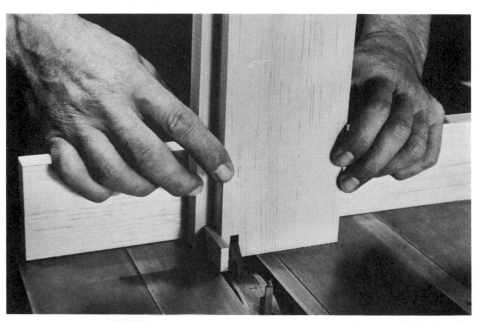

Cuts made are placed over the guide block to position the work for cuts that follow. Throughout the job, be sure that pieces are held firmly together and that passes are made slowly.

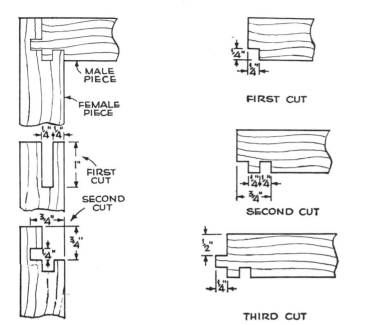

FIRST CUT

SECOND CUT

THIRD CUT

How to do a corner-lock joint. It is merely a series of straight cuts with $\frac{1}{4}''$ dadoes.

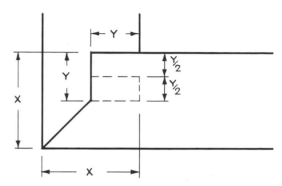

Study this formula before you attempt to do any of the rabbet-miter joints.

How to do the simple rabbet-miter is shown in the following photographs.

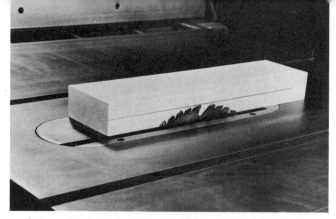

Set saw blade projection at half the stock thickness. Mark a piece carefully for use as a gauge. Check by cutting a kerf and measuring it. Accuracy is everything in this job.

Set the rip fence so the distance from it to the *outer* face of blade is equal to stock thickness. This means that distance from fence to blade equals stock thickness minus kerf.

Place the work against the miter gauge, butt the squared end against the fence, and make first pass. When more than one joint is involved, be sure to make same cut on similar pieces.

Make a second cut on the same piece but with work pulled away from the rip fence so the cut is more than halfway to end of the work. It's important to go beyond halfway point.

Make repeat passes to remove the material between the two kerfs. Although procedure here shows a saw blade in use, there's no reason why you can't use a dado assembly to speed this part of the job.

Using the same piece, leaving the saw-blade projection unchanged, reset fence so distance from it to the outer face of the saw blade equals *half* the stock thickness. The cut will be made on the *mating* part.

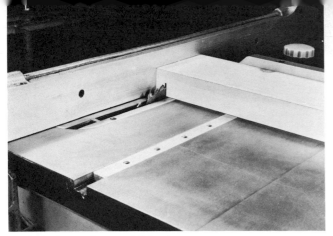

With the setting established as explained in the preceding photo, butt the end of the *mating* piece against the rip fence and use the miter gauge to advance it to make the kerf.

Set the saw blade at 45° and make the miter cut on the same piece. The miter cut and the inside bottom corner of the kerf should just meet. Blade projection is important so raise it a bit at a time until perfect.

The same miter cut is made on the mating piece with the contact point at the very corner of the work. Saw-blade projection on this step is not as critical.

If cuts are made accurately, the two parts of the simple rabbet miter will mate perfectly.

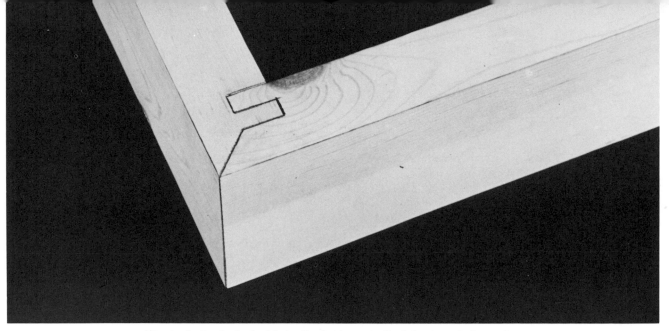

How to do the *locked* rabbet miter is shown in the following photographs.

It pays to draw a layout of the joint on a test piece. Here, blade projection is half the stock thickness, as is the distance from the fence to *outer* face of blade.

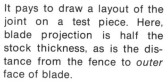

After the first cut on the *mating* piece, the groove is formed with the stock on end. Here, the distance from the fence to the *inside* face of the blade equals *half* the stock thickness.

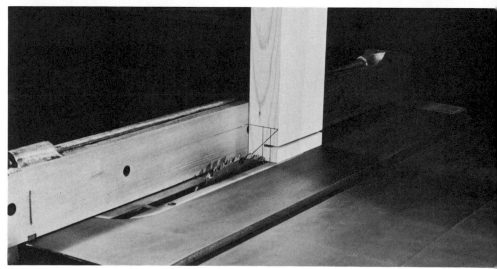

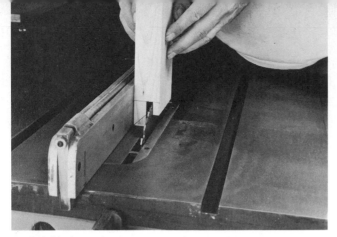

Set blade projection to *equal* stock thickness. Form the grooves by making repeat passes or by using a dado. Width of the groove should equal thickness of the tongue formed on the mating part.

The miter cuts on the parts of the *locked* design are made exactly as if the joint were a *simple* rabbet miter. Here the miter cut is shown being made on the same parts used in the first series of photos.

The mating part (the one you already grooved) gets its miter cut as shown here. Through this whole operation it would pay mightily to make trial cuts on scrap material similar to the good stock.

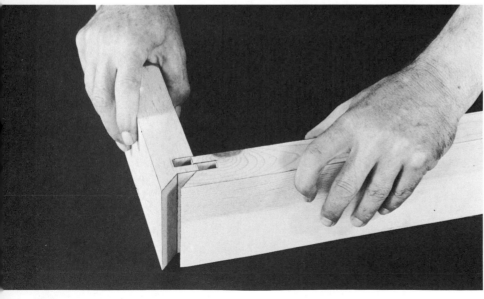

The locked rabbet miter fits together like so.

The *housed* rabbet miter is a good design for joining pieces that are different in thickness.

Start with the thicker piece. Blade projection equals thickness of this part *minus* that of the thinner one. Fence distance to blade's *outer* surface equals thickness of the thinner stock.

The miter cut on the thick stock starts exactly at the corner and just meets the bottom inside corner of the shoulder cut. Blade projection is critical.

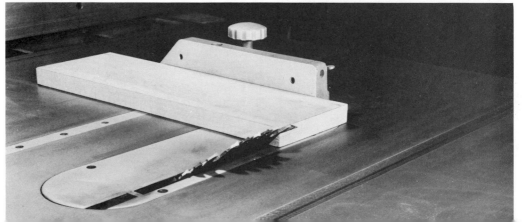

Final cut, on the thinner piece, is a simple miter. Where the fence can't be used as a stop, gauge the starting position by clamping stop block to table.

Splines are slim strips of wood that fit into grooves cut in the edges of mating pieces. Their basic purpose is to reinforce but on many types of joints they also help in assembly.

A V-jig, attached to the miter gauge, lets you groove across compound-angle cuts. The splines used here would be triangular and are thus called "feathers."

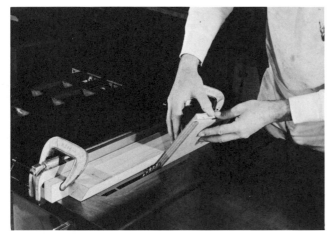

Here's a way to form spline grooves in compound-angle cuts. The beveled guide block is clamped to the rip fence so it forms a neat nook to snug the work in.

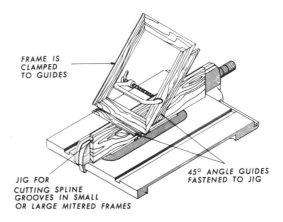

FRAME IS CLAMPED TO GUIDES

JIG FOR CUTTING SPLINE GROOVES IN SMALL OR LARGE MITERED FRAMES

45° ANGLE GUIDES FASTENED TO JIG

A "feathering" jig is nothing more than a tenoning jig with 45° angle guide to hold a pre-assembled frame so you can slot across the miter joint. A triangular piece is used in the groove that is formed.

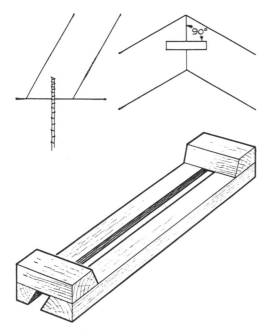

A slotted jig, cut to match the bevel angle, automatically holds the work at the proper slant. The spline grooves must be perpendicular to the bevel.

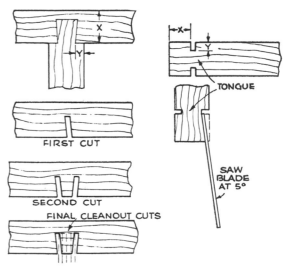

FIRST CUT

SECOND CUT

FINAL CLEANOUT CUTS

TONGUE

SAW BLADE AT 5°

How to cut a dovetail slot and tongue on the table saw. It can be done but the job is much easier to do on other tools.

DECORATIVE WORK ON THE TABLE SAW

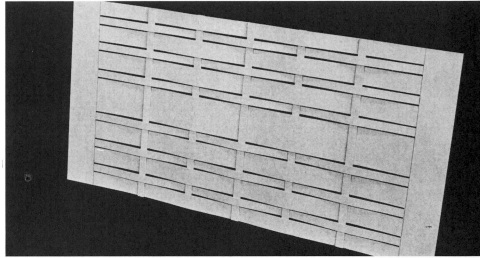

Multiple, parallel saw cuts make it possible to "weave" panels so they can be used decoratively in many ways.

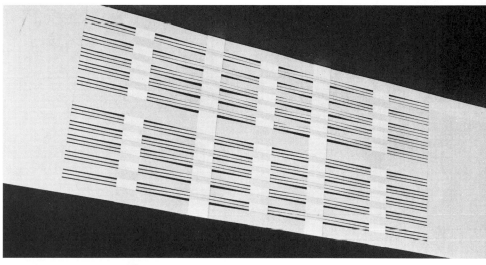

The more saw cuts you make and the closer they are spaced, the more flexible the material becomes. The weaving can be done with similar or contrasting material like colorful plastic strips or something exotic.

The multiple saw blade technique certainly finds good application for this kind of work.

Surface cuts on wide pieces that are then strip-cut produce slats for assembly into decorative panels. The kind of designs you can get are infinite.

The cuts on the original block to produce this pattern were all done with a regular saw blade.

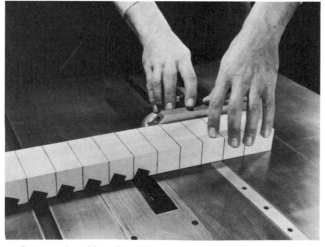

Cuts made with a tilted dado are the start for this pattern. Note the guide lines on the work.

Flipping the stock and making opposing cuts complete the basic block shaping.

with thin, wooden slats or another material. This procedure is a good place to employ the multiple-blade cutting technique.

The "doodles" technique calls for making matching cuts across opposite surfaces of a piece of lumber and then assembling strips that are rip cut from the board. The strips may be bonded edge-to-edge with contact cement, but for many jobs where the pieces might be enclosed with framing, you don't even have to do that. Pieces cut in such a manner make good slat material for tambour doors.

The third technique is a kind of "piercing." You make cuts on one side of a panel with the cutting tool projecting a bit more than half the panel thickness. Then you turn the panel over and make opposing cuts. Openings are created where the cuts cross. These can be almost any shape, depending on how you plan the design. Even diamond-shaped openings are feasible if you make angular cuts.

SPECIAL JIGS

A supersliding table. You can get very impressive accuracy when you work with this type of table-saw accessory. It also allows you to do some offbeat jobs safely. This accessory can be one of the most important tools in your shop. But you can't buy one; you have to make it. Even with the extra care you should use when making it, it's really not much more than a weekend's job.

Use a good grade of plywood for the table and the guides. Table size is not critical, but it should be larger than the saw table without becoming unwieldy. Plywood or hardwood can be used for other parts. Be especially careful when attaching the miter guides. Your best bet is to lay them out with accurate tools and then cut them a bit oversize. Finish off by sanding exactly to size. The miter-gauge V-blocks have to be a precise 90°. Similar attention to detail applies to all the construction since the accuracy you get from the table will be affected by how carefully it is made.

Be sure to start assembly by attaching the table guides to the table. Set the table squarely on the saw with the blade retracted, and then C-clamp the guides in place. Let the guides ride against the table edges just tightly enough to prevent any lateral play but without preventing the table from sliding freely. After the guides are attached, raise the blade so it cuts its own slot.

The crosscut fence is attached permanently, but the adjustable fence and both V-blocks can be moved. In each case, the locking device is the same. Slots are cut in the part and matching holes drilled through the table. Drive a Tee-Nut into each hole from the underside of

Flipping the stock makes opposing cuts in design. Note that the cuts produce both V's and slots.

After the "shaping" the blocks are strip cut and the resulting slats are joined edge-to-edge.

"Piercing" is done by making cuts on both sides of the stock with the cutter projection a bit more than half the stock thickness. Precision in blade-height setting is important.

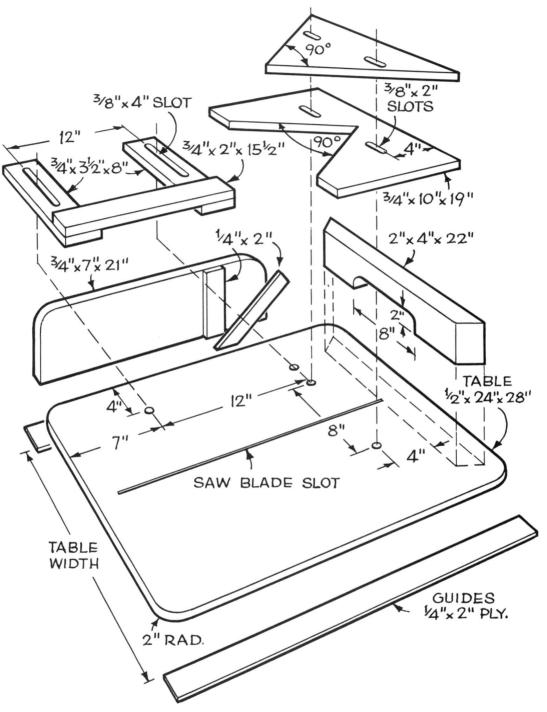

3/8" x 4" SLOT

3/8" x 2" SLOTS

12"

3/4" x 3½" x 8"

3/4" x 2" x 15½"

90°

90°

4"

3/4" x 10" x 19"

3/4" x 7" x 21"

1/4" x 2"

2" x 4" x 22"

2"

8"

TABLE
½" x 24" x 28"

4"

12"

7"

8"

4"

SAW BLADE SLOT

TABLE
WIDTH

2" RAD.

GUIDES
1/4" x 2" PLY.

Construction details of the sliding table.

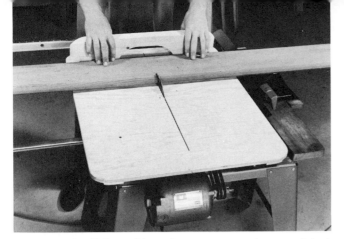

The basic sliding table makes a very good crosscut tool, especially for wide stock.

Slots for adjustment are cut in the V miter-guide. Attach it by pushing headless $\frac{1}{4}''$ bolts through the slots into holes in the platform. Wing nuts go on top, Tee-Nuts on the bottom.

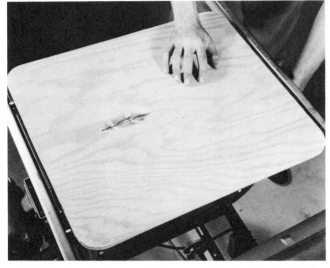

The blade cuts its own slot as you raise the blade with the sliding table in working position. A sharp, hollow-ground blade teams up fine with the table but any kind will work.

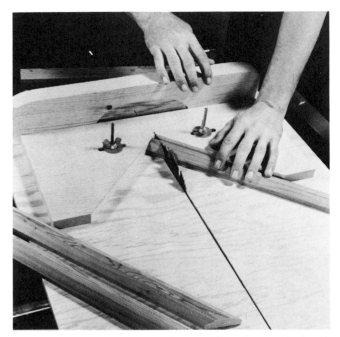

Finished pieces are mitered by guiding them with the V-block. Since the entire table moves, the work piece stays steady and you get a perfect cut.

Use a carpenter's square to set the crosscut fence at right angles to the saw blade. Once aligned, clamp the fence and drive countersunk screws upward through the table.

Miter uncut stock with the inverted V guide. Pieces can be cut anywhere along their length and you can work on either side of the blade.

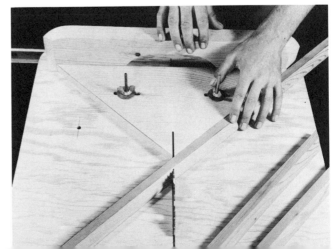

the table. The nut takes a headless $\frac{1}{4}''$ bolt inserted from above. A wing nut with a flat washer under it tightens down the slotted part.

This jig, as well as the others which will be shown, should be finished in good style. Sand all parts super-smooth and then apply several coats of sealer with a light sanding between each coat. Steel wool the final application. Use paste wax on the underside of the sliding table and on the surface of the saw table to reduce friction.

All-purpose jig. This jig is mounted on its own sliding table. It improves safety and accuracy on any cut where the stock must be held on its small edge, which includes tenons, grooves, tongues, and molding-head returns. The design is basically that of a tenoning jig, but because it's mounted on its own table, it's about as sophisticated as you can get without spending money for a commercial type.

Unless you own a very small table saw, the dimensions given in the accompanying drawing should be suitable. Do check the width of the sliding table against the distance between saw blade and table slot. If necessary, you can reduce the width or relocate the wooden bar that rides the slot. Leaving about $1\frac{1}{2}''$ between the left edge of the sliding table and the blade works quite well.

The position of the crosspiece on the table is critical. The angle between it and the saw blade must be 90°. The facepiece of the carrier assembly must be 90° to the saw-table surface. The handsaw-type handle is very convenient, but the clamp carriage is optional. If you have a good variety of conventional woodworking clamps, you can get by without it.

You will get the maximum use out of this jig if you visualize it as a holder and carrier for stock that requires being held on a small edge in order to be cut. Setting up is just a matter of situating the carrier face in relation to the cutter and the cutter projection in relation to required depth of cut.

A vertical table. This jig will do many of the jobs described for the all-purpose jig, but it's a unit you attach to the rip fence rather than to a table of its own. Also, it has its own miter gauge so angular settings can be infinitely variable between extremes.

Be careful of the setback at the base of the platform (the rabbet formed by the bottom miter-slide guide and the backup board). Determine this by the height of the rip fence; just a fraction less than the total rip-fence height is fine since you don't want the jig scraping the table when you position the fence.

The top edge of the bottom slide guide must be parallel

Make tenons and other difficult vertical cuts more safely and easily with a vertical guide on the table's rip fence for alignment and backing.

Tenoning, splining, or half-lapping a mitered piece requires a 45° guide in place of the vertical one. Guides are held in place with screws.

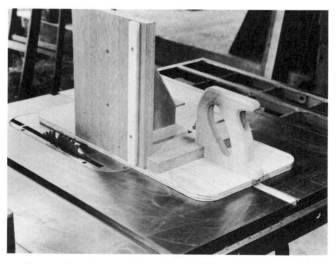

Mounted on its own sliding table, this jig vastly improves both safety and accuracy on any kind of cut where the stock must be held on the small edge.

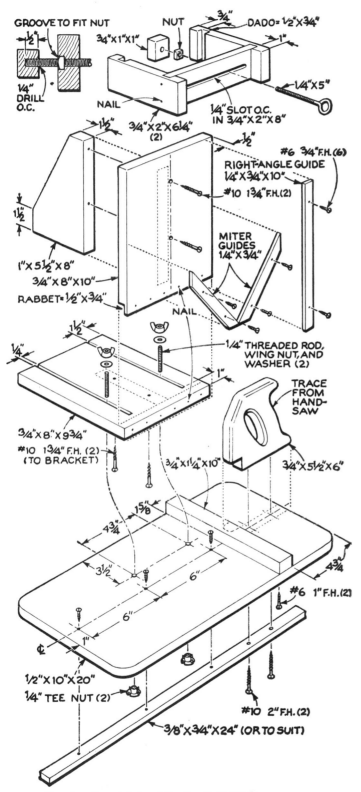

GROOVE TO FIT NUT
NUT
DADO = 1/2" X 3/4"
3/4" X 1" X 1"
3/4"
1"
1/4" DRILL O.C.
NAIL
1/4" X 5"
1/4" SLOT O.C. IN 3/4" X 2" X 8"

1 1/2"
3/4" X 2" X 6 1/4" (2)
1/2"
#6 3/4" F.H. (6)
RIGHT-ANGLE GUIDE 1/4" X 3/4" X 10"
#10 1 3/4" F.H. (2)

1 1/2"
MITER GUIDES 1/4" X 3/4"

1" X 5 1/2" X 8"
3/4" X 8" X 10"
RABBET = 1/2" X 3/4"
NAIL

1 1/2"
1/4"
1"
1/4" THREADED ROD, WING NUT, AND WASHER (2)
TRACE FROM HAND-SAW

3/4" X 8" X 9 3/4"
#10 1 3/4" F.H. (2) (TO BRACKET)
3/4" X 1 1/4" X 10"
3/4" X 5 1/2" X 6"

1 5/8"
4 3/4"
3 1/2"
6"
4 3/4"
6"
#6 1" F.H. (2)
1"
1/2" X 10" X 20"
1/4" TEE NUT (2)
#10 2" F.H. (2)
3/8" X 3/4" X 24" (OR TO SUIT)

Construction details of the jig-of-all-work.

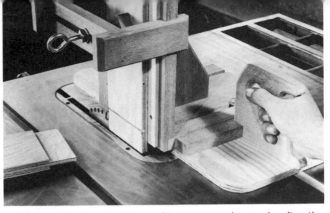

Cheek cuts on tongues and tenons can be made after the shoulder cuts are produced in conventional manner. Great advantage of jig is shown here where work would fall into insert slot if not supported.

Miter guides are used on the face of the jig for feeding stock that has an angle-cut end. Here, a spline groove is formed in a 45° miter cut.

Making the groove for a feather spline in a 45° frame joint. On such jobs you don't have to worry about centering the grooves if you have this type of jig.

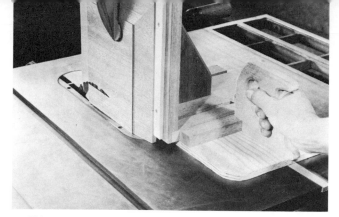

This panel-raising operation is accomplished with greater accuracy and far more conveniently because of the utilization of a carriage jig.

A true tenon takes four passes after the shoulder cuts are made. If you choose to work with a dado assembly, you can skip the shoulder cuts. The dado will do the whole job.

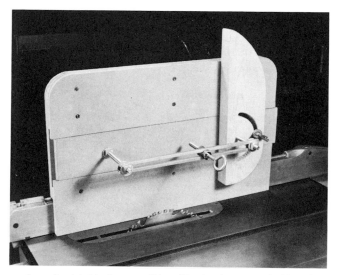

Another big job—shaping the top of a 4 × 4 fence post with the jig. When initial cuts prevent bottom edge of the work from resting on the sliding table (as here), use a scrap piece of wood to establish work height before clamping to the jig.

A vertical table is something like having a workable miter gauge on a plane that is 90° to the saw table.

A typical job is the cutting of tenons. The middle member of jig slides horizontally during pass, carrying work with it.

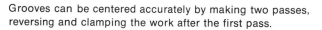

Grooves can be centered accurately by making two passes, reversing and clamping the work after the first pass.

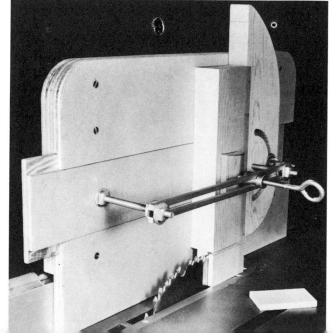

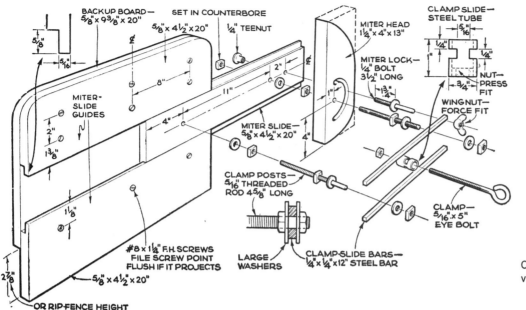

Construction details of the vertical table.

to the table surface. Your best bet here, after the rabbets are cut, is to clamp this piece in position against the fence and clamp the backup board to it while you drill holes for and then tighten the screws that hold the two pieces together. After that, you can remove the two pieces, put the miter slide in place, and screw on the top slide guide. The top slide guide should be fitted fairly snugly but not so tightly that the miter slide won't move easily. A coating of paste wax will help solve that problem.

The "thingamajig." For lack of a better term, we'll label this device a "thingamajig." It's a strange looking table-saw accessory, but there are times when it functions in fine style on jobs inconvenient to do any other way. It can be used in either table slot or against either edge of the saw table. It will handle odd-angle cuts or tapers, or it can be used parallel to the saw blade for ripping or crosscutting small stock.

Make the guide from $\frac{5}{8}''$ hardboard-surfaced plywood or a good hardwood. The arms are straight pieces $1\frac{1}{2}''$ wide x $16\frac{1}{2}''$ long. First cut the tenon on the end of each piece. This should be a snug fit in the slot cut in the guide. Repeat saw cuts will form the slots in the arms. The slight radius left by the saw blade at the ends of the cuts is not objectionable. Be sure that you hold the parts together when drilling the hole for the pivot. This should be a tight fit for a $\frac{1}{4}''$ bolt. Use hardwood for the table-slot bar and size it very carefully. Make it as tight a fit as possible without interfering with the sliding action. Be sure to recess the Tee-Nuts for a flush fit.

The rotajig. With this unusual tool you can form both round and square tenons on square or round stock,

and you can do this work on the table saw using a saw blade or dado. The rotajig also connects to the miter gauge and works like an extension of the gauge, permitting conventional-type cross or miter passes.

Work guides can be made to hold almost any odd-shaped piece so further cutting can be done accurately and safely. Each work guide you make becomes a permanent part of the setup for future use on similar applications. A critical dimension is the distance from the center of the holes in the guide holders to the table surface. As shown in the accompanying drawing, this tool is very good for a 10″ blade with about a 3″ projection. If your maximum blade projection is considerably less, you should probably adjust that one dimension to get maximum depth of cut on work held in the jig.

So that they will retain the work guides, make the holders from two pieces of stock with the hole in the thin piece a bit smaller than the hole in the thick piece. Then glue the two together. Use a fly cutter or hole saw to form the holes. If you don't have one of these tools, do the job on a jigsaw but make the cuts undersized so you can finish with a drum sander. This also applies to the retainers.

The work guides must fit well in the holders. Make them from the same material used for the holders and then reduce the thickness just a fraction by sanding. The kind of opening you make depends on the work, a square opening for square stock, a round opening for round stock, or a diamond-shaped, cross, quarter-round, or rectangular opening to correspond to the particular work shape. In some situations, guides can do double-duty. For example, if you have guides with a 1″ square

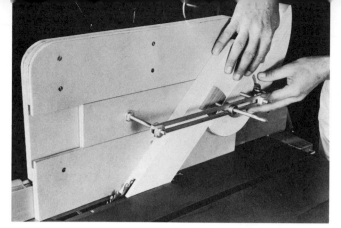

Since the head is adjustable you can do this kind of work without having to add extra guides to the vertical jig.

Taper legs by setting the thingamajig and cutting two adjacent slides of the stock. Reset the jig (the cutoff can be used as a gauge) and make the remaining two cuts.

Wider work can be cut like this using the edge of the saw table to guide the thingamajig. The jig may be used in either table slot or against either edge of the saw table. It may also be turned over and used backwards.

opening, they can be used to work 1″ dowels.

Be sure that you provide for the slot in the miter-gauge connection piece since this makes it possible to situate the jig close to the cutter for maximum work support.

LATHE WORK ON THE TABLE SAW

"Turning" bowls. With quite a variation of the coving technique, you can form troughs. Instead of an oblique feed (as in coving), the action here is rotary with the work jig-positioned over the saw blade. When the work and the saw blade are on the same center line, the depression you create by making repeat, circular passes is a true arc.

Be extra cautious! You can't use a guard here, and even though the work covers the blade when you are doing inside cuts, a miscalculation might bring it through. The blade is exposed for outside cuts so keep your hands pretty much on your own side of the work as you turn it. By doing this, the project is kept between you and the blade.

The overhead pivot jig is used for inside cuts; the simple bottom-pivot jig is used for outside cuts. With the two you can accomplish complete bowl turning. Overall dimensions of the jigs are not critical. If necessary, change them to suit your equipment. The thickness of the platforms, in effect, reduces the maximum blade projection so don't make them thicker than $\frac{1}{4}$″. Be sure the pivot support bar is well above the maximum blade-projection height. The distance between the vertical supports limits the size of the stock you can turn between them. However, this distance can be increased if you wish.

It's difficult to be precise about how much to raise the blade after each pass. Too little is much better than too much. Actually, you will know when you are trying to cut too deeply because you'll have to force the work, and this should never be necessary.

There is considerable freedom in designing, as shown in the accompanying sketches. The complete design is based on the pivot point of the work as it relates to the center line of the saw blade.

It's possible to do much of the inside turning with a V-block instead of a pivot. A pivot works satisfactorily, but the V-block demands that the work be a perfect circle to begin with and doesn't forgive error. The overhead pivot lets you work on square stock as well as round, and it keeps the work position constant.

Fence jig for spindle work. Strangely enough, many intriguing lathe effects can't be accomplished on the lathe itself or by using conventional turning tools. Most longitudinal details—cuts like reeding and fluting—

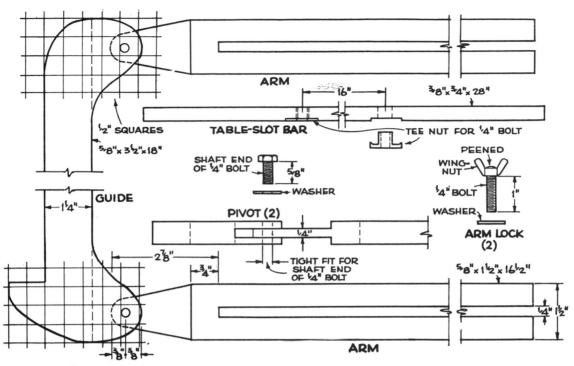

ARM

TABLE-SLOT BAR

$\frac{3}{8}" \times \frac{3}{4}" \times 28"$

½" SQUARES

$\frac{5}{8}" \times 3\frac{1}{2}" \times 18"$

TEE NUT FOR ¼" BOLT

GUIDE

SHAFT END OF ¼" BOLT

$\frac{5}{8}"$

WASHER

PEENED

WING NUT

¼" BOLT

1"

WASHER

ARM LOCK (2)

1¼"

PIVOT (2)

¼"

TIGHT FIT FOR SHAFT END OF ¼" BOLT

$\frac{5}{8}" \times 1\frac{1}{2}" \times 16\frac{1}{2}"$

$2\frac{7}{8}"$

$\frac{3}{4}"$

$\frac{1}{4}" \quad 1\frac{1}{2}"$

$\frac{3}{8}" \frac{5}{8}"$

ARM

Construction details of the thingamajig. Photos on opposite page show how it is used.

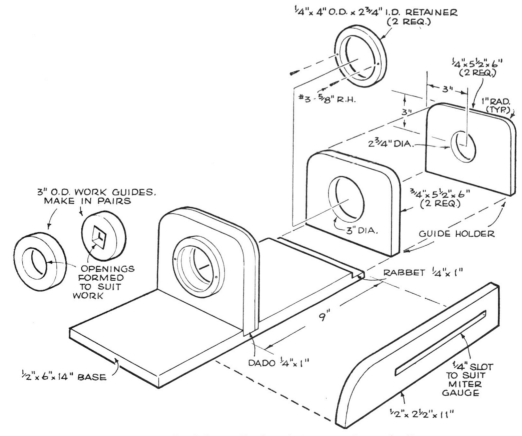

¼" x 4" O.D. x 2¾" I.D. RETAINER (2 REQ.)

#3 - ⅝" R.H.

¼" x 5½" x 6" (2 REQ.)

1" RAD. (TYP.)

3"

3"

2¾" DIA.

$\frac{3}{4}" \times 5\frac{1}{2}" \times 6"$ (2 REQ.)

GUIDE HOLDER

3" O.D. WORK GUIDES. MAKE IN PAIRS

OPENINGS FORMED TO SUIT WORK

3" DIA.

RABBET ¼" x 1"

9"

DADO ¼" x 1"

¼" SLOT TO SUIT MITER GAUGE

½" x 6" x 14" BASE

½" x 2½" x 11"

Construction details of the rotajig. See photos on next page for its uses.

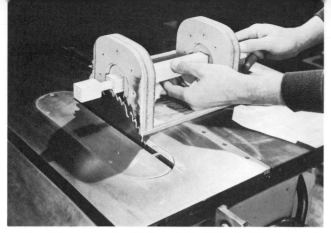

Here's how to work with the rotajig: While holding the work, you turn it in the guides to make the cut.

Substitute a sanding disc for the saw blade and you enter another big work area. Here, end of dowel is being angled. To get a conical point, rotate the dowel.

Work guides are all the same in outer diameter, but differ in inside shape to accommodate the work. Reduce outer diameter a bit so holders turn freely.

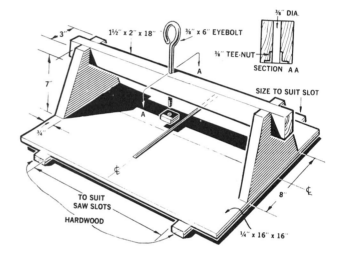

3"
1½" x 2" x 18"
⅜" x 6" EYEBOLT
⅜" DIA.
⅜" TEE-NUT
SECTION A A
7"
A
A
SIZE TO SUIT SLOT
¾"
C
8"
C
TO SUIT SAW SLOTS
HARDWOOD
¼" x 16" x 16"

Construction details of the overhead pivot jig.

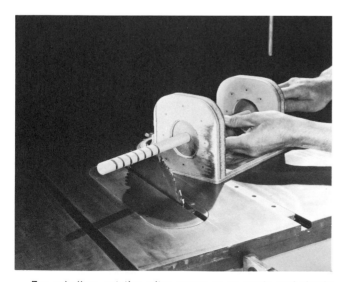

For spiraling, set the miter gauge at an angle and slowly rotate the work against the direction of rotation of the saw blade. The work will feed itself.

This cutaway view of a piece of work shows the arc formed by the blade as you rotate the work while you keep increasing the depth of the cut.

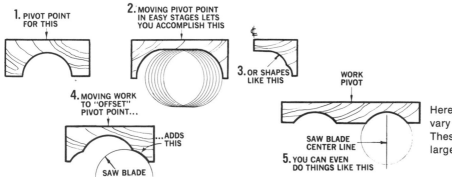

1. PIVOT POINT FOR THIS

2. MOVING PIVOT POINT IN EASY STAGES LETS YOU ACCOMPLISH THIS

3. OR SHAPES LIKE THIS

4. MOVING WORK TO "OFFSET" PIVOT POINT... ...ADDS THIS

SAW BLADE

WORK PIVOT

SAW BLADE CENTER LINE

5. YOU CAN EVEN DO THINGS LIKE THIS

Here are methods that permit you to vary the shape on the inside cuts. These ideas can be used to produce larger bowls.

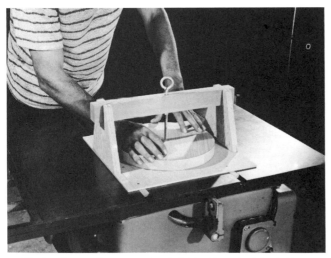

Work of any shape can be held by the pivot bolt. Form a slight depression in the center of the work by drilling into it with a countersink, and then turn the pivot downward until it rests snugly in the countersink.

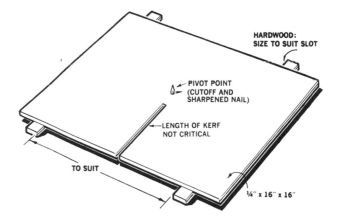

HARDWOOD: SIZE TO SUIT SLOT

PIVOT POINT (CUTOFF AND SHARPENED NAIL)

LENGTH OF KERF NOT CRITICAL

TO SUIT

¼" x 16" x 16"

The flat jig is simply a platform riding twin bars that fit the table slots. Sketch shows construction details.

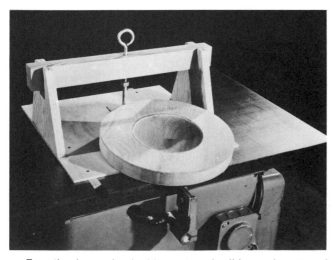

Even the depression in this section of solid core door turned out smoothly. The secret is not to take too deep a bite and to do the last few passes so the blade barely scrapes.

Outside shapes are varied by changing the distance from the center of the work to the blade. Blade height and tilt are also factors. Rotate work either left or right. Make repeat passes, raising the blade a bit after each.

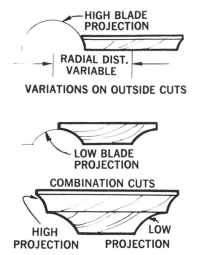

HIGH BLADE
PROJECTION

RADIAL DIST.
VARIABLE

VARIATIONS ON OUTSIDE CUTS

LOW BLADE
PROJECTION

COMBINATION CUTS

HIGH
PROJECTION

LOW
PROJECTION

Some ideas on how to do the outside cuts. Note that different types of cuts can be combined to add to shape variety.

You can "turn" square stock into a cylinder by making successive passes with a conventional saw blade—but only after you equip yourself with a jig like this.

poles. In addition, by using a regular saw blade, you can "turn" square stock into round and, by working with offset centers, form a tapered leg from square or round stock. Once you have become familiar with the tool, many other possibilities than the ones illustrated will occur to you.

Follow the construction details for the jig very carefully. Use a good grade of hardwood or a hardboard-surfaced plywood for the parts.

When adjusting the jig for work length, first set the

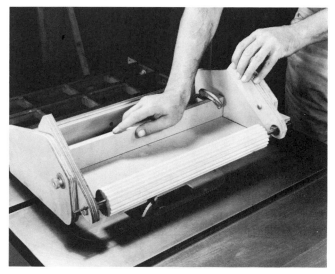

Reeding and fluting, the more common "after" jobs in lathework, are a cinch with the table-saw jig. After the cylinder has been mounted (above), make repeat passes over the cutter.

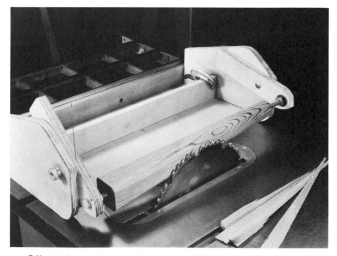

Offset the centers and you can "turn" a taper by making repeat passes with a regular saw blade. This is an ideal way to make multiple pieces for modern chair or table legs.

require a specially mounted and powered cutter, with the lathe—if it is used at all—merely a holding device for the work. Switching these functions to the table saw is really a logical alternative.

The rip fence is a ready-to-use guide. You have built-in depth-of-cut adjustment, and you can work with a molding head and its vast assortment of knives, a dado, or even a saw blade. Combine these assets with the fence jig, and you have a complete tool that is adjustable for work length and diameter. This jig also has mounting centers that can operate independently.

With the fence jig, you can make reeding or fluting cuts on stock that has been preshaped in the lathe or on ready-made cylinders such as large dowels or closet adjustable end in an approximate position and lock it in place with small C-clamps; then use the adjustable center for the final setting. Take up on the screw enough so the work will be held securely between centers.

Adjust the pivot arms for work height and lock in place. Set the rip fence so the center line of the work will be directly over the cutter. Raising or lowering the cutter gives you the depth of cut you want.

At all times, be sure that the work is locked in position, that all jig locks are tight, and that you feed with your hands well away from the cut area.

Jigs for circumference work. With this jig you can turn a block against an arbor-mounted molding head to achieve precise profiles that will rival the best efforts of a skilled woodturner.

Your "turning" patterns do not have to be limited by a meager assortment of molding knives. By utilizing portions of knife profiles and combining separate cuts, you can extend the basic shapes considerably. This jig can also be used with a dado to produce cylinders from square stock and to do many other jobs.

You can work with single, ganged, or spaced saw blades. You can even combine cutters such as a dado and a saw blade. Remember, with a saw blade or a dado that is set to cut a narrow groove, you can make deeper cuts than you should ever attempt with a shaped knife.

As a general rule, don't try to cut too deeply in one pass. Set the cutter below the table surface and after the work is mounted, raise the cutter slowly to make contact. Rotate the work very slowly against the rotation of the cutter while keeping your hands away from the cut area. The cutter should be raised slightly after each pass until you achieve the shape you want.

Round tenon on square stock can be formed by means of repeated passes over a regular saw blade. A dado assembly will make the job go faster.

Edge shaping on a rectangular block can be left as a decorative touch or the edges can be ripped off to make half-round, shaped molding.

Perfect beads can be machined on a cylinder. The octagonal block was mounted between centers and rounded with a blank cutter. Shoulder and beads were then cut with molding knives. A sure grip away from the cutting area, and a very slow feed against the cutters *are a must*.

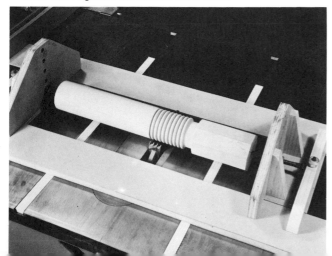

Tapered legs or spindles are turned in the same way that they would be on a lathe—with a true center at one end and an offset center at the other.

If you wish to use the jig for reeding or fluting, you can remove the miter-gauge strips so the jig can be run along the rip fence. Hand-hold cylinder and judge spacing by eye or make an indexing disc.

Upside-down-trolley version of the cylinder jig is for use with small diameter stock. This jig rides in the table slots and employs the rip fence as a stop. Be especially cautious on this and similar operations.

2 | RADIAL ARM SAWS

If you combine the rigidity of a large stationary tool with the flexibility of the portable circular saw, you get a fairly good picture of what a radial arm saw is. Of course, with this machine you always bring the work to the tool; but the fact that you can swing, tilt, raise and lower or adjust the cutting direction of the blade makes the tool-work relationship comparable to hand-held saw applications.

When the tool is ideally situated, it's easy to trim off the ends of 20′ long pieces of 2″ stock or to reduce such material to shorter lengths. This capability is a great feature of the radial arm saw and explains why the original model was generally a contractor's tool. The saw's table was extended to the left and the right to provide a total length of as much as 20′. Such support for long pieces that had to be crosscut, mitered, etc. made the tool ideal for people involved in house framing.

In modern versions, especially those designed for laymen's use, the tool still performs these basic applications well, but other features have been added and a wider range of applications devised so the inherent flexibility of the design is fully utilized. As a result, the radial arm saw enters the complete shop-in-one-tool category.

With the more advanced models, you can mount dadoes and molding heads, do shaping and routing, accomplish many drilling and sanding chores, use it as a power source to drive flex shafts and, sometimes, complement tools such as a lathe or a band saw. Some versions have built-in mechanisms to drive more than one arbor at different speeds. One type also has a variable speed changer.

Such features extend the tool's application to a variety of uses other than just sawing. However, if the tool is

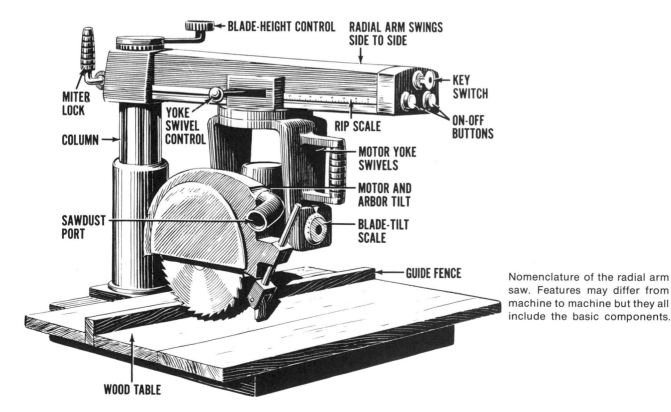

Nomenclature of the radial arm saw. Features may differ from machine to machine but they all include the basic components.

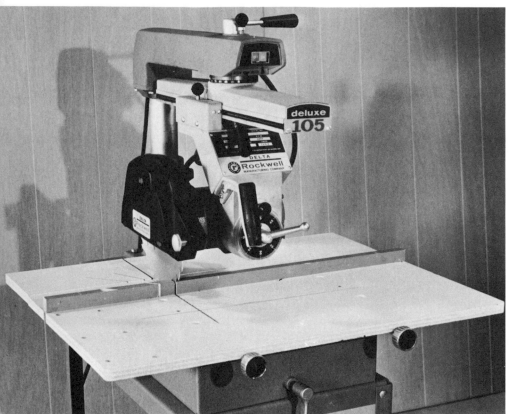

Radial arm saws range upward from an economy "under $100" model with an 8″ blade. This quality turret saw is equipped with a 9″ blade and has a $2\frac{1}{2}$″ depth of cut. Crosscut capacity is 14″.

Big 12″ machine has a 4″ depth of cut and develops $4\frac{1}{2}$ hp when run on 220-v. It can also be run on 110-v. It will crosscut up to 16″. Maximum rip cut is $26\frac{1}{2}$″.

limited to one arbor, one speed, and one direction of rotation, special adapters and cutting tools are usually offered as accessories.

As far as sawing is concerned, the big difference between the radial arm and the table saw can be demonstrated with a simple crosscut. On the table saw, you hold the work against the miter gauge and advance both the gauge and the wood past the blade to make the cut. On the radial tool, the work is set on the table and against a fence. The saw blade is pulled through to make the cut. Obviously, this procedure can have advantages in some areas—typically, on some angular cuts where a stationary workpiece can help achieve accuracy.

GENERAL CHARACTERISTICS

Design details may differ, but generally the motor is cradled in a yoke of sorts which in turn connects to a carriage that moves to and fro along an overhead arm. This is a basic cut action. You pull the motor unit toward you to make the cut, away from you to complete the pass action. The motor, the yoke, and the arm are all adjustable, and each component can be locked in a particular position to situate the saw blade for any cut you wish to make. For a miter, you simply swing the arm. For a cross-miter, you tilt the blade. When you do both, you get a compound cut.

The rotation of the saw blade is away from you. In essence, its action is to hold the work down on the table and against the fence as you make the cut by pulling the blade toward you. If you feed too fast, the blade will tend to "walk," much like a tractor tread. So feed speed is critical. For smoother cuts and safety, it's better to feed a little too slowly than too rapidly.

The yoke can swivel 360°. A 90° turn will place the blade parallel to the fence; this is the rip position. For ripping, you secure the blade in a particular position and move the work for the cut. When you turn the blade 90° toward the column, you set up for "in-ripping." When you turn the blade 90° away from the column, you organize for "out-ripping." The latter position is used for extra-wide rip cuts.

On rip operations, you feed the work against the blade's rotation. Therefore, the blade tends to fight feed pressure. This can cause kickback if you neglect to use the anti-kickback "fingers." This safety item is mounted on a rod that is situated in the saw guard. The fingers do not interfere with normal pass direction, but they dig in if the blade tries to fight you. It only takes seconds to set them up regardless of stock thickness.

It's normal on the radial arm saw for the blade to cut into the table; it has to in order to get through the stock. Each time you change the saw-blade position, for a miter

Some machines offer more than one outboard spindle. The upper one on this tool turns at 20,000 rpms—just great for shaping and routing.

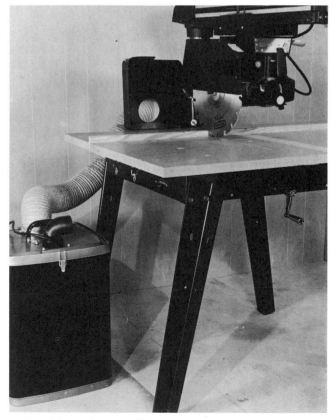

Special attachment will let you hook up to a shop vacuum cleaner so you can capture much of the waste produced when cutting.

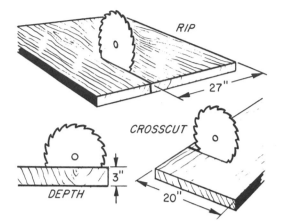

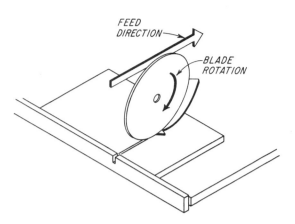

Capacities of the tool are listed as maximum crosscut, maximum rip, and maximum depth of cut. The smallest will cut through 2″ stock at 90° and at 45°.

How the blade cuts. Its rotation is away from you; you feed by pulling it toward you. You can see that pushing the feed might cause the blade to climb.

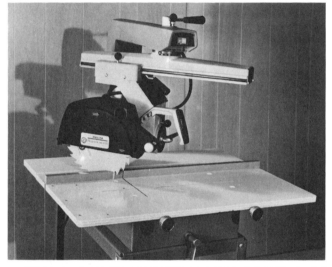

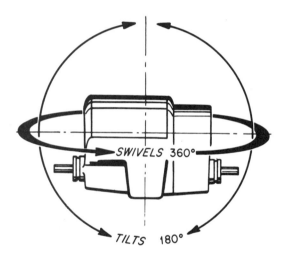

When you swing the arm (in this case the turret arm), you set up miter cuts. When the stock can be flipped, work in one miter position. If not, use both left- and right-hand positions.

When you swing the arm *and* tilt the blade, you get compound-angle cuts.

The motor unit swivels a full circle and tilts through 180°. It's this kind of flexibility that provides such an almost infinite number of tool-to-work positions.

For ripping, you set the saw blade parallel to the fence. This is an "outrip" setup.

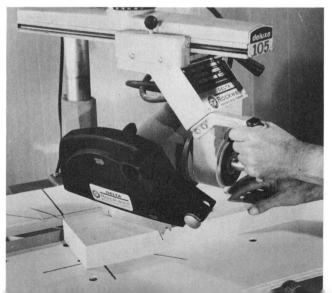

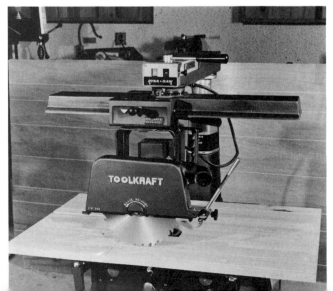

The guard covers about 50 per cent of the blade but may be tilted to cover more teeth on the operator's side. The rod supports anti-kickback fingers and it can be adjusted in relation to stock thickness.

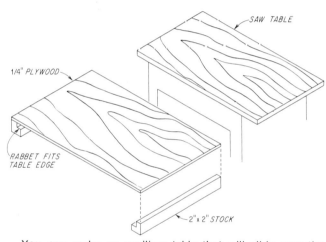

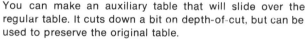

You can make an auxiliary table that will slide over the regular table. It cuts down a bit on depth-of-cut, but can be used to preserve the original table.

or a rip cut or whatever, you make a new cut in the table. This shouldn't bother you since it's routine; but for a lot of experimental cutting that might distress the table beyond normal needs, you can cover the table with a thin material to take the beating. This covering can be a piece of plywood that you tack-nail to the regular table or, as shown in the accompanying sketch, a cover with end pieces that allow you to slide the auxiliary table into place whenever you feel the need for it.

How much the saw blade penetrates the table is not critical; about $\frac{1}{8}''$ is sufficient for most cuts. Consider the fence an expendable item. If you did nothing but crosscutting on your radial arm saw, one fence might last forever; but if you use the saw for all types of cuts, the fence will take a beating and should be replaced when

necessary. However, it's nothing but a straight piece of wood, and you can quickly make a dozen as replacement parts or for use in particular applications.

WORK SUPPORT

One of the great advantages of the radial arm saw is the ease with which you can make cuts on long pieces of material. But this feature must be developed to make it wholly operational. A work support is the answer whether the tool you own is on casters so you can move it about or whether you place it in a fixed position.

A common work support is a roller-top floor stand, much like the one that is usable with a table saw. When used with the radial arm, it can be placed in position to support long work for crosscutting or for ripping. Since its height is adjustable, the independent stand may be used with other tools.

Contractors, who normally set the tool up outdoors and have no space limitations, and lumber-supply people, who also have no space problems, usually use roller-type extensions. When the tool is so equipped, it's no chore to square off the ends of pieces that are 20′ or more long. That example may seem extreme, but it is a fact that you may need a similar setup even if the lengths you ordinarily work with are only 6, 8, or 10 feet long.

Beyond the freestanding roller support, there are two other possibilities for work supports. Both are permanently attached to the saw. But the roller extension can be knocked down by removing a few screws, and the hinged extension flips down when not in use so it will take up little more room than the saw itself. Also, the hinged version won't interfere with mobility if you have the tool on casters.

The accompanying drawing gives specific dimensions for the roller type, but these dimensions can be changed to suit your own requirements. Two of these units, attached at either side of a 3′ saw table, will give you over 11′ of work support. If you want to make them longer, just supply more leg assemblies. If you work regularly with heavy structural lumber, you may prefer a stronger frame by substituting 2 x 4's for the $\frac{5}{8}''$ side pieces shown.

Suitable material for the rollers can range from antenna masts to seamless tubes. Just get something with enough wall thickness to be strong and with at least $1\frac{1}{2}''$ O.D. You can cut the plugs for the tube ends with a hole saw. Cut the plugs just enough oversize so they will fit tightly. The hole saw will also provide an accurate center hole. The bolt "axles" must be secured before the plugs are inserted.

For the hinged version, the length of the extension table must be related to the distance from the saw-table

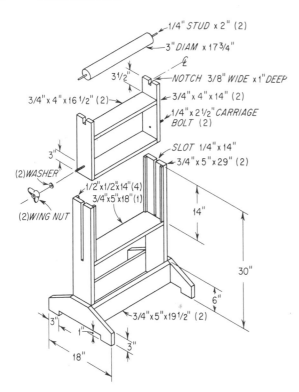

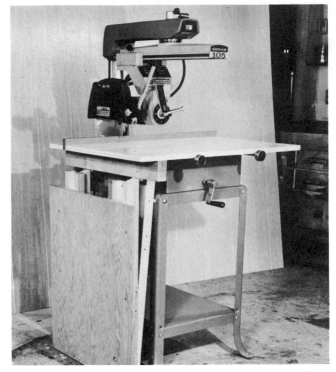

A roller top stand will provide good work support regardless of whether you are crosscutting or ripping.

In storage position, the extension table rests within the floor space required by the tool alone. Saw design and mounting determine the location of the attachment block.

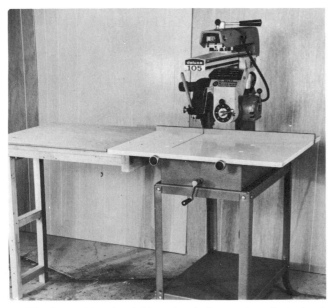

Flip-down extension table extends the work surface about $2\frac{1}{2}'$ but the design includes a sliding action that nearly doubles the support length.

Roller version, based on a conventional design, uses materials that are readily available. You can make it longer if you wish, merely by adding additional leg assemblies.

surface to the floor if the table is to be stored out of the way. This does impose limitations so a slide has been incorporated in the design. If you make it as shown, with one extension attached on each side of the main table, you can get 13′ of work support without sacrificing space-saving advantages.

Start this project by shaping the guides and the block that attaches to the table. Follow with the slides but dress down the dimensions just enough so they will move freely in the guide grooves. Attach the guides to the block by using 3″ T-hinges and set this assembly on a flat surface.

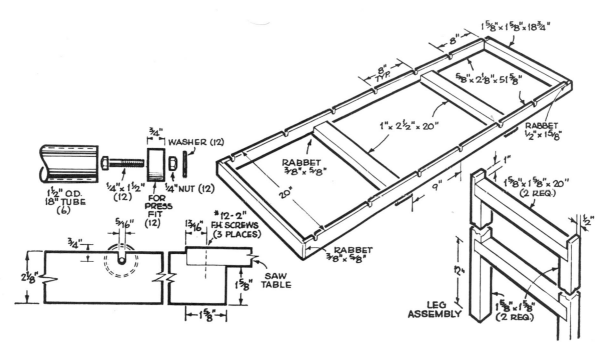

Construction details of the roller type extension table.

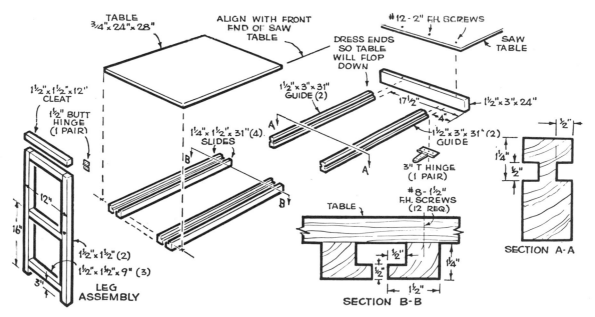

Construction details of the flip-down extension table.

After you cut the extension table to size, use clamps to hold it to the slides. Then, put this in place on the guides and make any necessary adjustment to be sure the table will move freely. Make the assembly permanent by using #8, 1½″ fh wood screws in place of the clamps. When you locate the extension table, be sure its forward edge lines up with the forward edge of the saw table.

Then you can cut and attach the cleat to the outboard end of the inner slides. When you make the leg assembly, adjust the height to match the distance from the saw-table surface to the floor. Attach to the cleat with 1½″ butt hinges.

Hold the block to the saw table with clamps and then drill for, and drive home, the #12, 2″ screws that secure it.

THE COMPLETE RADIAL ARM SAW SHOP

The design shown here is appropriate whether the radial arm saw is to be your only tool or one of many.

The plan is designed for efficient operation and easy construction. It doesn't require more than about 40 square feet of floor space yet provides ample storage facilities for the radial arm saw as well as accessories you need for other tools.

It isn't difficult to set up ideally for the radial arm since the average machine requires less than 3 square feet of space and is perfectly efficient when backed against a wall. Little maneuvering space is required in front of it, and you can get even more support than the benches provide by cutting an access door through an adjacent wall so extra-long boards can pass through the side of the building! For example, just about any length material can be handled in a shop that is little more than 10′ long because of an access door.

ALIGNMENT

To get the most out of your machine, check it immediately, and periodically thereafter, to be sure all components are in correct relationship. All machines have

(Continued on page 89.)

The complete shop, designed around a radial arm saw, provides lots of bench area and storage space while requiring a minimum of floor space. Long boards can poke out the access door on the left.

Cut carefully when you make the access, then you can use the cutaway material for the door itself. Note that the bottom of the opening is about $\frac{1}{2}''$ lower than the bench surface.

With this kind of setup, you have no problem when you must cut long material. When you have much to do, tack a strip to the bench top to extend the fence on the machine.

The perforated hardboard cabinet backs are a readymade means of hanging accessories. Many types of hooks are readily available so you can hang anything from saw blades to drum sanding accessories.

The drawers and the closet space beneath them are fine for larger accessories, supplies, etc. If your machine is not on a stand, set up a platform for it between the benches.

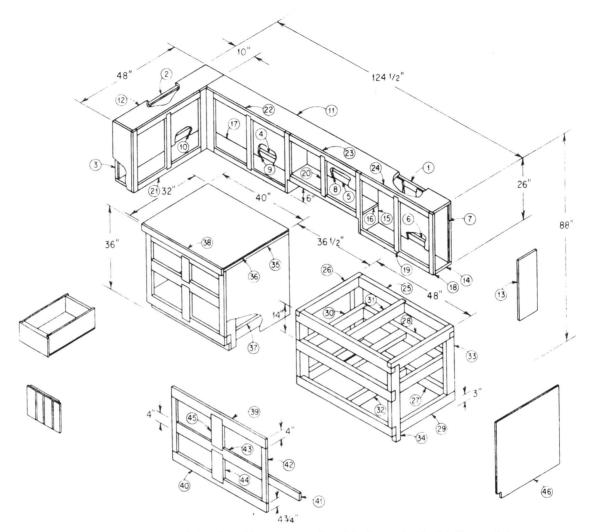

Construction details of the shop. The parts are keyed to the materials list. Some of the dimensions given are a bit oversize so you can trim to fit on assembly.

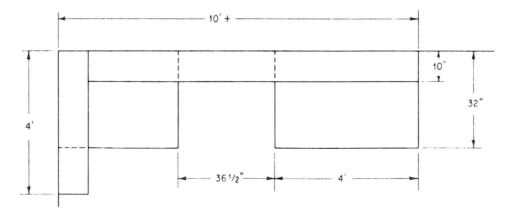

Floor plan of shop. It will fit in most oversize garages without interfering with cars.

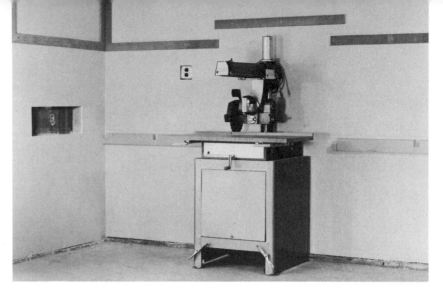

First step is to nail up the furring strips directly into the studs of the wall. Note how these pieces outline wall cabinet and floor unit positions.

MATERIALS LIST—RADIAL ARM SAW SHOP

No.	No. of Pieces	Size	Material
1	1	¾ x 2 x 122½	Fir lumber
2	2	¾ x 2 x 45¼	Fir lumber
3	2	¾ x 2 x 24½	Fir lumber
4	1	¾ x 2 x 39¼	Fir lumber
5	1	¾ x 2 x 36	Fir lumber
6	1	¾ x 2 x 36	Fir lumber
7	1	⅛ x 24½ x 46½	Perforated hardboard
8	1	⅛ x 17¾ x 36	Perforated hardboard
9	1	⅛ x 24½ x 40	Perforated hardboard
10	1	⅛ x 24½ x 48	Perforated hardboard
11	1	¾ x 10 x 113¾	Pine lumber
12	2	¾ x 10 x 47¼	Pine lumber
13	2	¾ x 10 x 26	Pine lumber
14	1	¾ x 10 x 46½	Pine lumber
15	2	¾ x 10 x 6	Pine lumber
16	1	¾ x 10 x 37½	Pine lumber
17	1	¾ x 10 x 40	Pine lumber
18	6	¾ x 2 x 26	Pine lumber
19	3	¾ x 2 x 24	Pine lumber
20	1	¾ x 2 x 18	Pine lumber
21	2	¾ x 2 x 34	Pine lumber
22	2	¾ x 2 x 30	Pine lumber
23	2	¾ x 2 x 36	Pine lumber
24	2	¾ x 2 x 46	Pine lumber

RIGHT-HAND FLOOR UNIT

No.	No. of Pieces	Size	Material
25	4	2 x 4 x 48	Fir lumber
26	2	2 x 4 x 31¼	Fir lumber
27	1	2 x 4 x 44	Fir lumber
28	1	2 x 4 x 40	Fir lumber
29	2	2 x 4 x 27¼	Fir lumber
30	2	2 x 4 x 29¼	Fir lumber
31	1	2 x 4 x 28¼	Fir lumber
32	2	2 x 4 x 27¼	Fir lumber
33	2	2 x 4 x 25	Fir lumber
34	2	2 x 4 x 33⅛	Fir lumber

LEFT-HAND FLOOR UNIT

No.	No. of Pieces	Size	Material
25	4	2 x 4 x 40	Fir lumber
26	2	2 x 4 x 31¼	Fir lumber
27	1	2 x 4 x 36	Fir lumber
28	1	2 x 4 x 32	Fir lumber
29	2	2 x 4 x 27¼	Fir lumber
30	2	2 x 4 x 29¼	Fir lumber
31	1	2 x 4 x 28¼	Fir lumber
32	2	2 x 4 x 27¼	Fir lumber
33	2	2 x 4 x 25	Fir lumber
34	2	2 x 4 x 33⅛	Fir lumber

RIGHT-HAND FLOOR UNIT

No.	No. of Pieces	Size	Material
35	1	¾ x 32 x 48	Fir plywood
36	1	⅛ x 32 x 48	Tempered hardboard
37	1	¾ x 31¾ x 48	Fir plywood
38	1	¼ x 2 x 48	Pine
39	1	¾ x 4 x 48	Pine
40	1	¾ x 4¾ x 48	Pine
41	1	¾ x 3 x 48	Pine
42	2	¾ x 2 x 26	Pine
43	1	¾ x 4 x 44	Pine
44	1	¾ x 2 x 14	Pine
45	1	¾ x 2 x 12	Pine

LEFT-HAND FLOOR UNIT

No.	No. of Pieces	Size	Material
35	1	¾ x 32 x 40	Fir plywood
36	1	⅛ x 32 x 40	Tempered hardboard
37	1	¾ x 31¾ x 40	Fir plywood
38	1	¼ x 2 x 40	Pine
39	1	¾ x 4 x 40	Pine
40	1	¾ x 4¾ x 40	Pine
41	1	¾ x 3 x 40	Pine
42	2	¾ x 2 x 26	Pine
43	1	¾ x 4 x 36	Pine
44	1	¾ x 2 x 14	Pine
45	1	¾ x 2 x 12	Pine
46	3	¼ x 32 x 36	Fir plywood

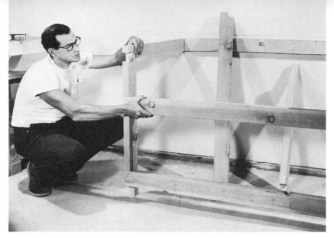

You can pre-assemble the front frame members and then set them in place as a unit. The simple end cuts provide a pretty good lock joint when the parts are assembled.

Be sure the bench frame is level. Check frequently as you proceed after you have installed the 2 × 4s on the walls. Work with a level—not a square.

It isn't necessary to make the bottom of the access opening level with the bench top. Keeping it a bit lower is better since it will assure adequate clearance for the work pieces.

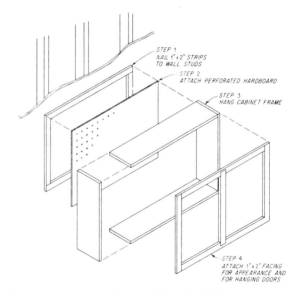

STEP 1
NAIL 1" x 2" STRIPS
TO WALL STUDS

STEP 2
ATTACH PERFORATED HARDBOARD

STEP 3
HANG CABINET FRAME

STEP 4
ATTACH 1" x 2" FACING
FOR APPEARANCE AND
FOR HANGING DOORS

How to set up the cabinets. Follow in 1-2-3-step order.

The center dividers of the wall cabinets will be stronger, and look better, if you notch them into the horizontal frame pieces. Use glue, and toenail through the divider.

built-in adjustment features so corrections can be made, when necessary, to maintain a high level of accuracy. How this is accomplished can vary from tool to tool, but the end result must be the same. Check your owner's manual for adjustment procedures to accomplish the following.

On a simple crosscut, the line of the blade must be 90° to the fence. Check by marking a wide piece of wood with a square and the cutting on the line. If the blade doesn't follow the line for the full length of the cut, you know adjustment is required. You can also check with a carpenter's square. Place the short leg against the fence and the long leg on the line of cut. Raise the blade to just clear the table and then, while pulling for a crosscut, see if the blade follows the line of the square.

The cut must be square to the work edge placed against the fence, but it must also be square to adjacent surfaces. This will occur if the vertical plane of the saw blade is 90° to the table surface. Use a square to check for this after you remove the saw guard. Be sure to place the blade of the square between set teeth on the saw blade.

When the "back" teeth of the blade do not cut on the same line as the "front" teeth, you get an undesirable result called "heeling." Check for this by crosscutting a wide piece of 2″ stock; halt the blade just short of leaving the stock. Check at the back teeth to see if there are pro-nounced radial marks on the cut edge. If there are, then adjustment is required. Adjustment is simply a matter of pivoting the blade a bit to the left or to the right. Heeling is something you can feel and see during normal cutting. The blade will seem to drag and cut edges will not be as smooth as they should be.

To check the angular settings—those for which the machine has auto-stops—work as you did for the crosscut. Mark the line on the work with a protractor and check to see if the blade follows the line as you make the cut. Actually, you could make gauge blocks from wide pieces of wood and keep them on hand for just this purpose.

The table surface should be parallel to the arm. Check by clamping or tack-nailing a large, flat board to the table. Adjust the saw blade to take a very light scraping cut, go through crosscut and miter passes, and swing the arm from one position to the other while the blade is turning. The shallow kerfs and coves you will make should be uniform in depth in all areas.

Check bevel-cut settings by making the cuts and checking the results with a protractor. Do this at each setting the machine has an auto-stop for.

You can and should check for all these factors as you work. Once in a while, put a square or a protractor on the cut you have made to assure yourself that things are

To get square cuts, the saw blade must travel a line that is 90° to the fence. To check this out you can use a wide board on which the cut line has been marked with a square.

To see if the blade is perpendicular to the table, use a square. Be sure the blade of the square rests between set teeth, then sight to see if the square is flush against the saw blade.

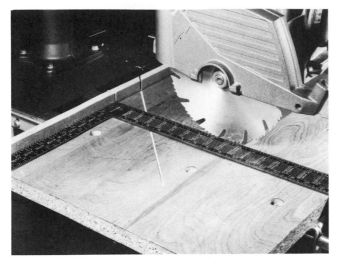

In checking angle, you can move blade along the long leg of a carpenter's square placed as shown. With this method, make sure that the machine is turned off.

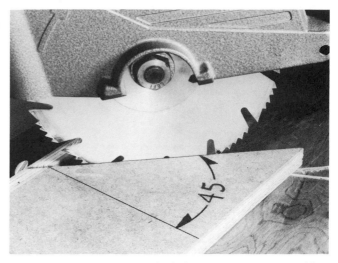

When you have automatic index stops on your machine, double-check them by setting them and then seeing if the blade will follow a line that you have marked on the work.

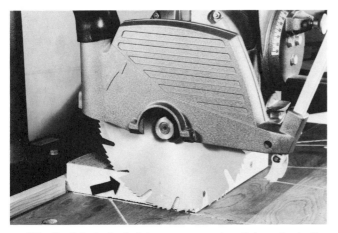

"Heeling" is indicated by pronounced radial marks in the area indicated by the arrow. When this is a fault, kerfs will be wider than they should be and you'll get excessive splintering on plywood.

as they should be. Machines do get out of alignment even during routine work sessions, and it's better to find out quickly when it does happen.

SAW BLADES

Everything said about saw blades in the chapter on table saws applies to blades for the radial arm machine, even feed speed as it affects smoothness of cut and choice of blade for a particular cut or material.

No matter what blade you use, forcing the feed will always result in a rougher cut than the blade will normally produce. If you want proof of this, make two cuts with the same blade. Feed as fast as possible on one without stalling the motor; feed easily and steadily

on the second. When you compare the two cuts, the effect of feed speed will be obvious.

On the radial arm saw it's not possible to get the free projection normally recommended for a hollow-ground blade. You can get around this, when you feel it's necessary, by placing a wide piece of plywood on each side of the cutline. This will raise the work and provide clearance under it for the blade. Place the plywood "elevators" so the gap between them is not much more than the normal kerf width.

CROSSCUTTING

When you start a crosscut, the saw blade should be positioned behind the fence. After you have placed the work snugly against the fence, you can turn on the machine and pull the blade toward you to make the cut. The total operation is not complete until you have returned the blade to the starting position.

It's usually a good idea to mark the cut line on the work. This gives you a point you can align with the kerf in the fence and provides a means for checking accuracy of the cut while you are working. Remember that the kerf has width and that it should occur on the waste side of the stock.

In most cases, you will use your right hand to do the feeding, your left hand to hold the work. Keep your left hand away from the cut line. If the workpiece is so small that holding it brings your hand close to the saw blade, you'd better have second thoughts about how to make that particular cut. If necessary, nail or clamp the work to the table and keep your hand in your pocket. When the work is held by hand, keep your hand in position until the blade has been returned to its starting position

The cut on the left was made with a combination blade. The other was made with a special plywood cutting blade. Difference makes obvious the wisdom of using the right blade for the right job.

behind the fence. The right hand holds the saw handle.

For extra-wide cuts—those beyond the capacity of the machine with the fence in normal-use position—do a normal crosscut to the full travel of the blade. After you have returned the blade to the starting position and have waited for it to stop, relocate the fence to its "back" position and position the work so the saw blade sits in the kerf already formed. Then make a second pass to extend the first cut.

You can do extra-wide crosscuts by flipping the stock after the first pass and making a second cut to meet the first one. A good job results when you are very careful about placing the work for the second cut. When the cut length cannot be solved by either of these methods, then you should plan to make the cut by using a ripping setup.

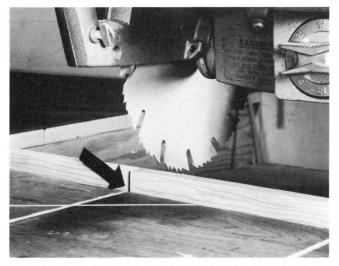

Make the guide cut in the fence after the fence has been locked in position. Thereafter, you can line up a mark on the work with this cut.

The "kerf" has width so be sure to situate the stock so that this occurs on the waste side.

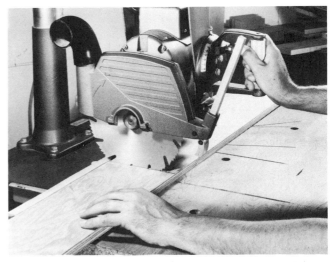

Good operator position is shown here. Use the left hand (well away from the saw blade) to secure the work—the right hand to pull the blade for the cut and to return it to its original position behind the fence.

When the cut is extra-wide, make one cut in the normal manner and then move the fence to the rear position. Situate the blade in the kerf and then make a second pass.

Stock that is thicker than the maximum depth of cut of the saw blade can also be crosscut by making two passes. Your best bet is to use a square to mark the cut line on opposite surfaces of the work. After you have made the first cut, flip the stock, line up the saw blade with the cut mark, and make the second pass.

When work size permits, you can do "gang cutting" to produce many similar pieces in one pass. Just butt the parts together and place them against the fence as if they were a solid piece. Then simply crosscut as you would normally.

Another way to produce similar pieces is to use a stop on the fence. The stop can be just a clamp, or you can make the special ones shown. To work, place the stop so it determines the length of the cutoff. Position the work against the stop and then cut. Avoid letting sawdust pile up against the stop, for the accumulation can throw off the accuracy of your setting.

On this kind of work, you'll probably leave the saw blade running as you position the work for each new cut; therefore, *be alert*.

With the blade set up for normal crosscutting, you can use a repeat pass technique to accomplish dadoes and rabbets. Elevate the blade above the table so the depth of cut will equal the depth of the dado or rabbet you need. When a lot of this work is required, it's best to use a dado assembly so you can accomplish the job faster and more accurately on similar cuts. But when you need just one or two, you can save setup time by staying with the saw blade and repeat passes.

Lastly, you can be guided by marks that you place on

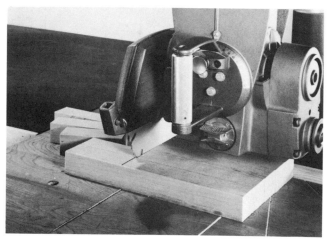

Gang cutting is just a question of holding several pieces edge-to-edge and then doing a normal cross-cut. A good way to produce many similar pieces with one cut.

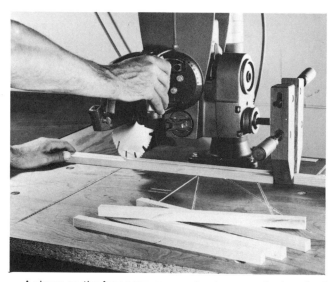

A clamp on the fence serves as a stop to gauge the length of the cutoff. Only a few seconds are needed to apply the clamp.

You can make adjustable stop blocks that slide smoothly along the fence. These become permanent accessories.

When the stock is so thick that you can't get through it in one pass, make a conventional crosscut, then flip the stock and raise the arm so you can cut from the other side, following a cut-line on opposite surfaces of the workpiece.

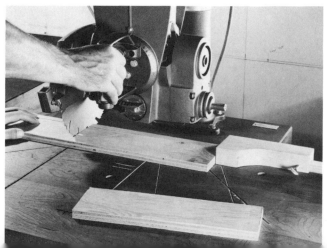

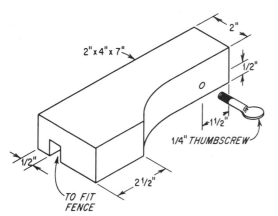

The stop block, made to these dimensions, is drilled for an undersize hole in which the thumbscrew is threaded.

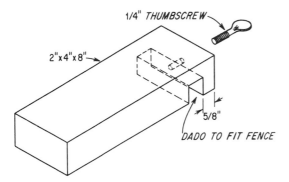

This type of stop block will extend farther out from the fence. On some types of cuts, it does a better job than the first one.

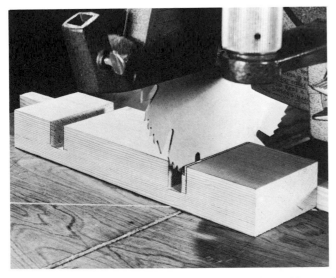

You can cut a dado with a regular saw blade by making repeat passes. It is best to do the outline cuts first and then clean away the waste stock.

the work, or you can use stop blocks to gauge the outline cuts and then clean away between them.

RIPPING

You do ripping by setting the saw blade parallel to the fence and locking it in position. Then you feed the stock against the direction of rotation of the blade. Adjust the anti-kickback fingers so they rest on the surface of the work; tilt the guard so the end nearest you covers a maximum amount of the saw blade. This is a safe position and one that will also capture most of the sawdust.

Because the motor unit can be rotated in either direction, you can set up for "in-ripping," which places the blade on the column side of the table, or for "out-ripping," where the blade is swung away from the column. The choice can be made according to the size of the work. The in-rip position is convenient for most work. If the width-of-cut range of the in-rip position isn't sufficient for the job, then set up for out-ripping. This allows you to get the maximum rip capacity from the machine.

The setup is made by measuring from the fence to the side of the blade that faces it. When the blade has set teeth, be sure to measure from the point of a tooth that is set toward the fence.

When the width of cut isn't sufficient to permit a safe hand feed, use a push stick. It's not a good idea to rely on a scrap piece as a push stick. The special one shown is designed to straddle the fence so it can't slip; it also has a long handle so you can push work past the blade without endangering your hands.

Use two passes to rip through a stock that is thicker than the maximum depth of cut of the blade. Raise the blade above the table so you get clearance between the bottom of the motor and the stock surface. Make a pass as you would for any rip cut. Then flip the stock and make a second pass. Since you are using a fence as a guide, the cut marks recommended for a similar operation when crosscutting are not needed here.

You can do a rip cut on stock that lacks a straight edge to ride the fence by tack-nailing a guide strip to its underside and then feeding so the guide strip rides the outboard edge of the table. The width of the cut is determined by the placement of the guide strip on the work and the position of the saw blade on the table. In most cases, it is best to set the blade in an out-rip position. Be sure to keep the guide strip snugly against the edge of the table throughout the pass.

HORIZONTAL SAWING

This feature is peculiar to the radial arm saw because of the many ways you can situate the saw blade. To set

When ripping, feed the work against the direction of rotation of the saw blade. Keep the right hand hooked over the fence, the left hand away from the blade.

For "outripping," the blade is positioned at the front edge of the table. This gives you the maximum rip capacity. Note that here, feed is from left to right. This does not interfere with safe set up of the guard and anti-kickback fingers.

A pusher stick is the way to go when work is narrow enough to get your hands too close to the cut area.

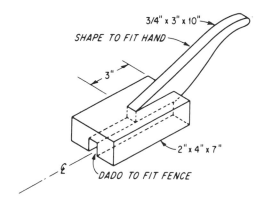

This pusher stick rides the fence so it can't slip. Cut the dado so the tool will slide easily.

To rip through extra thick stock, flip the work and cut again after you have made the first pass. Since the fence is a guide, you don't have to mark the stock for the cuts.

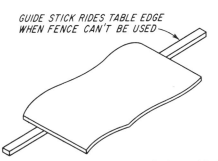

When the work doesn't have an edge that can ride the fence, tack-nail a guide strip to its under side. Then make the pass so the guide strip rides the front edge of the saw table.

up for horizontal sawing, raise the blade well above the table, turn it to the in-rip position, and then tilt it parallel to the table surface. Its position in relation to the fence can be adjusted by using the arm, pivoting the motor, or altering the position of the fence itself. After you have made the setting, be sure that all components are firmly locked.

For horizontal cutting, it's often necessary to raise the work above the table surface. This can be accomplished by placing the work on a board that you move along with the work or by tack-nailing a piece of plywood to the table.

With this method and similar techniques discussed later, it's often a good idea to use a special, high fence through which the cutter protrudes. Your best bet is to lock the fence in place and make the opening for the cutter by pulling it through slowly while it is turning.

Special tables can be made for horizontal cutting operations. These tables are especially useful when you hold the work still and pull the blade through for the cut. Used in such a manner, these tables provide a means for you to elevate the work as well as supply a fence that positions the work for an accurate cut.

A typical operation, made possible by combining horizontal cutting on one of the special tables and simple cutting with the blade in normal crosscut position, is the shaping of a wide two-pass rabbet. The width of the rabbet is established by cutting with the blade positioned horizontally and the work resting on the special table. The second pass, the shoulder cut, is done in normal crosscut position with the blade height set to meet the depth of the first cut.

More details on horizontal cutting will be given later in this chapter.

MITER CUTS

A miter cut is accomplished with the saw blade in normal crosscut position but with the arm of the tool swung to the angle required. On most machines, common angles such as 45° will have auto-stops. Settings for angles between the automatic stops have to be gauged by using a miter scale usually situated at the top of the column. Since the joining of miter cuts in good fashion relates directly to how accurately the cuts are made, it's good practice to check the first cut with a protractor before you proceed to cut all the pieces. In a picture frame, for example, being "off" just a second or two will result in quite a gap when you try to assemble all four pieces.

Hold the stock firmly against the fence and make the pass even more slowly than you usually do. On the radial arm saw, you don't have the amount of movement

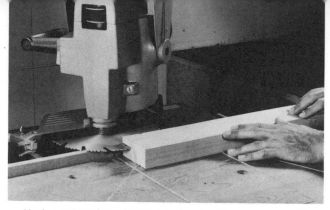

Horizontal cutting will prove convenient for some operations. You must be especially careful with hand placement when doing this kind of work.

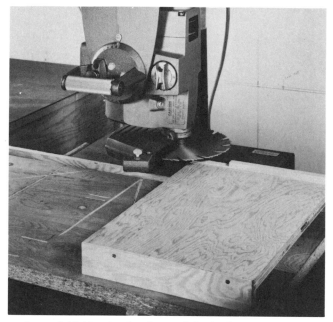

A special table elevates the work for horizontal cutting.

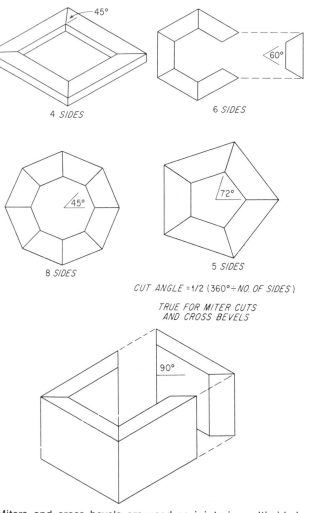

CUT ANGLE = 1/2 (360° ÷ NO. OF SIDES)

TRUE FOR MITER CUTS AND CROSS BEVELS

Miters and cross bevels are used as joints in multi-sided projects. The formula lets you select the correct cut angle for any number of sides.

from the cut line that you can encounter on a table saw. Even so, many professionals use a special fence as an aid in keeping the work stationary. This special fence is no more than a regular fence with nails or screws driven through from the back so the points protrude just a bit at the front. These protrusions help to hold the stock still as you pull the blade through.

Making miter cuts at each end of the stock is no problem when the material is flat and can be flipped for alternate cuts. This is not the case when mitering moldings. Then you must make both left- and right-hand cuts which means swinging the blade to achieve the positions. Therefore, you have twice as much room for error, which calls for being especially careful when setting up the machine and for making test cuts to prove the settings.

One possible method is to cut the frame pieces to overall size first and then miter the ends. This will waste some material, but you have to judge the cost of the waste

The simple miter is done by swinging the arm to the angle required and then pulling the saw blade as you would for a crosscut. Here, the setup is shown on a turret arm machine.

in terms of better accuracy. The use of a stop block makes the procedure even simpler. Cut the first piece and use it as a gauge for setting the stop block on the fence. The stop then positions other pieces correctly so the cuts will be duplicated.

You can also make and use special mitering jigs. When you do a good job making them, the accuracy of the cut will be assured. Whether you use precut pieces where you just miter the ends or make consecutive cuts along the length of a single piece, the saw blade position is for normal crosscut work. Thus, work placement, assured by the jigs, establishes the accuracy of the cut.

Cross Beveling. The cross bevel is often called a miter (or the reverse, if you wish). Whichever, you accomplish it with the blade in a crosscut position but tilted to the angle required. Whenever it is necessary to tilt the blade, elevate it above the surface of the table and, after tilting, lower it as it is turning to take the $\frac{1}{8}''$ bite in the table surface. When you run it through the fence, you get a kerf that you use like the one needed for crosscutting.

To cross bevel a number of pieces quickly, place them together as you would for a simple crosscut. Hold them firmly together in place and pull the blade across the whole batch.

Rip Beveling. The rip bevel is done with the machine in rip position but with the blade tilted to the angle required. Follow all the rip-cut rules about anti-kickback finger position, guard position, and safe hand placement. Feed the stock through as you would for a rip cut but be even more careful about keeping it snug against the fence throughout the pass. Use the push stick when necessary and always feed against the direction of rotation of the saw blade.

Chamfer Cuts. The chamfer cut is just a partial bevel. You can make it along an edge or across an end. When working on an edge, set the saw up for a rip-bevel operation. However, since you won't remove the entire edge of the stock, keep the blade elevated above the table. When the chamfer is across an end, set up as you would for a cross bevel.

V-grooves. Do V-grooves by setting up for a rip bevel but adjust the blade height to provide for the groove depth required. Two cuts are required for each groove. When the "V" is in the center of the board, you can turn the stock end for end to make the second pass. When it's located elsewhere, you must reset the blade in order to mate the second cut with the first cut.

Compound Miters. You cut a simple miter when you swing the arm but keep the blade in a perpendicular

When you can flip the stock, the saw blade can remain at the one setting for all the cuts. Perfect accuracy is required if the parts are to join correctly.

A stop block on the fence can be a big help when you cut miters on similar pieces. The operation calls for cutting the parts to correct length first.

V-shaped mitering jig positions the work at the correct angle, lets you do a mitering job as if it were a simple crosscut.

BEVEL CUTTING

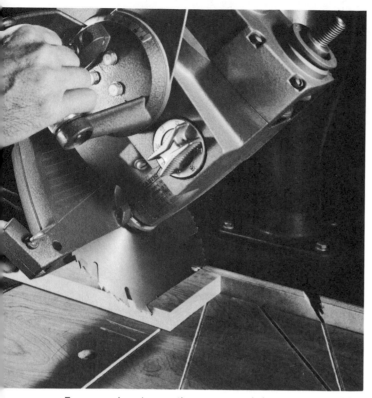

For cross bevel operations, you work in crosscut position but with the blade tilted to the angle you need.

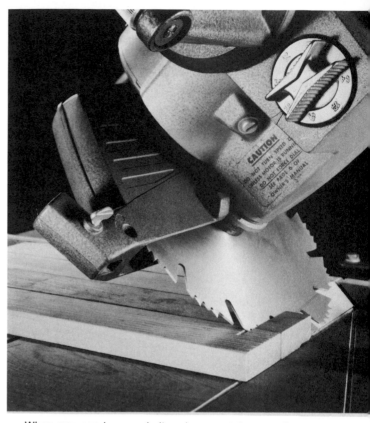

When you need many similar pieces, set them up for gang cutting. Hold the work pieces firmly together as you cut.

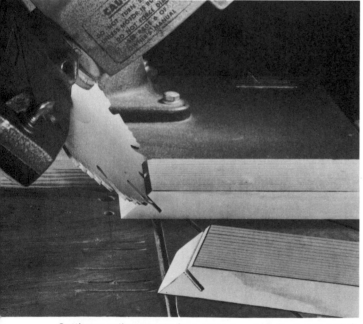

Cutting a spline groove in a cross bevel. Splines can match the kerf width of a regular saw blade.

position. If you swing the arm and also tilt the saw blade, you get a compound angle cut.

Compound miters are probably the toughest kinds of cuts to make simply because of the perfect accuracy they require. Everything we said about care when doing the simple miter has double the emphasis here. Work slowly, doublecheck each setting before you make the cuts, and test the setting by cutting first on scrap stock.

Sometimes, when you are cutting parts of similar length consecutively from one long board, you can use the first piece cut as a template for making the succeeding cuts. Flip the first piece over and place it on the board so you can mark the cut line with a very sharp pencil. Place the stock so the next cut you make will just remove the pencil line.

Being able to flip the stock will allow you to work exclusively with right-hand cuts. Othertimes, you must change the settings and make half the cuts on the right side and half the cuts on the left side. This situation should make it more obvious than any number of words that care in setting up is the primary factor.

If you first establish the slope angle of the work by

For rip bevels, work as you would for any ordinary rip cut but tilt the blade. There is greater tendency here for the work to move away from the fence so keep it secure throughout the pass.

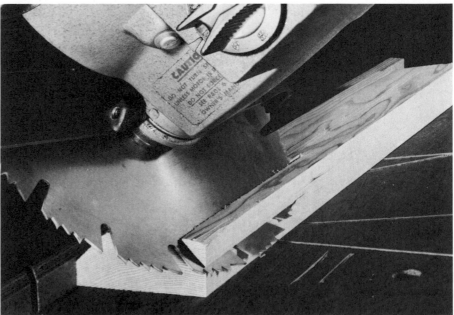

Do chamfer cuts the same way —just elevate the blade so it removes just part of the edge.

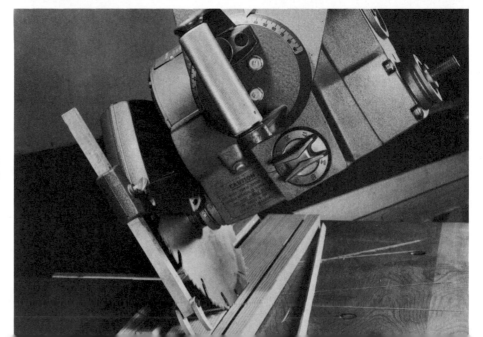

Do V-grooves by making matched cuts. Be careful when you position the saw blade.

SETTINGS FOR COMMON COMPOUND-ANGLE CUTS

Work Slope, Deg	Four-Side Figure		Six-Side Figure	
	Blade Tilt, Deg	Arm Angle, Deg	Blade Tilt, Deg	Arm Angle, Deg
15	43¼	14½	29	8¼
25	40	23	27¼	13½
30	37¾	26½	26	16
40	32½	32¾	22¾	20¼
45	30	35¼	21	22¼
50	27	37½	19	23¾
60	21	41	14½	26½

Blade-tilt and arm-angle settings for the most common compound-angle cuts.

making bevel cuts on the edges, you can use the simple miter jig to do compound cutting. The work is put in position against the guide but resting on the bevel. The blade is set in normal crosscut position and pulled through in the usual fashion. The cut is compound simply because the work is tilted to begin with.

As shown in an accompanying photo, you can also use a height-block to establish the work angle. In this case, the blade is set up for a simple 45° miter. This method is not as accurate since the thickness of the height-block can be arbitrary. However, a few degrees in the work angle one way or the other shouldn't be that critical.

You can also work with a U-block jig. This is made especially for pieces of particular width and is clamped to the table at a 45° angle to the saw-blade path. The work nestles between the verticals of the jig and is held at a fairly close slope angle. Then you make what amounts to a simple crosscut, but you get a compound angle. Of course, both the height-block and the U-jig can be organized to produce a very specific work angle. Either one of these two methods might be used if you require a particular compound-angle frame in more-than-one quantity.

ODD ANGLE CUTS

To cut angles you can't handle in the usual fashion — whether it's because the work is too large or too odd-shaped to begin with or the angle is too extreme — use a guide strip that can ride the outboard edge of the table. This is tack-nailed to the underside of the work and positioned so that it parallels the line of cut you want. Thus, you can handle the job like a simple rip cut.

If you own a turret arm radial arm saw, in this kind of situation the work can be clamped to the table and the blade pulled through for the cut. Naturally, the length of the cut will be limited by how far the carriage can travel along the turret arm.

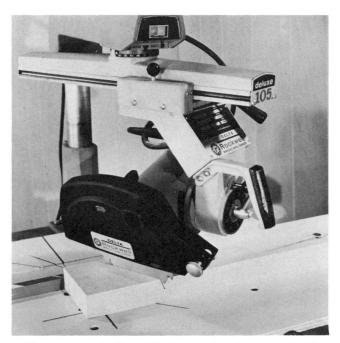

The compound miter calls for swinging the arm *and* tilting the blade. These are probably the roughest cuts to do but only because of the precision that is required.

You can use the mitering jig if you pre-bevel the work pieces to provide the correct slope angle of the work. The cut is then done like a simple crosscut.

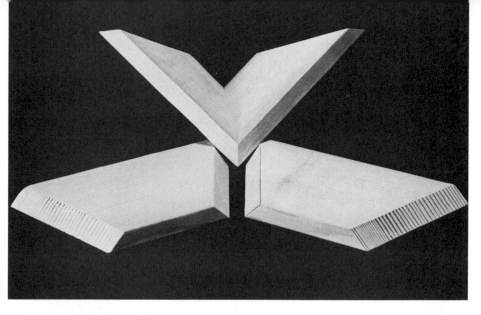

Typical compound-angle cut and how the parts join. The cut-parts must mate perfectly and the angle between any two pieces in the frame must be 90°.

When you cut consecutively from one length of stock you can use the first piece as a template for marking the others. . . .

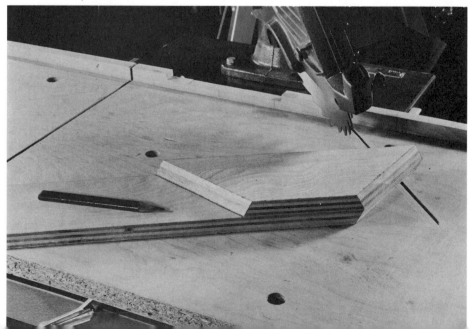

Flip the piece and place it as shown. Use a very sharp pencil. On the next cut, the kerf will be on the waste side and should just remove the pencil line.

USING THE DADOING TOOL

The dadoing tool is not used to part the stock, so it is always elevated above the table surface to form a U-shape that is a "dado" when done across the grain, a "groove" when done with the grain. The cut depth can be gauged easily if you mark it on an edge of the stock and adjust cutter height to match the mark.

The dado assembly is used much like a saw blade. However, since it removes considerably more wood, the feed speed should be minimized. If you feed too fast, the dado will tend to "climb" and "walk" along the work instead of cut. While the normal feed direction is the same as for a saw blade, there are times when pushing the cutter through instead of pulling it may be better. This means that you position the dado at the front of the table instead of behind the fence and, after the work is placed, push the dado toward the rear of the machine to make the cut.

No matter which way you feed, whether you are cutting across the grain or with it, make all dado cuts at a speed that will permit the cutting edges to do their job without clogging. As with all cutting tools, one rule concerning good feed speed and pressure is paramount: keep the tool cutting constantly but without strain.

When the same dado is required on many pieces, it's wise to use a stop block on the fence to gauge the position of the cut. This method is much better than marking the pieces individually and then gauging each cut by eye. If you require an extra-wide cut, such as a half-lap on wide pieces, the stop block can be used to set the work for the outline cuts. The material between is then removed by making repeat, overlapping passes.

A kind of "gang cutting" may also be employed to assure accuracy of dadoes on mating pieces. For example, in dadoing opposite sides of a bookcase for horizontal shelves, cut the first dado in the parts, butt them edge-to-edge, and use a small piece of the shelf material in the dado already formed. This will keep the pieces in alignment for the following cuts. Often you can combine this kind of gang cutting with a stop block on the fence for faster, more accurate work.

The "stopped" dado or "blind" dado is a cut that does not go across the full width of the stock. This is done,

Some of the cuts you can accomplish using a dadoing tool on the radial arm saw.

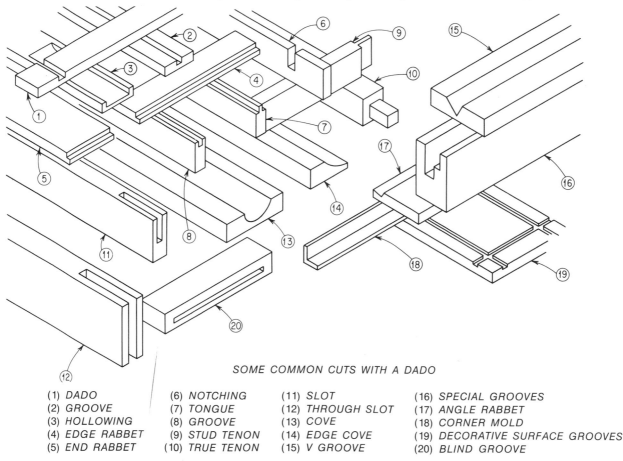

SOME COMMON CUTS WITH A DADO

(1) DADO
(2) GROOVE
(3) HOLLOWING
(4) EDGE RABBET
(5) END RABBET
(6) NOTCHING
(7) TONGUE
(8) GROOVE
(9) STUD TENON
(10) TRUE TENON
(11) SLOT
(12) THROUGH SLOT
(13) COVE
(14) EDGE COVE
(15) V GROOVE
(16) SPECIAL GROOVES
(17) ANGLE RABBET
(18) CORNER MOLD
(19) DECORATIVE SURFACE GROOVES
(20) BLIND GROOVE

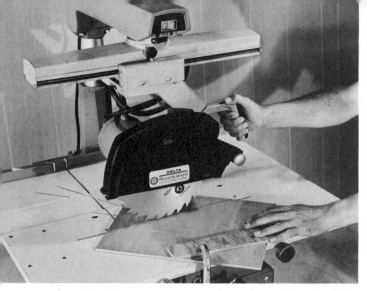

On a turret arm saw, you can clamp the work and pull the blade through for the cut. Of course the length-of-cut is limited by the length of the arm.

Simple dado is done with the machine in crosscut position. When the cut is deep, it's okay to feed as indicated by the arrow. This is opposite to normal feed direction. Feed so the tool keeps cutting, but never force it.

Grooving job being done with a dado assembly. Note that guard and anti-kickback fingers are organized for maximum protection of the operator.

for example, when you use the joint to hang a shelf but wish to conceal the cut at the front edge. All you have to do is draw a line on the work to indicate the length of the cut, then stop when the dado reaches that point. Since the cut so formed ends in a radius, you will have to clean it out by working with a chisel or shape the end of the shelf to match the radius.

To do groove shapes, you organize the saw for ripping and feed the stock into the cutter as if you had a saw blade mounted. To get the correct depth of cut, work as explained for dadoing. Use the guard and the anti-kickback fingers (even though they are not always shown in the illustrations) as if you were doing a normal rip cut.

Whenever possible, work with the machine in the in-rip position. Feed steadily but, since the dado removes more wood, a little more slowly than you would when ripping. To do extra-wide grooves, just make repeat, overlapping passes. To do stopped grooves, use a stop block on the fence to limit the length of the cut. After you hit the stop block, retract the work carefully until it is clear of the cutter. For angular cuts with a dadoing tool, situate the machine as you would for miters.

Cutting rabbets. The dadoing tool is fine to use when you require a number of rabbet cuts that are too many to be done by the repeat-pass regular saw blade method. When the rabbet is required across the end of the stock, use the crosscut position; when it follows a long edge, use the rip position. Procedures are approximately the same as for dadoing; the difference is simply in the shape you produce. To do a "bevel rabbet," a shape that is handy when you wish to join two pieces at an angle, work with the machine set up for horizontal sawing but tilt the cutter to the angle you need.

Variable-depth cuts. You can use this technique on both dado and rabbet cuts when, for example, you want the side members of a bookcase to slope inward. How much slope you can get will depend on the thickness of the stock you are using. To do the job, tack-nail a strip of wood under one edge of the work or to the saw table so the top surface of the workpiece is no longer parallel to the table.

Since the cutting tool moves on a parallel plane, the cut will be deeper at one end of the stock. The difference in depth from one end of the cut to the other is controlled by the thickness of the elevating strip.

Some decorative cuts. When you do intersecting, shallow dadoes and grooves in the surface of the stock, you come up with a panel effect that can be simple or very fancy, depending on the number of cuts you make.

If you want to extend the idea to the point where the

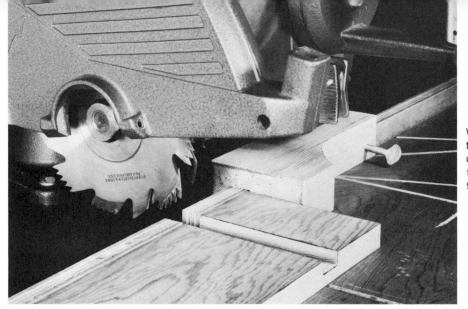

When you have the same dado to cut on many similar pieces, use a stop block on the rip fence to gauge cut position. (See page 93 for stop block details.)

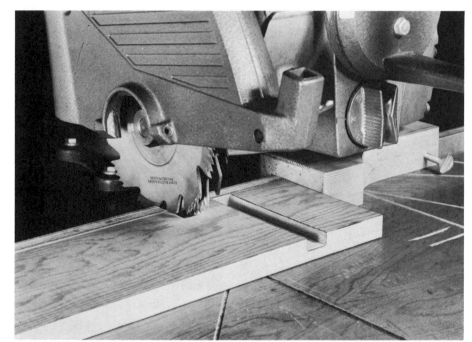

The stop block may also be used when you are doing extra-wide cuts. Set the block up to gauge the outline cuts, then remove the waste between. Work this way especially when you need to repeat the same cut on many pieces.

To do matching cuts on opposite surfaces, you can use a nail-stop in the fence. It can't be seen here because of the work. Of course you can also work with the regular fence stop-block, or a clamp.

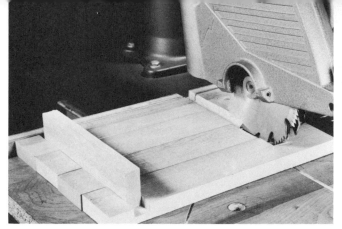

Repeated gang cutting of dadoes uses a dado-sized piece of wood in the first notch to hold and align the pieces for any following cuts on the stock.

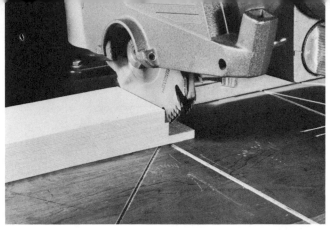

To do rabbet cutting on the end of stock, use the crosscut position. When the rabbet is extra-wide, just make repeat passes. For rabbets along an edge, use the rip position.

For blind dadoes, cut to a line on the work or use a C-clamp on the arm of the machine to limit the travel of the carriage.

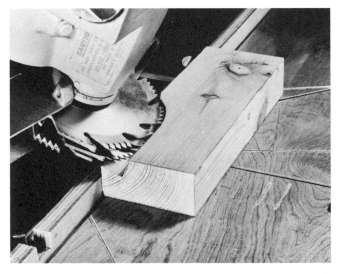

To get an angled-rabbet, saw head is set as for horizontal cutting, but with required tilt.

One-piece, variable width dadoing tool may also be used to cut grooves, dadoes and rabbets on the radial arm saw.

Sloped dadoes and rabbets are accomplished by using a height block as shown here.

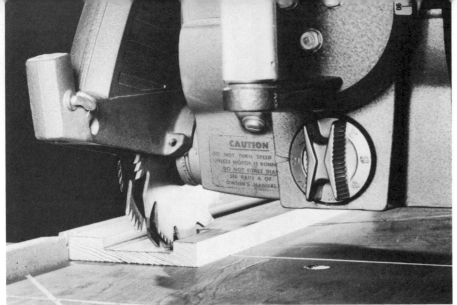

For extra wide grooves, work as you do for ripping, adjusting the position of the cutter after each pass. Don't neglect to use a pushstick when necessary.

To do stopped grooves, use the stop block on the fence.

For angular dadoes, set the machine up as you would for miter cuts. Always make the passes slowly—give the tool a chance to work.

results come close to resembling some intricate chip carving, work approximately the same way but with the dado tool tilted. This requires that you make matching cuts to create facets instead of flat-bottom grooves.

It's also possible to hold the workpiece snugly against the fence while you pull the turning cutter toward you. When you stop the cut, the result is an arch plus a cove shape. When you go completely across the stock with equally spaced cuts, you produce simple cove shapes. Such a part can be used as it is, or it can be strip cut to make many pieces with the same profile.

Working with the machine in crosscut position, but with the dado tilted, will produce "V's." Experimentation here will result in many intriguing effects. For example, if you stop the cuts, you get a knife-point design. When you form two of these back-to-back on a common center line, you create an arch.

Horizontal operations. The dado tool can be used in a position that places it parallel to the table. For this kind of work, it's a good idea to make a special fence so the only part of the dado that will be exposed will be buried in the work. Plywood ($\frac{1}{2}''$) is fine for the fence; if you make the slot in it oversize, you'll have room for adjusting the dado position. Some of the accompanying photos show the tool completely exposed while in use; however, this is mostly for photographic reasons.

When used as previously described, the dado tool does a good job of producing scallop cuts. These can be individual cuts, equally spaced, or one extended cut done by feeding the stock forward after you have made firm contact with the fence. In each case, you can be guided by marking the work or by using stop blocks to control spacing or cut length.

Scallop cutting generally falls in the area of decorative cuts, but the horizontal dado setup can have more practical applications. As is shown in the accompanying photos, grooves, rabbets, and spline cuts are all possible.

Circular work. To do a rabbet on the perimeter of a disc, use the horizontal dado position and work in one of the following ways.

Use a V-block setup with the special fence. The blocks that form the "V" can be tack-nailed to the table or secured to the fence. Set the width of the cut by the position of the blocks and by the projection of the cutter; set the depth of the cut by the height of the cutter above the table.

A second possibility is to use a piece of the waste, which is cut off when you form the disc, as a guide. This is clamped or tack-nailed to the table as a guide for the cut. It's assumed that cutting of the disc is done carefully enough so the waste and the work are fairly well matched.

Intersecting, shallow grooves will result in a "paneled" effect. Procedure may involve both crosscut and rip setups.

To get faceted effects, use both crosscut and rip positions, but with the cutter tilted. Do the crossgrain cuts first. Be careful to make cuts meet perfectly.

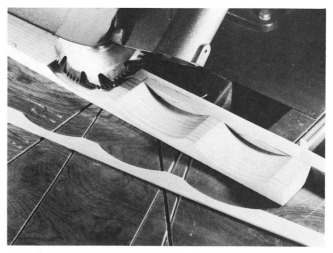

Keep the work very secure, even if you must clamp it for each cut, for horizontal dado cutting with the tool tilted to produce matching coves. The part can then be ripped into thin strips like the one in the foreground.

In either case, to do the cutting, rest the work solidly on the table and ease it forward gently to make the initial contact. Then, rotate it slowly against the direction of rotation of the cutting tool.

Slots. To cut a slot by using the dado, set up in a rip position but place the work before you lower the cutter to make contact. Do this slowly and, after the cutter has penetrated the work, feed until you have the slot length you require. Such slots will begin and end in a radius. If you want those points to be square, finish up with a chisel.

Using a V-block. You can form notches across a corner post by using a V-block to situate the work and pulling the cutter across as you would for a simple dado. The block doesn't have to be more than a length of 2x4 with a "V" cut down its center. When you need such a cut on many pieces, it's a simple matter to tack-nail a strip across the "V" for use as a stop. In such cases, it's probably a good idea to secure the V-block to the table or to the fence. Your concern will then be to hold the work still as you make the cut.

THE MOLDING HEAD

The flexibility of the radial arm saw increases the usefulness of a molding cutterhead. When you consider the number of knives available, each one's capability of providing various shapes, and the positioning of the head vertically, horizontally or at an angle, you realize the infinite number of cut possibilities.

For a basic kind of molding-head work, organize the machine as you would for horizontal sawing. A conventional fence may be used as long as the center area is

Form scallops by using the machine in horizontal cutting position. Adjust the depth setting with care.

V-blocks will let you rabbet the edge of circular pieces. The arrow indicates the direction of feed which should be against the direction of rotation of the cutter.

Make a high fence through which the dado can poke so you can work more safely on many kinds of horizontal dado-cutting operations. This is last pass of a four-edge rabbet cut.

To cut a slot, place the work in position with the cutter raised above it. Then lower the cutter slowly and feed the work forward. Use a scrap piece between work and saw table.

reduced to provide turning room for the knives. It's also possible to use a two-piece fence with the sections situated so the gap between them allows room for the cutter.

To establish knife height and projection for a particular shape, put the work in position and turn the cutter-head by hand until one knife butts against the edge of the work. In this way, you can actually see what the results will be.

To make the cut, hold the work flat on the table and snug against the fence. Move it slowly to engage the cutter and keep the feed action steady throughout the pass. Most molding cuts remove a lot of material so don't force the feed. Try to work so that you are cutting with the grain of the wood. Cuts made in this manner will always be smoother than cuts made against the grain or across it. When you can't work with the grain,

A V-block lets you position square stock for cross-corner dadoes. The work is done with the machine in crosscut position. You can even use the V-block to form a dado in a cylinder. Clamp or hold the work firmly.

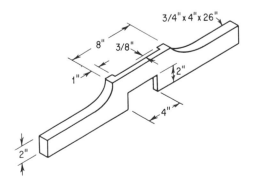

Make this special fence, which you can use as is for all straight-line cuts that do not remove entire edge of stock.

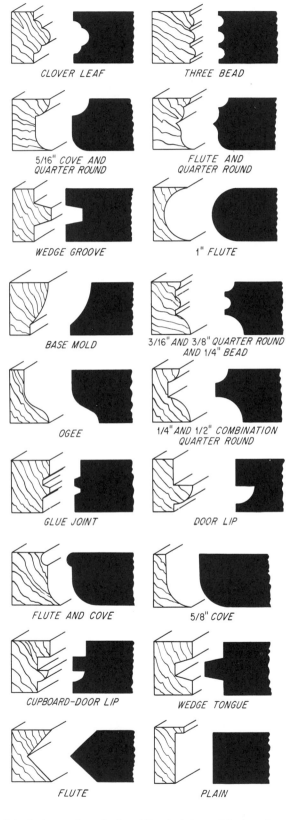

CLOVER LEAF

THREE BEAD

5/16" COVE AND QUARTER ROUND

FLUTE AND QUARTER ROUND

WEDGE GROOVE

1" FLUTE

BASE MOLD

3/16" AND 3/8" QUARTER ROUND AND 1/4" BEAD

OGEE

1/4" AND 1/2" COMBINATION QUARTER ROUND

GLUE JOINT

DOOR LIP

FLUTE AND COVE

5/8" COVE

CUPBOARD-DOOR LIP

WEDGE TONGUE

FLUTE

PLAIN

A typical assortment of molding knives and their cuts.

CUTTING WITH THE MOLDING HEAD

The molding head locks on the arbor just like a dadoing tool. Most heads require knives in sets of three. Here are some typical molding knives.

To get an idea of how the edge will look after you have made the cut, set one blade flat against the stock's edge.

When you do the cutting, make the pass very slowly; let the cutter work. Note how only a portion of this knife's profile is being utilized to get the shape that is required.

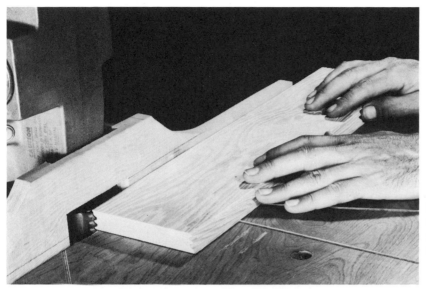

Sometimes, in order to use a specific part of the profile on a knife, it would be necessary to cut into the table.

At other times, you can work so that the knife is completely clear of the table.

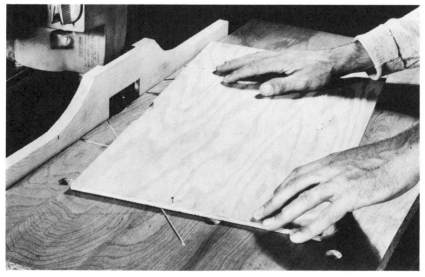

You can also work with a small sheet of plywood tack-nailed to the saw table. This raises the work, and permits much greater latitude in the depth-of-cut adjustments without chewing up the surface of the saw table.

make the passes even slower than normal. This will let the knives take smaller bites, and they will pass over a given area of the wood a greater number of times.

The special fence shown in the accompanying sketch will provide more safety than a conventional one and can be used on any cut that does not remove the entire edge of the stock. Such a partial cut leaves enough of the original work edge to ride the outfeed part of the fence when the fence sections are in line. A full cut removes the entire edge of the stock.

For a partial cut, either a one-piece fence or a two-piece fence with the bearing surfaces in line will do. On a full cut, the work will lack support after it has passed the cutters so you must make some compensation. The easiest solution is to use a two-piece fence with the infeed section shimmed back an amount that equals the depth of cut. Cut the shim so it does not project above the table.

When a part requires cutting on each of its four edges or on two adjacent edges, do the cross-grain cuts first. The final with-the-grain cuts will remove the end-area imperfections that are almost inevitable on cross-grain passes.

On any cut where the work is narrow, be sure to use a backup block to feed the stock across the cutter. This will keep the work square and allow you to complete the pass safely. It also helps to minimize the splintering that normally occurs at the end of a cross pass. Don't work on stock that is so narrow that even a backup block won't help. In such cases, it's best to do the job on a wide piece and then rip off the section you need.

Narrow moldings. When you need just one piece, you can work by shaping the edge of a wide board and then ripping off the width you want.

To turn out narrow moldings in quantity, it's best to pre-rip pieces to the size you want and then run them through a special fixture. This is no more than a long, heavy piece of stock in which you form a rabbet to suit the size of the basic strips. The block is clamped in place to cover the cutter; the work is fed into one end (the infeed side) and pulled out the other. To avoid chatter as you make the pass, be sure the L-shaped cut in the block matches the size of the precut strips quite closely.

Circular work. The V-block technique described for rabbeting discs with a dado tool can be used to shape the edge of circular pieces. For greater flexibility, you can attach each block to a half-fence. Thus, you have a two-piece arrangement you can situate to suit the size of the work.

Ease the work in slowly to make initial contact and, when the piece is firmly settled in the "V," rotate it slowly against the direction of rotation of the cutterhead.

Irregular work. To work on irregular pieces, you need a special half-circle guide that is attached to a fence so that it can be situated under the molder. This guide does approximately the same job performed by collars on a shaper. Depth of cut is controlled by the relationship between the cutting knives and placement of the guide.

To minimize cutterhead exposure on this kind of work, make an overhead plywood guard like the one

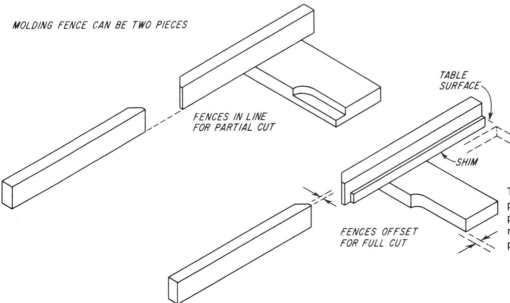

MOLDING FENCE CAN BE TWO PIECES

FENCES IN LINE FOR PARTIAL CUT

FENCES OFFSET FOR FULL CUT

TABLE SURFACE

SHIM

The difference between full and partial cuts. Use a shim to compensate for the stock that is removed on a full cut. This will provide support *after* the cut.

Crossgrain cuts are always made first. On narrow stock, use a back-up block as you would a miter gauge. The block helps keep the work in alignment and checks excessive splintering at the end of the cut. A sheet of plywood will help in protecting the saw table from the cutter blade.

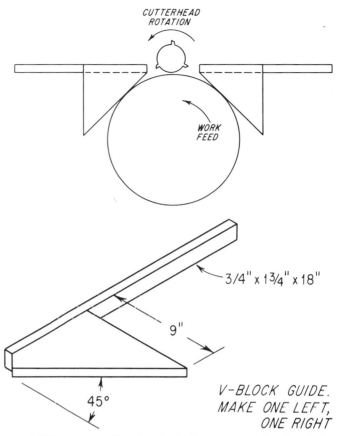

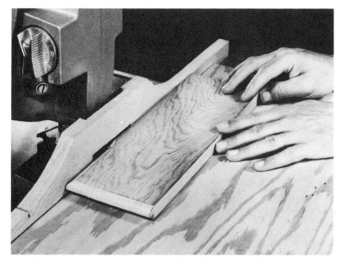

The passes that are made with the grain of the wood will remove the slight imperfections at the ends of the crossgrain cuts. The particular shape being cut with the molding head here is a cabinet-door lip.

A V-block setup (top drawing) lets you shape the rim of circular pieces. The arrow indicates direction of turn after full contact with the cutter. The two-piece fence permits adjustment to suit the size of the work and minimizes the gap around the cutter. Bottom drawing shows dimensions of V-block guide. Make one left, one right.

Use this setup to do fast, safe production of similar strip moldings. The rabbet in the guide block is sized to match the piece to be shaped, with just enough clearance to feed the work through with complete freedom.

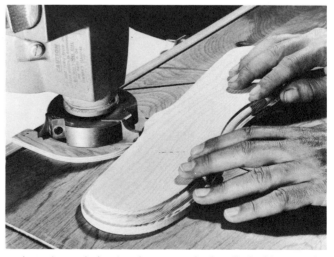

Irregular and circular shapes can be handled with a special cutter guide. Be sure to keep the work flat on the table and snug against the guide throughout the pass.

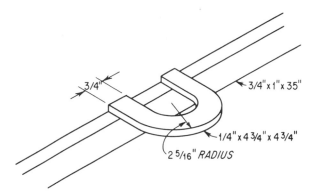

How to make the special molding cutter guide.

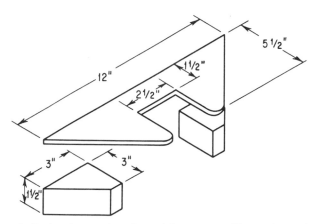

Cutterhead cover is extra safety measure. The parts can be put together with glue and nails.

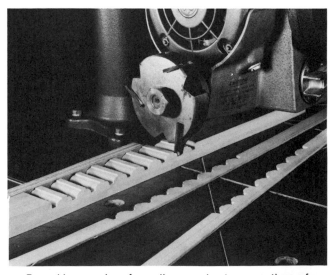

By making a series of equally spaced cuts across the surface of the stock and then strip cutting, you can produce a great quantity of slim moldings.

shown in the accompanying sketch. Even with this safety device, don't try to mold pieces that are too small to be held safely with your hands.

Angular cuts. To increase the shapes you can get from an assortment of knives, try working in a horizontal cutting position with the cutter tilted. Because a setup like this presents an unusual knife angle, it may be difficult to visualize the shape and the depth of the cut. So use even more care than usual, starting with a very light cut and increasing depth as you make repeat passes. When the cut you wish to make is a critical one, do the preliminary setting up and cutting on scrap stock.

Strip moldings. With the machine set up in crosscut position, you can do a repeat-pass pattern across the stock's surface and then rip the piece into slim sections. This kind of cutting should be done very slowly with the stock held firmly. It's not a good idea to try to cut deeply in one pass. It's better to achieve full depth of cut by making repeat passes.

A special fence, drilled to take a nail stop, is almost a necessity for this kind of work. Using it, you have a mechanical means for work placement to gauge equally spaced cuts. Space the holes in the fence about $\frac{1}{2}''$ or $1''$ and drill them so they will be a tight fit for the nail you will use as a stop.

Coving. Coving cuts with a molding head are accomplished by setting up the machine in an in-rip position and feeding the stock against the direction of rotation of the cutter. Different types of knives may be used, but in all cases the basic procedure is the same. Achieve full depth of cut by making repeat passes.

The cuts can be made on the edge of the stock or somewhere along the surface. Variations are possible by tilting the cutter. More about coving will be given later in this chapter.

TAPER CUTS

There are several ways to cut tapers on the radial arm saw, and each of them calls for a special arrangement that will position the work for the cut. You can make a step jig to suit the job or a variable jig that can become a permanent accessory for use on just about any tapering job.

The step jig can be a production tool, used when you require many similar cuts. It has an advantage in that the steps, which determine the taper, are fixed. Any number of pieces you cut will be exactly alike. When the taper is required on opposite edges or on all four edges of a piece of stock, the jig must incorporate two steps. For four edges, the first step in the jig will position the work for cuts on adjacent sides. The second step,

Tilting the head will allow you to produce additional shapes. Be sure the work bears against the fence throughout the pass, especially near end of the cut.

Surface cuts can produce interesting and exclusive panel designs. Don't set up for jobs like this without using every possible safety precaution you can.

You can surface cut a wide board and then cut out the shaped section to use as a piece of molding, all in a few minutes.

A special fence, with equally spaced holes drilled through it, will let you use a naíl as a stop to position the work for each cut if you must do repetitive work.

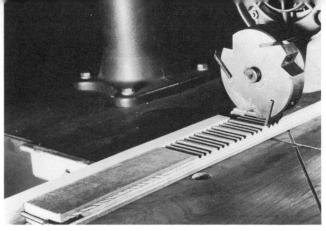

Work is placed against the nail at each position. Surface cuts done like this should never be too deep. If you must cut deeply, do it by making repeat passes.

Cove cuts are made possible by using the cutterhead in ripping position but angling it about 10°. The full depth of cut you want must be achieved by making repeat passes.

The same thoughts apply whether you are coving an edge or cutting somewhere along a surface. Many variations are possible depending on cutterhead tilt and angle.

This panel-raising operation is being done with a knife that was designed especially for the purpose. It makes sense to spend for such items when you intend to do much similar cutting and the quantity of the work you do justifies it.

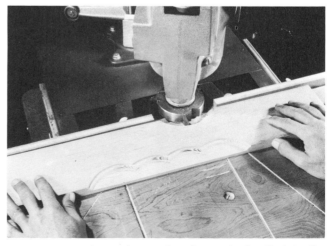

Do scallop shapes by moving the work directly into the cutter, then pulling back. By using the molding head on your radial arm saw, you can get more intriguing results on this kind of work than with a dado tool.

which doubles the first setting, sets the work for the two remaining cuts.

With the variable jig, you work about the same way, setting the angle for the first cuts and then re-setting for the final ones.

Make taper cuts approximately the same way you do ripping. The work is snugged in the jig; both the jig and the work are moved past the blade for the cut. The distance between the fence and the blade should equal the width of the jig plus the width of the work where the taper begins.

Notched guides, as shown in the accompanying photos, are also possibilities for taper cuts. Since these are used with the machine in crosscut position, the work length will have to be within the crosscut limits of the machine.

PATTERN SAWING

Pattern sawing is a fast method of cutting any number of odd-shaped pieces. It's a good method because it sets up a mechanical means of gauging cuts; therefore, the size and the shape of the workpieces are determined by the pattern. All pieces will be exactly alike, since the pattern is a precise example.

The stock is first roughly cut to approximate size and then, for the cutting, each piece is tack-nailed to the pattern. Feeding is done by guiding the pattern along a guide block that is secured to the table in line with the saw blade. The blade cuts the work so that it matches the pattern.

KERFING ON THE RADIAL ARM SAW

Kerfing for bending. Kerfing for bending is done with the machine in crosscut position but with the blade raised so it doesn't cut through the stock. Since many kerfs are required, usually equally spaced, it's best to make a special fence if a lot of work is to be done or use a nail-stop in a conventional fence for an occasional job.

Kerfed moldings. The same kind of kerfs made for wood bending and variations of them can be used to produce many types of distinctive moldings. The idea is to strip cut the pieces after they have been kerfed to produce the design you have in mind.

Since you are not concerned with bending the wood, the depth and even the width of the kerfs can be varied arbitrarily to suit your design.

A simple variation is to flip the stock for each cut or after each two cuts. You can use a dado for this kind of work, or you can combine saw kerfs with dado cuts.

COVING

For coving on the radial arm saw, organize the saw for

A step jig is used for tapering. The steps are equal in size, so flipping the stock and placing it into the second step for the next cut determines that cuts on opposite sides are similar. Use guard and anti-kickback fingers for all rip cuts, including tapers.

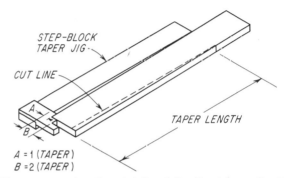

Here are construction details of the fixed taper jig. If the work is square and a taper is required on all four sides, you would still need but two steps in the jig.

You can clamp a notched guide on the table to do taper work on small pieces with the machine in crosscut position. To do your cutting on opposite sides, just flip the stock over. Don't change the position of the jig.

VARIABLE TAPER JIG

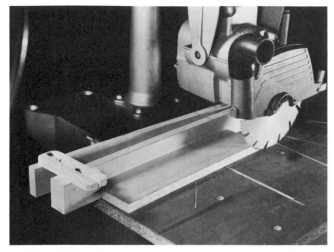

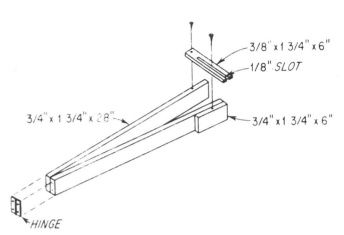

3/8" x 1 3/4" x 6"

1/8" SLOT

3/4" x 1 3/4" x 28"

3/4" x 1 3/4" x 6"

HINGE

The variable taper jig can be set for any taper within its capacities. The distance between the fence and the saw blade must equal width of the jig plus width of the work.

Construction details of the variable taper jig.

Keep the jig snug against the fence as you make the pass. Set the guard down closer to the work than it is shown here—use the anti-kickback fingers. Note that the saw dust ejection elbow points away from the operator.

Make a mark on the legs of the jig 1' away from the hinged end. Measure across at this point to set the jig for taper-per-foot.

PATTERN SAWING

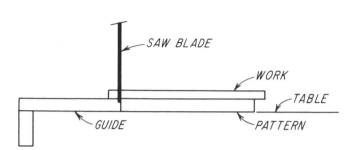

The basic setup for pattern sawing is shown here. The thickness of the pattern should be at least equal to the thickness of the guide for best results.

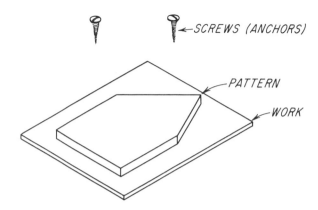

The work is tack-nailed to the pattern. You can use screws just long enough to project through the pattern; then the work can be pressed down on the points.

The outside edge of the kerf made by the saw blade must be flush with the outside edge of the guide.

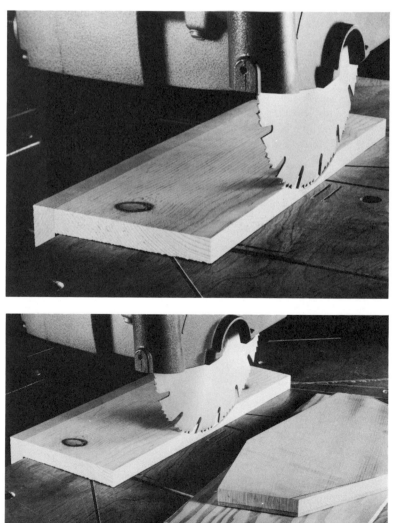

It is necessary to rough-cut the work to approximate size before you secure it to the pattern. The outside edge of the kerf made by the blade must be flush with the edge of the guide.

KERF CUTTING

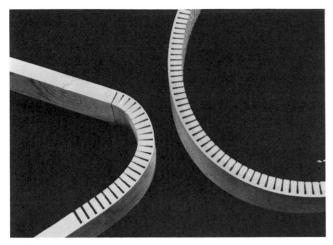

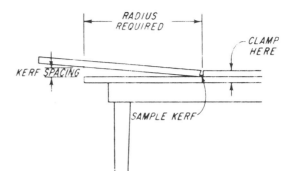

The kerfing method provides an easy way to bend wood without having to steam it. The cutting must be done carefully and evenly at just the right intervals to make sure the wood will bend easily and will not break.

This method will help you determine kerf spacing for the job you are doing. Lift the wood until the sample kerf closes, then measure from the bottom of the work to the table surface. Not foolproof, but a good place to start.

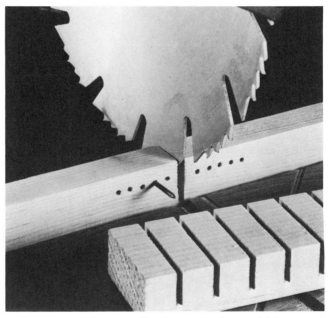

A regular fence can be used to space the kerfs if you install a nail as a stop.

Or you may take some time to construct a special fence and save it for jobs like this.

To bend wood in a spiral turn, cut the kerfs at an angle. The degree of the angle will determine the tightness of the spiral.

crosscutting but tilt the blade to between 10° and 15°. Lock the blade over the center of the work and adjust its height to take a shallow bite (between $\frac{1}{16}''$ and $\frac{1}{8}''$). Feed the work slowly past the blade as if you were making a rip cut. Be sure to hold the work snugly against the fence throughout the pass. Repeat the procedure several times, lowering the blade a maximum of $\frac{1}{8}''$ for each pass. The cove will begin to take shape immediately, getting wider and deeper with each pass you make.

To get an idea of what the cove will be like before you start to cut it, make and use the parallel rule shown in the accompanying drawing. To use the rule, set the distance between the long arms to equal the width of the cove you want. Pivot the blade so the "front" and "back" teeth just touch the arms. You can judge the depth of the cove as you do the cutting. When you set up the work for cutting, be sure the center line of the cove you want is on the center line of the saw blade.

All cove cuts should be accomplished by making repeat passes. Remember that the action involves a lot of scraping by the saw blade; therefore, make passes slowly and keep depth of cut to a minimum. The final pass should be made with the saw blade barely touching; this will produce the smoothest end result.

CIRCULAR CUTS

You can cut circles with an ordinary saw blade if you set the machine up for in-ripping and use a pivot-guide system so the work can be rotated against the direction of rotation of the blade. The cut you get is actually a small cove, so the cut depth on each pass should be limited to about $\frac{1}{8}''$.

The distance from the pivot point to the saw blade determines the radius of the circle. When the work is very large, you can set up the pivot off the saw table by using a sawhorse or some kind of improvised stand.

For some kinds of circular cuts, it's possible to clamp the work securely and move the cutting tool.

SAUCER CUTS

A saucer cut is a unique operation that is somewhat related to coving in that the blade is used more in a scraping action than in a cutting one.

To try a simple saucer cut, clamp the work to the table and raise the blade (while in crosscut position) until it is high enough to be swung through the full tilt range without hitting the work surface. Lower the blade about $\frac{1}{16}''$ and swing it through the tilt while the blade is turning. Keep your hands well away from the cut area, be sure the work is firmly clamped, and achieve full depth of cut by making repeat passes. If the saucer cut

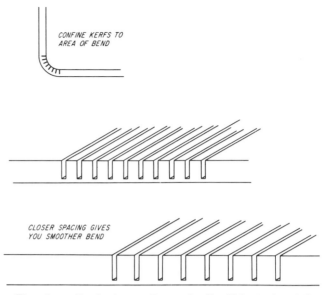

The closer the kerfs are, the easier it will be to bend the wood. Over-doing it though can weaken the wood too much.

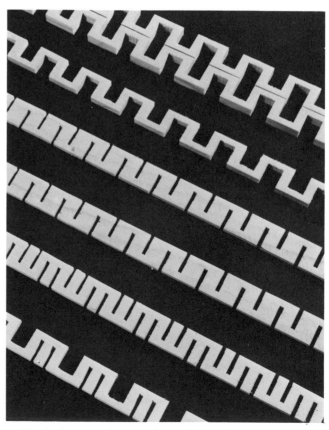

The kerfing technique can be used to produce many varieties of dentil-type molding strips. Top one was done by joining two similar pieces edge-to-edge.

COVE CUTTING

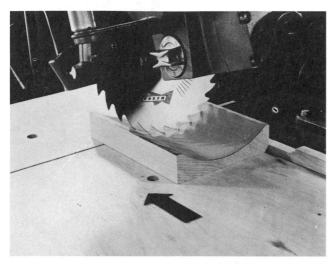

Get a true cove by setting the blade at right-angles to the work centerline. Tilt the blade toward the direction from which you will be feeding the stock. The radius of the arc will be determined by the size of the saw blade.

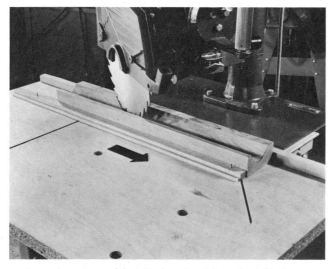

A good way to work is to tack-nail a strip to the table to create a feed-trough between it and the regular fence. Feed slowly —make many passes to get full cut-depth.

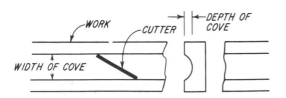

The angle at which the blade is set determines the width of the cove. Its depth depends on how many passes you make.

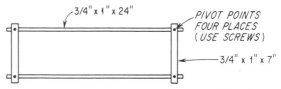

Making a parallel rule and using it as described in the text will help you pre-determine cove size.

Coving can be accomplished on stock-edges. Same techniques apply. Be sure to feed so your hands are always away from the blade.

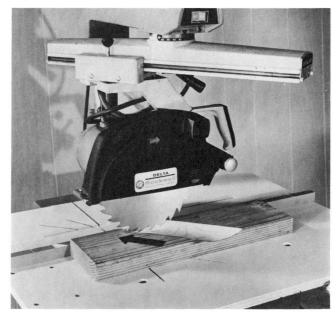

You can form crossgrain coves by working this way. The arrow indicates the direction of feed when you are using a setup like this.

CIRCLE CUTTING

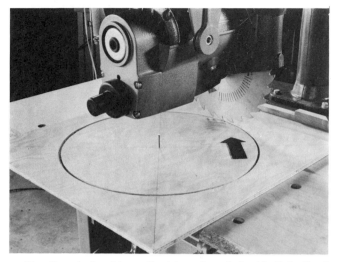

Use the pivot-guide method to cut a circle. Limit depth of cut to about ⅛″ for each pass. Feed (arrow) against the direction of rotation of the blade. Hold the work firmly.

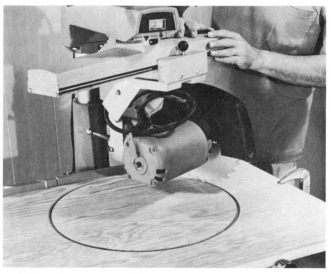

With a turret arm machine, you can clamp the work to the saw table and make the cut this way. Feed in the direction the teeth of the blade are pointing.

You can actually cut a disc by working in the crosscut position and turning the pivot-mounted work for each pass you make. Final passes should be made by turning the work just a few degrees for each.

You can form curved grooves and slots like this. Clamp the work to the table—don't cut too deeply—feed as indicated by the arrow.

SAUCER CUTS

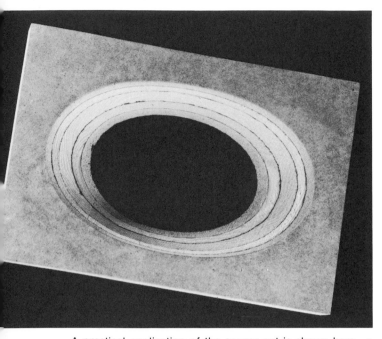

A practical application of the saucer cut is shown here—a unique picture frame. The concentric circles resulting from cutting of layers in the plywood make an interesting pattern.

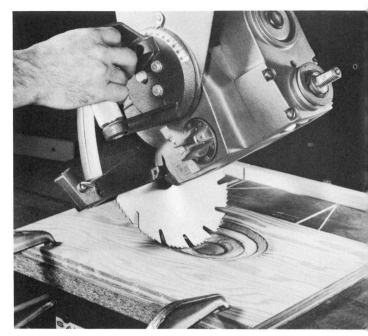

Swing the blade through its tilt range and make repeated, slight scraping cuts in the stock. If the cut is to go through, use scrap between the work and the saw table.

By using the auto-stops built into the machine, you can do a stopped saucer cut. When you do the full ones, you must keep the auto-stop button (or whatever) depressed.

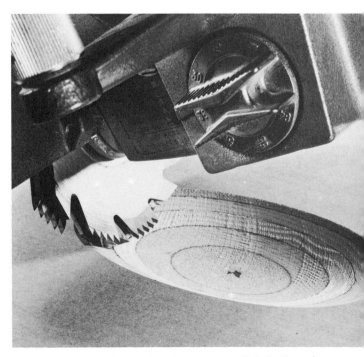

A dado can also be used to do a saucer cut. Actually, using one, you can cut deeper and faster than you can with a conventional blade.

Since the power unit can be rotated 360°, you can cut a small circle this way. Tilt the dado to 10° or 15°—take small bites.

Diamond-cut pieces can be assembled to make effective decorations. Proceed carefully with the cutting as explained in the text. Use a blade with little set, or a hollow-ground one.

Variations are possible. These individual pieces can be used as door or drawer pulls, or they may be assembled to create design overlays.

is to go completely through the work, be sure to use a scrap block between the work and the saw table.

CUTTING "DIAMONDS"

Diamond-shaped pieces that can be assembled into many-pointed star shapes can be cut as follows:

First, bevel the stock so that a cross-section would be an isosceles triangle. Actually, any bevel may be used, but the given method that produces certain results is best to start with before you attempt variations. Once the stock is so formed, a series of compound angle cuts are done to form the individual pieces. If you swing the arm to 45° and tilt the blade to the same angle used to cut the bevel, you'll get an eight-point star. If you want a specific number of points, divide the number required into 360° and set the arm to this figure.

Make the first cut on the end of the stock with the work positioned on the left-hand side of the blade. Then move the work to the right-hand side of the blade and make a second cut to mate with the topmost point of the first cut.

Return the work to the left-hand side and again make a cut; then return the work to the right side for the second cut. The piece cut off when the work is on the left side of the blade is scrap. Continue the procedure until you have the number of pieces you require.

SAW-BLADE PANEL RAISING

You can "raise" a panel with a conventional saw blade if you work in the horizontal position with the blade tilted up a few degrees. If the very tip of the cut is set to hit the surface of the work, you can do the panel

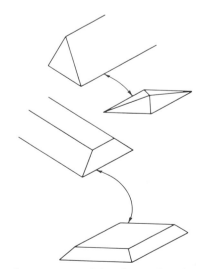

Two ways to prepare stock for diamond cutting. Experimenting can lead to infinite variety.

raising in one pass. The disadvantage, however, is the angle on the shoulder that is the result of the blade tilt. To eliminate it, make slight surface cuts with the blade perpendicular to the table, either before or after you make the angle cut. Of course, the two cuts must meet exactly.

MULTI-BLADE IDEAS

There are advantages in being able to mount two saw blades on the arbor. For example, using two blades in making kerfs for wood bending reduces the cutting time by 50% because you need just half the number of passes.

Of course, there are limits because the arbor is just so long. However, for kerfing and some similar operations, the double-blade idea works fine. You can also use blades with different diameters: for example, you could do a cutoff and form a shoulder cut for a rabbet at the same time. This technique can be applied when you need a number of similar drawer fronts. You can also work with a dado and a saw blade to do the same thing. In this case, the rabbet would be completely formed during the one cut.

Finally, remember that you do want to be careful about what you put on the arbor. You must always leave enough threads exposed so the lock nut can be tightened securely.

ROTARY PLANER

It's easy to use a rotary planer on a modern radial arm saw because most of these accessories have outboard spindles that rotate in a direction compatible with the cutting action. If they were to turn the other way, they simply wouldn't cut.

In addition, a rotary planer is handy to use on the radial arm saw because of the infinite number of ways you can position it in relation to the work. The operations shown in the accompanying photos illustrate only a few of these ways.

Be sure to read the instructions that come with the accessory. Such matters as depth of cut and number of cutters can vary from tool to tool, and these factors will affect the number and scope of applications. Generally, a slow feed speed with shallow depth of cut works best. Cuts will always be smoothest when you feed the stock (or the cutter) so that the tool cuts with the grain of the wood.

PIERCING

You can do piercing with a saw blade or a dado by making cuts on both sides of the stock. Depth of cut is a little more than half the stock thickness. Thus, openings through the work are created where the cuts cross each

To set the stage for panel raising, work in the horizontal cutting position but tilt the blade up a few degrees. If necessary, use a "platform" under the work to raise it.

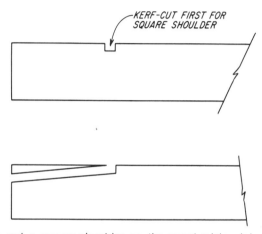

To get a square shoulder on the panel-raising job, cut a shallow kerf to meet the angle cut.

Double production by using two blades. The blades are separated by washers that fit the arbor. Never mount so much that you don't leave sufficient thread for the nut.

When you mount a dado with a saw blade, you can cut off and form a rabbet at the same time. Since you are removing a lot of material, make the pass slowly.

The rotary planer can be used for panel raising, rabbeting and the like. Always feed against the direction of rotation of the cutters. The planer may be used with the machine in cross-cut position, but with the cutter parallel to the table.

To do piercing, make cuts on both surfaces of the stock with the cutter set to cut a bit more than half the stock's thickness.

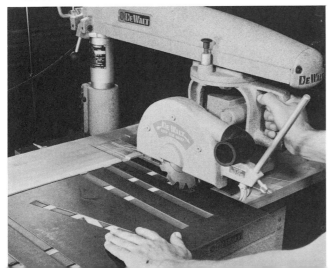

other. The shape of the openings is determined by how you do the cutting. You get squares when the cuts are of equal width and at right angles to each other, diamond shapes when they are angled, etc. The possibilities are infinite.

DADO "TURNING"

The illustrations in this section demonstrate a method of mounting work between the centers of a special jig so you can accomplish some jobs you would ordinarily do on a lathe. The system calls for rotating the stock by hand against the direction of rotation of a turning dado assembly.

You can use this system to form integral tenons on cylinders or square stock, round a square piece of stock for its full length or in a limited area, or even do tapers.

The rear part of the jig is clamped in place of the fence. The forward part is secured to the table with clamps after the work has been mounted between the centers.

This kind of cutting calls for caution since it's natural for the cutter to try to turn the work. Make the initial contact between the cutter and the work very slowly and be sure to grip the work firmly with your hands well away from the cut area. Adjust the guard for maximum tool coverage and be sure to rotate the work very slowly when you are cutting.

Don't try to make deep cuts in single passes. Instead, make repeat passes, lowering the cutter a bit after each until the job is finished.

Always check twice before starting to work to be sure that the stock is very secure between the centers and that the jig is tightly clamped to the saw table.

DRILLING

You can do quite a bit of drilling on the radial arm saw, but there are factors to consider that might affect the kind and the size of the tools you can use. For example, if you have a single-arbor machine, its rotation won't be good for conventional tools. The solution is to use special cutters that are designed to function under those conditions. Some machines have an outboard arbor in addition to the saw arbor; for these you can buy special adapters and chucks for mounting conventional tools. You might be limited to one particular speed which means, of course, this is not an ideal setup for overall drilling operations. Because of these factors, be sure to read your owner's manual carefully. It will provide important specifics concerning the particular machine you own. Also, check the chapter on drill presses for general information concerning drilling tools.

Simple drilling. When work size permits, it's some-

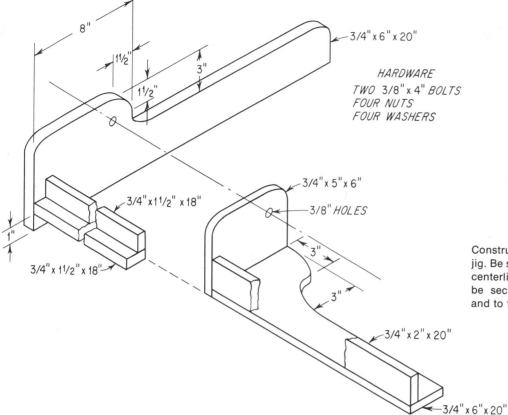

8"

1½"

3"

1½"

3/4" x 6" x 20"

HARDWARE
TWO 3/8" x 4" BOLTS
FOUR NUTS
FOUR WASHERS

3/4" x 5" x 6"

3/8" HOLES

3/4" x 1½" x 18"

1"

3/4" x 1½" x 18"

3"

3"

3/4" x 2" x 20"

3/4" x 6" x 20"

Construction details of "dado turning" jig. Be sure the $\frac{3}{8}''$ holes have the same centerline. Both parts of the jig must be securely clamped to each other and to the table.

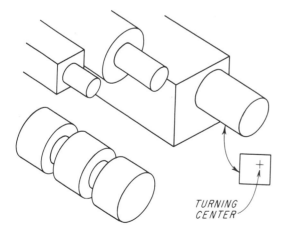

TURNING CENTER

MOUNTING FOR TAPER

WORK   CUT LINE

TRUE CENTER   "OFF" CENTER

Here are cuts you can make by doing dado turning. Also how to mount the work for turning a taper.

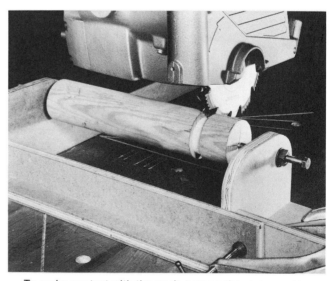

To make contact with the work, turn on the motor and lower the cutter slowly. Then turn the work against the direction of rotation of the cutter. Check frequently to be sure the work has not begun to jiggle loose.

The bolts (used as ''centers'') are pointed on a grinder. The double nuts let you secure the bolt. Check frequently as you work to be sure the work does not loosen.

To form an integral tenon just limit the cutting to that area of the work. Always adjust the guard to cover as much of the cutter as possible on the operator's side, for safety.

Form a taper by using one offset center. The cutter is moved for each pass. Work slowly on this kind of stuff—be sure, always, that centers and jig are secure.

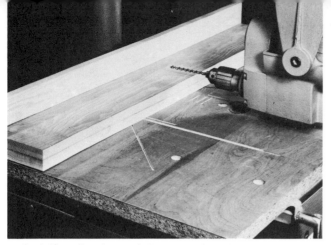

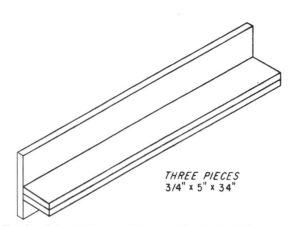
THREE PIECES
3/4" x 5" x 34"

A platform for the work is a good idea. The vertical piece extends below the platform (not shown in photo) so that it can be gripped like a fence.

Details of the platform, which consists simply of three pieces of wood. If necessary, change dimensions to suit the measurements of your own equipment.

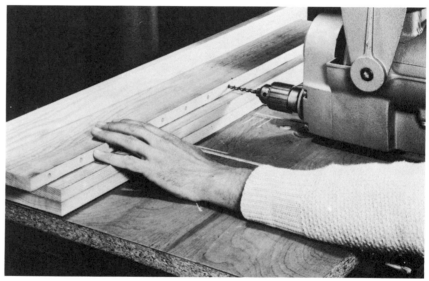

Place work flat on the platform and adjust the drill height by using the arm-raising crank. To control hole-depth, you can use a C-clamp on the arm. This, to limit travel of the power unit.

Do angular drilling in the same fashion simply by swinging the arm of the machine. On extreme angles, make the initial contact very carefully to avoid having the bit wander.

When work size permits, you can drill by using the arm-raising lever. If the hole is to go through the stock, use scrap between the work and the table.

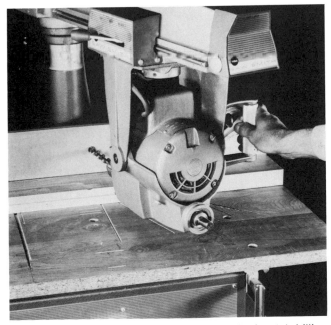

The radial arm saw makes a pretty nice horizontal drilling machine. You can do straight drilling or, by swinging the arm, angular drilling.

times possible to place the work on the table and do the drilling by using the arm-raising crank. The fence can be used as a gauge to control edge distance when you require a number of holes on the same center line. When the holes must go through the stock, use a scrap block between the work and the saw table.

Horizontal drilling. One type of horizontal drilling is done by organizing the machine so the cutting tool points to the rear. You do the drilling by feeding the power unit in that direction. Often, it's possible to secure the work itself in place of the regular fence. Other times, especially for edge drilling, it's better to work with the special platform arrangement that we show in an accompanying sketch. What this does is elevate the work so the power unit will have clearance above the table. The vertical part of the platform provides for backing up the work and for securing the unit to the table as you would a regular fence.

Actually, this arrangement functions as accurately as any horizontal drill. It's ideal for edge-to-edge dowel joints because you know that all the holes will have exactly the same edge distance. If you mark each piece of stock so a similar surface will be kept uppermost, it won't matter if the holes are not centered exactly.

Adding the gadget that is also shown makes it possible to automatically position the work when you have a number of equally spaced holes to drill. To control hole depth, you can use a C-clamp on the arm of the tool to limit travel of the carriage. The same setup can be used to drill mortises merely by doing a series of overlapping holes and to form radial holes in round stock.

To drill radial holes on a surface, you can make a vertical pivot jig that is clamped to the vertical part of the horizontal drilling platform. This permits you to turn the work while it is in a position that is perpendicular to the saw table. Of course, your work size is limited by the maximum distance between the table and the arm.

For horizontal end drilling, you work with the drilling tool pointing to the left of the machine. The simple table you need takes the place of the platform used for edge drilling. For these procedures, lock the position of the tool and feed the work to do the drilling. Be sure to keep the work flat on the table and snugly against the fence. To control the depth of the hole, clamp a stop block to the table. On this table, the fence is in a fixed position, so adjustments for hole location are done by situating the drilling tool. The setup is also usable for drilling into the ends of miter cuts. You do need guide blocks to hold the work at the correct angle.

Circular work that requires edge holes can't be fed along the fence. Therefore, for such work you make

A simple attachment like this provides a drilling gauge so you can automatically position the work for a series of equally spaced holes.

This is the setup you need for drilling into a circle. Since the work is mounted on a pivot, all the holes will be exactly the same distance from the center.

A series of overlapping holes clear away most of the waste for a mortise. Finish up with a sharp chisel.

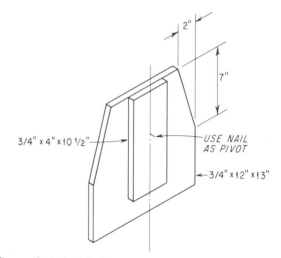

The vertical pivot jig is constructed this way. Clamp it to the backboard of the horizontal edge-drilling platform.

A back-up platform, secured in the fence groove, raises and supports work in this fashion. To control hole depth, use a C-clamp on the arm of the tool. This will limit carriage travel.

A sliding table permits end drilling in pieces that can't be fed along a fence. The work is clamped to the jig and the whole bit is fed forward into the drill.

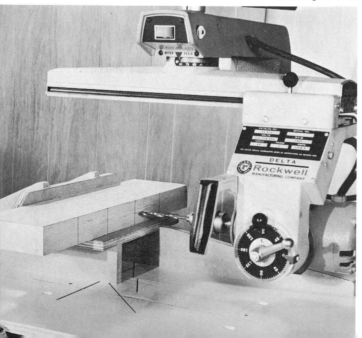

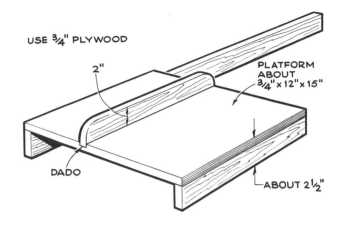

USE ¾" PLYWOOD

2"

PLATFORM ABOUT ¾" x 12" x 15"

DADO

ABOUT 2½"

This table is needed for horizontal end-drilling. The table and its fence must be parallel to the drilling tool.

How to construct the table for horizontal end-drilling. It can be made out of ¾" plywood. Cut the back piece long enough so it can be secured in place of the regular fence.

To gauge the depth of the holes, clamp a stop block to the table.

You can use the same setup to drill holes in miter cuts.

what amounts to a sliding table to which you can clamp the stock. Then, both the work and the table are moved forward to do the drilling.

ROUTING

Most manufacturers of radial arm saws list special chucks so router bits can be used in their machines. It's a good idea to use these chucks as opposed to the conventional three-jaw chucks because the bits develop considerable side thrust and are best held in the special devices. If your machine has spindles that turn at different speeds, use the highest available for routing jobs. When you are working at saw speed, which is all right but not ideal, use a slow feed speed so the cutting tool will have a chance to do its job.

Many routing operations can be done with the bit set in a vertical position. Adjust for depth of cut by using the arm-elevating crank. Routing a groove is simply a matter of placing the work on the table snugly against the fence and moving it forward against the cutter. The depth you can cut in one pass will depend on the material. Soft, grainless wood permits deeper cuts than hardwoods. But, no matter, if you must force the feed to get the cut done or if you feel excessive chatter in the work, you can be fairly sure that you are trying to do too much in one pass. It is better to achieve full depth of cut by making repeat passes.

To do cross-grain cuts, such as dadoes and end rabbets, use the machine as you do for crosscutting. The work stays put; the cutting tool is moved. Cross-grain cuts are always a little harder to do simply because you encounter more resistance. Feed the cutter slowly.

A good deal of horizontal routing can be done by using the same platform you made for horizontal drilling. The difference in this situation, most times, is that you keep the tool locked and move the work. Forming tongues and grooves, round-end mortising, and angular routing are examples of the jobs you can do.

Pattern routing. For pattern routing you need a guide pin that is the same diameter as the bit. The best way to set up is to tack-nail a sheet of $\frac{1}{4}''$ or $\frac{1}{2}''$ plywood to the saw table and then use the arm-elevating crank for the bit to form a hole in the plywood. Glue a dowel pin in the hole so it projects above the auxiliary table about $\frac{3}{16}''$. The pattern, which is the shape of what you wish to cut in the project, is tack-nailed to the underside of the workpiece and then placed over the pin. Position the router bit to the depth of cut required and do the cutting with the pattern in constant contact with the guide pin. Since the cutting tool is directly over the guide pin, the pattern design will be duplicated in the work.

Router bit on the radial arm saw can cut grooves and rabbets. Always feed so the cutting action of the bit tends to hold the work against the fence. Special chuck limits side thrust.

The platform that you made for horizontal drilling can be used the same way for routing jobs. Here the cutter is locked in position and the work is fed to make a groove.

To form a tongue, just make two passes. It isn't necessary to re-position the cutter, just flip the stock for the second cut. Work is supported on platform.

Do rabbet cuts by feeding so the bit action tends to hold the work against the fence. When the width of cut you need is wider than your largest bit, just make more passes.

Do dado-type work by holding the work still and pulling the cutter across as in crosscutting. Crossgrain cuts are always rougher to do so make the pass slowly and steadily.

Do end rabbets the same way. Repeat passes will give you wider cuts than the diameter of the bit you are working with.

Do a mortise by using the router bit to "drill" overlapping holes, then lock the cutter in position and move the work back and forth to clean out the cut.

Pivot cutting. You can do circular grooves or rabbets on the edge of circular pieces easily if you use a nail as a pivot guide. All you have to do is drive a nail through the center of the work so the point can penetrate the saw table about $\frac{1}{4}''$. The distance from the nail to the cutter is the radius of the circle you will rout.

Decorative cuts. Router bits offer many opportunities to make surface grooves for purely decorative purposes. A series of equally spaced, stopped grooves on slim stock will produce pieces that can be used as moldings. To limit the length of cut on operations like this, you can feed to a line on the work or use a C-clamp on the arm to limit the travel length of the carriage.

Curved grooves. You can rout grooves parallel to a curved edge if you use a triangular piece of wood as a guide. This is tack-nailed to the saw table with one point in line with the router bit but spaced away to equal the edge distance of the groove. Move the work so its edge bears constantly against the guide. As you make the pass, keep the work positioned so that a tangent to the curve at the point of cut will be perpendicular to the center line of the guide.

Freehand routing. Since a router bit will cut in any direction, it's a logical tool to use for cutting intricate designs, house numbers, names, etc. Since a freehand operation has feed going in many directions, the results will depend on how well you follow the design. It isn't difficult but does demand careful feed and sharp tools. Success will come faster if you do some practicing in soft wood with minimum grain.

SHAPING

The radial arm saw does a very efficient shaping job. Like the drill press, its drawbacks may be less than ideal speed and the fact that the spindle is situated over the work. However, slow feed will help compensate for lack of speed, and the overhead cutter position is not going to interfere with the bulk of the work you will do.

How you put the cutters on your machine and what kind of adapters you need can depend on the design of the tool you own. So, again, check your owner's manual for pertinent details. Most tools provide an auxiliary arbor so the cutters can rotate in a conventional manner. Therefore, with the cutter set vertically and situated behind a fence, the feed direction would be from left to right as it is on a drill-press setup.

Straight shaping. Chances are that most of the shaping you will require will be on straight edges so it can be done against a fence. On the radial arm saw this fence can be two pieces of wood set in place on the regu-

The guide pin and the router bit must be aligned perfectly. Best way to be sure of alignment is to use the router bit itself to drill the hole for the pin.

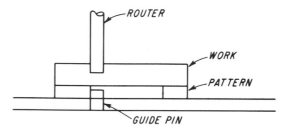

This is the setup for pattern routing. The guide pin must not project more than the thickness of the pattern.

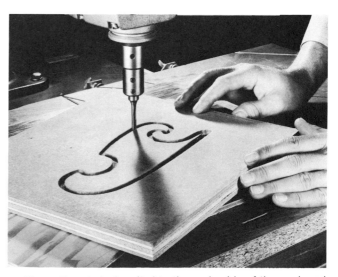

The pattern is tack-nailed to the underside of the work and you do the cutting by keeping the pattern in constant contact with the pin. The router then duplicates the pattern.

You can do perfect circular grooves made by the pivot-guide method. You can cut through to form a disc or a ring, by making repeat passes.

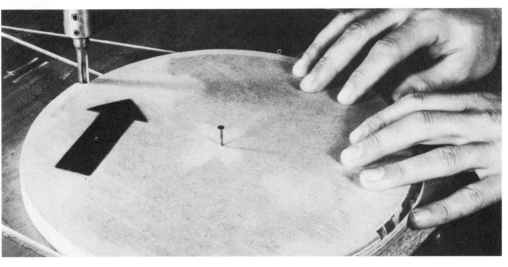

You can rabbet circular edges by working the same way. The arrow indicates direction of feed. Keep the work firm and feed steadily.

Making stopped grooves at a slight angle to form a strip of molding. You can work to a line on the work or use a C-clamp on the arm of the tool as a stop.

The cut can go across the work —the stock can be inverted for alternate cuts. Decorative possibilities are similar to those achieved when making dentil moldings with a saw blade.

This is the way to form a groove parallel to a curved edge. The idea will work for inside as well as outside curves.

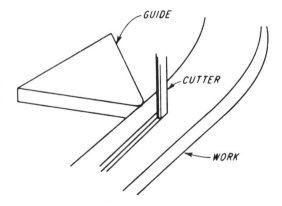

Picture the center line of the guide as being perpendicular to a line that is tangent to the curve at the cut area. Maintain this relationship throughout the pass.

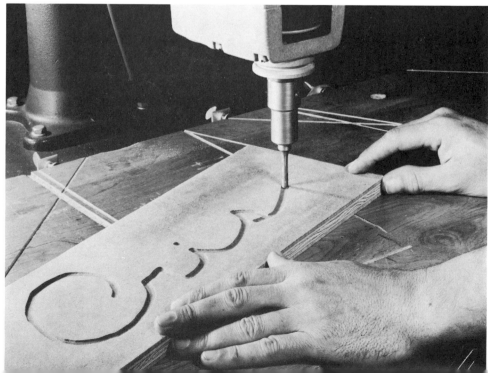

Do some practicing before tackling an important job freehand. Work slowly and be sure the cutter is sharp. If you had many similar designs to do, it would be wise to set up for pattern routing.

COLLARS

COLLARS MAY BE USED BELOW OR ABOVE THE CUTTER, BETWEEN TWO CUTTERS, OR IN OTHER WAYS THAT ARE CONVENIENT TO THE WORK

SHAPER ADAPTER

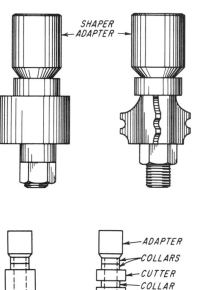

ADAPTER
COLLARS
CUTTER
COLLAR
CUTTER
NUT

Except for some fences and special jigs that you can make yourself, adapters like this, on which you mount three-lip shaper cutters, are about all you need to do shaping work on the radial arm saw.

lar fence. Adjust the gap between the two pieces to minimize the amount of cutter that is exposed.

When the cut removes just a portion of the work edge, the two pieces of the fence are in line. When the cut removes the entire edge of the stock, then you must compensate to provide support after the cut. You can do this by using a shim against the outfeed fence. The thickness of the shim should equal the depth of cut. The same thing is accomplished when you use a shim between the table and the infeed fence.

You can preview the cut by placing the workpiece flat on the table and against the fence and turning the cutter by hand until the face of the blade rests against the edge of the stock.

Whenever possible, feed so the cutter works with the grain of the wood. This will give you the smoothest cuts. Also, it's a good idea to set up so the cutter is under the

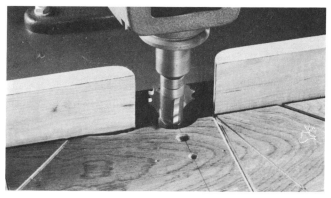

Two boards that you can clamp in place of a regular fence make a practical setup for straight line shaping. Slight in-cut in the table is a help for vertical adjustments.

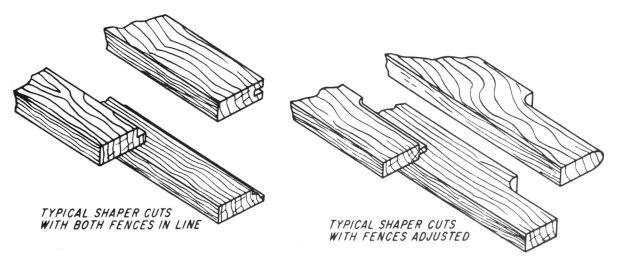

TYPICAL SHAPER CUTS WITH BOTH FENCES IN LINE

TYPICAL SHAPER CUTS WITH FENCES ADJUSTED

On the left are partial cuts—some part of the original stock edge remains *after* the cut. On the right are full cuts that call for consideration to support the stock after the cut.

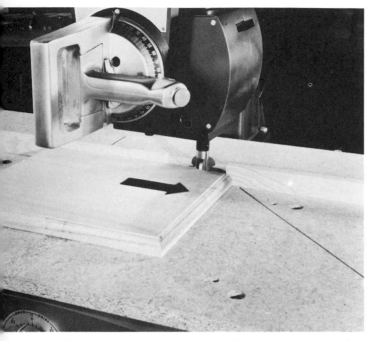

Simple shaping cut is done by holding the work snug against the fence as you move forward for the cut. Keep the feed slow but steady. Cut *with* the grain whenever possible.

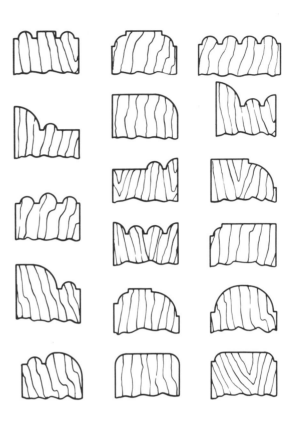

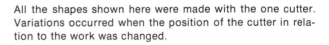

All the shapes shown here were made with the one cutter. Variations occurred when the position of the cutter in relation to the work was changed.

To preview the cut, turn the tool by hand until one blade rests against the edge of the stock.

work, even though some of the accompanying photos don't always show it this way. Having the cutter under the work affords greater protection and avoids gouging the work should you accidentally lift it during the pass. It isn't always possible to work this way, but it's wise to do so whenever the operation permits.

In shaping, the following are general rules to keep in mind. Keep feed speed at a minimum but keep the tool cutting. Try to cut with the grain. Always feed against the direction of rotation of the cutting tool and keep your hands away from the cutting area.

To do cross-grain cuts on stock that is too narrow for good bearing surface against the fence, use a backup block as if it were a miter gauge. If you must shape all edges or two adjacent edges, do the cross-grain cuts first. These will end with slight imperfections to be

When you tilt the cutter, which is possible on the radial arm saw, you extend even further the results you can get from standard cutting tools.

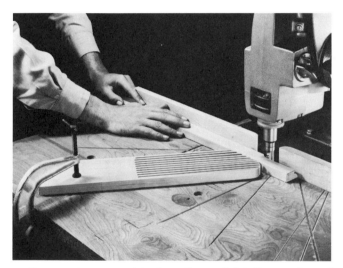

You can do narrow strips in pretty good style if you make and use a spring-stick hold down. Position it to hold the work snug against the fence just in front of the cutter position.

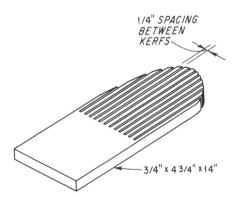

1/4" SPACING BETWEEN KERFS

3/4" x 4 3/4" x 14"

Straight grain fir is a good material to use for spring sticks. All you have to do is slot a board as shown here.

removed by the final with-the-grain passes.

Narrow moldings. Never attempt to shape slim pieces of wood without taking special precautions. A spring holddown that you can make yourself is good to use for an occasional piece; but when you require many similar parts, it's better to make a special guide and holddown that is clamped to the fence so that the entire cutting area is enclosed. All you do is feed the pre-cut pieces of stock into one end and pull them out the other.

Stopped cuts. To do stopped cuts, use stop blocks or clamps on the fence. To operate, place one end of the work against the stop on the infeed fence and swing it in slowly to engage the cutter. Then feed as you would normally until the work hits the stop on the outfeed fence.

Many decorative cuts can be accomplished using the stop-block technique. The idea is to brace the work against a stop on the infeed fence and swing the work in slowly to engage the cutter. This results in a semi-circular cut with its profile shape determined by the cutter you are using. The stop is positioned for each new cut. A special fence with holes drilled in it for a nail stop can be very useful in this kind of work.

Freehand shaping. Circular work and work with curved edges can't be handled against a straight fence. Instead, make the special table that is shown and work against collars that are mounted on the shaper adapter. These control the depth of the cut and provide a surface against which part of the work edge can bear while you make the pass.

Since the collars turn with the cutter and bear on the work edge, it's necessary to keep them smooth and clean. Otherwise, they can contribute to uneven cuts and burning of the wood.

Making the initial contact when shaping against collars has an element of danger unless some means of support for the work is provided at the very start of the pass. The table shown incorporates a left-hand and a right-hand bolt to serve as fulcrum pins. When you start the operation, you support the work against the infeed fulcrum pin and then move slowly to engage the cutter until the work rests solidly on the collar. Once the cut is full, you can bear against the collar only. At the end of the cut, take advantage of the outfeed fulcrum pin to provide work support.

Don't work in this manner when the pieces are too small to be safely held by hand. If you do require a slim, curved molding, do the shaping on the end of a wide piece and then cut off the part you need.

To do inside cuts, place the work before you lower

When you have many similar slim moldings to do, it's best to make a special guide hold-down like the one we described for doing similar kinds of work with a molding head.

For stopped cuts, use clamps or stop blocks on the fence. Brace the work against the left-hand stop before you engage the cutter. Then move forward until you hit the right-hand stop.

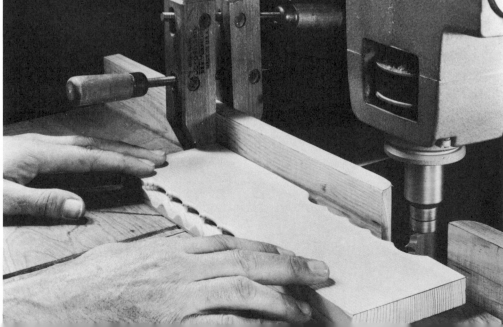

You can use stops to do decorative cutting. The work is moved into the cutter and then pulled back. Then it is repositioned for the next cut. A drilled fence for a nail stop can be a big help here.

the cutter to its correct position. Sometimes you can use the fulcrum pins, sometimes you can't. So extra caution is called for. Always hook your hands over the workpiece edges so it's difficult for them to slip. Always keep them on the outside edges as far from the cutting area as possible. As previously mentioned, it just isn't good practice to attempt jobs on pieces that are too small to be held safely.

THE RADIAL ARM SAW USED AS A SANDER

Disc sanding. Be sure to use a disc that is listed as an accessory for the machine you own. It will be designed to operate safely at the speed (or speeds) that your machine can provide. The best way to utilize it fully is to make a special table that imitates a conventional disc sander setup. Ours incorporates a groove for a miter gauge and has a leg so the entire unit can be locked in place as you would a conventional fence.

Always operate so the work is placed on the table on the "down" side of the disc. Working the other way will cause the disc rotation to lift the work. What is shown in the accompanying illustrations are simply "quick-thoughts." Many of the ideas illustrated in the chapter on disc-sander use also apply to the radial arm saw.

Drum sanding. To work efficiently with a drum sander, you can operate freehand, with the special table designed for freehand-shaping operations, or even with the table you made for disc sanding. To get the most out of the unit, check the drum sander applications shown in the drill press chapter and apply them to the radial-arm-saw setups.

OTHER USES

You can use your radial arm saw as a grinder as long as you check to be sure the wheel you wish to mount is designed for safe operation at the speed or speeds that are available to you. So that you can hold tools in correct relationship to the grinding wheel, make the tool support that is shown in the accompanying sketch. The operations illustrated are examples of what you can do. For more information on grinder use, check the chapter on grinders.

If you consider the tool as a power source, then you can think in terms of using wire wheels, buffing wheels, even flex shafts. Information on specific uses of these items will be found throughout this book. It is important that whatever you mount on the arbor of your radial arm saw be designed to operate safely at the speeds you must work with. It's wise to check your owner's manual carefully and work with accessories listed by the manufacturer for that particular tool.

This is the setup you need for freehand shaping against collars. The work is supported by the fulcrum pins—depth of cut is controlled by the collars that situate with the cutter on the adapter.

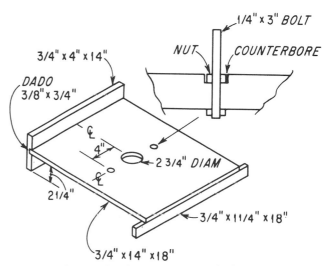

Construction details of the special table for freehand shaping. Adapt dimensions, if necessary, to your machine.

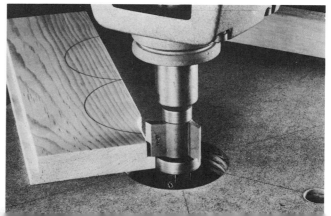

This is how the collar controls the depth of the cut. You can see, since they turn with the cutter, why the collars should be clean and smooth.

The radial arm saw can be a pretty efficient disc sander if you set up for the job like this. Always place the work on the "downside" of the disc, keep the work moving steadily.

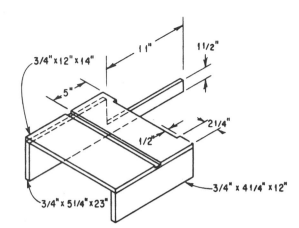

How to make the special table for disc-sander operations.

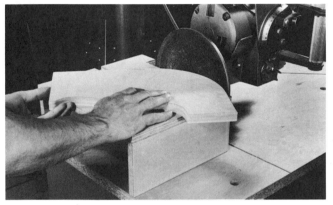

When doing the sanding, keep the work moving. If you hesitate with feed, you may get a flat spot where you don't want it.

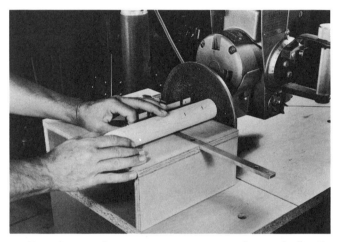

By using a miter gauge, you can move the work directly forward to engage the disc. This will assure a square edge on what you are sanding.

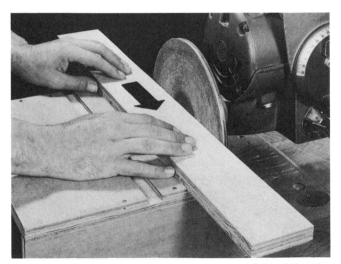

You can do edges too. Try to angle the work just a bit so the cutting will be done on the "down" side.

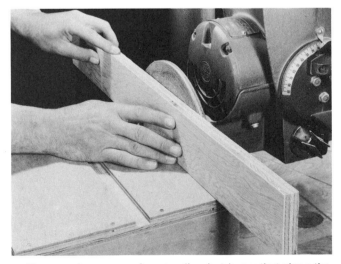

You can do some surface sanding but know that since the action is a rotary one, the results will not match the smoothness you will get when you use a tool that permits in-line sanding for finishing work.

The table you made for disc sanding can be used for drum sander operations also.

To sand inside edges, situate the work before you bring the sanding drum down. Sand so you are feeding the work against the direction of rotation of the drum. Move the work slowly but steadily.

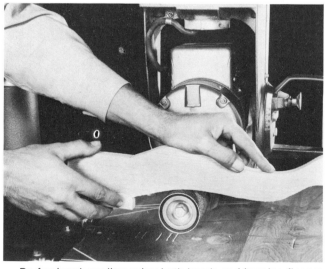

Do freehand sanding using both hands and keeping fingers well away from drum. Move work smoothly over drum and don't hesitate at any one point.

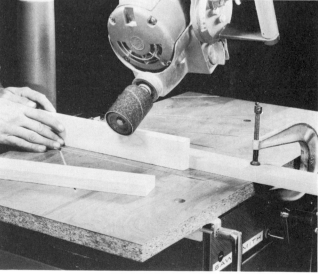

You can do angular sanding by tilting the drum. Clamp a guide strip to the table to help hold the feed direction.

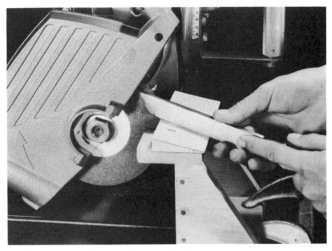

Use a tapered block to provide the correct edge angle for a lathe skew chisel. This photo illustrates typical grinding wheel operation. Wear goggles for all grinding operations.

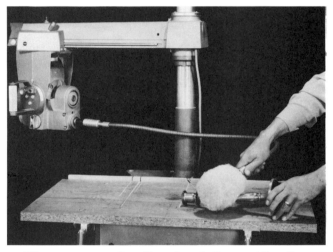

A grinding wheel will let you renew and maintain the edges on tools. Lock stand securely to table. Adjust guard for maximum protection without obstructing visibility.

When you use an item like a flex shaft, mount it so the machine provides the correct direction of rotation. Also, be sure the flex shaft can operate at the available speed.

3 | THE JIGSAW

The jigsaw, by means of a crankshaft arrangement converts a rotary motion into an up-and-down blade action. Not all units operate in this way but, regardless, they cut because the blade strokes vertically. The jigsaw's greatest asset lies in extremely fine and intricate curve cuts. Also, it is the only stationary homeshop tool with which you can do piercing, the technique that permits making internal cuts without a lead-in kerf from an edge of the stock.

The jigsaw should not be viewed as a toy machine. Since you can mount heavy blades and common depth-of-cut capacities run to about 2″, you can handle some quite heavy stock. The truth is, within its capacities, the jigsaw can do band-saw jobs, but there is no comparison in cut speed; the band saw will win everytime when compared solely on that basis. On the other hand, the jigsaw is king when it comes to very short-radius curves and extremely fine kerfs.

That's why it is such a special tool for scrollwork and fretwork. Inlay crafts, marquetry, intarsia, and jewelry-type projects in metal are much easier to do when a jigsaw is available.

Because it is relatively easy and safe to use, the jigsaw is also a logical choice if you wish to introduce a youngster to the art of power-tool woodworking.

GAUGING CAPACITY

Depth-of-cut capacity is figured in terms of the maximum stock thickness it can handle. The second capacity factor is the distance from the blade and the support for the upper structure. This is throat capacity, and the figure is used to designate jigsaw size. For example, an 18″ jigsaw can cut to the center of a 36″ circle. It's possible with some tools to use an accessory extension arm to increase the throat capacity, but more often the design permits removing or swinging down the upper structure to remove the support interference. Then, in effect, capacity is unlimited and the setup is called "saber sawing." More will be said about this topic later,

BASIC PARTS OF THE JIGSAW

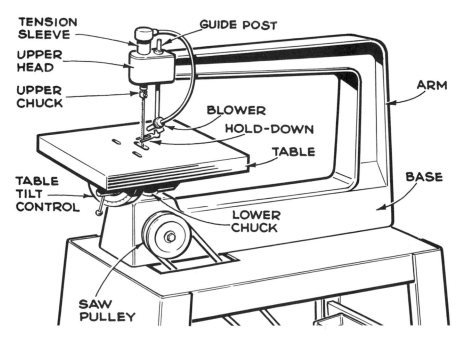

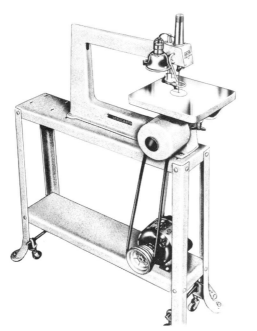

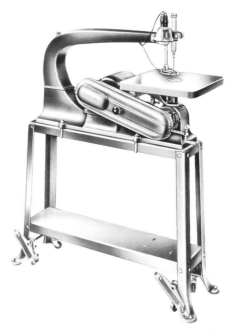

Typical homeworkshop jigsaw has stepped pulleys to pro-vide various speeds. The light attached to the upper arm is a worthwhile addition because of the extremely fine cutting you will often do on the machine.

Larger unit has a variable speed mechanism. This is ideal since it permits infinite changes between the extremes and also eliminates the bother of having to change V-belt posi-tion for different jobs.

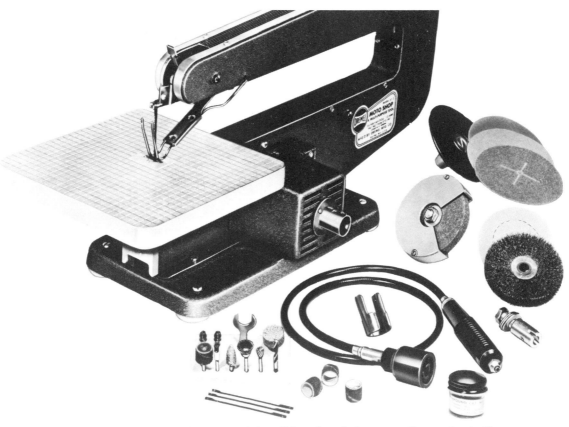

Dremel Moto-Shop includes a power take-off for a flex shaft to run a disc sander, buffing wheel, etc. A very nice tool for a youngster to have.

but generally this feature is made possible by gripping a heavy-gauge blade in the lower chuck only.

HOW BLADES MOUNT

Two chucks are provided. One is in the upper arm, the other below the table. Although designs may differ, the purpose of the chucks is to hold the blade taut between them. The amount of adjustment in the chuck and the method for achieving blade alignment can vary from tool to tool. Usually, a set of chuck blocks is provided. A setscrew on one side of the chuck lets you position one of the blocks in a more-or-less permanent position for most normal cutting; a setscrew on the opposite side moves the second chuck block so that the blade can be gripped securely. Some designs provide a permanent position for one of the blocks. You can get specific information about your tool from the owner's manual.

The important thing is to install the blade so it will "jig" in a true vertical line throughout the stroke travel. It must be vertical when viewed from the front and the side. One way to do this with assurance is to make yourself a guide. This guide is no more than a squared wood block (about $\frac{3}{4}'' \times 4'' \times 4''$) with a straight kerf cut down the center of one edge. Holding the blade in the kerf as you tighten the chucks will assure alignment.

The blade backup is at the bottom of the guide post. Some of these are *universal*, being a slim, steel disc with various blade-size slots cut in the perimeter. You choose the slot that is suitable for the blade you are going to cut with and then adjust the device so the steel sleeve (or something similar) bears against the back edge of the blade. The degree of bearing should be a light-touch contact. Another design provides a split sleeve encased in a tube. The blade sits in the slot of the sleeve; the tube is used as the backup.

Whatever the method, be sure the blade can move easily in the guide and that the backup is not pushing.

A spring affair is provided as a work holddown. Without it, the wood would move up and down with the blade. Adjust the spring mechanism so it just touches the top surface of the work. Too much pressure can cause the spring to mar the work and interfere with a free feed. Too little pressure will be apparent because the work will chatter excessively.

Check the table for correct alignment. At "0," the angle between it and a side of the blade should be 90°. If your machine has a tilt scale and a table-stop screw, adjust them, if necessary, after you have checked the angle between the blade and the table.

BLADES

Many types and sizes of blades are available, but they all fall into one of two general categories. Those that must be gripped in both the upper and lower chuck are called "jeweler's blades." Others, heavy enough and wide enough so they can function while gripped in the lower chuck only, are called "saber blades."

There is a little bit of overlap here because some of the jeweler's blades are heavy enough to work as saber blades. The general rule is to use the heavier blades as the stock thickness increases. Choose the widest and the fastest cutting blade as long as it does the job for you. Think about saber blades and the heavier jeweler's blades when the stock reaches maximum depth-of-cut thickness and, of course, when you are working on large material that makes it necessary for you to remove the upper arm of the machine.

The accompanying blade chart does not list all the blades that are available, but the selection is an excellent assortment to begin with. If you use the blade chart together with the speed chart that is given, you'll be quite well organized for most of the jigsaw projects you're likely to encounter.

Quite often, it's possible to use discarded band-saw blades and still-sharp sections of used hacksaw blades. These must be cut off or "snapped" to a suitable length. When the width of such items doesn't permit mounting in the jigsaw as is, you can always grind down the ends to the chuck size of your jigsaw.

Use wide blades with few teeth at slow speeds for heavy cutting. Use narrow blades with many teeth at high speeds for thin material and for smooth cuts.

Most jigsaws provide a device that permits you to

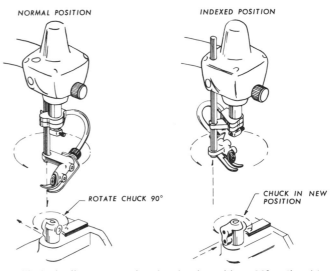

NORMAL POSITION INDEXED POSITION

ROTATE CHUCK 90° CHUCK IN NEW POSITION

"Indexing" means turning the chuck positions 90° so the side of the blade will then be parallel to the rear arm of the machine. Thus you can cut long stock without interference.

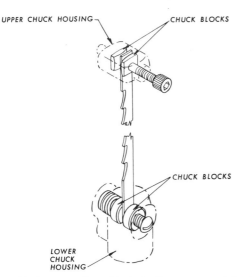

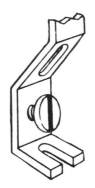

Jig saw blades are gripped in both the upper and the lower chuck. When you install the blade, be sure that the teeth point downward.

A very simple guide and backup is shown here. The blade passes through the upper slot and rides in the lower one. The screw is turned either in or out to suit blade width or position.

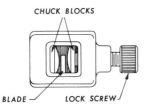

Turning the "lock screw" grips the blade between "chuck blocks".

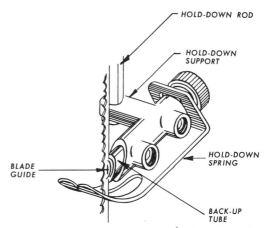

Another type (found on the Shopsmith jig saw) has a split tube as a blade guide. This is encased in an adjustable sleeve that serves as the backup.

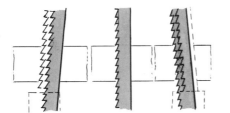

When the blade is locked in the chucks and viewed from the side, it must not lean either forward or back. The most efficient setting is shown in the center sketch.

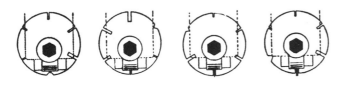

A universal guide is a disc with a slotted perimeter. You turn the disc and so choose a slot that is right for the blade. The backup roller is set to lightly touch the back edge of the blade.

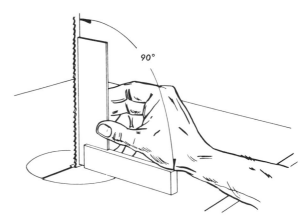

Angle between the side of the saw blade and the table must be 90° when the table is set at zero.

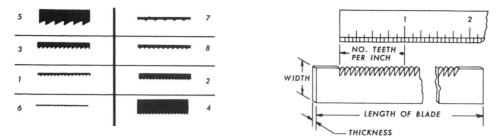

The eight examples of jig saw blades represent a good assortment to have on hand. The numbers are defined in the chart below.

BLADE	BLADE DIMENSION			OPERATION				R.P.M.
	THICKNESS INCHES	WIDTH INCHES	TEETH PER INCH	STOCK THICKNESS (Inches)	CUT RADIUS	KERF	BEST FOR	
5	.028	.250	7	1/4 & up	large	coarse	soft & hard wood — pressed wood	745
3	.020	.110	15	1/8-1/2 in metal, 1/8 & up in other material	medium	medium	metal — wood — bone — felt — paper	1175
1	.010	.040	18	1/16-1/8	small	very fine	wood — bone — plastics	1600
6	.012	.023	20	up to 1/8	very small	fine	plastics — bone — fiber — comp. board	1050
7	.020	.070	7	up to 1/4	medium	medium	plastics — bone — hard rubber	1400
8	.010	.070	14	1/8-1/2	medium	very fine	wood — plastics — bone — hard rubber	1525
2	.020	.110	20	1/16-1/8	medium	medium	aluminum—copper— mild steel	940
4	.028	.250	20	3/32-1/2 (1/4 max. in steel)	large	coarse	aluminum—copper — mild steel	830

Select the blade for the material you are working on and choose a speed that is close to the recommended one.

One way to store jig saw blades. The body of this box is just a block of wood with wide saw kerfs in it. Back it up with plywood. Make the block about 4″ high and as wide as you need for your own blade assortment.

"tension" the blade after it has been secured in the chucks. In most cases, it's merely a matter of pulling or pushing up on a cylinder that is part of the upper chuck assembly arm. It's even possible that the cylinder may be scaled for different blades. Whatever the case, more tension is needed on fine blades than on heavy ones; however, producing too much tension will just result in premature blade breakage. Probably the least tension that will do the job is the best to use. The operator's judgment is critical when deciding the degree of tension. You can easily be guided by well-defined indicators of poor tension adjustment. Cuts that are not square, blades breaking quickly, difficulty in following the cut line, and obvious off-vertical movement of the blade when you are cutting clearly indicate the need for tension readjustment.

BASIC WORK HANDLING

Be relaxed and comfortable. Many jigsaw jobs take a long time to do so a strained position will tire you quickly and will affect the quality of your work. At most times, use the left hand as a guide to keep turning the work so the blade stays on the line; use the right hand to feed. However, there is so much twisting and turning involved with jigsawing that it is difficult to abide by one set rule.

It's not out of line to use both hands in a combination action that provides both guiding and feeding. Many times, even during a cut, you'll find it convenient to move from in front of the machine to one side of it. Just be aware that the main job is to keep the blade on the line.

Never crowd the blade but, on the other hand, do not be overly cautious. The teeth on the blade are there to cut, not to burnish. A steady, even feed that constantly produces sawdust is ideal. Don't force a wide blade to turn a corner that is too small for it. You'll end up burning the wood, breaking the blade, and probably running off the line. Keep feed in a from-you-to-the-back-of-the-machine direction. It's the work you must keep turning, not the blade. Most jigsaw blades can be twisted when forced; and they will make cuts you never planned for, especially the finer, more flexible blades.

A good rule is to keep the side of the blade tangent to all curved lines. Worry about the teeth of the blade and the business of staying on the cut line.

If you feel that you are doing everything correctly and are still having difficulty making true cuts, check the relationship of the blade to the guides and the backup, as well as the degree of tension. If problems do occur, it will be mostly when you are doing intricate cutting with

Good "normal" hand position is shown here. But, when cuts are as complicated as this, the operator's position as well as the hand position may be changed frequently.

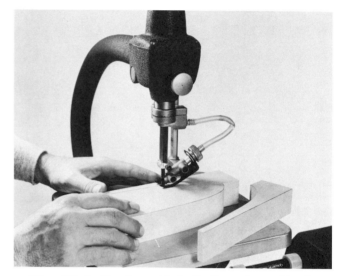

When fitted with a heavy blade, the jigsaw is capable of cutting wood stock up to 2″ thick.

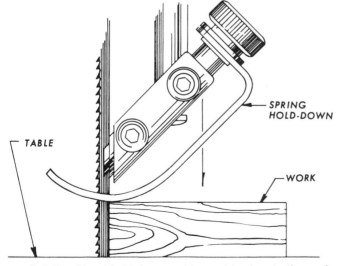

SPRING HOLD-DOWN

TABLE

WORK

Relationship of hold-down, guides and backup to the work and to the blade. Set the hold-down so it bears lightly on the work. The guide must not "pinch"; the backup must not push the blade forward.

It is even possible to do compound cutting. This technique is described in the band saw chapter.

small jeweler's blades. The heavier blades will function in pretty good order even with some maladjustment. This is not the case with the others. A good deal of what will be said in the bandsaw chapter about backtracking and in-cutting apply to the jigsaw. However, because the jigsaw can negotiate extremely tight radii, the degree of backtracking and in-cutting possible is not nearly the same.

PATTERNS AND LAYOUT

A "pattern" can be simply an attractive picture that you snip from a magazine and cement to plywood. You can cut it out in profile to produce a silhouette-type project or you can cut in intricate, interlocking pieces to make a jigsaw puzzle.

When you work with an original design, you can draw it full-size on the wood or on a piece of paper that you then cement to the stock. The latter method destroys the pattern so if you need duplicates or wish to save the pattern for possible future use, transfer it to the wood by means of carbon paper. In the case of duplicate pieces, the first part you cut can be the template you use for marking other stock.

The transferring-by-squares method is still a fairly effective method when you have a ready-made pattern that you wish to transfer to wood whether you wish to keep the same size of the original pattern, enlarge it, or reduce it. What you do is mark off the pattern in squares of one size and mark off the work with same, larger, or smaller squares. Then you just transfer the design square by square. This makes it easy to duplicate any design or pattern. If you make 1″ squares on the original and 2″ squares on the stock, you double the pattern size. And of course it works the opposite way when the work must be smaller than the original.

Many of the methods of work layout that are shown in the accompanying sketches can be used to minimize waste. Sometimes, through planning and good layout, it's possible to cut small pieces from scrap so they may then be joined to form a large part. When you are cutting many parts from a single panel, it's wise to first make all the patterns you need and then lay them out on the panel. Thus, you can minimize waste and, maybe even more importantly, plan for a compatible grain direction on each of the pieces.

PIERCING

It's possible to do piercing on a jigsaw because the blade is straight and secured at each end. Therefore, the blade may be passed through a hole in the work before it is secured in the chucks. This is intriguing because you can produce an internal design without a lead-in cut

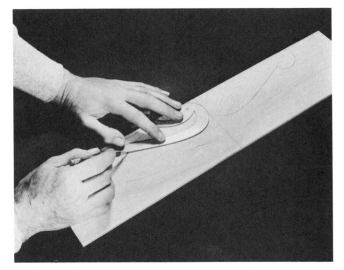

Various French Curve templates are helpful for creating any variety of jigsaw designs.

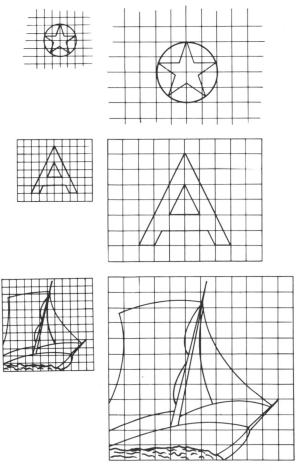

The enlarging-by-squares method is demonstrated here. Squares on the work are drawn 2x, 3x, etc., the size of the squares of the original. It can work the other way as well.

from an edge of the stock. The common procedure is to loosen the blade from the upper chuck, pass it through the blade-insertion hole, and then secure it in the upper chuck. Usual cutting procedures follow, but you do have to repeat the blade-insertion process for each cutout in the design.

The accompanying sketches show good feed direction for various shapes. When the cut is circular, the insertion hole may be drilled anywhere in the waste, but it does make sense to locate the insertion hole near the line simply because it reduces cutting time. Quite often, the insertion hole can be planned as part of the design; one example would be when you need a round corner. Choose a bit that will produce the radius you require and be accurate when you form the hole.

To cut a square corner, start from the insertion hole and approach the corner from one direction. Then backtrack to the hole and approach the corner from the second direction. Often, when you are using a fine blade, it's possible just to turn the corner. It will not be square; but when a tiny radius is not critical, this does not really matter. Wise jigsaw use calls for visualizing the shape and the cut before you start, if only to minimize the amount of cutting you must do to achieve a particular shape.

Choose blade sizes as you would for normal cutting: heavy blades for thick stock, smaller blades for thin material.

STRAIGHT CUTS

For most straight cuts, you will be working freehand, but there are occasions when setting up a guide can be useful. For example, when cutting squares for a checkerboard, doing slots, or even cutting dowels to length, using a guide is most helpful.

The guide you use can be an improvised rip fence, simply a straight piece of wood that you clamp to the jigsaw table. In the case of cutting similar pieces, it's a good idea to use a squared block of wood to feed with.

Piercing enables you to make internal cutouts without a lead-in kerf from the side of the stock.

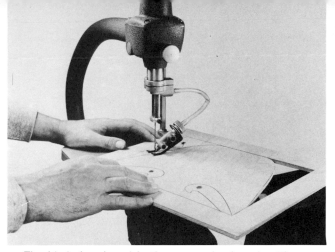

The blade is gripped in the upper chuck and cutting proceeds in normal fashion. You need a blade-insertion hole for each cutout in the design.

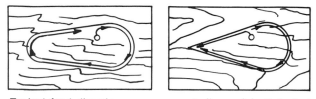

Typical feed direction on an example jigsaw job. Note that when the corner is acute, you clean it out by approaching from two directions. Follow the arrows.

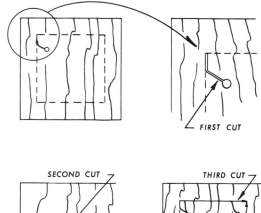

FIRST CUT

SECOND CUT   THIRD CUT

FOURTH CUT

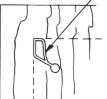

WHEN ROUND CORNER IS NEEDED, MAKE ONE CONTINUOUS CUT

A couple of ways to turn corners. The technique varies depending on whether the corner is square or round.

The fence will gauge the length of the cut, and the feed block will assure squareness.

Unlike the table saw, you can use a fence on the jigsaw as a stop for gauging duplicate cutoffs. Since the blade moves up and down, there is no kickback and no dangerous binding.

A fence is good to use when cutting slots, especially if you must do them in many pieces. When the slot has round ends, drill holes at each end of a common center line with the hole diameter matching the width of the slot. Insert the blade through one of the holes (as in piercing) and clamp the fence in place to guide the cut. After you have cut the first side, adjust the fence so you can cut the second side. If you require the same slot in many pieces, do the first-side cut in all of them before you adjust the fence.

If the slot has square ends, then you must do some freehand guiding after the slot sides are cut. Many craftsmen, when they require a lot of square-end slots, work as has been described for round-end slots; but they use a mortising chisel instead of a bit.

Remember that the jigsaw is not a speed tool. Feed slowly when using a fence and choose the heaviest blade that will produce the job you want. Guided cuts are tougher to do with the finer blades because they can twist so easily. When that happens, the blade simply moves off the line. Also, the work can move away from the guide. The answer is to use a good blade and a feed that permits the blade to cut without choking.

PIVOT CUTTING

You can cut accurate circles by using an auxiliary table that you clamp to the regular table. A nail that you drive through the auxiliary table acts as the pivot. It is very important for the pivot to be in line with the blade. The blades, because they are somewhat flexible, will tend to drift if you don't do a good job of locating the pivot point.

The extra table doesn't have to be more than a sheet of $\frac{1}{4}''$ plywood or hardboard. Drill a hole through it so you can insert the jigsaw blade and, if you wish to use the same one for various size circles, drill a series of holes about $\frac{1}{4}''$ apart on a common center line. Then you can insert the pivot through the hole that will give you the correct radius distance from the pivot to the blade.

A long nail as a pivot means you must drill a center hole through the work. If you wish to avoid this, just use a very short nail instead. Then you can simply press the work on it.

Thin blades, when used for pivot cutting, have more tendency to drift than heavy ones. If you must work with a thin blade, apply a bit more tension than you

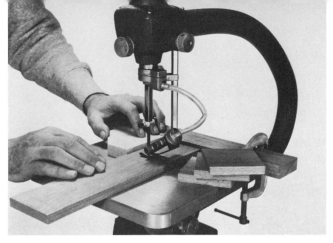

An improvised fence and a backup block is a good setup for doing work like this. Unlike the table saw, you can use a fence as a stop to gauge work length.

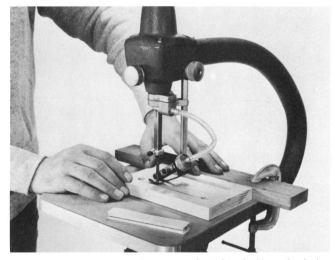

The same setup but without the feed block. Note the holes that have been drilled on a common center line. These provide for blade insertion and also for rounded slot ends.

This is a good way to cut dowel to length. Be sure to use a squared feed block.

155

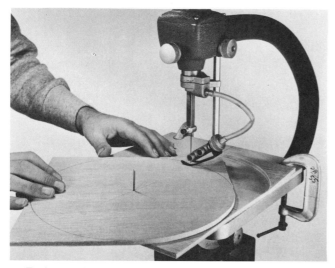

Typical setting for cutting circles. The pivot pin must be in line with the blade. A slow feed is essential, especially when working with a fine blade. A little extra tension helps.

A blade insertion hole is required for each ring, drilled at the bevel angle you will use for the sawing.

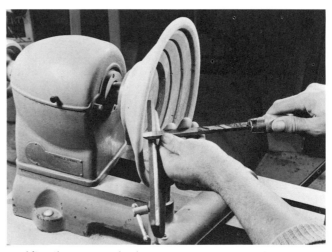

After the concentric rings are glued together in their projected position, the work can be face-plate mounted and turned. Thus you can get a deep bowl from a flat board.

might normally do. In all cases, rotate the work slowly.

BEVEL CUTTING

Bevel cutting with a jigsaw enables you to form, among other things, a deep bowl from a flat board.

If you jigsaw a disc in the center of a board, the disc will fall through. If you do the same thing but with the table tilted about 5°, the beveled disc will fall only part way through the beveled opening. The disc will jam like a stopper in a barrel.

If, instead of a single disc, you cut a series of concentric beveled rings, each would sink part way through the opening it was cut from; and you would end up with a cone shape. The more rings you cut, the deeper the cone will be.

When can this technique be used? Well, some of the things you can make include planters, raised bases, hollow hulls for boat models, trays with raised lips, signs with raised letters, panels with raised sections, drawer pulls cut directly from the drawer front, and blanks for lathe-turning bowls, plates and trays. There are many possibilities to discover after you have tried the technique.

The shape you get depends on the contour of the sections, the wall thickness of the rings, the number you cut, and the projection of each. For example, if you cut six concentric rings in a $\frac{3}{4}''$ board that is 6″ square, and each ring projects $\frac{1}{2}''$, you get a bowl shape that's 6″ across and $3\frac{1}{4}''$ high. There is little point in trying to figure out beforehand just how much projection you'll get; it depends on the stock thickness, the table tilt, and the

kerf width. It's easier to make a trial cut in some scrap and then measure it.

The less table tilt you use, the greater the projection of each individual piece; the more pieces you cut, the greater the total projection. Using too little table tilt can add up to a difficult glue job when you assemble the rings. Try a table tilt of 2° to 5° in materials from $\frac{1}{4}''$ to $\frac{3}{4}''$ thick but don't use a blade that makes a heavy kerf. A blade that is .020″ thick by .110″ wide by 15 teeth to the inch works fairly well on the jigsaw. As we show in the photographs, you can do this kind of thing on the band saw too. When working on that tool, choose a $\frac{1}{8}''$ or a $\frac{1}{4}''$ blade with a slight set.

These recommendations are just to get you started

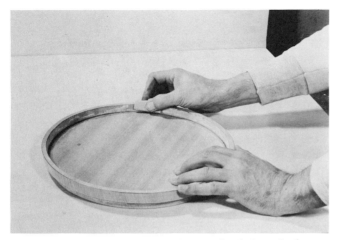

Trays and plates with raised lips are simple to make from a flat board when you use the bevel-cutting idea. They can be sanded and used as is, or lathe-mounted for more shaping.

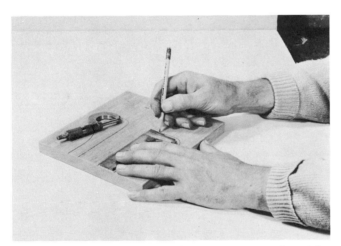

You can bevel cut for tool pockets. Trace the outline of the tool as shown here and then bevel-cut.

After the glue dries, plane or sand off the part of the cutout that projects. This is a good way to make sliding shelves with tool pockets.

since there is no law that says you can't use heavier blades or lighter blades should they be compatible with the stock thickness.

When you cut, be sure to *always* keep the inside piece (the part that will project) on the same side of the blade. If you don't, you will change the bevel direction, and the parts will not fit.

SABER SAWING

To do saber sawing, grip a special saber-saw blade or a very heavy jeweler's blade in the lower chuck only. You might wish to do this in the following two examples: when the work is heavy and tough and you feel a saber blade will do the job best and when work size requires that you remove the upper arm of the machine. In the latter situation, you have no choice since there is but one chuck to work with.

How you set up for saber sawing depends on the machine you have. The chuck grip should be normal, but some tools have a special backup device for saber-blade use. Check your owner's manual.

When doing pierced work in heavy stock where the use of a fine blade would be out of line, using a saber blade can speed up the job because you don't have to go through the business of releasing from the upper chuck, inserting through the hole, re-securing in the upper chuck, etc. With the saber blade you merely jump from one opening to another. The insertion holes, of course, are still required.

Don't force the work. Although the blades you use for this application are stiffer and heavier, they can still bend or twist. Feed so that the blade is doing the cutting at a speed it was designed for.

INLAY WORK

The most common type of inlay work on the jigsaw is a kind of pad sawing. It calls for a selection of wood veneers that are fastened together between top and bottom boards with nails driven through the waste areas. The design you wish to inlay is drawn on the top board. Since all the veneers are cut at the same time by pad sawing, any piece cut out of one layer will fit the corresponding piece in another layer. The veneers, of course, must be selected for contrast both in color and in grain.

As the cutting proceeds, situate each separated piece on a flat board in the same position it occupied in the pad. This will eliminate having to search for and fit the pieces.

When the cutting is finished, the pieces are joined

SABER CUTTING

Saber blades are held in the lower chuck only. Some machines provide a special, under-the-table backup.

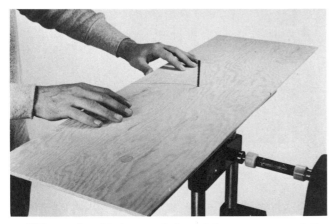

With a saber blade mounted, and the upper arm of the machine removed, you can handle any size workpiece on the jigsaw. Feed just fast enough to keep the blade cutting.

Sometimes, piercing on heavy stock is best done with a saber blade. It eliminates the chore of frequent re-chucking at the upper end.

together by placing them on a sheet of gummed paper or something similar. The fully assembled picture is glued, paper side up, to a backup board. After the glue has dried, the paper is dampened with water and rubbed off. Then the exposed, inlaid picture is sanded and finished as desired. In most cases, a smooth, clear coating is used so the beauty of the veneers will not be hidden.

You can see that if the pad is made up of ten different sheets of veneer, you can actually get ten pictures. This is fine for wide-scale production, but a single-version selection of cut pieces should be made for the most promising results. Yes, this produces waste, but it is done for art's sake.

Another possibility is to work without making a pad.

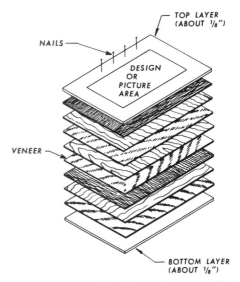

Pad-sawing veneers provides the parts you need to do intricate and fascinating inlaid pictures. Any piece cut from one veneer will fit the corresponding hole in another.

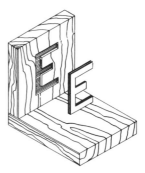

Intarsia is another type of inlay work. You cut the design on the jigsaw, rout or carve out a recess to fit it. Best to use the jigsawed design as a pattern for the recessing.

Then you cut each part of the picture from separate sheets of veneer. It can be done, but it calls for a lot more accuracy than you need when pad sawing. For all inlay work of this type, use a very fine blade. The kerf width must be minimal.

CUTTING SHEET METAL

Metal cutting on the jigsaw is similar to cutting wood except you select a blade that is best for the material. Metal cutting blades are available in both jeweler's and saber-blade types. It doesn't hurt to lubricate them with something like beeswax since this will help to make tight turns and reduce the possibility of breakage.

If you work directly on the regular table, you will find that burrs will accumulate as the blade cuts. This means a jagged edge and possible feed interference. Very thin material may actually bend because of the up-and-down blade action.

A simple way to get around all of this is to sandwich the sheet metal between pieces of scrap plywood. Another way is to use the auxiliary table shown for pivot cutting or to make a special table insert.

SHEET METAL, PLASTICS, PAPER

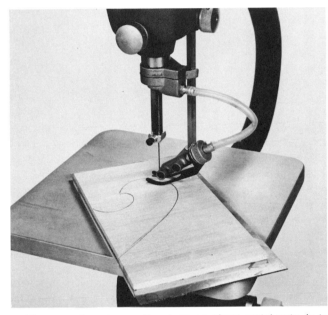

Easy way to get smooth edges on sheet metal cuts, is to sandwich the work between pieces of scrap plywood. Tape will hold the pieces together.

For cutting sheet metal, make a special insert to minimize the opening around the blade, thus providing full support to cut down on burred edges in the metal.

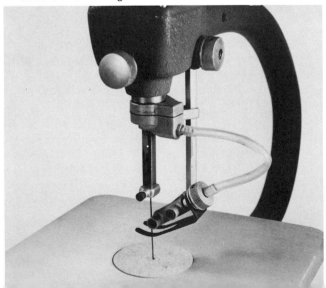

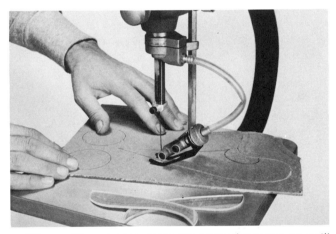

When cutting plastics, leave the protective paper on until after you have done the cutting. Ordinary wood-cutting blades will work, but a skip-tooth design is better.

To cut paper, sandwich the sheets between scrap wood. A hundred sheets or more of 20 lb. bond can be cut at a time.

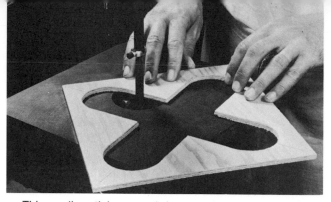

This sanding stick was made by mounting an emery board on a stiff metal backing. Shape at each end for gripping in the chucks. Files also can be used, held in the chuck V-block.

PLASTICS

Certain plastics (phenolics) can be sawed easily with results about what you might expect from a hardwood.

When working with materials like Plexiglas or Lucite, use a coarser blade than you would normally and work at a slower speed. Speed and narrow kerfs combine to create enough heat to melt the plastic.

Although woodworking blades may be used, it's wiser to use a skiptooth design. The spaces between the teeth help clear away the chips, and this helps to avoid overheating the work. Some plastics are soft enough so they actually weld directly behind the blade and cause it to bind.

Since most plastic you will use comes with a protective layer of paper, you have a ready-made surface for marking lines and designs. It's wise not to remove the paper until all the cutting has been done.

PAD-SAWING PAPER

You can saw paper cutouts easily if you sandwich the sheets of paper tightly between pieces of $\frac{1}{8}''$ or $\frac{1}{4}''$ plywood. The idea is to end up for cutting with what is the equivalent of a single, solid block. The tighter the pad, the better the results will be.

Use a blade that will take the turns you must do but try to work with one that is not too coarse. The other

extreme is a blade so fine that the paper particles clog it quickly. This can result in burning the work. Properly done, paper cut in this fashion will have remarkably smooth edges.

FILING AND SANDING

As was shown at the beginning of the chapter, special accessories are available for both filing and sanding. The standard sanding attachment has a semicircular shape like a piece of half-round molding. Thus, it may be used for both flat and curved edges. The abrasive is the same as a sleeve you would use on a normal drum sander.

The machine files come in a variety of shapes and with either a $\frac{1}{8}''$ or a $\frac{1}{4}''$ shank. Both the files and the sander are held in the lower chuck only. Most jigsaws provide a block in the lower chuck that has a V-cut in it. The shanks of files and sanders should be gripped in the "V."

Do these abrasive operations at slow speeds. Fast speeds will glaze the paper very quickly; files will simply scrape, which is not the way they should work. Remember, they are cutting tools. In general, you can use a higher speed as the abrasive gets coarser. In most cases, it's wise to make a special insert for the tool you are using to minimize the opening around the cutter. This is especially important when you are filing or sanding very small pieces. With large work, it's often possible to work without any insert at all.

Don't jam the work against the abrasive. Since you work without a holddown, it's easy for the tool to lift the work from the table. Besides, trying to speed up the operation by forcing will gain you nothing. A gentle feed with fingers holding the work down on the table is best. The feed should be just strong enough to keep the abrasive cutting.

There are various ways you can improvise filing and sanding attachments. Some craftsmen make use of broken files by grinding a shank on one end. It's even possible to use "needle" files. But do be careful since these can snap easily, and most of them have sharp points. A sanding attachment can be just a length of dowel with abrasive paper glued on it. One handy gadget is made from an emery stick. This item and a backup piece of stiff sheet metal are cut to jigsaw-blade length and shaped at each end to fit the chucks. The unit is then gripped like a jigsaw blade.

If you check the standard, small drum sanders, you will find that many of them can be used in the jigsaw even though they are intended for use in a drill press or portable drill. Remember, however—and this is true of filing and sanding generally—production speed on the jigsaw will be slower.

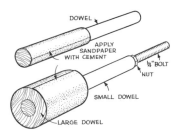

DOWEL

APPLY SANDPAPER WITH CEMENT

$\frac{1}{4}''$ BOLT

NUT

SMALL DOWEL

LARGE DOWEL

You can make an assortment of "sanding drums," each with a center hole. Then, anyone of them can be mounted on an arbor made by using a $\frac{1}{4}''$ bolt and nut.

4 BAND SAWS

In depth-of-cut capacity and in cutting speed, the band saw is unequaled by any other home-shop woodworking machine. While you probably think of it mostly to be used for sawing curved lines, you'll discover its importance for straight-line operations and will be impressed by its ease in doing other jobs that are very difficult, if at all possible, to do on other equipment.

The band saw is not designed to be competition for a jigsaw even though, when it is equipped with a fine blade, the applications of the two machines can overlap. With a cut either tool can do, the band saw will do it faster. On the other hand, the jigsaw is the only stationary tool you can use for piercing (internal cutting without a lead-in cut from an edge). Actually, piercing can be done on a band saw, but it would require breaking the endless blade and then welding it together again after it has passed through the stock. While this kind of thing is done in industry, it's really not a home-shop technique.

Some of the more impressive capacities of the band saw include resawing to make thin boards out of thick ones, compound cutting to make anything like a cabriole leg, and sawing through a stack of pieces to make many duplicate parts.

As with most woodworking machines, you may buy a band saw because of some job it does especially well, but once you have it in the shop, you'll find dozens of other practical uses for it.

Band saw size is determined by the distance from the blade to the throat and by maximum depth of cut. The average home-shop machine will run from 10″ to 12″ and can make a 6″ thick cut. An 18″ band saw is not out of line for a home shop, but perhaps the biggest advantage in choosing that size machine is not as much in the increased depth of cut as in the increased width of cut. Of course, the larger the machine, the more powerful it will be; increased power usually permits driving wider blades, an advantage on resawing jobs.

Table size is never too great and actually shouldn't be a major factor in the choice of a tool. However, it would be advantageous for the table to have a miter-gauge groove and even provisions for mounting a fence. The table should be adjustable for angular cuts.

GENERAL CHARACTERISTICS

The blade must be *tensioned* relative to its size and must *track* correctly. The tensioning is accomplished by moving the upper wheel, which is done by turning a screw, a lever, a crank, or whatever and will depend on the design of the machine. Getting the correct tension is easy since most machines have built-in tension scales. You simply adjust the upper wheel until the scale pointer indicates the right setting for the blade you are mounting. If you lack the tension scale, adjust for maximum tension and then slowly slack off until you can flex the blade about $\frac{1}{4}″$ with light finger pressure. Make this test above

BASIC PARTS OF THE BAND SAW

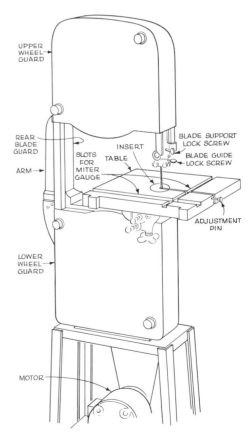

The ease with which a band saw can cut through heavy material is impressive. It is the fastest cutting, and has the greatest depth of cut of any home workshop machine.

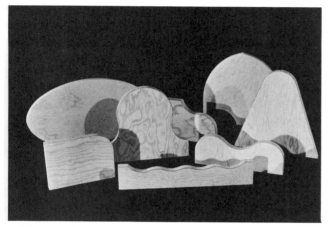

When equipped with a small blade, the band saw will do many jobs you might associate with a jigsaw, but it really isn't intended as an out-and-out competitor.

This 18" band saw was put together from a kit that provides all the parts that can't be made in a home shop—wheels, bearings, castings, etc. You supply all the wood parts and the assembly work.

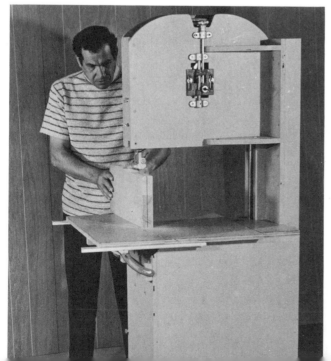

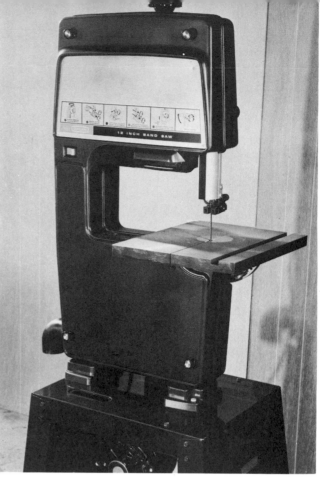

Typical home-shop machines fall in the 10" to 14" category. That dimension indicates the distance from the throat to the blade. Most all such machines have a 6" depth of cut. That is the maximum thickness of stock that can pass between the table and the upper guides.

Most modern band saws have a table slot so you can use a miter gauge. This one has a slot going two ways so you can use the miter gauge (with an extension) as a fence.

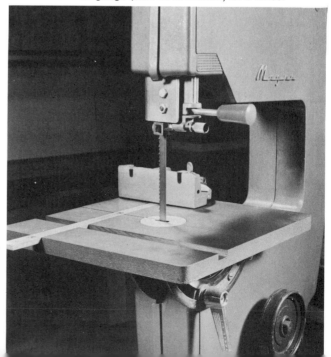

the table with the upper blade guard raised as high as possible.

Blade tracking is usually accomplished by tilting the upper wheel so that the blade will remain centered on the wheel rims as it is turning. On some machines, the tracking is automatic. The blade moves to a correct position regardless of its width. Always go through the blade tracking routine by turning the wheels by hand.

Blade mounting, tracking, and tensioning should be done with the upper and lower blade guides and back-ups out of the way so that these items will not interfere with the procedures and so you will be able to adjust them correctly to the new blade.

After the blade is mounted, the angle between it and the table should be 90°. You can check this with a square and adjust the table if necessary. Most band saws have a built-in stop for the normal table setting, and it should be fixed at this time.

The blade guides must be adjusted so they will prevent the blade from twisting without actually being in contact with the blade when it is free-running. The best way to achieve this is to use a piece of paper as a spacer when you lock the guide in position. The forward position of the guides must be adjusted to the width of the blade. Don't bring them so far forward that they contact the teeth; adjusting to depth of the space between adjacent saw teeth is fine.

The blade support (backup) should not be in contact with the blade when it is free-running. This will only contribute to blade breakage. It is best to leave a gap of $\frac{1}{64}''$ to $\frac{1}{32}''$ between the back edge of the blade and the support. In this way, the support will work only when you are cutting.

Normally, when you are making a simple cut, the kerf will be straight and parallel to the side of the table. If you feed straight and the blade runs off the line so that it becomes necessary to compensate by adjusting the feed angle, it's wise to check the blade mounting and all the guides again. If these check out well, then it's reasonable to assume that the problem is caused by something else. This can be incorrect set of the teeth, a condition that can be the result of a poor sharpening job or a saw cut that caused the blade to dull on one side. The blade does not cut in a straight line because the sharp side "leads" off. When this condition is excessive, it can be remedied only by removing the blade and having it resharpened and reset.

When the "lead" is slight, you can do a salvage job by lightly honing the sharp side. This procedure is not a positive approach since you are dulling the sharp side to match the other, but it can save you in a situation where you don't have a replacement blade or the time to get

ADJUSTING THE BLADE

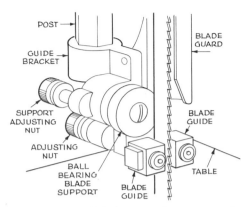

Typical blade guide and blade support arrangement.

The blade guard and upper guides should be positioned about $\frac{1}{4}''$ or $\frac{1}{2}''$ above the work. Many times we don't show it that way but only so the cut can be seen more clearly.

Blade tension is achieved by vertical adjustment of the upper wheel. Usually, you set to markings on a built-in tension scale, as in the photo below.

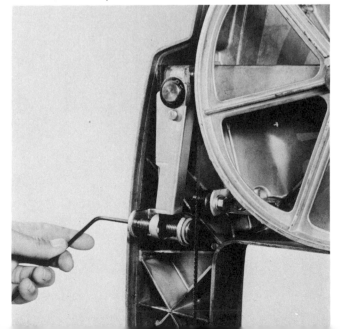

ADJUSTING THE BLADE (Cont.)

When the blade is correctly mounted, adjust the table so the angle between it and the blade is 90°. The miter gauge slot should be parallel with the kerf line.

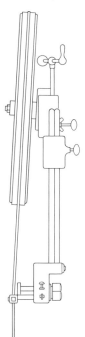

Tracking the blade is done by adjusting the upper wheel until the blade is running centered on the rim.

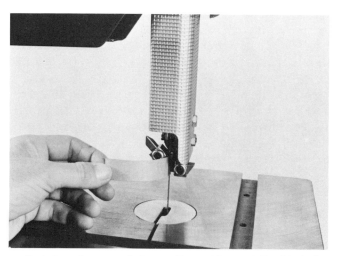

Test the clearance between the guides and the blade by placing a piece of paper between them. Provide this clearance on each side of the blade.

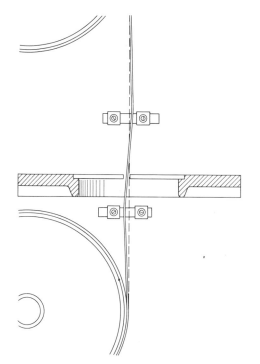

The blade guides and the blade supports should be positioned after the tracking procedure. If the guides are not set correctly, the blade can be twisted out of alignment.

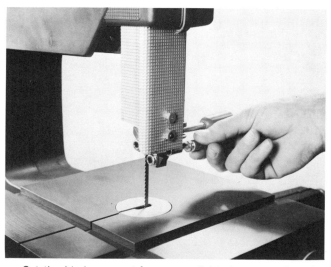

Set the blade support for a very slight clearance when the blade is free-running. This support backs up the blade when you are using the saw for a cut.

the mounted one fixed. Of course, you can work with the "lead" problem temporarily by compensating for it as you feed the stock. To do the honing, back up the blade on the dull side with a block of wood and lightly touch the sharp side with a honing stone as the blade is running.

BAND-SAW BLADES

Blades for home-shop band saws fall into the "narrow blade category" which ranges from $\frac{1}{8}''$ wide up to $\frac{1}{2}''$ wide. You would not be wrong, considering routine band-saw applications, if you selected a $\frac{1}{4}''$ wide blade as the one you'd most like to commonly use.

The two most popular blade designs are the "standard" and the "skip-tooth." The latter is so called, logically enough, because every other tooth is skipped. It cuts fast and throws waste out quickly. A third blade to know about is called a "roll-chip." It resembles the skip-tooth and is an excellent all-purpose blade that also does a fairly good job on plastics and metals like aluminum, including the do-it-yourself variety. A very new blade in the field is the toothless blade, but it has an edge that is coated with grits of tungsten carbide. This blade is fine for metals, ceramics, and plastics; it can also be used on wood. On wood, however, although the cut is very smooth, cut speed is greatly reduced.

A thin blade with light set will give you the smoothest cuts while a heavy blade with heavy set provides maximum cutting speed and freedom from binding because of the wider kerf that provides more freedom for the blade.

A band-saw blade will leave its mark in the cut, and this is called "washboarding." It can be slight or so pronounced that it is impractical for some applications. This effect wouldn't bother you, for example, if you were cutting firewood; but it wouldn't be right on the edge of a cornice. Your control over the degree of washboarding rests with choice of blades. For a smooth cut, choose a blade with minimum set. The washboard effect will be there, but minimized.

A band-saw blade will cut better across the grain than with it. In the latter situation, cut speed is reduced, and there will be a tendency for the blade to follow the grain of the wood instead of a marked line. Such things will not affect your productivity, but they are band-saw facts of life and you should be aware of them.

BAND-SAW BLADE STORAGE

It's advisable to "fold" band-saw blades and to hang them on pegs in a cabinet where they will be protected until you need them. Of course, you can hang them full-length, but this practice makes quite a demand on storage facilities. Folding isn't difficult and once you get used to doing it after carefully following the accompanying

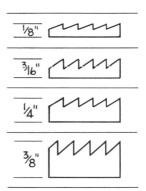

Actual size of four commonly used band-saw blades.

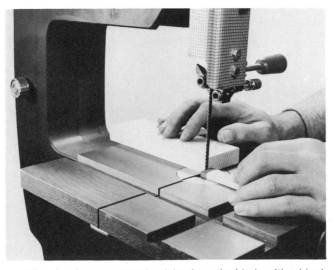

When honing to correct lead, back up the blade with a block of wood. Apply the stone with a very light amount of pressure to the sharp side of the blade.

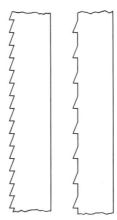

The standard blade pattern is shown on the left. The other is a skip-tooth or "buttress" design.

illustrations, you'll be able to do it blindfolded.

After the blade is folded, tie it with a piece of string or soft wire. If you think it's going to hang unused for a long time, coat it with a light oil. Band-saw blades are expensive so using them and storing them correctly can save you money.

The blades are flexible and do have considerable spring, which you will discover when you unfold them. Therefore, unfold them carefully, especially wide blades. Hold them away from your body and turn your face away.

Also, when you fold and unfold them and when you place them on the machine, be very careful not to bend them. Kinks in a blade are not easy to work with.

BASICS OF CUTTING

The usual position for band-saw cutting will place you behind the left side of the table. Your left hand will be on the work doing most of the guiding while your right hand will feed the stock. You'll notice in many of the accompanying illustrations—and you will soon discover it in your own work—that this is not an invariable rule. The size of the work, the kind of cut, and the direction of feed required will all affect how you stand and where you place your hands. There is little point in following this rule when, for example, a considerable overhang at the rear of the table makes this positioning difficult or even hazardous.

A better rule to be strict about is to keep your hands away from the blade while you keep the blade on the line. A sharp blade and a steady feed are good safety

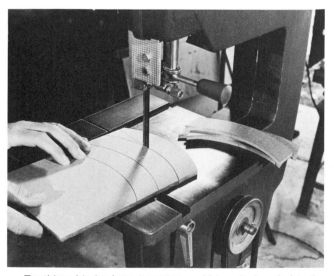

Toothless blades have tungsten-carbide grits bonded to the cutting edge. They are very fine for plastics and other non-wood materials.

BAND-SAW BLADES

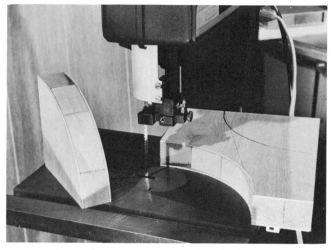

You will get the smoothest cuts when the blade has a lot of teeth and minimum set. When smoothness is not critical, you are better off working with a coarse blade and much set.

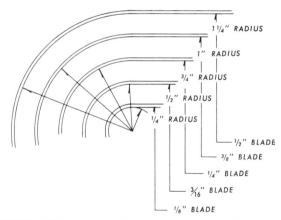

Typical turning radius of various size blades. These are not invariable since the type of blade and the amount of set are factors that effect the actual radius.

factors. Try to keep fingers of the feed hand hooked over the edge of the work. This will guard against slippage that could move your hand to a dangerous area. The sharper the blade, the less feed pressure you need; this factor also reduces the possibility of hand slippage.

Band-saw cutting is basically a simple procedure, but you can easily box yourself in on some cuts so that you must saw your way out or do considerable backtracking in order to get back to the cut you want. This can happen because you get into a spot that the blade can't handle or because the throat of the machine interferes with feed direction.

A partial solution is to visualize the cut and plan how you will accomplish it before you do any sawing. Often,

FOLDING THE BLADE

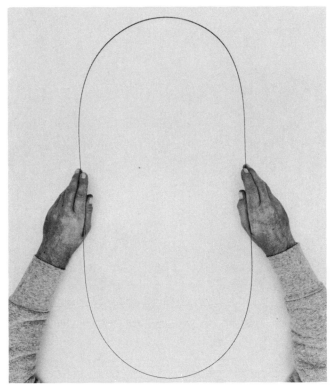

To start folding a blade, hold it like so with its teeth pointing away from you.

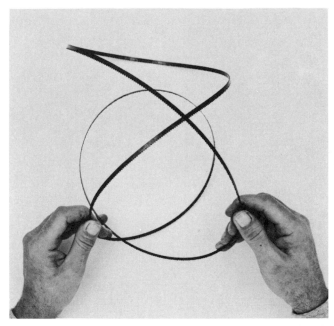

Let the upper loop fall into the lower one. Bring your hands together so you can trade the loop in one hand for the loop in the other. As you do this (see below) . . .

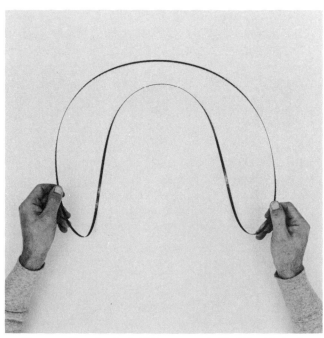

Use your thumbs to fold the upper half of the blade down toward the floor while your fingers twist a bit to turn the teeth outward, as in the photo above.

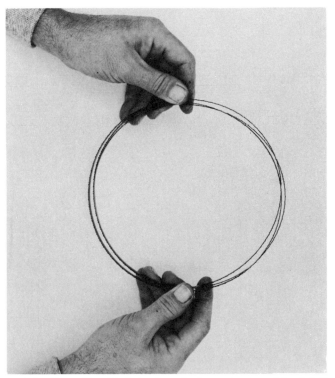

bring the coiling blade back against your body and it will fall into three uniform loops. Tie with soft wire or tape. When folding, be careful not to kink the blade.

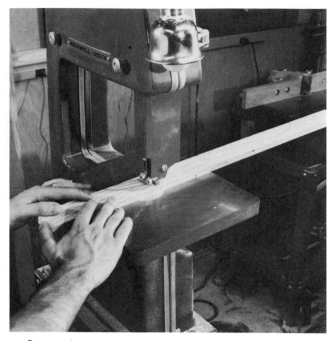

Operator's position will vary with the cut. Normal procedure calls for guiding with the left hand and feeding with the right.

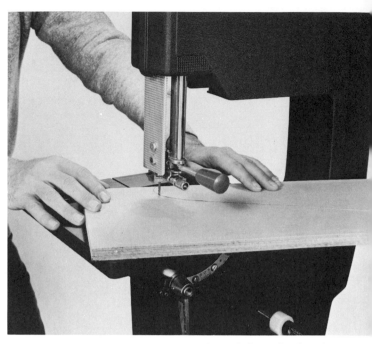

Visualizing the cut beforehand will often eliminate the throat interference occurring here.

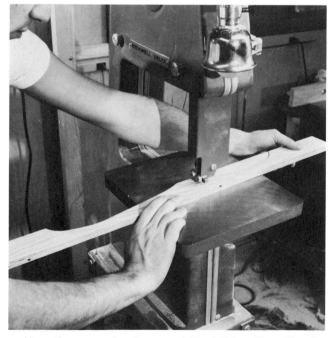

Here, the reverse has happened. The left hand is pulling the work, the right hand is guiding. The important thing is to keep the blade on the line without putting yourself in danger.

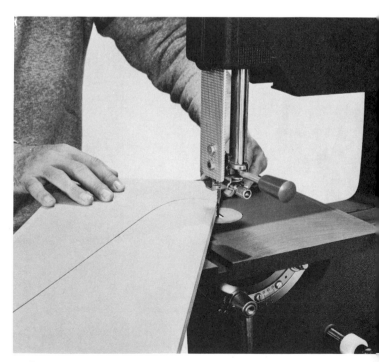

If the cut had been started like so, it could have been made in a single pass.

you will find that the cutting is simplified if you do the layout either totally or partially on both sides of the stock: flipping the stock can occasionally make an "impossible" cut possible.

On complicated jobs, it's more difficult to eliminate backtracking entirely than when the cuts are short. Frequently, it's better to saw out of a situation than it is to backtrack. This simply means leaving the cut line at a point and exiting at an edge of the stock. Then you re-enter close to the problem point and continue the job.

Corner cuts and turning holes can be done in advance with other tools in order to save time and, occasionally, material. You can form square corners with a mortising chisel or just drill holes. Drilling holes isn't a bad idea when you have many to do, especially when the turning radius is tight. This can reduce the band-saw chore to simple cutting while giving you accurate radii and smooth, drill-produced corners. In either case, whether you use square openings or holes, they must be located accurately to fit in with the design.

Radial and tangent cuts can make it possible for a blade to get around a turn it couldn't do otherwise. Radial cuts are simply cuts made from the edge of the stock to the line you have to follow. What they do is permit waste stock to fall away as you are cutting and so provide more room for the blade to turn. Tangential cuts are run-offs. You follow the line until you feel the blade is binding, move off to the edge of the stock, and then come back to where you had left the line and continue to cut in similar fashion.

FREEHAND CUTTING

When cutting freehand, you guide the band saw by hand and by sight. The bulk of what has been said so

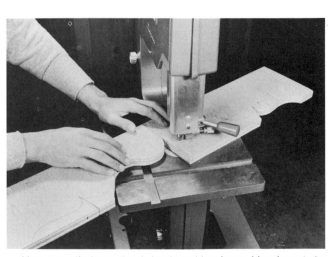

You can eliminate much backtracking by making in-cuts to begin with. This permits waste pieces to fall off as you go.

far applies to operator control over the work-to-blade relationship. The basic cutting rule is to keep the blade on the line that you have drawn. The mechanics of the machine are involved in achieving this: correct blade tension and tracking, good blade-guide settings, and sharpness of the blade. Beyond this, making an accurate cut depends on providing good feed direction. It's almost like driving a car. Don't overshoot the curves. Lead into them as they come up. Slacking on feed pressure in such situations will make it easier to be accurate simply because it will provide more time to do the maneuvering.

When you approach a curve from a straight line—this applies mostly to rounding off of corners on sized stock—follow the straight edge for an inch or two before you enter the curve cut. When you do start to turn, ease up on feed so the blade can do its job.

On thick cuts the blade works harder. In such situations you should ease up on feed. When you can, use a wide blade with much set to do the job. If the cut is being done, for example, to prepare a piece of stock for lathe turning or for a part that you know will require much sanding, then the rough results of the heavy blade won't matter. When smoothness of cut of the band-saw job is critical and you choose to work with a narrow blade, be aware that the blade can "bow" in the cut, especially on wood that has a strong grain pattern. The only way to protect against this, other than changing to a heavy-gauge blade, is feed the work extremely slowly. The smoothness of cut on such operations, especially when you are turning a circle, will not be consistent regardless of how you feed. You'll find differences, and the roughest areas will be where the blade quarters the grain.

BASIC GUIDED CUTS

You can use a miter gauge or a rip fence for guides on the band saw but remember that when the work is so guided, you can't compensate for lead. So the blade must be in good shape in order to work without problems.

If the band saw does not provide for a miter gauge, you can get by with clamping a straight piece of wood to the table to act as a fence and then moving a backup piece of wood along it to feed the work for the cut. And, of course, you can make the special table shown at the end of this chapter. This table provides a groove for miter-gauge use.

Band-saw crosscuts are limited by throat interference. In a normal setup, crosscut length can't be greater than the distance from the blade to the throat. To get around this, make an angle cut as close to the line as you can get. Then make a second cut on the line. This process does waste some wood, but it is a solution. When work

FREEHAND CUTTING

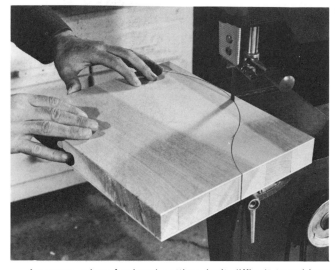

Accuracy, when freehand cutting, isn't difficult to achieve when the blade is in good condition. Feed speed can be up to the maximum cutting capacity of the blade but don't work so fast that you lose control.

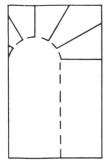

Radial cuts are like incuts. You do them first so the waste pieces fall off and this gives the blade more room to turn.

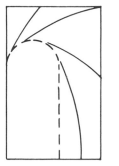

Tangential cuts means moving off the line and out of the work whenever you feel the blade begin to bind. To get the smoothest end result possible, start each new cut as carefully as possible and proceed slowly.

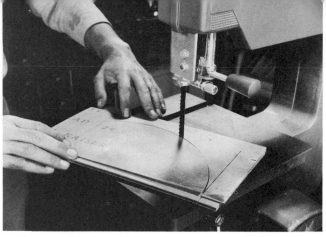

You can do a layout job so the cut pieces may be joined to form a particular shape.

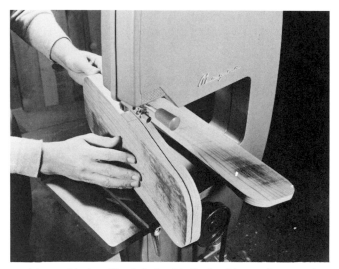

A heavy blade with a lot of set is the best to use for resawing jobs. A light blade will have more tendency to bow in the cut. To prevent it, slow up on feed pressure.

width permits, you can use this technique with the stock on edge. The end result is the same, but wood waste is kept to a minimum.

Another way is to offset the blade so you can feed the stock at an angle and get a straight cut without throat interference. This can be accomplished simply by making a twist-board. Cut into a piece of $\frac{3}{4}''$ stock until the kerf is about 9″ or 10″ long and then turn off the machine while the blade is still in the cut. Back off the guides, turn the board about 20° or 30° and clamp it to the table. Of course, the blade twists with the board, and this permits an oblique feed so you can handle longer stock. Don't use the blade guides for this operation but do use the blade supports. Such a setup is good for a limited number of cuts since the blade will tend to return to its normal position by cutting through the twist board.

A more permanent answer is to make special guides that will hold the blade in the twist position.

If the band saw is equipped with a rip fence, lock it

This band saw provides for the miter gauge to be used as a fence. Other saws have regular rip fences, or you can clamp a straight piece of wood to the table.

in place to obtain the cut width you need and then pass the work between it and the blade. This will be difficult to do if the blade has "lead." Actually, the heavier the blade and the more set it has, the easier it will be to do guided rip cuts.

CROSSCUTTING TO LENGTH

On the band saw you can use the rip fence as a stop when cutting pieces to length. When the work is wide enough, simply place one end against the fence and move forward as if you were making a rip cut. On narrow work that could rock during the pass, use a backup block behind the work to do the feeding.

ANGLE CUTS

When a fence is used in beveling operations, position it on the right-hand side of the table so that both the fence and the work will be "below" the blade. The fence-table combination creates a "V" that provides excellent work support.

This setup is fine for work procedures such as chamfering, removing corners from a block that you will then spindle-turn in the lathe, and ripping squares into triangular pieces.

When cutting circular blocks for faceplate mounting on a lathe, making the cut with the table tilted will remove much of the material you would ordinarily have to cut away with lathe chisels. The idea is especially good for lathe projects that have a taper, or for bowls.

Quite often, the fence-table setup is a good substitute for a V-block. Try it, for example, when you need to completely cut through the workpiece or when you need

to slot the end of a cylinder. On such work you must be very careful to keep the wood from turning as you are making the pass.

SPIRALING DOWELS

Dowels so treated have superior holding power in glued joints. To do the job, tilt the band-saw table anywhere from 10° to 20° and lock the miter gauge in position as shown in the accompanying photograph. Its distance from the band-saw blade is what controls the depth of the groove. When you hold the work firmly against the miter gauge and make contact with the blade, the work will immediately begin to feed into a perfect spiral. However, don't give up hand control; the work can be twisted along the gauge faster than the blade can do the cutting. The idea is to let the work be guided automatically while you control the speed.

The same idea can be used as the first step when you wish to form the kind of spirals shown in the lathe chapter. The band-saw job can mark the line of the spiral and also cut the depth of the groove.

RESAWING

Resawing is ripping a heavy board into thinner pieces. The best blade for the job is wide, has coarse teeth, and plenty of set. Such a blade has enough "tail" to help keep it on a straight line and a nice wide kerf for blade room. A skip-tooth blade, the widest your machine can handle, is recommended. This blade will not produce smooth cuts, but that is not the purpose of resawing.

On the other hand, you will often use a smaller blade

A fence may be used as a stop when you wish to cut similar pieces. When the parts are narrow, use a back-up board to do the feeding. Push the work free of the blade before you return the backup.

MAKING ANGLE CUTS

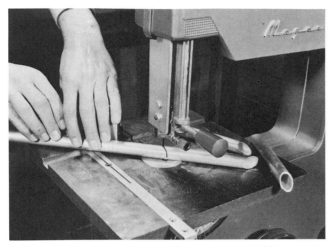

The miter gauge may be used to do angle cuts. Here, a conventional blade is used to cut do-it-yourself aluminum tubing. The edges will require clean-up work after the cut.

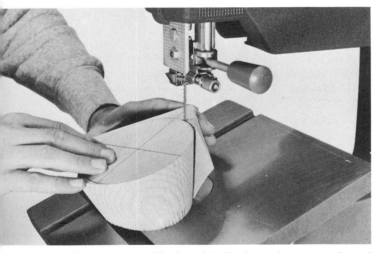

Circular cuts, with the table tilted, produce cone-shaped blocks. This is a good way to prepare stock for lathe turning.

Fence on tilted table create a V-block arrangement that provides good support for jobs like chamfering or cutting off corners before lathe turning.

because you want the smoothest cut possible or because the blade happens to be on the machine and the resaw job required doesn't justify a change. This will work but do be aware that there will be more tendency for the blade to bind and to bow in the cut. A sharp blade and a slow feed are essential. Naturally, the less depth of cut involved in the job, the less critical is the blade-width factor. After all, if you are resawing 1″ square stock, it would be no different than a routine cut.

Resaw jobs can be done freehand, and that is probably the method to use if the blade is not in ideal condition. Guiding the saw freehand, you can compensate to some extent for lead. After you have entered the cut and discovered that the blade is cutting fine and free, you can speed up feed as long as you keep within the blade's cutting capacity.

You can also do resaw jobs against a fence, which is a wise method when you have many pieces of equal thickness to produce. In this situation there isn't much opportunity to compensate for lead, so the blade should be a good one.

If you discover that the resaw job is putting a lot of strain on the motor, you might still be able to accomplish it if you first cut guide kerfs on the table saw. These kerfs are saw cuts on the resaw line, and they reduce the amount of material the band-saw blade must cut.

MULTIPLE PIECES

To produce multiple pieces, pre-shape a thick piece of wood that you resaw into thinner, duplicate pieces or assemble thin pieces of wood into a pad and saw them all at the same time.

The resaw method involves simply drawing the shape

Spiral-cutting of dowels on tilted table. Spiral pitch will be constant if you hold the work firmly while rotating.

RESAWING

Resawing jobs can be done freehand, but if the blade is in good shape, it's best to work against a high fence. You can make one like this, or screw a high board to a regular fence.

of the part you need on the stock and then cutting it out. The shaped piece is then resawed against a fence. After the fence is adjusted to maintain the thickness of the cut, you run the pre-shaped part through as many times as possible or until you have produced the number of pieces you want.

The pad method involves putting pieces of wood together in a stack and then sawing them as if they were a solid piece. The easiest way to accomplish this is to drive nails through waste areas. On a common, home shop band saw, you can stack as many as 24 pieces of $\frac{1}{4}''$ plywood and produce 24 duplicate parts in the one cutting operation.

In some situations you can use clamps to hold the pieces together as long as they don't interfere with the cutting. A little trick that can be used is to place double-faced tape between the pieces. The tape will usually hold the parts together well enough for the cutting.

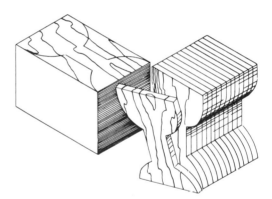

The grain pattern you get on each piece will depend on what side of the block you did the original layout and cutting.

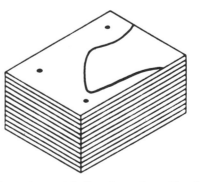

Table-saw kerfs, cut on the resaw lines, will reduce the amount of stock the band-saw blade must cut.

Resawing isn't limited to slicing thick boards. Here, a piece that was "pierced" on the drill press is being sawed into thin strips to make a number of decorative pieces.

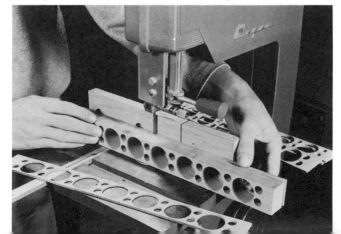

You can also get many similar pieces by nailing thin boards into a thick pad and sawing as if it were a solid piece of wood, then separating the pieces.

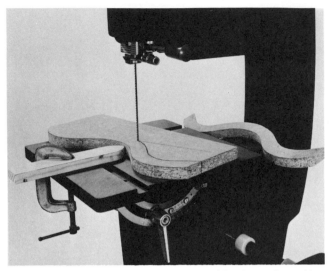

Parallel curve-cutting calls for the guide shown here. You must keep the work in constant contact with the end of the guide. Of course, the blade guard is set much too high here.

COMPOUND CUTS

Shapes that result from cuts that are made on two or more sides are classified as "compound cuts." The most common example is the cabriole leg and its variations, but the techniques may be employed to do unsymmetrical shapes and ornamental work as well as to prepare stock for lathe turning.

The basic procedure involves making a pattern of the shape you want and using it to mark two adjacent sides of the stock. Cut the work on one side, but do it to produce a minimum number of waste pieces. These are then tack-nailed back in their original positions, and the stock is cut on the second side. The waste pieces from the first cut must be replaced in order for the work to have a base and to reproduce all the original pattern markings for the second cut. When you replace them, drive the nails so the part you are cutting out will not be marred. After the second cut, discard all the waste pieces. Some of the facts on post blocking contained in the lathe chapter can be employed on band-saw compound cutting, especially when you are doing cabriole legs and similar jobs.

How you can apply this technique when preparing stock for lathe-turning jobs is demonstrated in one of the accompanying sketches. Here, the task is to turn a ball, but the method will work on any project that requires a spherical shape. As with any compound cutting, the profile you want is laid out on two adjacent sides. You want to be careful with the layout so center lines will match. In this case, be sure to leave sufficient stock

at each end of the piece so you can mount it in the lathe after you have accomplished the band-saw cuts.

PATTERN SAWING

Pattern sawing is required when the curves on the parts you need are not extreme. The technique to be used lets you cut duplicate pieces without having to do a layout on each and should probably be considered when the job can't be handled by either resawing a shaped piece or by pad sawing.

The idea is to set up a guide block that is undercut at one end to permit passage of the work. The end of the guide on the undercut side is notched just enough to snug the blade and is shaped in concave or convex fashion to suit the job being done. It is important for the center of the curve to be in line with the teeth of the blade.

Parts to be shaped are roughly cut to size and then tack-nailed to the pattern. When you are doing the cutting, concentrate on keeping the pattern in constant contact with the guide. Be sure on your first test cut that the blade does not cut into the pattern. If it does, make the notch in the guide arm just a bit deeper. The blade should just barely clear the pattern.

PARALLEL CURVES

Cutting parallel curves can be as simple as following the lines that are marked on the work; and if only a few cuts are involved, that's probably the best procedure to use. However, when you have to make many of these cuts, you can set up a guide system so you can come up with as many duplicate pieces as you want without having to do a layout for each.

When the curves are slight, you can use a fence to gauge the width of the cut. Make the first cut in the work freehand; make the others by passing the stock between the fence and the blade. The one important rule is to keep the arc tangent to the fence throughout the pass.

You can't use a fence as a guide when the job involves reverse curves, but a pointed guide block that you clamp to the table in line with the teeth on the blade can be used in its place. The distance between the point on the guide and the blade controls the width of the cut. It's essential to do the feeding so that contact between the guide and the side of the work is constant. With this setup, it's not likely that the cut could be oversize; but unless you handle the job carefully and feed easily, you can move off the guide. This would result in the cut being narrower than you want.

CUTTING CIRCLES

A pivot jig can be advantageous when you have many circular pieces to do; it can also be handy when you have a single oversize circular piece that might be difficult to do freehand. Any circle-cutting jig is nothing more than a pivot point around which you rotate the work to make the pass. In order for the cut to be right, the pivot must be on a line that is at right angles to the blade, and it must be aligned with the teeth. If these rules are not followed, the blade will track to the inside or the outside of the line, depending on the kind of misalignment you have. It's also important for the blade to be in good condition.

There are two ways to start the job. Make a freehand lead-in cut to the line and then set the pivot or cut the work square to begin with (the sides of the square must match the diameter of the circle) and rest one edge of the work against the side of the blade to start the procedure. There should be some pressure against the blade to begin with, and this can cause the blade to crowd a bit until it enters the cut and becomes "positioned." After that, it's just a question of turning the work.

The accompanying photograph shows an oversize piece that is mounted on an off-the-table pivot point. For smaller jobs you can use the setup that is part of the special band-saw table shown at the end of this chapter.

WOOD BENDING

On the band saw, you can do wood bending by "kerfing" or by "thinning out." The kerfing idea is the same one that is described in the table saw chapter even though the method of cutting the kerfs differs. On the band saw,

you do the job with the stock on edge and angled to clear the throat. This means the kerfs will be at a slight angle, but the angled kerfs will not interfere with how they allow you to bend the wood. You can feed the work freehand, or you can use a miter gauge that is set at the angle you need to clear the throat.

Thinning out is really a resaw job that you limit to the area of the work you wish to bend. What you are doing is reducing the stock thickness at that point to make it flexible. Such areas are seldom used as they are since they lack strength. Instead, they are backed up with blocks. The thinned section is a "veneer" that carries the appearance, and the blocks provide the strength. For example, you would use this method for the rails of a table that has straight sides but semi-circular ends.

SANDING

To set up for sanding, a special accessory kit is required that, in most cases, is used in place of the regular guides. The abrasive is an endless belt just like a band-saw blade, and it is fitted over the wheels with just enough tension to keep it tight.

The accessory kit will contain a backup plate which serves to support the belt when you move work against it. For some jobs, like contour sanding, it's possible to work without the backup plate; but you must be careful to apply the work so that you don't cause the belt to move off the wheels.

Pivot cutting is a good technique, especially on large work that would require outboard support anyway. The pivot here is a rod held in a photo light stand.

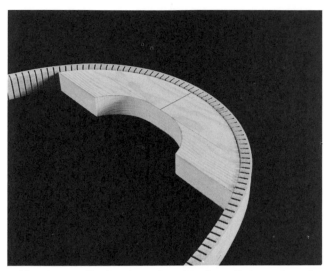

You can use the band saw to cut kerfs so that wood can be bent without having to be steamed.

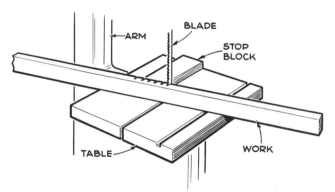

To do kerfing on the band saw, you must feed the work at an angle in order to clear the throat. This does not affect how the wood will bend.

The "thinning out" method involves cutting away part of the stock to leave a very flexible veneer.

CUTTING SHEET METAL

If you are working with a material like do-it-yourself aluminum, you can use a regular woodcutting blade. For other materials you should get either a special metal-cutting blade or a combination blade that can be used for either wood or metal. In either case, the job is done best when you use a backup board under the work. This will minimize, if not eliminate, the jagged edges that will occur when you work with the sheet metal directly on the table.

Special toothless, carbide-tipped blades can be used without the backup. The action in this case is more abrasive so the cut will be quite smooth without taking precautions.

A SPECIAL TABLE

The unit shown in the photograph and drawing on page 177 was designed for the average home shop machine. If your unit has an 11″ to 12″ throat and a table that measures in the 12″ × 12″ area, you should be able to make one as shown. The depth of cut on your machine is not a factor.

Before you start construction, follow all the recommended procedures for setting the blade-to-table angle to 90°. It's also important to be sure the angle between the blade and the miter-gauge slot is 90°. If your table does not have such a slot, then make certain that the outer edge of the table is 90° to the blade.

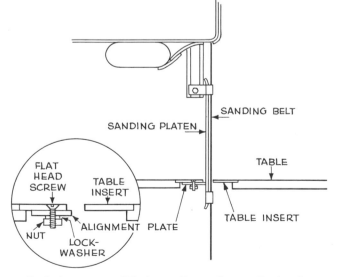

Typical arrangement that permits sanding on the band saw. Special accessory kits are available. The platten backs up the sanding felt, except when working on compound curves.

Make the table halves of $\frac{3}{4}''$ hardboard-surfaced plywood or something similar. After you slot the adjoining edges and fit the spline, assemble the parts without securing them as a unit and locate the center of the table opening so you can scribe a 3″ circle at that point. You can use a saber saw to cut the half circles but do stay inside the line and finish up with a drum sander. Use glue to assemble the parts permanently but keep the spline in that part of the slot that runs from the hole to what will be the inboard table edge.

Make the circle insert as shown in the drawing. The seat for it in the table can be done with a router or on a shaper.

The next step is to work on the table saw and make the 1″ opening down the center line on the outboard side. Then, lower the saw blade to $\frac{1}{2}''$ projection and form the rabbets on each side of the opening. Cut the blade slot directly on the center line of the table hole and make the L-shaped cut on the inboard edge.

To fit this table to the machine table, shape the table guide from a strip of hardwood. This strip should fit in the machine's table slot just snugly enough to avoid lateral movement but still be able to slide smoothly. Put the guide in the slot and position the new table so the saw blade is approximately in the center of the hole. Be sure the outboard edge is perfectly parallel with the kerf line. Clamp the table to the guide and then attach the guide with glue and screws.

Make the two table clamps and attach them so the table can be moved one way or the other about 1″. The table can not have a fixed position because some of the

pivot-guided work you will do with it will require good alignment between the blade teeth and the pivot point. Being able to adjust the table position will let you provide for this.

Shape up the stiffener and drill holes for the attachment screws. Drill for and install the T-nut for the pivot-slide lock. If your machine table lacks a miter-gauge slot so that you can't use the table guide, adjust the width of the stiffener to ride against the edge of the machine table.

Make the table tie from hardwood and install it about $1\frac{1}{2}''$ in from the forward edge of the table to straddle the blade slot.

Now that the table is solid, you can work on the table saw to form the miter-gauge groove. Size this for a gauge you already have on hand or one that you buy for the purpose.

Before you replace the unit on the band saw, drill for and install the two, 10-32 T-nuts that are located on the center line on the inboard side. These should fit flush on the underside.

Critical factors concerning the fence are its overall length and the angle between the fence and the base. The length of the fence, including the base, must miss the front edge alignment by $\frac{1}{16}''$, and the fence-to-base angle must be 90°.

Use hardwood to make the parallel-curve guide and the pattern-cutting guide. Actually, these designs are merely samples. Once you've started using them, you'll come up with designs that will be more suitable for particular applications.

Table is made in halves (see drawing). Cut ¾″ hardboard-surfaced plywood into two pieces exactly 13⅛″ by 26¼″. Be sure edges are parallel, corners exactly 90 deg. Cut a slot, join pieces with plywood spline.

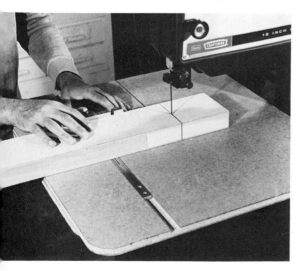

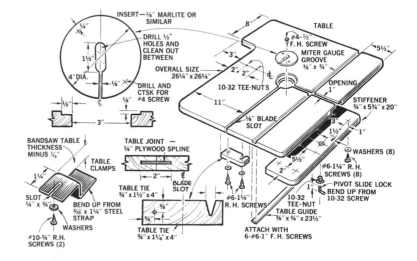

5 DRILL PRESSES

To buy a drill press based only on the need to drill holes is no longer realistic. If you use good techniques and choose wise accessories and jigs, the drill press can become one of the most versatile tools in your woodworking shop. Furthermore, it can easily become the second most important piece of equipment in your home workshop.

Its essential mechanism is a spindle that has a gripping device at the free end. In most cases, a key-operated, three-jaw chuck is used; but there are times when a substitution is necessary or wise. Such a substitution can be needed when you are using mortising bits and chisels, which require special holding items, or when you are using router bits, which develop sufficient side thrust to warrant a special kind of chuck.

The *head* of the tool is composed of all the parts attached to the top of the column. The *table* is movable vertically, may be swung aside and, on some units, can be tilted. The *quill* houses the spindle and is moved downward by means of the *feed lever*. The return of the quill to normal position is done automatically through a spring action. There is usually an adjustment procedure so this action can be strengthened or weakened. Normally, the quill should return smoothly and without great shock.

It's possible to lock the quill in any extended position or to limit its extension through the use of the *depth stop*, almost always located on the outside of the quill housing. Cone pulleys allow you to select speeds. The more expensive drill press can have a built-in, variable speed mechanism.

The *base* of the drill press is the table-like casting on which the unit stands. The length of the *column* determines whether the drill press is a *bench model* or a *floor model*. The capacity of a drill press defines the distance from the column to the spindle center and from the chuck to the base. When the capacity is specified as 15″, the column-to-spindle distance is 7½″, which permits you to drill in the center of a 15″ wide board.

Adjustments on a drill press are mostly operational; the tool has to be accurate to begin with. If the table is adjustable, then you should check to see, when it is in normal position, that the angle between it and the spindle

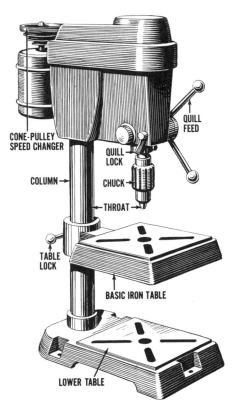

BASIC PARTS OF THE DRILL PRESS

is 90°. One way to do this is to insert a length of ½″ drill rod in the chuck and then work with a square to achieve the correct angle.

TYPICAL DRILL-PRESS TOOLS

The most common drill-press tools are those you will use to form holes. These can range from the smallest twist drill to good-size fly cutters. Although you will use twist drills quite a bit, they really don't do the very best job in wood. They have to be used simply because no other hole-forming tools with special wood-cutting features are available in the variety of sizes that you can find in twist drills.

Bits that have spurs and a point are better than twist drills. The point locates the hole center; the spurs cut through wood fibers cleanly so you get a smooth hole to exact size. Flutes in these types of tools provide channels for chip removal so it's never wise to bury the bit to the point where this can't happen. On most jobs, it's good practice to retract the bit frequently as you work. This practice will clear chips from the hole and keep the cutter cool to prevent burning.

Spade bits are also excellent tools. They have long, sharp points and slim shanks. The blades are flat and good ones have relieved edges. A set will range from $\frac{1}{4}''$ up to $1\frac{1}{2}''$. A relatively high speed is necessary to use them efficiently. Even the largest size should be run at about 1,500 rpm's.

When you want to drill large holes, you can think in terms of fly cutters and hole saws. The fly cutter is an adjustable item that rotates a vertical bit at the end of a horizontal arm. Here, slow speed is essential. Clamp the work and keep your hands clear as you start the machine at the slowest speed. If you have variable speeds, you can pick up a bit at a time until the tool is cutting smoothly without vibration.

There are various types of hole saws, some fixed, some adjustable. All of them saw through wood. Feed should be minimal, speed slow.

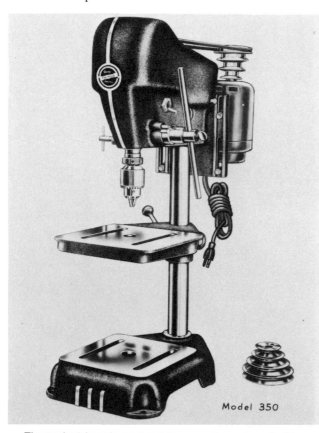

Model 350

The typical bench-model drill press is equipped with cone pulleys to provide three or four specific speeds. You change speed by moving the V-belt from step to step on the pulleys.

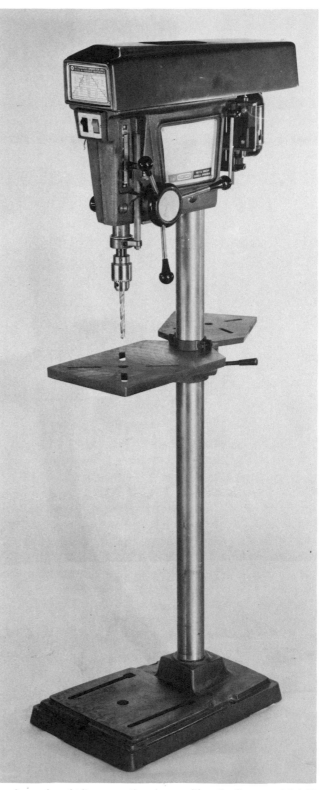

Assuming similar operational capacities, the floor model drill press differs from the bench model only in the length of the column. This unit has an accessory table that tilts for angular work, a useful item for advanced shop work.

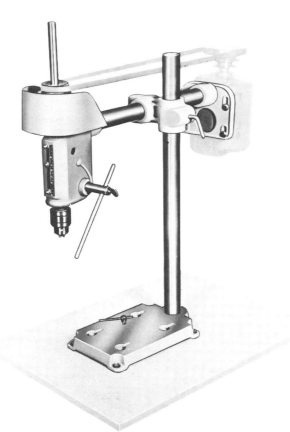

Economy version of a radial drill press. Such a design is excellent for angular drilling since the head may be tilted. It also provides greater chuck-to-column capacity.

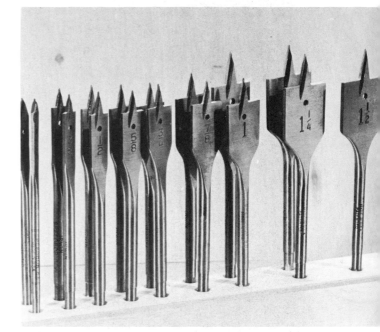

Spade bits (right) compare in size to auger bits and are available in sets that increase by sixteenths from $\frac{1}{4}''$ to 1" and by eighths from 1" to $1\frac{1}{2}''$. They are excellent hole forming tools whether you use them in a drill press or a portable drill.

Cutting tools with screw points are seldom used on a drill press in the home shop since you can't achieve the critical feed-to-screw-pitch relationship points are better, safer.

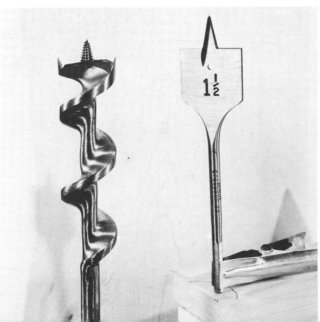

Nomenclature of the twist drill. For optimum performance in wood the point angle should be as shown.

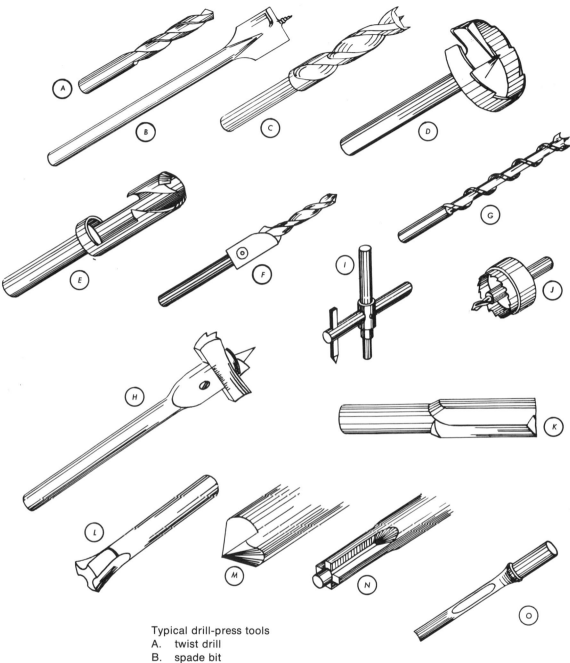

Typical drill-press tools
A.   twist drill
B.   spade bit
C.   spur machine drill
D.   multi-spur machine bit
E.   plug cutter
F.   twist drill w/ adjustable countersink attachment
G.   solid-center bit
H.   expansive bit (w/ brad point)
I.   fly cutter
J.   hole saw
K.   router bit
L.   dovetail cutter
M.   countersink
N.   counterbore (w/ pilot)
O.   mortising chisel

Other drill-press tools will be shown in the sections of this chapter that deal specifically with their use.

SPEEDS AND FEED

Excessive speeds on some tools can be dangerous. The general rule is to use slower speeds with larger tools. Sometimes this is not the most efficient way to use a particular tool, but it is done because the safety factor is as important. Be aware that the most efficient setup causes the tool to cut steadily. Unless it's designed to work that way, it should not scrape. Chatter, excessive vibration, rough results, and stalling of the motor can all be signs of the wrong speed, the wrong feed, or both.

At the other extreme, a speed that is too slow on some materials and with some tools, together with a hesitant feed, can cause the tool to rub, which won't do anything but dull the cutting edges. A slow speed with heavy feed

Another type comes with various saw-edged bands that lock in grooves in the head. Thus, the one tool will do various size holes. Each band, when used, is held in with lock screws.

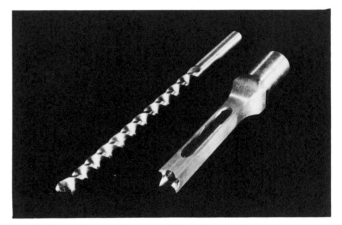

Mortising bit and chisel set. The bit works inside the square sleeve. It removes most of the waste while the chisel cuts away the corners. Together, they form a square hole.

Hole saws are available so various diameter cutters can be used on one arbor. This is an expensive way to set up for large hole forming.

An adjustable hole saw is a single tool that can be set to cut holes up to about 3″ in diameter. It comes with two sets of blades, one set to be used for metal cutting.

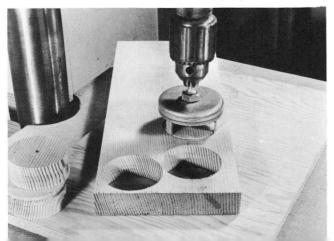

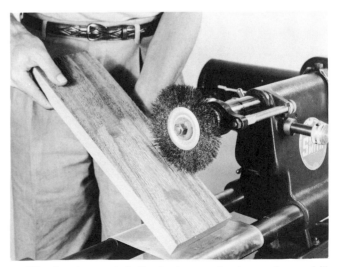

Wire brushes and similar tools may also be used on a drill press. Here, on a horizontally situated ShopSmith, a wire brush is used to sculpture a wood surface. On such operations, goggles are a must.

can make the tool dig in, which can stall the motor or even cause breakage of the cutting edges.

There is an ideal speed and feed for any tool and any material, but drill-speed charts, such as the one given, should be used only as a general guide. Most importantly, the tool should be cutting steadily, smoothly and without excessive vibration, no matter what the material. Increasing or decreasing rpm's can even be justified by differences in boards from the same species.

Feed is the amount of pressure you apply to control penetration. It goes hand in hand with speed, and the best general rule to follow again is to keep the tool cut-ting, taking a bite evenly and without strain.

In any event, when doubt exists, always start at a slow speed. Increase the speed to the point where the situation is as ideal as you can make it.

WORK SUPPORT

When the underside of the piece you are drilling doesn't matter, you can rest the work directly on the table and drill through when the table opening is aligned with the spindle. It really isn't a bad idea to use a scrap block between the work and the table, no matter what the job. The scrap block will protect the table and provide

DRILL PRESS SPEEDS

MATERIAL	OPERATION	SPEED (rpm)
wood	drilling—up to ¼"	3,800
wood	drilling—¼" to ½"	3,100
wood	drilling—½" to ¾"	2,300
wood	drilling—¾" to 1"	2,000
wood	drilling—over 1"	700
wood	using expansion or multi-spur bit	700
wood	routing	4,000-5,000
wood	cutting plugs or short dowels	3,300
wood	carving	4,000-5,000
wood	using fly-cutter	700
wood	using dowel-cutter	1,800
hardwood	mortising	2,200
softwood	mortising	3,300
metal	fine wire-brushing	3,300
metal	coarse wire-brushing	1,000
wood	coarse wire-brushing	2,200
soft metals	buffing (cloth wheel)	3,800
hard metals	buffing (cloth wheel)	4,700
plastics	buffing (cloth wheel)	2,300
metal	using fly-cutter	700
metal	grinding—3"-4" cup wheel	3,100
glass	drilling with metal tube	700

Drill-press speed chart is a good guide. Stay as close to the suggested speeds as you can—on the "under" side whenever you are in doubt.

backup so the cutting tool will not splinter the underside of the work as it emerges.

It's permissible to hold the work by hand if the work size permits and the hole size is not excessive. Often, on long work, you can brace one edge of the work against the drill-press column, and this setup is sufficient to counteract any twist caused by the cutting.

Don't hesitate, however, to use clamps to lock the work to the table. Using clamps provides a guarantee that, should the cutter grab in the hole particularly at the breakout point, the work will not be twisted out of your grasp. Such a possibility should be considered if you wish to avoid having your fingers rapped.

Many times, a fence, in addition to being a guide, acts as a safety mechanism. The fence doesn't have to be more than a straight piece of wood clamped to the table in position to gauge the edge distance of the hole. With such an item in place, any twisting force exerted by the drill will be taken by the fence, not your hands.

DRILLING TO EXACT DEPTH

Drilling exactly to a predetermined depth can be done in one of two ways.

Set the work on the table and extend the drill so that its point contacts the work. Then set the nuts on the stop rod the additional amount needed to achieve the hole depth.

Another possibility is to make a mark on the side of the work to indicate hole depth. Extend the quill so the drill point touches the mark and set the stop-rod nuts accordingly.

After you have set up in one of these two ways, you can drill any number of holes knowing that each will be to the same depth.

WORK LAYOUT

Be careful and accurate when you are measuring and marking lines. The pencil you use should be about 3H and should always be sharp.

The easiest and most accurate method of marking a hole location is to draw intersecting lines that tell you the center of the hole. Puncture this point with an awl and position the point of the drill there. A combination square can be used to draw lines at right angles to an edge and may also be used as an edge-marking gauge. Dividers (or a compass) do a good job when it is necessary to pick up a dimension from one piece (or a drawing) so you can carry it to another. Dividers are also a good tool to use when you wish to divide a line into a number of equal spaces.

There are many ways to proceed with work layout and what you do depends on the job and whether you

No matter what the material, the tool should be cutting constantly, taking a smooth, even bite. Correct speed and feed let you accomplish this easily.

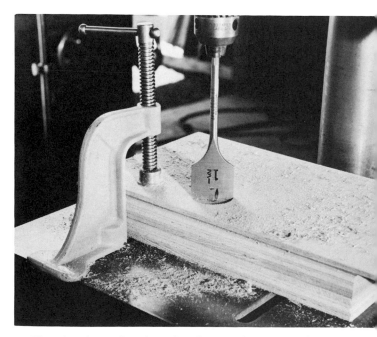

Clamping the work makes a lot of sense when you are forming large holes. It is good for both safety and accuracy. This type of clamp is made especially for drill-press work. It locks through the table slots and so may be positioned just about anywhere in relation to the work.

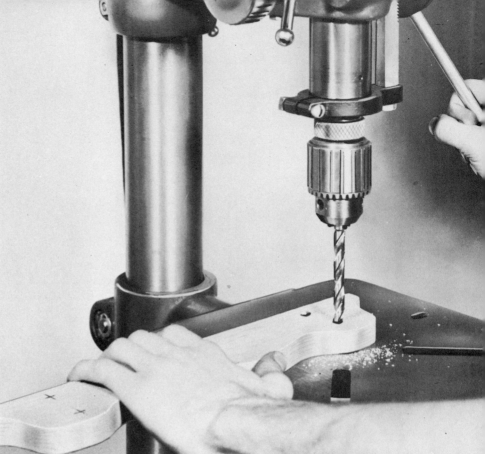

You can place work on the table when the bit is centered over the table opening. This, however, leaves a rougher exit than you would get by using a backup block under the work. Hand holding is okay when work size and the tool you are using permit it.

Making special setups for repetitive operations is good practice and usually eliminates much layout work. ShopSmith is used here to drill dowel holes in miter cuts.

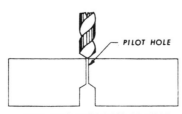

PILOT HOLE

DRILL FROM BOTH SIDES OF WORK

On thick stock, you can drill a through pilot hole and then open up to full size by drilling from both ends.

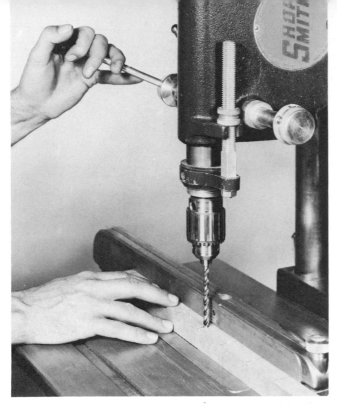

A fence, which doesn't have to be more than a straight piece of wood clamped to the table, is an excellent guide for maintaining hole edge-distance.

When rip fence and miter gauge are part of the table, they can be used to form jigs. Lacking such accessories, you substitute wood pieces to accomplish similar chores.

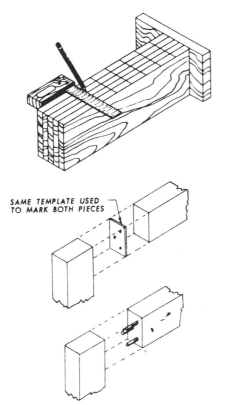

SAME TEMPLATE USED TO MARK BOTH PIECES

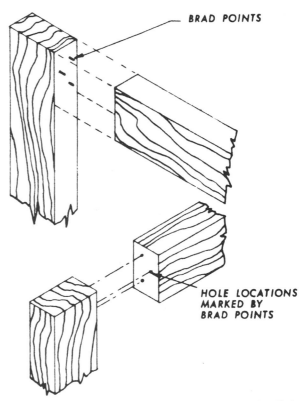

BRAD POINTS

HOLE LOCATIONS MARKED BY BRAD POINTS

Drilling accuracy depends greatly on careful layout. When the same marking is required on many pieces, it pays to make a template instead of laying out on each part.

If you tap in brads at location points and then snip off the brad heads, you can press one part against another to get the correct mating locations.

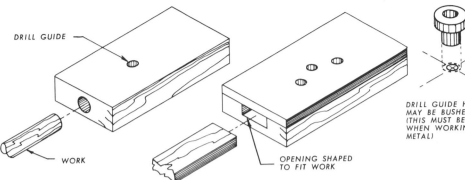

DRILL GUIDE

WORK

DRILL GUIDE HOLES
MAY BE BUSHED.
(THIS MUST BE DONE
WHEN WORKING WITH
METAL)

OPENING SHAPED
TO FIT WORK

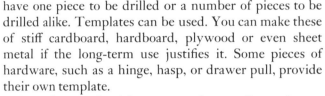

When needed, you can design fixtures to guarantee accurate placement of holes. Such items should be made only when the quantity of work justifies it.

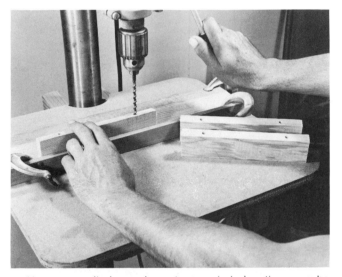

You can easily improvise setups so hole locations can be gauged automatically. Here, C-clamps on a wooden fence act as stops to gauge hole locations automatically.

have one piece to be drilled or a number of pieces to be drilled alike. Templates can be used. You can make these of stiff cardboard, hardboard, plywood or even sheet metal if the long-term use justifies it. Some pieces of hardware, such as a hinge, hasp, or drawer pull, provide their own template.

An often-used trick to use when ordinary layout proves impractical or too time consuming is to insert headless nails in appropriate locations in one of the pieces. When this piece is pressed against the mating part, the nails provide drill location points.

To mark hole locations on a series of boards that will be joined edge-to-edge by doweling, align the board edges and butt them surface to surface. Mark hole locations on one edge and carry the line across all pieces by using a square.

Use a fence as a guide whenever you must drill a series of holes with a common center line. Such a fence can be two pieces of wood joined to form an L-shape. C-clamps can then be used as stops to position any number of pieces that require the same hole in the same place. When you can use a fence and a miter gauge (as you can on a ShopSmith, for example), any number of setups can be created to position work for drilling. In fact, pieces of wood can be used on any drill press as substitutes for built-in accessories.

AUXILIARY TABLES

Such tables can serve dual purposes. They are instantly available setups for, in one case, drum sanding, which is a very good drill-press application; and they are handy tool shelves when work is being done on the regular drill-press table. A one-piece table is probably more convenient for a small drill press while a split-table model will go with almost any tool. Actually, either would be easy to scale to suit your equipment.

In either case, the attachment design is a split-clamp arrangement. A turn of a wing nut enables you to position the accessory anywhere, vertically or horizontally. The clamps must lock tightly on the drill-press column. If you have a hole saw or a fly cutter that will cut the

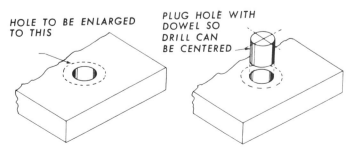

HOLE TO BE ENLARGED
TO THIS

PLUG HOLE WITH
DOWEL SO
DRILL CAN
BE CENTERED

When a drilled hole must be enlarged, plug the original hole so you can center the bit for the new drilling.

TABLE JIGS

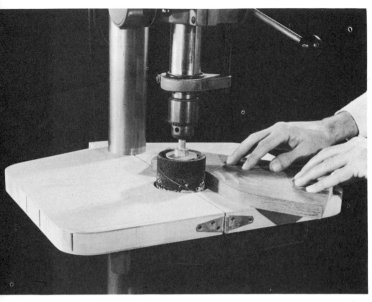

Easy-to-make hinged table permits the use of a drum sander.

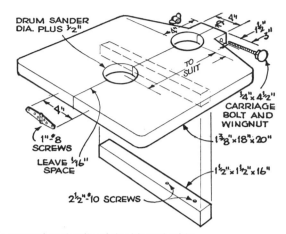

Construction details of the hinged table.

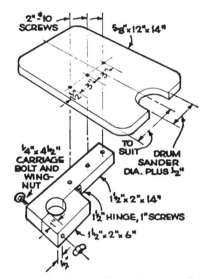

Construction details of a similar table that might be more convenient for a smaller drill press. It is also good for drum sanding but the design makes it necessary to stay on one side of the drum as you work.

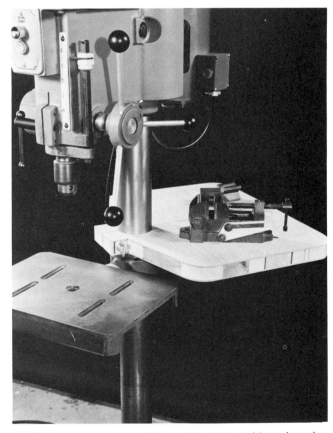

When not needed, the table can be swung aside and used as a holding platform. It will not interfere with normal drill-press activities.

correct size hole, it's a good idea to form the support arms from a single piece of stock. Then you can cut on the hole center line, and the material removed by the saw cut will be just enough to give you good, split-clamp action.

COLUMN STORAGE RACK

Drill-press work will be easier if you keep frequently used tools close at hand so you don't have to walk, stretch, or stoop every time you need one. That's the objective of a column storage rack. It is not a substitute for a large cabinet, but if you analyze your work and out-fit the case to suit your needs, you'll find it a big help.

The split-clamp lock described for the auxiliary tables

The case has space for many small tools but don't outfit it haphazardly. Instead, lay out small tools you use frequently and design holders to use the space efficiently.

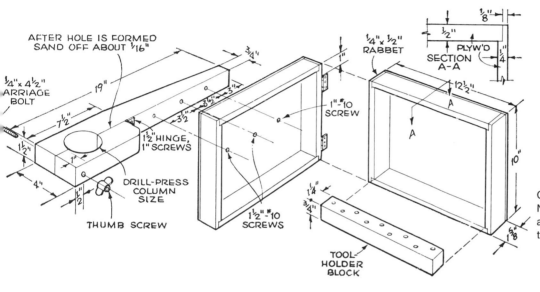

Construction details of the case. Note that it is made as a unit and then cut in half to make the two parts.

also applies to this storage case. Actually, you might be able to mount both the case and a table without critically reducing the distance between the spindle and the table proper.

TWO ADVANCED JIGS

A couple of very professional jigs will be described here even before the main material about drill-press work is given. For one thing, it seems a good way to demonstrate immediately how flexible the drill press can be. Also, a good many of the operations shown later in this chapter will be done on these jigs rather than on commercial units you might have to spend a lot of money for.

After you have read the whole chapter, you can return to this section and make a decision on which of the two jigs will be most useful to you. You might base your decision on the accompanying construction details or

particular operations. Whatever, jigs like these are what make the drill press flexible. Otherwise, it wouldn't be useful for anything but drilling holes.

Jig #1 is basically a table attached to a base that is secured to the regular drill-press table with two C-clamps. The table hole centers under the drill-press spindle and permits the use of drum sanders and three-lip shaper cutters. Individually adjustable fences are used for shaping straight-line work. Fulcrum pins support curved work that must be shaped freehand.

This jig has a drilling fence that can be used in place of the shaping fences for drilling holes at equal distances from the edge of the work. A built-in spacer can be used to automatically gauge the distance between holes. It is organized for a pivot guide for rotational passes against a cutter and has an indexing head. These and other features have prompted it to be called the "Woodworking Champ of any Shop."

ADVANCED JIG #1

Advanced jig #1. Here it is set up in the shaping mode. Other applications will be shown as we go along.

The pivot guide must fit precisely in the table's T-slot. A roofing nail makes a good pivot pin. Recess the underside of the pivot guide for the head of the nail.

The indexing head mounts on the pivot pin. Since this pin must go through the indexing head in order to hold the work-piece, keep several lengths of roofing nails on hand for different jobs.

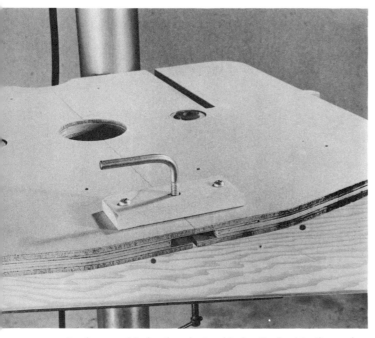

Lock assembly for the pivot guide is attached to the underside of the table with roundhead screws. A ¼" bolt is bent up to make the L-shaped lock handle.

Once made, the jig becomes a lifetime tool so it makes sense to construct it accurately to begin with. Start by making the base assembly, checking its dimensions against the size of the table on your drill press. The only change that might be necessary is a reduction or increase in the overall width. Once the base is assembled, you can add components. If you are a beginner, it would be wise to pause after the basic table construction. You can add other items to it after you have become involved in drill-press work.

Jig #2 contains a drawer that provides for storage of tools that you use with the tool. Actually, this design evolved from a simpler version that was made for drum sanding and drum-sander storage. The drill press is a great tool for such work, but the regular table just won't do. For rotary sanding only, you could get by with nothing more than an inverted, U-shaped structure; holes at the top allow the drum to pass through.

Since the same general construction serves for other

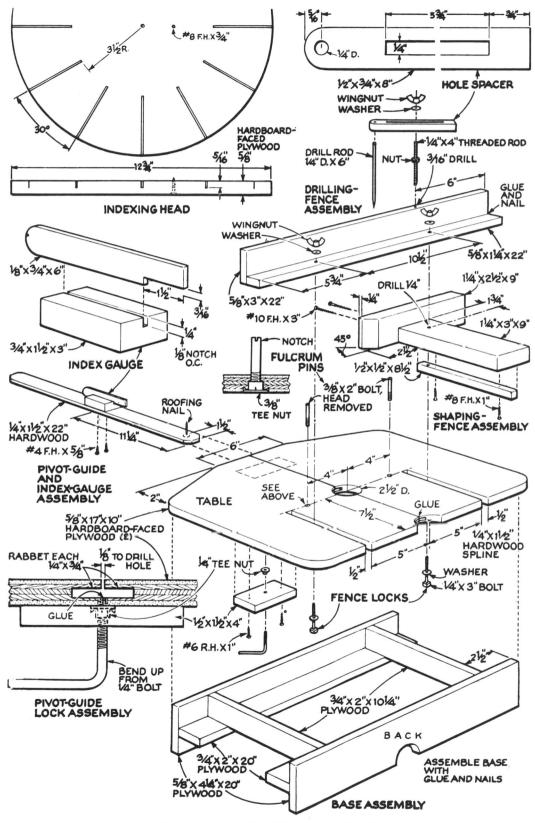

Construction details of the advanced jig #1.

ADVANCED JIG #2

The drawer back has a peculiar shape because it must clear the cutter and keep waste out. The pocket so created collects a good percentage of waste from the drill and, so captured, it is easy to clean away.

Design of the drawer interior is something you can do in line with the bulk of your work. A 1″ board, perforated with various size holes, will store many types of straight shank tools and other accessories.

Advanced jig #2 will align automatically if you make the back cutout carefully and install the clamp ledge accurately. Built-in drawer has ample room for storage.

rotary tools, it is logical to provide for different size table inserts.

Critical construction points of this jig follow. Cut the table to size and bisect the long dimension with an accurate center line. On the center line at the rear of the table, make an accurate half-circle cutout to fit the column.

With the table in place, use the drill press to form a small hole on the center line. This hole is the center of the table opening.

Work on a table saw to form the slot and the groove for the slide. The slide should not fit loosely; provide for a good fit even if it means having to exert a little pressure to move the slide to and fro. Shape one end of the slide support to conform to the table opening.

Shape and attach the rails with glue and screws that are driven up through the underside. The rails provide location points for the case sides which you can attach after forming the rabbets along the bottom edge.

Cut the case bottom to size and assemble, without gluing, what you have done so far. Put the unit in place on the drill press with the center line exactly so and scribemark the location of the front edge of the regular drill-press table so you will know exactly where the dado for the clamp ledge must go. This factor is critical for automatic jig alignment; therefore, take the time needed to do it correctly.

A point about the drawer is its peculiar shape at the back. This design prevents the drawer from becoming a receptacle for dust and chips. The U-shape actually collects a good percentage of waste which is easily brushed out or vacuumed away.

HOW TO DRILL FOR WOOD SCREWS

Normally, two holes are required for a wood screw. These holes permit the screw to be driven and allow for maximum holding power. The body hole equals the screw gauge; the smaller lead hole provides entrance for the screw end.

A good procedure is to drill lead holes first and then

For much more you can live with a solid insert of the large one needed for drum-sander work. For small work and small tools it's best to be prepared with a variety of inserts to minimize opening around tool.

A fly cutter can be used to form the discs that are used as inserts. Various size bits can make the center holes. If the inserts are made as a tight fit in the table recess, you won't have to worry about a means of holding them down.

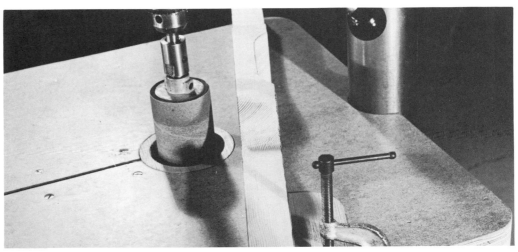

The pivoting fence is as functional as any more elaborate parallel type. Make the hole for the pivot bolt a fairly tight fit. A C-clamp at the free end provides security for the setting.

Different types of guides, all designed around store-bought 10-32 screws, lock into the aluminum slide and facilitate sanding and cutting operations. Polish guides with emery cloth.

open up the top portion to body-hole size. Countersinking is done so flat-head screws can be driven flush. Control the countersink depth by using the stop rod. On hardwoods, countersink to the full depth of the screwhead. On softwoods, stay a bit on the minus side. The screw will pull flush as you finish driving.

When you are driving very small screws in softwood, you can often simply make a starting hole with an awl. It's also possible to do this with some hardwoods. Make a judgment after testing with one or two screws.

A counterbore is required when the fastener head must be set below the surface. The counterbore is no more than a shallow hole sized to suit the head of the screw or bolt or whatever. Special counterboring tools are available, but you can form the counterbore first, using a spade bit or something similar instead, and then do the lead and body holes.

Such holes are often sealed with plugs cut from the same type of wood. Special tools for cutting out such plugs are available, and they will be discussed in the section on plug cutters in this chapter.

EQUI-SPACED HOLES

A simple way to equally space holes is to pencil mark the distance between the holes and to use a fence to establish edge distance. The fence doesn't have to be more than a straight piece of wood clamped to the drill-press table. The distance from it to the drill point must equal the edge distance required for the job.

Jig #1, an advanced jig previously described in this chapter, provides an attachment so you can gauge distance between holes automatically. After drilling the first hole, set the work for the spacing you want and set the guide pin in the hole already drilled. By repeating the procedure, you can drill as many equally-spaced holes as you need without a layout. If you need holes that are larger than the $\frac{1}{4}''$ pin, simply regard the holes as pilots that you then enlarge.

RADIAL HOLES

Drilling radial holes can be simply a matter of layout on the work, or you can use pivot guides like those shown on the two advanced jigs. Without the jigs, drive a nail through a board that you then clamp to the regular drill-press table. The nail is the pivot on which you center the work. If you don't want a center hole through the wood, cut the nail short and use it as a stud on which you press the work.

Edge holes are different. Only on a ShopSmith, which

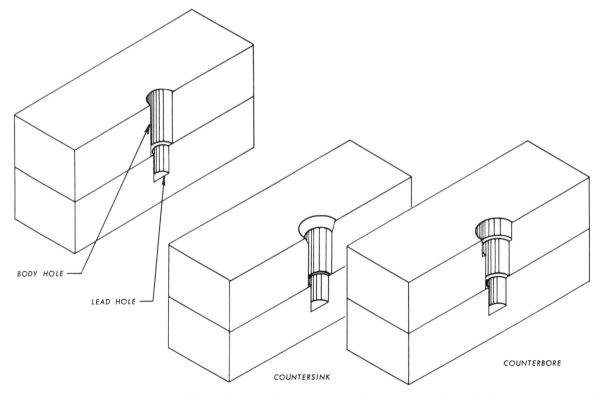

BODY HOLE

LEAD HOLE

COUNTERSINK

COUNTERBORE

Nomenclature of holes required for screws is shown in these cut-away drawings. A countersink is used when screw-heads must be flush. Use a counterbore when the screw is set below the surface and then concealed with a plug.

HOLE SIZES FOR WOOD SCREWS

SCREW GAUGE	BODY HOLE	LEAD HOLE	SCREW GAUGE IN INCHES
0	53	—	.060
1	49	—	.073
2	44	56*	.086
3	40	52*	.099
4	33	51*	.112
5	1/8	49*	.125
6	28	47	.138
7	24	46	.151
8	19	42	.164
9	15	41	.177
10	10	38	.190
11	5	37	.203
12	7/32	36	.216
14	D	31	.242
16	I	28	.268
18	19/64	23	.294
* In hardwoods only.			

Correct holes sizes to drill in relation to the size of the wood screw. If you don't have the right size drill, stay as close as you can on the minus side.

Simple-angle holes like this are easily done by tilting the table. Spade bits with long points are good to use since they will be centered before the tool starts cutting.

can be used as a horizontal drill press, can you position the work flat while you drill into its edge. On a conventional drill press, you tilt the table so its surface is on a vertical plane and clamp the work to it. If the work is round, you can make a V-block and use it as shown in the accompanying sketch. Be sure to line up the center of the "V" with the point of the drill.

ANGULAR DRILLING

Three kinds of off-vertical holes can be drilled; the position of a chair leg in each type of hole best illustrates each type of angle. At a simple angle, the leg tilts in one direction. The angle is obvious when you view it from one side. The equal compound angle has the leg tilting the same amount in two directions. The angle will be the same whether you view the leg from the front or the side. With an unequal compound angle, the leg tilts two ways but a greater amount in one direction. The angle viewed from the front is different than the angle viewed from the side.

When the work size permits, the simple angle is done by tilting the drill-press table. If this is not feasible, then you must leave the table in normal position and use a height block under one edge of the work. Size the height block to give you the angle you want.

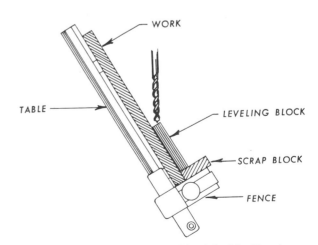

On an extreme angle, where the side of the bit will make contact before the point, use a leveling block to keep the bit stable and prevent it from wandering.

REPEAT DRILLING

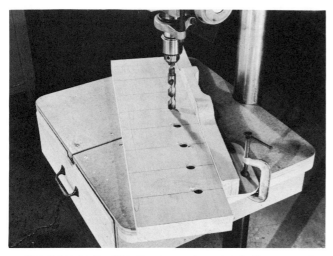

The fence on jig #2 is fine to use to maintain the same edge distance on a series of holes.

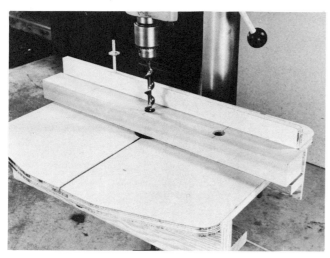

This also applies to jig #1. Work can be placed on the table if the holes are not through. Otherwise use a scrap block between the work and the table.

The fence accessory provides automatic gauging of equally spaced holes. The pin seats in each hole drilled to position the work for the next one.

The equal compound angle is popular. It has some overall factors that are interesting and that can make many jobs easier to do. If you mark perpendicular diameters on a circular piece of wood or corner-to-corner lines on a square piece of wood and then drill simple angles with the layout lines in line with the spindle, you will have a compound angle position for what you insert in the hole.

What makes many of these jobs difficult is not the operation but the size of the workpiece. However, even considering size, you can facilitate matters through careful designing. Let's assume you have a round or square table on which you wish to splay the legs. Picture the understructure as legs attached to two crosspieces. If you drill simple angles at the end of each crosspiece and then assemble the crosspieces with a centered half-lap joint so that they are at right angles, what you inset in the holes will be equally splayed about the table.

On all angular drilling, be aware that the side of the cutter may contact the work before the point does. This can lead to wandering of the drill unless you make contact with an extremely slow feed until the drill is firmly positioned. On extreme angles, it pays to use a leveling block which will provide a flat for the drill to enter.

LARGE HOLES

What is a large hole? Arbitrarily, you might say it's anything above the maximum size you can do with a spade bit, which is $1\frac{1}{2}''$. Going above this measurement is a question of having the tool that will do the job. Fly cutters provide a good solution simply because you can bore any size hole between the minimum and maximum settings. Fixed hole saws can be used, but being equipped for anything can be expensive; few, if any, of the adjustable types go above approximately $3''$. Fly cutters can produce up to a $6''$ diameter. Above this, you might regard the job as a piercing assignment for a jigsaw or a saber saw.

There is a drill-press solution with the appropriate technique and jig. However, the chore is really a routing operation. A center hole drilled in the work is placed over the dowel pin in the adjustable jig. The jig is secured to gauge the radius of the hole, and then the work is rotated so the $\frac{1}{4}''$ router bit forms a circular groove. On thick work it may be necessary to rotate the work several times, cutting a bit deeper after each pass.

Large hole forming, no matter what the cutter, calls for maximum security for the work and ample clearance for your hands. Position the work and then clamp it solidly to the drill-press table. Use a slow feed and a slow speed. The outboard, cutting end of a fly cutter

Within its limits (the number of slots that you cut) the indexing head automatically positions the work for the various radial hole locations.

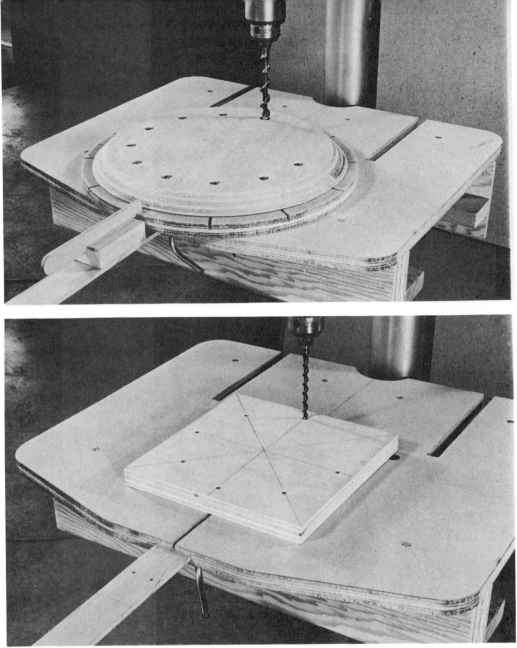

Pivot guide alone can be used for radial holes but this provides for radial distance only, not spacing. For this reason, layout lines are needed.

If a center hole doesn't matter, then the pivot pin can go through the work. Otherwise, use a short pin and impale the work on it.

LARGE HOLE DRILLING

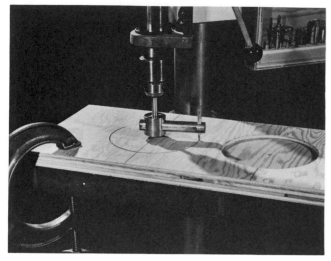

A fly cutter can be used for holes up to 6″ in diameter. Keep feed and speed at a minimum and always clamp the work securely. Never place hands near the cutting area.

Fly cutter is used here for a double cut to create a wooden ring. Be very careful at break-through for the ring will be free in the hole.

can be just a blur even at slow speeds, so keep your hands well away.

DEEP HOLES

The maximum depth of a hole you can normally drill is limited by the maximum extension of the quill regardless of the length of the drilling tool. When, for example, quill extension is 4″ and the bit is 6″, you can get the full cut by drilling 4″ first, then raising the table so the bit is in the hole that extra 2″ and drilling again.

You can form a hole that is two times the maximum by working from both sides of the stock so opposing holes have the same center line. This can be accomplished by accurate layout or by providing a hole-size guide pin on the table over which the work can be placed after the first hole is formed. This technique positions the work accurately for drilling from the opposite side.

Extension bits can be used for very deep holes, but they are not too usable on bench model machines because of the limited chuck-to-base capacity. Some operators get around this limitation by swinging the drill-press head so it projects over the edge of the bench. Thus, they get a chuck-to-floor capacity.

Be careful with extension bits because they can whip. Use a slow speed and have the point of the bit embedded in the work before you turn on the tool.

CONCENTRIC HOLES

Picture concentric holes as longitudinal openings through the center of a cylinder. The techniques to use don't differ too much from those described for deep holes. Differences arise, sometimes, in methods for holding the work. A very useful holding device can be made from a screw clamp merely by cutting matching "V's" in the jaws. This permits round work to be gripped securely. If the screw clamp is large enough, one of its handles can be braced against the drill-press column to counteract any twist created by the cutting action. Further security is achieved by using a C-clamp to lock the screw clamp to the drill-press table.

If you have an adjustable lathe chuck, it makes a very fine holding device for concentric drilling because it is heavy enough to provide very good support. Even tubing can be gripped for drilling should the I.D. be too small for your needs.

THE COUNTERSINK

The countersink is a tool that forms an inverted cone to seat the heads of flat-head screws flush with adjacent surfaces. They are available with different bevel angles to suit the fastener. All wood screws require one angle; machine screws require another.

When you need a number of countersunk holes, it's best to set the drill-press stop rod to control depth. This method is theoretically wrong, but a countersink is often used to form the seat for the screw head and also a counterbore for a plug to hide the screw. This simply means going deeper with the countersink than you need

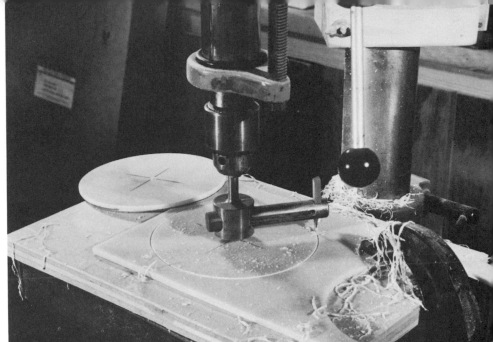

Fly cutters can be used on other materials, like this new plastic ''Corian''. Steady streams of ribbon-like waste indicate good feed pressure and correct rpms.

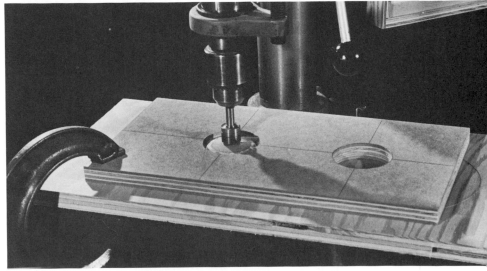

This kind of fly cutter has a sloping bit to cut away waste. It does not cut a disc. More about it in the section on Decorative Cuts.

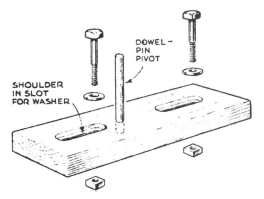

The jig that permits a router bit to be used for cutting extra large holes is shown here. A center hole drilled in the work fits over the dowel pivot. The work is then rotated against the direction-of-rotation of the cutter.

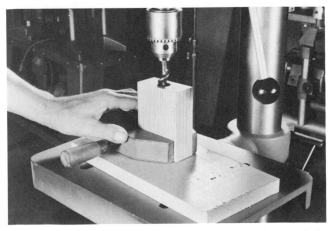

No matter how long the bit you are using, the deepest hole you can drill in one pass is limited by the maximum quill extension on your machine.

COUNTERSINK BORING

There are many styles of countersinks but they all make inverted cone depressions so you can set screw heads flush.

You can continue to countersink to below the work's surface. By doing so, you also form a counterbore for a plug.

But retract frequently when doing this. Also, be sure you have, or can form, plugs that will match the overall diameter of the countersink.

To some extent a countersink can be used like a router bit to do chamfering on stock edges and things like these V-grooves. Keep depth of cut light, speed high, and feed slow. Repeat passes can lead to deeper cuts.

On deep holes, it is important to retract the bit frequently to clear chips from the hole. This will result in a smoother job and will reduce heat buildup in the tool and the work.

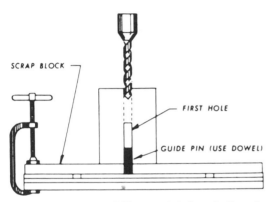

SCRAP BLOCK

FIRST HOLE

GUIDE PIN (USE DOWEL)

How you can set up to drill accurately from both ends of the work in order to double hole depth. In this case the guide pin is secured in a board that is clamped to the table after pin and bit have been aligned.

Screw clamp with matching Vs cut in its jaws makes holder for concentric drilling of either round or square stock. Handle of clamp is braced against column to counteract twist of the cutter.

to go for the screw head alone. Consider two factors. Be sure you have a plug-cutting tool that matches the O.D. of the countersink. Be aware that you are burying the countersink more than you should so retract frequently to clear waste from the hole and thus avoid burning the tool and/or the work.

Countersinking in thin sheet metal calls for a "dimpling" procedure. Using a countersink in normal fashion would simply form a sloppy hole for the screw head. To get around this, shape the end of a hardwood dowel so it matches the angle of the countersink you need. Use the countersink in a backup block. Chuck the dowel and use it, more or less, like a press to form the metal into the countersink shape. Success depends greatly on the gauge and the softness of the metal. It works fine on, for example, do-it-yourself aluminum. Using a slow speed and putting a dab of paste wax on the end of the dowel are also helpful.

ROTARY RASPS

Rotary rasps are little tools; but when you use them on a drill press, you can do good-sized jobs. Such jobs include making joints, doing shaping and pattern forming, or accomplishing pesky short-run chores, especially on small pieces that might be difficult to handle by other means.

Most common types are rasps designed primarily for use as rough-cutting files under power. Many of those shown here are System Zenses, products imported by Dal-Craft, Inc. The Surform is a Stanley product that you might already be familiar with.

The imported types differ from the common rasp image in that each of the units is meant to do a particular job. The primary purpose usually indicates the shape of the tool, but imagination can lead beyond the single application.

Imported types cut differently, too. On most of the tools, the teeth are like raised chisel edges so they shave rather than scrape. This action leads to faster, smoother cutting that under correct feed-speed conditions produces edges requiring little additional attention. To get the most out of these imported rotary rasps you should have a couple of easy-to-make jigs (see accompanying drawings).

When you make the end cut, miter and vertical guides, check your cuts with a square and be sure the blocks that will be used to position the workpieces are exact.

The System Zenses tools are made of case-hardened cutting steel and can operate between speeds of 1,500 and 10,000 rpm's. A range of 2,000 to 3,000 rpm's is recommended. Very high speeds, especially in hardwoods, can cause burning and in soft, gummy woods can

CUTTING WITH THE RASP

These types of rotary rasps are pretty new. Each is designed for a specific job but capabilities overlap. With them you can do jobs like those shown in the photo below.

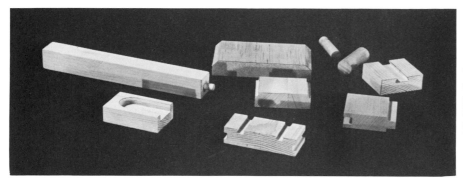

With rotary rasps, you can do chamfering and beveling, grooving, edge shaping, forming dowels, integral tenons, dovetails cuts, etc.

Dowel mills are designed so a plug (or dowel) cut by one will fit the hole formed by the next size up.

Best way to use the rotary rasps on a drill press is to make a special table and some other simple guides that are used along with it.

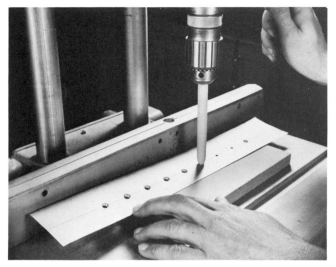

"Dimpling" to form screw-head seats in thin sheet metal with hardwood dowel in which the end is tapered. Use slow speed and a wax lubricant.

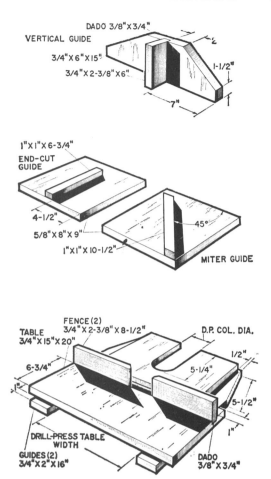

Construction details of rotary rasp table and some guides that make it easy to do accurate cutting.

clog the teeth quickly. Moderate speeds plus light feed pressure will help keep the teeth sharper, longer.

When you use a shape that must be buried in the work, regard it as a drill, retracting frequently to remove waste.

Don't try to cut too deeply. As an example of how much material the tool can remove in one pass, figure a groove about $\frac{1}{4}''$ wide by $\frac{3}{8}''$ deep in pine as an approximate standard.

Even under ideal conditions, the teeth will clog; but you can clean them easily with the same kind of brush you use on your hand files. For problem clogging, first dry-brush the tool and soak in paint thinner for a minute or two; then brush again.

SHAPING ON A DRILL PRESS

The drill press makes a good shaper as long as you are aware of two limiting factors. The highest speed doesn't match the rpm's you can get from an individual machine; the spindle is above the table instead of being under it. Since you can compensate to a great degree for lack of speed simply by slowing up the feed and since the above-the-table spindle position is not critical for the bulk of shaping work, you can get along quite well.

The drill press does require a shaping table accessory. This accessory can be a commercial unit you buy or an attachment you make to use with the advanced jig. Beyond this, you need an adapter to use in place of the regular chuck, depth collars that are used on the adapter, and the cutters themselves.

Several general rules apply when using the drill

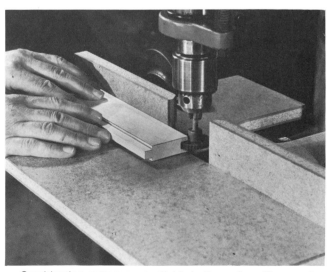

Combination cutters are available in three sizes. They can be used to form T&G joints and for light surface planing jobs.

A 45° angle cutter can be used to chamfer edges and to do similar jobs. Feed slowly, *with* the grain. On four-edge cuts, do the crossgrain ones first.

The heavy-duty mill looks like a stubby dowel mill but has thicker walls and is good to use for fast removal of stock on such jobs as rabbeting. Note use of end-cut guide.

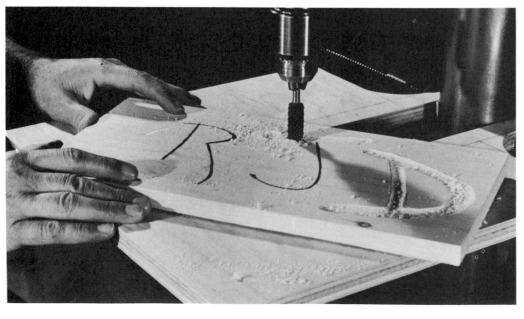

More conventional type rasps are just like deep-cutting files designed to be used under power. With a slow feed and a reasonable depth-of-cut, you can do some pretty good freehand ''carving.''

The dovetail groover can also be used to form matching tongues. The latter by passing stock on edge across the cutter.

The combination cutter may also be used to form integral tenons. Use a very slow feed to avoid burning. Note use of vertical guide.

press as a shaper. Always use the fastest speed you have. Work against a shaper fence whenever possible. Try to keep the cutting tool under the work if at all possible (even though it may be shown in accompanying illustrations over the work for the sake of clarity). One reason is for safety; the other is to guard against gouging the work should you lift it accidentally during the pass. Feed the work into and against the rotation of the cutting tool. Hold hands away from the cutting area and try to feed so fingers are hooked over work edges to guard against slippage. Don't force the work; make all passes with a slow, steady feed. Don't try to shape pieces that are too small to be held safely.

The one-piece, three-blade cutter is the most practical type of tool for homeshop use. Like molding head knives, these may be designed for full profile cuts to produce a specific shape or they may be combination cutters where you use part of the edge to achieve a form. No law says that you can't use either type in any way you choose if a variation of the standard leads to the end result you want.

Straight pieces should be shaped against a fence. When only part of the edge is removed, the fences are set on the same plane. When the entire edge of the stock is cut away, then the outfeed fence is brought forward an amount that equals the depth of cut. Both practices allow the work to have full support both before and after the cut.

Freehand shaping, necessary when the work has an inside or outside curve, is done against fulcrum pins. These pins are vertical "dowels," one on each side of the cutter. To start the cut, brace the work against the infeed pin and gradually move it forward to make contact with the cutter. You can still hold against the infeed pin as you continue to make the cut. As you near the end, swing the work to brace against the outfeed pin and finish the job. On all such jobs, collars are used on the adapter together with the cutter to control depth of cut.

ROUTING

Routing is done with special bits, best secured to the spindle with a router chuck. A good many of the rules described for shaping apply to router work, especially the advice about speeds and feed.

Router bits don't have to be straight-shank affairs. Many are available that will produce shaped edges, even dovetail slots. Actually, if you are going to set up for both shaping and routing, you want to be careful that you don't duplicate coverage.

Routing cuts are smoothest when you work with the grain of the wood. Cross-grain cuts, especially when they must be straight, are the most difficult to do. Use a fence

Surform tools (made by Stanley) can be used on the drill press at between 1,500 and 2,500 rpms depending on the hardness of the wood. Clamp locks the special table to the drill press column.

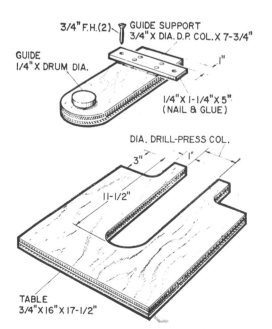

Construction details include those for a guide so you can do pattern forming. The guide must equal the diameter of the Surform drum and be aligned exactly with it.

SHAPING ON THE DRILL PRESS

Typical setup for shaping on a drill press using commercial accessories. Auxiliary table bolts to the regular table. Fences are individually adjustable. Such units are available for most any drill press you buy.

Work is braced against the infeed fulcrum pin and slowly advanced to contact the cutter and to bear against the collar. Arrow shows direction of feed. At the end of the cut, brace against the outfeed pin.

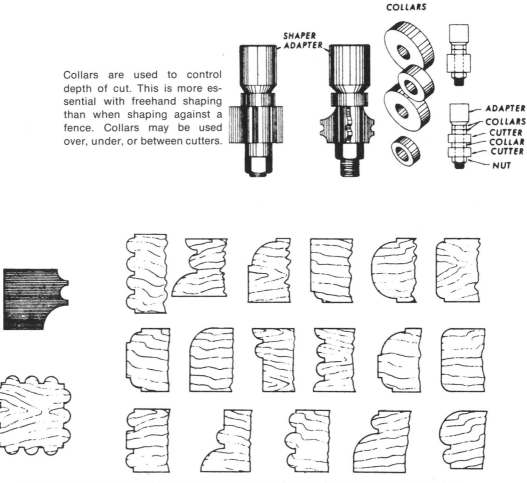

Collars are used to control depth of cut. This is more essential with freehand shaping than when shaping against a fence. Collars may be used over, under, or between cutters.

Important factor in three-lip shaper cutter use. All of the designs shown here were done with a single combination quarter-round and bead cutter. Variations made possible simply by changing relationship of work and cutter.

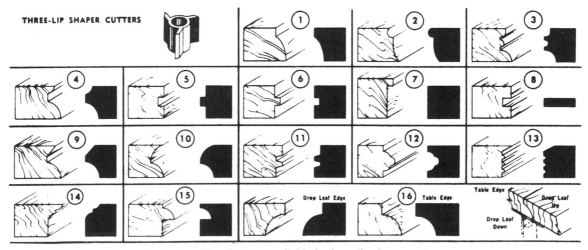

Typical profiles that are available in three-lip shaper cutters.

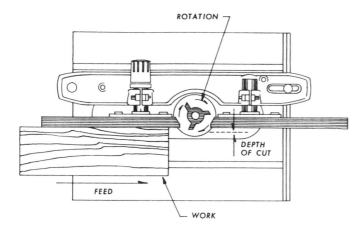

ROTATION

DEPTH
OF CUT

FEED

WORK

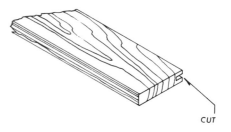

WITH FENCES IN LINE,
CUT REMOVES PART
OF WORK EDGE

CUT

WRONG

WHEN ENTIRE EDGE
OF STOCK IS REMOVED,
OUTFEED FENCE IS
ADJUSTED TO PROVIDE
SUPPORT AFTER WORK
HAS PASSED CUTTER

CUT

NO SUPPORT
HERE

FEED

WORK SUPPORTED
HERE AFTER CUT IS MADE

FENCE MOVED BACK

CUT

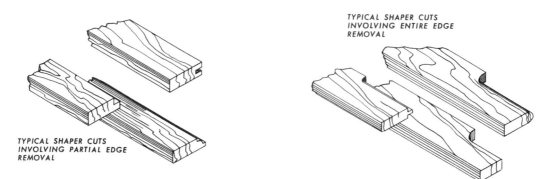

TYPICAL SHAPER CUTS
INVOLVING ENTIRE EDGE
REMOVAL

TYPICAL SHAPER CUTS
INVOLVING PARTIAL EDGE
REMOVAL

Some of the important points regarding fence alignment when doing shaping operations are shown here.

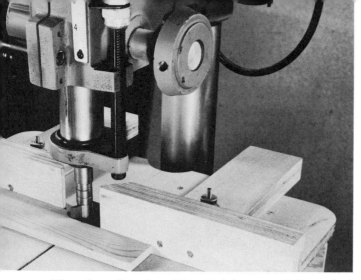

When the entire edge of the stock is removed, the outfeed fence must be brought forward a distance equal to the depth-of-cut. Note use of #1 jig.

When only part of the edge is removed, the fences are set on the same plane. Use high speed, feed slow from left to right and, whenever possible, feed so you cut *with* the grain.

Fulcrum pins are very essential when you do freehand shaping. Equally important, awareness of where you place your hands which should never be too close to the cutter.

or guide for either type of cut.

For much cross-grain work, it's best to prepare a special setup. This is no more than an auxiliary table with a fence guided by rails that move along opposite edges. The idea is to guide the work so the line of cut is at right angles to the work edge.

When doing freehand routing, you must be very careful to hold the work firmly as you guide it. Cutting action will vary with differences in grain structure, and it's quite easy for the work to move away from the line you are trying to follow. The deeper you try to cut in one pass the more obvious the movement away from the line will be.

Pattern routing is a way to do intricate shapes with good guarantee of accuracy. It is also a good method to use when you require many similar pieces.

For this type of routing, secure a router bit-sized post in a board that you attach to the drill-press table so the post is exactly aligned with the cutter. Cut the pattern you wish to reproduce in a piece of plywood or hardboard. The pattern is tack-nailed to the work and situated over the post. Bring the cutter down to the depth you want. Move the work and pattern so the pattern is constantly bearing against the post. Since the post and cutter are in line, you duplicate the shape of the pattern.

To rout parallel to a curved edge, you need a guide that will maintain the correct distance between work edge and cutter. The guide can be a pointed piece of wood that you clamp to the regular table or nail to a board that is then clamped to the table. It can also be the more sophisticated version designed for use with the advanced jig #2.

V-blocks, semi-circular guides, or specially made shapes that are made to fit the work can be used advantageously. One of the accompanying, illustrated examples might well do for a job you may encounter.

DRUM SANDING

A drum sander is the tool to use for many edge-smoothing operations, and the drill press is a fine tool to use it on. Since the regular drill-press table won't do for this technique, you can make an auxiliary table with a U-shaped cutout. Thus, the drum can be situated so its bottom edge is below the work that rests on the new table, and the entire edge of the work can be brought to bear against the drum. This setup also assures a right-angle relationship between work and drum so the sanded edge will be square to adjacent surfaces.

While this primitive jig is appropriate as a quick solution, it is not ideal since it doesn't allow for use of all the abrasive surface. An improvement would be to elevate the auxiliary table so the drum could be set

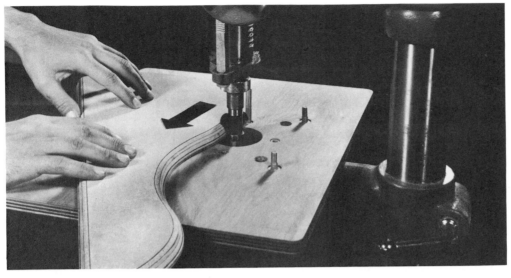

Some pretty intricate forms can be shaped when you work free-hand. Sometimes it's necessary to remove the outfeed pin—if so, be especially careful at the end of the cut.

For internal cuts, set the work in place before you adjust the cutter. Feed direction must always be the same. You *can* make repeat passes for exceptionally deep cuts. Just adjust the cutter after each.

You can do pivot shaping with either of the jigs but you must be very careful to hold the work firmly. The cutter will try to treat the work as if it were a wheel.

Multiple-cutter setups are possible like this shaped edge and rabbet being formed in one pass. The collar controls the depth-of-cut. This setup is for illustration only. When you need a slim piece, it is much better to shape the edge of a wide board and then cut off that part which you will be using in your work.

Similar job being done with a bead-and-cove cutter and a $\frac{1}{4}''$ blank knife. This gives you a decorative edge plus a panel insert groove in a single pass. Since you remove a lot of material, such cuts should be made very slowly.

Some special items are available for drill-press shaper work. This set of special collars lets you use molding knives like three-lips shaper-cutters. Be sure to read carefully instructions that come with such equipment.

ROUTING ON THE DRILL PRESS

1. Router bits require high speeds to cut smoothly. Use the highest drill-press speed available—at least 5,000 to 6,000 r.p.m. If you have a speed changer, you can go up to 9,000 or 10,000 r.p.m., but don't tax the quill by going any higher.

2. Always use a special router chuck to hold the bits. Conventional three-jaw drill chucks are not designed to take the side thrust of router bits.

3. Always feed the work *against* the cutter's direction of rotation. If you feed it the other way, the bit will try to pull the work with it and won't cut as well.

4. When you use a fence, be sure the thrust of the cutter, which is in its direction of rotation, is *toward* the fence. This gives a cleaner, more accurate cut because the thrust holds the work tightly in place. If the thrust is away from the fence, it tends to pull the work away with it.

5. Never cut deeper than about ⅛" at a time or it will strain the cutter and result in a poor job. Make deep cuts in successive passes, lowering the cutter slightly on each pass until you reach the desired depth.

Five good general rules for routing operations on the drill press.

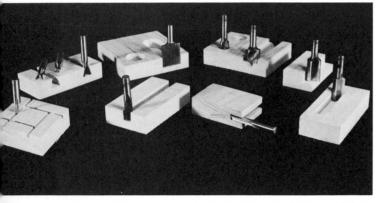

Router bits come in various shapes and sizes. All of them should be run at the highest speeds possible.

You can add decorative touches to pre-shaped work whether it is something you have made or purchased. Feed the work by using the fence—use a stop block to control length of cut.

higher or lower at will. This feature, as well as other advantages, is possible with the advanced jigs.

To do pattern sanding, you can make a guide to match the diameter of the drum. This guide is attached to a board, and the board is clamped to the drill-press table so the guide is in perfect alignment with the sander. Correct alignment can be accomplished by using jig #2 to make a special insert which is secured to the guide.

To use the guide, shape one piece of work as a pattern and cut the others roughly to shape. The rough pieces are tack-nailed to the pattern. Since the pattern rides the guide, the drum sander cuts down the rough pieces to match the pattern.

The remaining illustrations show a few other sanding techniques that can be accomplished in good style on a drill press.

DECORATIVE WORK

You can do luxurious carving, as well as create such items as drawer fronts and door pulls with a custom look, on your drill press. The accompanying, illustrated samples of such work are simply a place to start; you can go much further by adapting the technique to your own projects and tools.

Much of what is shown is done with a fly cutter that has a sloping bit rather than a vertical cutter. As the tool is fed, its pilot drill makes a center hole and the blade makes a circular recess with a sloping bottom. When a second cut is done close enough to overlap the first, new angles and interesting patterns result. The cutter (called Adjust-A-Drill by Jet Tool Company) is available in two sizes. Since both have adjustable bits, a wide range of designs is possible.

This kind of decorative work can be done on almost any wood, but stock such as maple and birch is best to use.

Work with a ruler and compass to plan designs. Mark

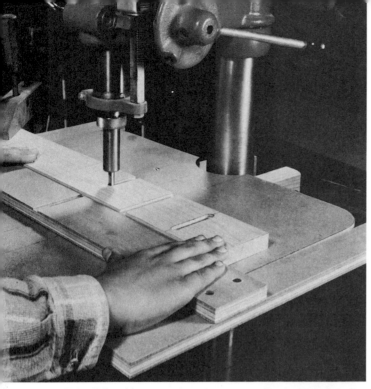

This sliding fence, used on the router table, lets you feed the work at right angles to the cutter. To guarantee a straight cut, clamp the work to one of the fence guides (notice the clamp in upper left corner of photo).

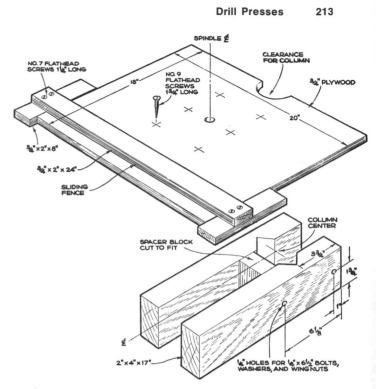

Construction details of the router table and the special fence.

Make the base for the table from stock 2×4s V-notched at the rear to fit the drill-press column. After you make the base, clamp it in place with the set screws and then attach the table.

Like other table-type jigs we've shown, this one can be swung aside when it is not needed to serve as a holding platform during other operations.

The essence of pattern routing is shown here. The pattern rides a pin that is set in a table (or a board) directly in line with the router bit. The work is tack-nailed to the pattern . . .

. . . and, as the pattern rides the pin, the shape is duplicated in the work above it. Best way to align the pin is to drill its hole with the router bit you will use for the job.

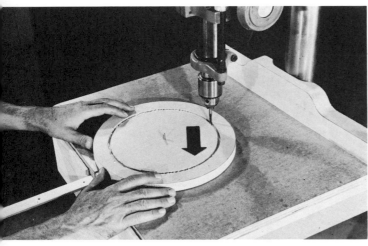

You can do pivot routing with either of the advanced jigs. After you set the slide, hold the work firmly as you lower the cutter. Lock the quill position and rotate the work slowly in the direction indicated by the arrow.

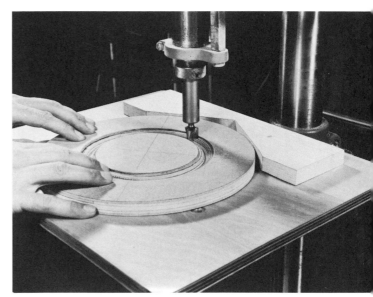

You can do circular routing by rotating the work against a V-block. A shaped bit is used here but full depth-of-cut was achieved by making repeat passes.

Work against a fence to do "freehand" routing chores. Feed from left to right.

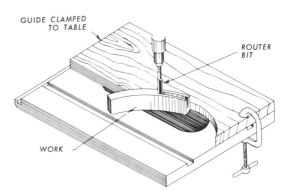

Specially shaped board is helpful for "odd" shaped pieces that would be difficult to control.

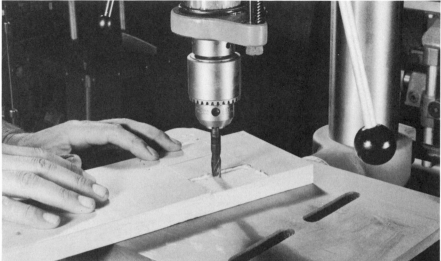

You can do freehand routing if you are especially careful about gripping and feeding the work. When you wish to freehand cut a straight line, it helps to first incise the line with a knife.

This looks like a shaping operation and the setup is pretty much that. Difference is that a router bit is used instead of a shaper-cutter. It's included to show you can employ a shaper-fence setup if it makes the operation more convenient.

Same thing applies here where a wide, straight router bit is forming a rabbet. Arrow indicates direction of feed. Deep, wide cuts like this can be achieved in one pass if your drill press has a lot of power. Otherwise, make repeat passes.

A router bit can be used much like a drill to make vertical, overlapping cuts as the preliminary step to form a round-end mortise. After the "drilling" the work is moved to-and-fro to clean ridges from the slot.

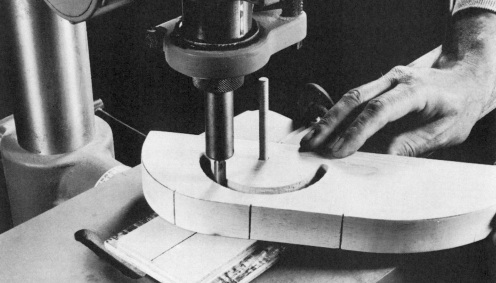

An improvised type of pivot guide that works pretty much like the one we showed for doing large holes. Radial distance is controlled by where you situate the jig.

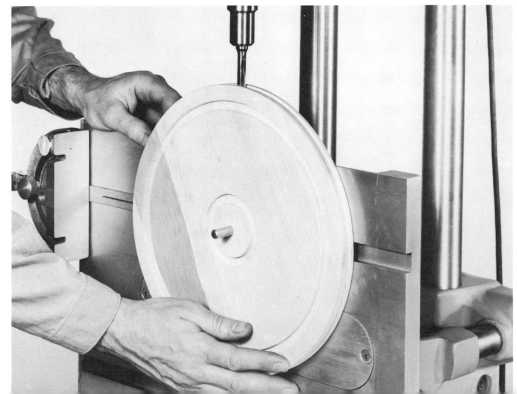

You can use pivot guidance to do grooves in circular edges, if you make a setup that is similar to this one on a conventional drill press. All you need is a board with a pivot pin.

DRUM SANDING

Basic drum sander assembly. Taking up on the nut when the parts together, expands the rubber sleeve to grip the abrasive band that is placed over it.

This L-shaped jig locks with bolts that are pushed through the slots in the regular drill-press table. Be sure the vertical piece is perpendicular to the table surface.

Best way to use a drum sander is to establish a setup so work can be held flat while its edge is smoothed.

Inside or outside curved edges can be passed through between the guide on jig #2 and the drum. This is the way to go when you have many pieces that should be exactly alike. A single piece can be handled freehand.

When doing inside edges, place the work before you situate the drum. Use 1,500 rpms with coarse paper—2,000 to 3,000 rpms with fine paper for best results.

Sanding circular pieces like dowels is done best when the free end of the work is snugged in a hole drilled in a board clamped to the table. This will keep the work from whipping.

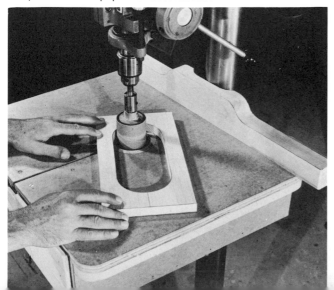

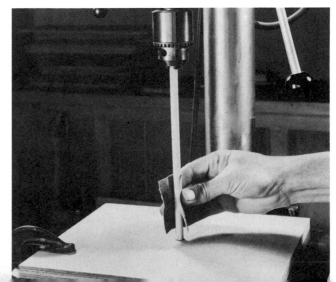

You can sand edges in fine style when you run the work between the drum sander and a fence. *Don't* try to remove a lot of material in one pass.

This is an excellent way to smooth surfaces on very thin materials. Use a slow, no-stop feed. Pausing at any point might cause the drum to gouge and mar the work.

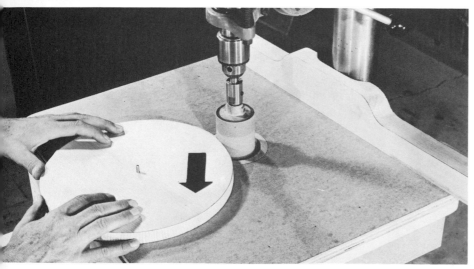

You get perfect circles when you pivot-guide the work. Best way is to advance the work until the drum is cutting. Then lock the slide and rotate the work in the direction of the arrow.

You can do freehand drum sanding too. A good way to distress edges when you want that hand-hewn look on a project.

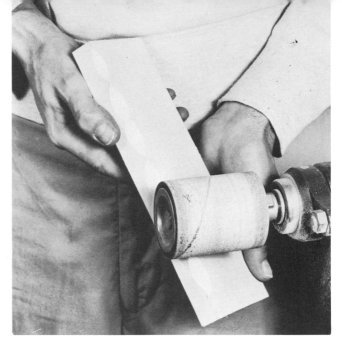

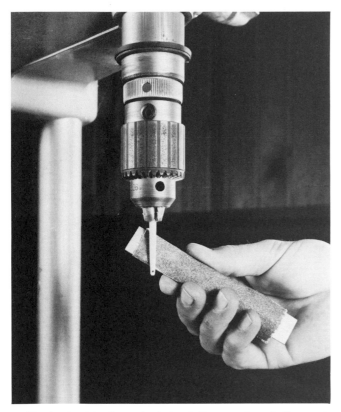

To do shorter pieces, just chuck them and apply the sandpaper. Sandpaper wrapped around a block of wood will produce a more uniform finish.

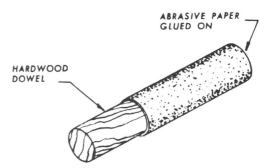

ABRASIVE PAPER
GLUED ON

HARDWOOD
DOWEL

You can make your own special size drum sanders by gluing abrasive paper around a length of dowel.

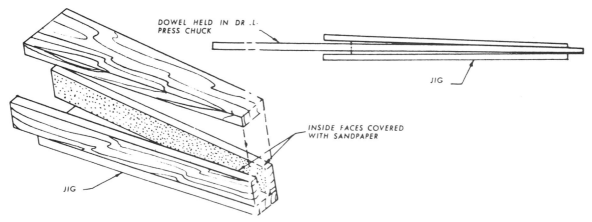

DOWEL HELD IN DR .L.
PRESS CHUCK

JIG

INSIDE FACES COVERED
WITH SANDPAPER

JIG

For special applications think about special jigs, like this one for tapering dowel to be used for ship model masts.

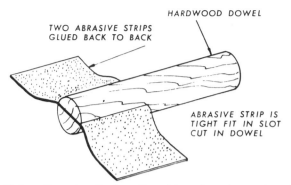

Make a flap wheel by inserting strips of sandpaper in a slot cut in a dowel. Such a flexible sander can be used on odd-shaped pieces or to smooth small holes and plastics.

Uniform cuts on four sides with the fly cutter (see opposite page) can result in attractive lamp bases, railings, posts, etc. Use the quill stop to control cut-depth. Clamp the work securely and be accurate with layout.

Boring decorative concentric circles is done in successive steps with the cut-diameter reduced for each. After boring, the outside of the part can be shaped as a circle, oval, square, whatever.

centers accurately and drill pilot holes first, either by working with a similar size bit or by taking the cutting blade out of the tool and using the pilot drill alone.

Always clamp the work and run the drill press at a slow speed. Do larger circles first and use the quill stop to control depth of cut. As with all fly cutters, keep hands away from the cutting area. Use a slow feed; and when the tool is at full depth, hold it there a second or two. A burnishing effect results that helps produce a smooth finish.

You can increase speed as you decrease the hole diameter. If the wood you are using leaves a rough nap, try dampening the wood after the initial cuts. When it dries, make a very light smoothing cut to remove the fuzz raised by the moisture.

The pilot-drill holes can be left open for a lacy effect; or they can be plugged with dowels, discs or buttons. Such pieces can have a contrasting tone. While the finished jobs can be spray painted, natural finishes seem more appropriate, especially on hardwoods.

Decorative effects can be achieved by drilling on the center line of two boards that are clamped together. After the boards are strip-cut, the slats can be joined edge-to-edge to form fancy, pierced panels.

Sometimes, simply a pattern of overlapping holes can create a special design. Mortising bits and chisels can be used to pierce stock that is then cut into slats.

V-BLOCK WORK

V-blocks make excellent holders for drilling diametrical holes through cylinders and tubes. The V-shape is formed with saw cuts; the holder is clamped to the drill-press table so the point of the bit is on the V's center line. The result is that the longitudinal diameter of the work is put on the same plane.

When drilling a series of holes, it's best to draw a line on the work to help keep you from rotating it as you go. When the job calls for a series of equally spaced holes, you can drive a nail through the first hole drilled: the distance from the nail to the bit equals the hole spacing.

MORTISING

Mortise-and-tenon combinations account for some of the strongest and most durable joints in woodworking. The closest competition is the dowel joint, but only when two dowels are used. Twin dowels are necessary to gain the anti-twist strength that a tenon in a mortise provides automatically.

The tenon is an easy table-saw job, but the mortise sometimes puzzles the beginning craftsman. The mortising bit forms a hole much like a drill bit, but it is encased in a square, steel sleeve that is really a four-sided

Clamp two similar pieces together and bore deep holes on the joint line. Separate the pieces and strip cut to produce slats that you can join edge-to-edge for open work panels.

The intersection of two V-cuts makes a good holding situation for drilling into or through, ball-shapes.

The mortising bit can be turned in the chuck so you get a "diamond" shape.

Then, strip cutting produces the slats that you join edge-to-edge to make a continuous pattern.

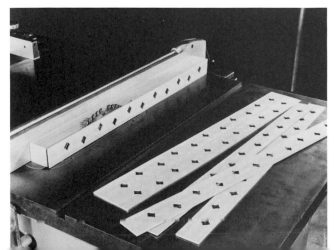

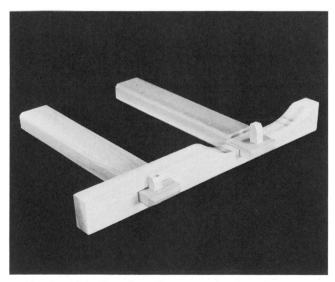

The "tusk" is like a key. The square hole you form for it is spaced so placing the tusk forces the rail against the shoulder of the tenon. Exposed tusk and tenon-end are used on some furniture styles as decorative details.

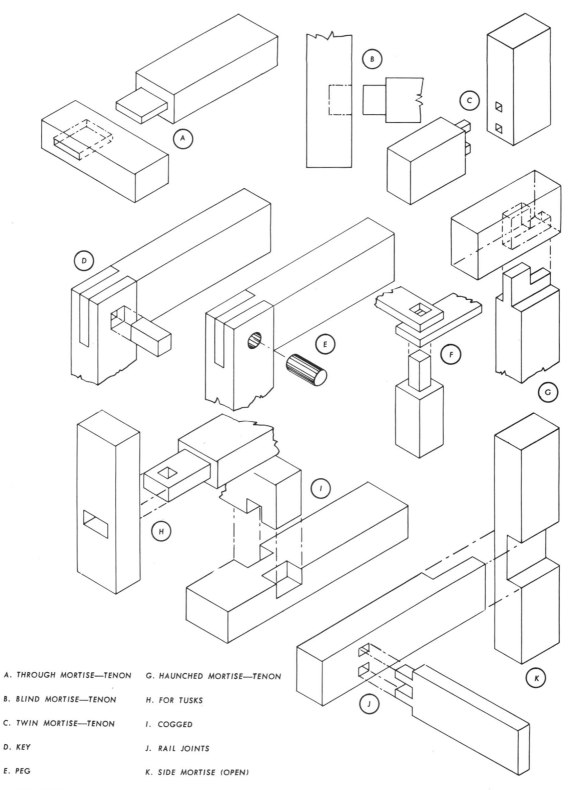

A. THROUGH MORTISE—TENON

B. BLIND MORTISE—TENON

C. TWIN MORTISE—TENON

D. KEY

E. PEG

F. THREE WAY

G. HAUNCHED MORTISE—TENON

H. FOR TUSKS

I. COGGED

J. RAIL JOINTS

K. SIDE MORTISE (OPEN)

Various types of joints you can do using mortising equipment on the drill press. The "key" and the "peg" are additions that lock the basic joint.

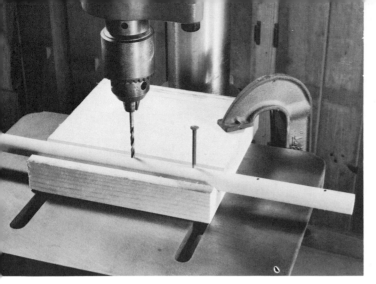

A setup like this will provide for automatic spacing. Drill the hole for the nail guide in the V after drilling the first hole in the work. Then drill successive holes.

There is bound to be some splintering where the chisel breaks through. This is minimized by using a scrap block under the work; but for a perfect job, work on stock that is slightly thicker than the part needed. After mortising, do a light shaving cut on the table saw to remove the imperfections.

When you get to the tenon, don't size it so it must be wedged into the mortise or cut it too long. There must be room for excess glue. Keep the tenon shorter by about $\frac{1}{16}''$ or chamfer its end.

The mortising bit and chisel set does two things. The bit forms the round hole to remove most of the waste—the chisel cuts away the remaining corners to produce the square hole.

chisel. The job of the chisel is to clean out the corners left by the bit, and the result is a square hole. Since one side of the chisel is slotted, waste chips can escape.

In order to use the chisels, you must have a special casting that locks in some fashion to the end of the quill. Usually, this component is part of a kit you buy that includes a special fence and a hold-down.

Two factors apply no matter what your equipment is. The chisel must be square to the fence so cutting will be done parallel to the work edge. There must be at least $\frac{1}{32}''$ — but not more than $\frac{1}{16}''$ — clearance between the spurs on the bit and the cutting edge of the chisel. Keep this clearance to a minimum but not so tight that you create excessive friction between bit and chisel. Not enough clearance will result in overheating and damage to the tools. Too much clearance is needless and can result in large waste chips that may clog inside the chisel.

An interesting variation of the basic technique is shown here. The fingers may be done as long slots which are then cut apart on the table saw.

Generally, the larger the chisel, the slower the speed should be, especially in hardwoods. For chisels up to $\frac{1}{2}''$ size, use a speed range of 1,700 rpm's to 3,500 rpm's in softwood and a maximum of about 2,000 rpm's in hardwoods. These rules apply best under ideal conditions. There are differences in softwoods and hardwoods, even in boards cut from the same tree. You must also consider whether you are cutting across the grain, with the grain, or into end grain.

Regard these rules as generalizations and break them according to how the cut is going. Stay away from excessive feed pressure; but, on the other hand, a feather touch won't work since the chisel cuts under quill-feed pressure only. The rate of feed and speed are probably correct when the waste chips move smoothly up the flutes of the bit and easily out through the escape slot in the chisels. Retracting can also help to keep things going well. Control the depth of blind mortises by using the quill-feed stop rod.

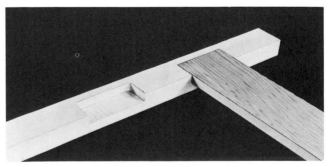

A side mortise provides for flush rail insertion. When the cut is required on matching pieces, you can often do two at once by clamping the parts together face-to-face.

SPECIAL MORTISING JIG

You don't have to restrict mortising to square stock. If you make a V-jig accessory to replace the conventional fence arrangement, you can form square cavities on round stock or on the corners of square pieces. Operational considerations don't change, and you use all the items that normally attach to the quill.

These procedures make it possible, for example, to mortise rails into round legs, to attach corner-to-corner stretchers or rails when square legs are used, and to install shelves on round posts by forming radial mortises.

When you make the jig, be careful of the dimension from the center of the "V" to the back edge of the jig. It should equal the distance from the center of the spindle to the back edge of the table to easily achieve alignment each time the jig is used.

When you use the jig be sure that the spindle and "V" have the same center line and that the chisel is square. Place your work in the "V" and trap it with the hold-down. Similar cuts on multiple pieces can be gauged easily by tack-nailing a stop block across the "V." The same idea applies when you do radial mortising. Alignment of repeat cuts when forming slots is controlled by drawing a longitudinal line on the work after you have formed the first cavity. Thereafter, keep the edge of the chisel on the line.

Concentric mortises are feasible if you devise a means of holding the work in relation to the cutting tool. The same modified screw clamp that was shown for simple concentric drilling can be used. It will work fine on either round or square stock.

Mortising equipment can also be used for making large interior cutouts in panels of wood or other materials. Unlike drilled holes, the mortises give the cutouts square corners. After the cuts are made, make straight cuts along the sides of the cutout by working on the table saw.

SPIRALING DOWELS

Drill a horizontal hole through a block to fit the dowel being grooved. Drill a vertical hole through the surface of the block until it meets the horizontal hole. The vertical hole is for the router bit that will do the cutting. Run the drill press at high speed and push the dowel through the horizontal hole. After you make contact with the router bit, rotate the dowel as you continue to feed it through. This is a good way to do grooves for gluing in any common dowel.

PLUG CUTTERS

Concealing a screw or bolt hole with a plug cut from an ordinary dowel that you buy in the local hardware

USING THE MORTISE CHISEL

Typical mortising setup on a drill press. Special casting attaches to the end of the quill and is used with the regular chuck. U-shaped foot holds the work down, L-shaped rod keeps it against the fence.

To remove the stock between the end cuts, make successive overlapping cuts. Ideally, these should be about three-quarters of the full chisel width. Stay as close to the ideal as you can. Mortises give the cutouts square corners.

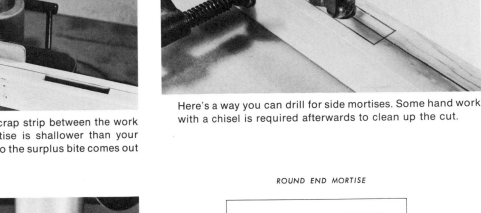

Here's a way you can drill for side mortises. Some hand work with a chisel is required afterwards to clean up the cut.

To do a side mortise, place a scrap strip between the work and the fence. If the side mortise is shallower than your smallest chisel, make the setup so the surplus bite comes out of the back-up strip.

ROUND END MORTISE

TWO END HOLES ARE DRILLED FIRST.
HOLES BETWEEN ARE DRILLED NEXT (SOLID LINES)
CLEAN-OUT HOLES ARE DRILLED LAST (DOTTED LINES)

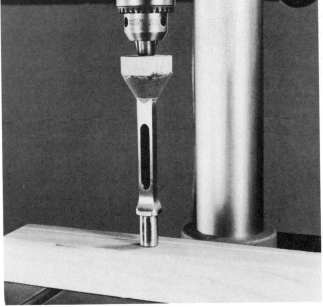

Chisels must be sharp, since pressure of the quill is the only push behind them. An emery wheel makes a good sharpening tool. Make one by shaping a cone to match the chisel bevel. Glue on emery paper and then use as shown here. Just a light touch is required.

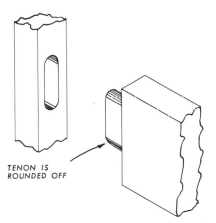

TENON IS ROUNDED OFF

Working in the round is no trick at all if you use standard mortising equipment and a V-jig we developed for the purpose. Place your round work in the V and secure it with the hold-down. Proceed with cutting in normal fashion making end cuts first and then cleaning away the stock between.

Forming mortises with a drill or a router bit, results in round-end slots. It's okay to go this way but the tenon must be rounded off to fit.

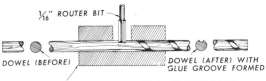

⅟₁₆" ROUTER BIT

DOWEL (BEFORE)   DOWEL (AFTER) WITH GLUE GROOVE FORMED

GUIDE BLOCK CLAMPED TO DRILL PRESS TABLE

How to cut spiral grooves in dowels. A special guide block is required for each size dowel you wish to treat this way.

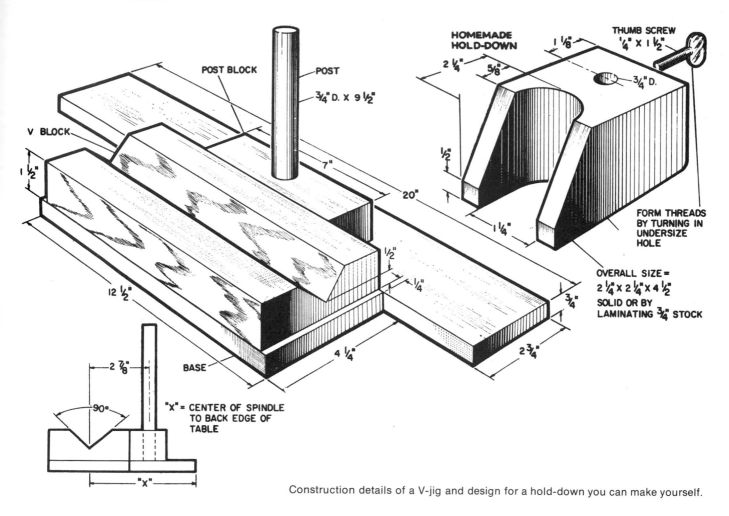

Construction details of a V-jig and design for a hold-down you can make yourself.

store is not the best method to use. Such items are not always accurate, and you can't find them in all kinds of wood. Furthermore, it would be too much to expect that the grain of the plug would match that of the wood you are using. Plug cutters are good solutions to this little headache since you can cut plugs from the same material you are working with and match the grain so closely that the plug would be hard to find.

The plug cutter used in the drill press can also make dowels. Length is limited to about two inches, but this is long enough for dowel joints. You can use scrap pieces of lumber as stock; and since hardwood dowels are not inexpensive this alone helps justify the cost of the tool.

In addition to forming plugs and dowels of wood, the plug cutters can be utilized to form integral tenons whether the stock is square or round.

METAL DRILLING TECHNIQUES

When you drill metal, establish firm support for the work as close to the cutting area as possible. You can place work directly on the table. Center the bit over the table hole or place a scrap block under the work as you do when drilling wood. Parallel supports are often used under the work, but it's an error to separate them by much. Metal drilling develops considerable twisting action, especially when the drill breaks through. Therefore, keep the work clamped at all times or provide stops that will do a similar job.

Good operating speeds will vary with the size of the drill and the material being worked. The accompanying chart is a reasonable guide for most types of work you might do. If the speed suggested is not available, use the closest low speed possible.

Good speed and correct feed when done with a sharp cutter will curl a ribbon of metal out of the hole. The bit should cut constantly or you will merely rub the metal, accomplishing nothing but dulling the tool.

Twist drills are available in fractional, letter or number sizes. Since you probably won't be completely equipped with all three, you can work from the chart of decimal equivalents to select a size that comes close to what is called for.

PLUG CUTTERS

Crossgrain plugs cut from the same material as the project are not easily seen when they are used to fill screw or bolt holes. You can match the grain direction, even the tone when you work carefully.

This type of plug cutter is strictly for drill-press use. It will cut plugs or short dowels as shown here. They are cut in the end grain of the wood so the dowel will have a strong cross-section. Run between 1,200 rpms and 1,800 rpms. Feed slowly and retract frequently.

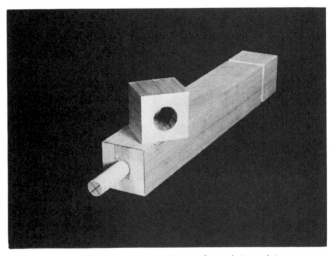

By using the plug cutter you can form integral tenons on square or round stock.

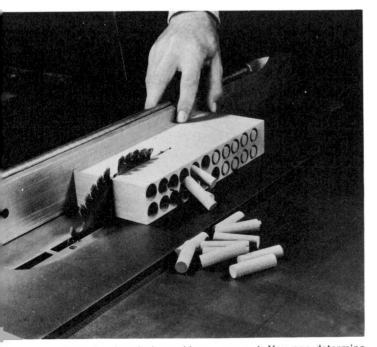

Free the dowels by making a saw cut. You can determine dowel length by this cut. *Don't* make this kind of cut so the loose dowels will be between the saw blade and the fence.

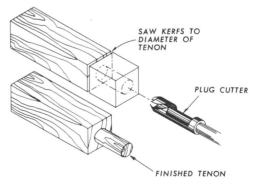

SAW KERFS TO DIAMETER OF TENON

PLUG CUTTER

FINISHED TENON

The idea is to saw kerfs to match the diameter of the tenon and then to plug-cut to meet the kerfs.

227

Work with a sharp scriber to do layout work. On some metals a scribed line doesn't show too clearly. In addition, it's often poor practice to incise the line, so surface-coaters are used. By using these and scribing lightly, you can do layout work without cutting into the metal surface.

Always use a prick punch to mark hole centers. In addition, a center punch can be used to form a slight well into which you seat the drill point when you start drilling. Without it, especially on round surfaces, the drill point can wander off the mark.

You can work with extreme precision if you use the prick-punch mark as the center for scribing the hole size you want. The scribed circle is a guide to tell you if the drill is moving off-center. To get to a $\frac{1}{2}''$ hole, it isn't uncommon to start at $\frac{1}{16}''$ or $\frac{1}{8}''$ and then work up through several other sizes to get to the final $\frac{1}{2}''$.

DRILLING IN METALS

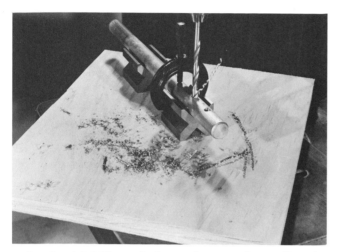

Good metal drilling calls for maximum work security and a feed-speed combination that causes the waste to emerge as a twisting ribbon.

Good way to counteract twist when drilling metal is to use a nut-and-bolt setup like this. This is especially good when you must do a number of similar pieces.

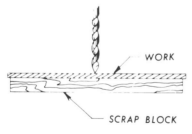

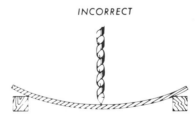

Good support is achieved by using a scrap block under the work as you do with wood drilling. When using parallel supports, keep them close to the cutting area.

MATERIAL	DYE
Rough Metals	White or blue chalk, rubbed on surface.
Castings	Whiting (mixture: 50-50 white lead and turpentine).
Smooth Steel	Copper sulfate (2 tablespoons in 1 cup water—crystals available at drugstore or chemical house) or layout compound (purple coating, available at hardware store).
Bright Sheet Metal	Layout compound.

Keep layout dye in discarded shoe polish bottle—one with dauber which may be used to apply the dye. Apply dye evenly and smoothly on the surface of the metal.

Suggested surface-coaters you can use when preparing various types of metal for layout work. Keep scribe marks light—just barely enough to scribe through the coating.

DRILL SIZE	MATERIAL			
	SOFT METALS	SOFT CAST IRON	MILD STEEL	PLASTICS AND HARD RUBBER
1/16	6,000—6,500	6,000—6,500	5,000—6,500	6,000—6,500
3/32	6,000—6,500	4,500—5,500	4,000—5,000	6,000—6,500
1/8	6,000—6,500	3,500—4,500	3,000—4,000	5,000—6,000
5/32	5,000—6,000	3,000—3,500	2,500—3,000	4,000—5,000
3/16	5,000—6,000	2,500—3,000	2,000—2,500	3,500—4,000
7/32	4,500—5,000	2,000—2,500	2,000—2,500	3,000—3,500
1/4	4,500—5,000	2,000—2,500	1,500—2,000	3,000—3,500
9/32	4,000—4,500	1,500—2,000	1,500—2,000	2,500—3,000
5/16	3,500—4,000	1,500—2,000	1,000—1,500	2,000—2,500
11/32	3,000—3,500	1,500—2,000	1,000—1,500	2,000—2,500
3/8	3,000—3,500	1,500—2,000	1,000—1,500	1,500—2,000
13/32	2,500—3,000	1,500—2,000	1,000—1,500	1,500—2,000
7/16	2,500—3,000	1,000—1,500	400—1,000	1,500—2,000
15/32	2,000—2,500	1,000—1,500	400—1,000	1,500—2,000
1/2	2,000—2,500	1,000—1,500	400—1,000	1,000—1,500
9/16	1,500—2,000			1,000—1,500
5/8	1,500—2,000			1,000—1,500
11/16	1,500—2,000			1,000—1,500
3/4	1,500—2,000			400—1,000
FEED	Medium	Medium	Heavy	Light
LUBRICANT	Dry or paraffin oil	Dry	Lard oil	Dry

Speed and lubricant suggestions for various kinds of non-wood drilling. The "feed" refers to how strongly you bring the cutting tool to bear. Notice, it isn't recommended that you go over $\frac{1}{2}$" in iron or steel.

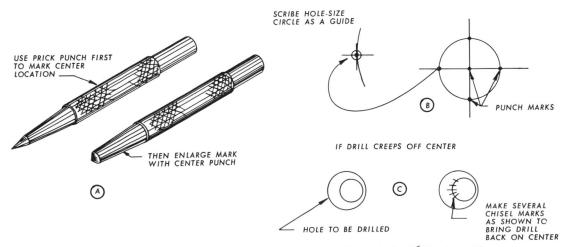

Hole locations should be marked with a prick punch and then indented further with a center punch. This is not too critical on very small holes.

A sure way to locate work so the hole mark is centered exactly with the drill is to work with a centering pin. This doesn't have to be any more than a short length of $\frac{1}{8}''$ or $\frac{1}{4}''$ drill rod sharpened at one end. In practice, you secure the pin in the chuck and lower it so the point engages the center-punch mark. Then you clamp the work and substitute the drill for the pin.

TAPPING

The drill press may be used to overcome the difficulty of keeping a tap square to the work. Any of the three kinds of taps, when secured in the drill-press chuck, will be square to the work surface throughout the job.

However, tapping is never done under power. The drill press merely assures squareness; the tapping is done by turning the chuck by hand as you apply very light feed pressure. To do this, use a short length of metal rod (or a suitable bolt) in the chuck holes normally used by the chuck key.

The tap works by cutting metal. To remove waste, turn the chuck to the right about one-fourth turn for every half turn to the left. Use a drop of oil on the tap as you go. Be careful when withdrawing the tap. Keep some feed pressure as you continue to turn the chuck to the right until the tap is clear.

SPOT POLISHING

Getting an attractive finish on a metal surface by "grinding" overlapping spots is spot polishing. The tools can be made as shown in the accompanying drawing. The abrasive you use can be judged in relation to the hardness of the metal. The plain rod that is illustrated can be used when a mixture of emery dust and light oil is applied to the work. Abrasive paper or steel wool can be worked dry.

Always do some test work first on scrap stock. Use a fence so you can move the work in a straight line and try to overlap the spots evenly. Feed pressure should be very light; and speed must be judged on the basis of the abrasive, the material being worked, and the results you are getting. Start at a slow speed and increase the speed gradually to what does the job you want.

When you make the tools, be sure that the working end will bear flat against the work.

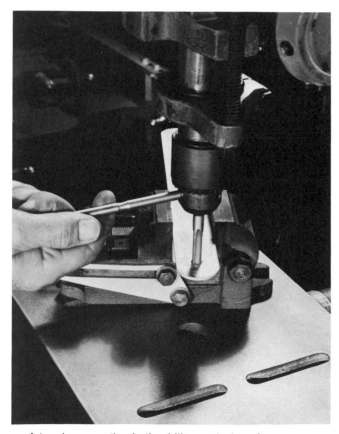

A tapping operation in the drill press is done for accuracy— it is *never* done under power, not in the home workshop anyway. Tapping is done by turning the chuck by hand.

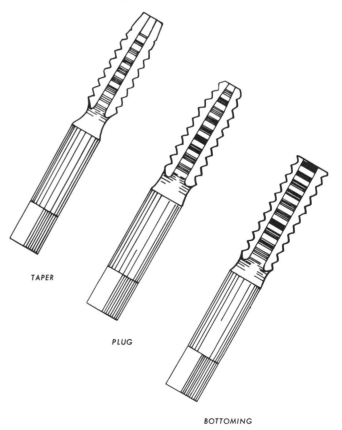

TAPER

PLUG

BOTTOMING

When you thread a hole that is clear through the material, use the "taper" or "plug" tap. When the hole does not go through, start the job with the "taper," use the "plug" to the bottom of the hole, finish up with the "bottoming" tap.

TAP			TAP DRILL		DRILL FOR CLEARANCE
NO. OR FRAC-TION	NC	NF	NC	NF	
0		80		3/64	51
1	64	72	53	53	47
2	56	64	50	50	42
3	48	56	47	45	37
4	40	48	43	42	31
5	40	44	38	37	29
6	32	40	36	33	26
8	32	36	29	29	17
10	24	32	25	21	8
12	24	28	16	14	1
1/4	20	28	7	3	Same as tap
5/16	18	24	F	I	Same as tap
3/8	16	24	5/16	Q	Same as tap
7/16	14	20	U	25/64	Same as tap
1/2	13	20	27/64	29/64	Same as tap
9/16	12	18	31/64	33/64	Same as tap
5/8	11	18	17/32	37/64	Same as tap
3/4	10	16	21/32	11/16	Same as tap
7/8	9	14	49/64	13/16	Same as tap
1"	8	14	7/8	15/16	Same as tap

Drill the correct size holes for each tap you plan to use. This is important for easy work and good threads. The clearance hole will remove threads should this ever be necessary.

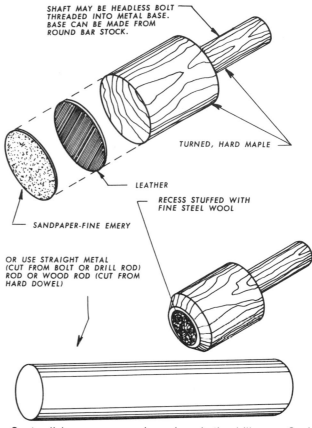

Spot polishers you can make and use in the drill press. Such an operation is often referred to as "damaskeening."

To polish rods, chuck in the drill press and apply an abrasive strip as shown here. You can work down through progressively finer abrasive and end up with steel wool if you wish a super finish.

Special tools are available for forming threads in wood. The drill-press technique is usable here too.

LATHES

The lathe is one of the few woodworking machines on which you can turn out a finished project. For example, work held between its centers might become a lamp base; a block mounted on a faceplate might become a salad bowl. Shaping, smoothing, and finishing are all done right in the machine.

Reactions to the lathe differ. Some people immediately operate the tool without regard for some basic considerations; others assume that a long period of apprenticeship will be required before they dare try an actual part or project. The latter approach is safer, but it should not be carried to an extreme. The truth is that a beginner can form a good piece of work immediately as long as he uses lathe chisels in a simple fashion. The professional uses a "cutting" action whenever he can whereas the learner should stay with a "scraping" action, a technique that enables him to use any chisel right from the start. In so doing, he can accomplish quality work even though he won't win any speed contests. He can be immediately productive while taking an occasional crack at more advanced chisel usage.

GENERAL CHARACTERISTICS

In concept, all lathes are the same. They differ in features, weight and capacity. The main parts include a *headstock* that is in a fixed position, a *tailstock* that is movable, and a *tool rest* that is adjustable. All parts are mounted on a *bed* or *ways*. The tool rest and the tailstock are movable laterally so they can be situated to suit the size of the work.

Spindle turnings are mounted between the headstock and the tailstock. Bowls, trays and the like are mounted on a *faceplate* that secures only to the headstock. When work can't be mounted between centers and is too small to do on a faceplate, a *screw-center* can be employed. This too secures only to the headstock and is designed so small pieces can be worked. In addition, universal chucks, three-jaw chucks and holding devices that you can make yourself can be used with the lathe. Therefore, on a lathe you can fabricate projects or parts for projects that range from corn cob holders to heavy bed posts.

Lathe capacities are figured in terms of maximum spindle length and the maximum diameter of the work

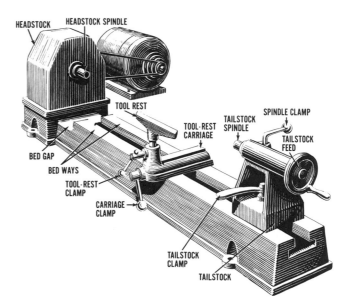

BASIC PARTS OF A WOODWORKING LATHE

that can be swung over the bed. Usually, the latter is used to indicate lathe size. On a 12″ lathe, the bed is approximately 6″ from the headstock. Thus, you can swing a 12″ faceplate turning. The greater the faceplate work you can mount, the longer the distance will be between centers.

The spindle capacity does not limit what you can do in terms of a project. To go beyond the basic work size you can mount, you simply do two turnings and then join them. On many lathes you can do outboard turning. For such work, the workpiece is mounted on the outboard side of the headstock so the work radius is limited by the distance from the center to the floor. Therefore, even the lathe-size figure given in catalogs isn't a true picture of maximum work size.

Safety. Generally, the lathe is a "safe" tool. Of course, the usual clothing precautions apply. Half sleeves are good; long sleeves are fine as long as they don't flap and the cuffs are tight around the wrists. Follow the rules concerning handling chisels and hand position on the

Work that doesn't go between centers and is too small to mount on a faceplate can usually be handled on a screw-center. Here, a duplicate has been turned for an exact match of an existing drawer pull.

These are typical lathe jobs, ranging from delicate rings to maximum-size spindles and outboard-turned trays. The beginner, by using a recommended chisel action, can do things like this right off.

Other attachments, like this universal chuck, may be used in the headstock. Note the use of a file to shape up a length of metal which is held in the chuck.

"Heavy-duty" lathe is all cast iron construction. "Gap" in the bed permits turning 12″ on a faceplate. The maximum capacity between centers is 37″. Multi-step pulleys provide a speed range from 700 to 4,250 rpms.

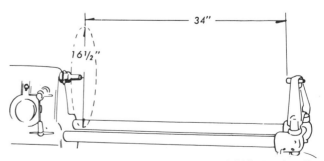

Lathe capacities are figured in terms of "A", 2× the distance from the center to the bed and "B", the maximum distance between the headstock and tailstock centers.

233

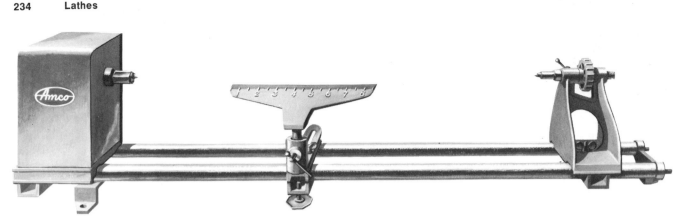

Low-priced, "unadorned" lathe with 12″ × 36″ capacity. Even though such designs are light and basic, you can do efficient turning with them.

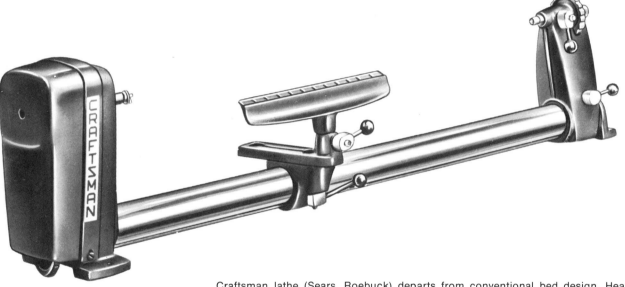

Craftsman lathe (Sears, Roebuck) departs from conventional bed design. Headstock, tailstock, tool-rest base, all mount on a single, heavy tube. Tube is keyed for component alignment. Adjustments are made by turning knob-levers.

tool rest. Be extremely careful with speeds, especially when doing roughing operations. Wearing goggles is a good idea although they are more important for preliminary steps than they are for final sanding and finishing.

Check how secure the mounted work is before you start cutting and, occasionally, during the turning. Do this even more on softwood than on hardwood. Always spin the work by hand before you flick the switch. Keep all chisels sharp.

Adjustment. The one major lathe adjustment is alignment of the *spur center*, which is in the headstock, with the *cup center*, which is in the tailstock. How this is accomplished and maintained may vary from tool to tool, and you'll find instructions for doing it in the owner's manual. The important thing is for the points on

the centers to meet when they are viewed from above (vertical alignment) and when they are viewed from the side (horizontal alignment). Since the spur center has a fixed position, any necessary adjustments are made by moving the cup center.

Speeds. The basic rule is to use slow speeds for large work and fast speeds for small work. On all jobs speed changes should be made during the work. You'll notice in the accompanying speed chart that the lowest speeds are suggested for roughing operations and that the rpm's move up as you get into the shaping stages. The high speeds are used for final cuts and for finishing. The exception occurs when you get to maximum-size workpieces. Actually, this restriction is more a safety factor than anything else.

You can get quite close to the suggested speeds if your

For spindle turning, the work is mounted between the spur center in the headstock and the cup center in the tailstock.

For bowls, trays and the like, the stock is mounted on a faceplate that secures to the headstock in place of the spur center.

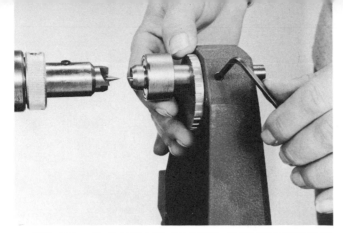

The main adjustment puts the points of the two centers on the same vertical and horizontal centerlines. Some lathes require this adjustment, others do not. Check your owner's manual to see if yours requires this alignment.

lathe is equipped with a variable speed changer. In most cases, however, you'll be working with belts and will have to use specific speeds provided by the relationship between pulleys. Stay as close to the suggested speeds as you can. If you must (at least until you acquire good skills on the lathe), use a lower speed rather than a higher one.

At all times, let the action of the lathe and of the work be your best guide. If it's difficult to hold the chisel or if the work or the lathe vibrates excessively, it's a good sign that you are going too fast.

Centers. The drive center in the headstock has a point for centering the work plus spurs that dig into the wood. The spurs must always seat firmly in order for the wood to turn. It's a good idea to work on one of the spurs with a file, making a very small half-round shape or forming a bevel at one end. In doing this, if you ever have to remove a spindle turning from the lathe before it is complete, you'll be able to re-mate it with the spur

center, placing it back in the original position.

The center in the tailstock can be plain or cupped. The cupped design is better simply because it provides more bearing surface and thus less chance for the mounting to loosen. With either one, you should check occasionally, especially on softwoods, and tighten the fit if necessary. Many craftsmen use a tiny drop of oil on the dead center as a lubricant. However, don't overdo it since the oil can stain the wood. Paste wax works fine but don't use too much of it; just polish the point on the center.

The best method is to use a ball-bearing live center in the tailstock. The point on this turns with the work and, therefore, eliminates the loosening and burning problems you can encounter with a dead center.

Faceplates. Faceplates come in different sizes, ranging from about 3″ up to 10″. They are always mounted in the headstock and make it possible to turn work that can't be mounted between centers. In this way you can do such work as bowls, trays, round boxes, and bases for spindles.

Screws are used to attach the work to the plate. The important consideration is to use screws that are heavy enough to provide security but not so long that you may cut into them when shaping the project.

The tool rest. The tool rest is an adjustable ledge on which you rest the chisel when you apply it to the work. It can be moved either laterally or vertically and will pivot so you have complete freedom of adjustment in relation to the work whether it is a spindle turning or a faceplate job.

The ideal position for the tool rest is about $\frac{1}{8}$″ away

MATERIAL AND DIAMETER	ROUGHING CUT	SHAPING CUT	FINISHING CUT
	revolutions per minute	revolutions per minute	revolutions per minute
wood up to 2″	910	2,590	4,250
wood 2″ to 4″	810	2,375	3,380
wood 4″ to 6″	650	1,825	2,375
wood 6″ to 8″	650	1,200	1,825
wood 8″ to 10″	650	910	1,025
wood over 10″	650	650	650
plastics up to 3″	2,200	3,125	3,875
plastics over 3″	1,025	1,200	1,680
non-ferrous metals up to 3″ (with carbide-tipped tools)	650	1,300	3,125

Suggested lathe speeds for various operations.

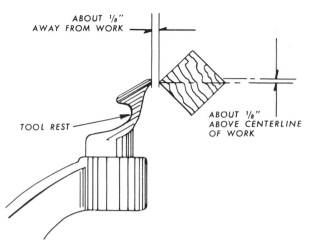

ABOUT ⅛" AWAY FROM WORK

TOOL REST

ABOUT ⅛" ABOVE CENTERLINE OF WORK

The theoretically correct position for the tool rest. It's not always possible to work this way but stay as close to it as you can. Let the chisel play against the rest.

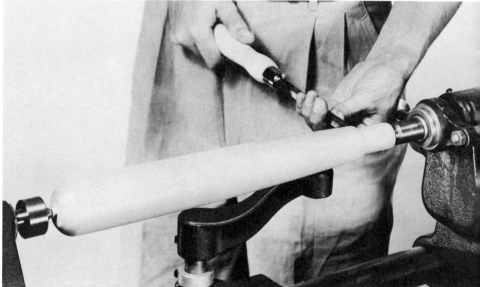

The important consideration is to place the tool rest to provide maximum support for the chisel near the area to be cut.

This applies to faceplate work and to any other job.

from the work and about ⅛″ above the work center line. It's a difficult position to maintain constantly unless you are doing work such as straight cylinders or tapers. Still, it's generally a good rule and should be remembered at least as a guide post.

Lathe chisels. A good set of chisels should include a *gouge*, a *skew*, a *squarenose*, a *parting tool*, a *spear point* and a *roundnose*. Perhaps the least important of these are the squarenose and the spear point. An ordinary butt chisel can be used in place of the squarenose; the skew, when placed on its side and used in a scraping action, will do many of the jobs performed by the spear point.

If you don't maintain a keen edge on the chisels, you'll be working under a handicap. Your best bet is to study the shape of the tool before you start using it. Keep a stone handy and, as you work, touch up the cutting edge occasionally. You'll find, if you do this, that *re-grinding* jobs, necessary when the chisel must be re-shaped, will be required very infrequently.

Carbide-tipped tools are available in various sizes but mostly in roundnose or squarenose shapes. The cutting edges are made of an extremely hard material that will hold sharpness much longer than steel. They can be used on wood but, more importantly, they make it possible to do freehand turning on metals and plastics at wood-working speeds. More about them later.

Hand positioning. The basic rule is to hold the forward end of the chisel in your left hand, the handle in your right hand. Don't use your left hand like a fist. Instead, rest the tool toward the tips of the fingers with your thumb gripping against the side or on the top of the blade. Your index finger should rest comfortably on the tool-rest ledge.

When you are making a cut that is parallel to the work, the index finger acts as a depth gauge. Both hands and the chisel move as a unit. For many types of shaping cuts, view the contact point between the chisel and the tool rest as a pivot. This point is just about maintained as the right hand provides the cutting action. On many types of scraping cuts, the tool is held at right angles to the work and simply moved forward.

Always feed the chisel slowly and steadily; you don't want to force it and you don't want to jab it into the work. Make the initial contact cautiously; then get a little bolder as you cut. You don't want to overdo it, but on the other hand, just rubbing the tool against the wood won't get you anywhere.

It's a good idea to keep tools so they are behind you or to one side to avoid reaching over the lathe. Don't check work for roundness with your fingers, especially on roughing jobs. Stop the lathe to check or rest the blade

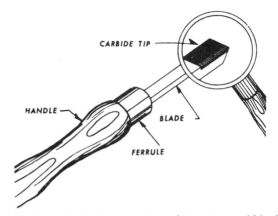

Carbide-tipped tools have an edge of tungsten-carbide. It is an extremely hard material that holds a keen edge for a much longer time than ordinary metals.

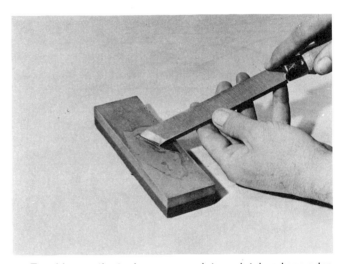

Touching up the tools as you work to maintain a keen edge is good practice. An occasional touch on an oil stone will do much in this area.

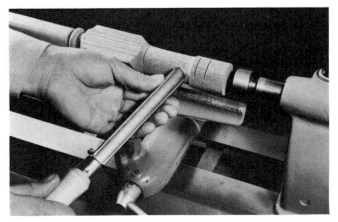

This is correct and safe, hand and chisel position. Note how the index finger of the left hand rides the tool-rest ledge.

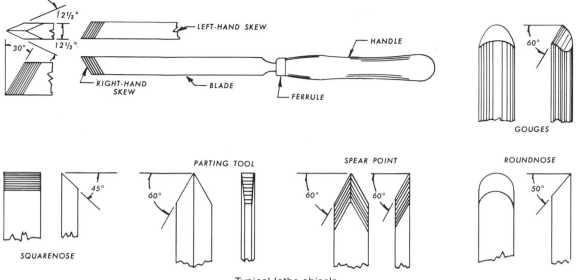

Typical lathe chisels.

of the tool lightly on the turning wood. You can tell by vibration of the tool whether the work is approaching roundness.

Three actions of lathe chisels. Lathe chisels scrape, cut, or shear.

Scraping is the easiest and safest of the three and the best for the beginner to use. All the tools can be used in such fashion but the technique, even by professionals, is most applicable to the roundnose, the parting tool, the squarenose and the spear point.

The action gives good results and minimizes the chances of gouging. The idea is to place the tool on a horizontal plane and to advance it slowly into the work. The cut that is made is the reverse of the chisel shape. For example, a roundnose tool will produce a cove. The cove size is not limited to the chisel size. You can, as you penetrate, pivot the cutting edge in a uniform arc. This has to produce a cove that is broader in its radius than a straight feed would produce.

The scraping action is not limited to shaping. The gouge for roughing (bringing square work to round) can be used in similar fashion. What you do is advance the gouge until it is making a slight cut (from $\frac{1}{16}''$ to $\frac{1}{8}''$); then, while maintaining the penetration, move the cutting edge parallel to the work. Repeat this until the work has come to full round.

When you do a straight scraping action with a spear point, you get a V-shape; with the parting tool, you get a groove. A squarenose, depending on the number of cuts you do, will produce a fillet or a band.

You can work a bit faster if you start the scraping action of the tool with a point just a bit below the work center line and move it upward as you move it forward.

You will never get as smooth a finish with a scraping action as you will with a shearing action, but all you need do to bring the work to par is apply sandpaper.

As you can see in the sketch on page 240 of the three techniques, the cutting action calls for bringing the tool edge up by lowering the handle of the chisel. The edge of the tool will remove material in much the same way that a hand plane cuts the edge of a board. This is a situation where it's easy to "dig" the tool so, more than elsewhere, keep the feed light and make the cut slowly. Jabbing the chisel in suddenly or too deeply can wrench it from your hands. It's also possible to ruin the work by lifting large chunks of it.

The cutting action is something you should try after you have done enough with the scraping action to be really familiar with each of the tools. When you first try it, be cautious. Don't become bold until after you have done enough practicing to build up your confidence. A good cutting action should produce a finish that requires little touchup. This can vary from wood to wood. A grainy species will not impress so much and will require sanding even after a professional cutting action.

The shearing action can separate the expert from the amateur, not in terms of ultimate quality but in production speed. It's done best with the gouge and the skew.

It's an action that requires the tool edge to be moved laterally. It takes a consistent bite, removing a layer of wood from the surface of the stock. This varies, of course, since manipulation of the chisel in a shearing action is relative to the shape you must produce.

When first trying this technique, do it with a gouge on

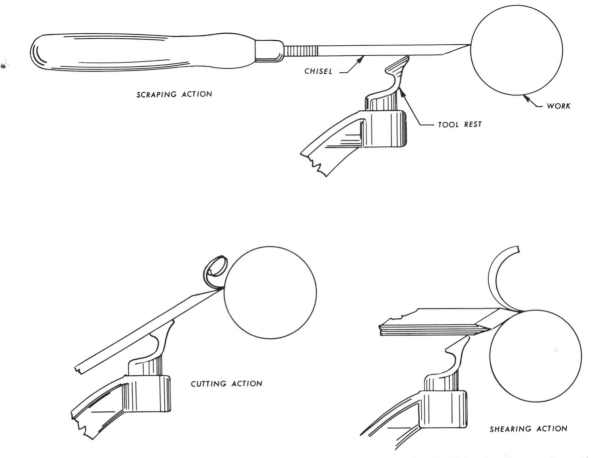

The three chisel actions. The beginner can do a fine job using the scraping action almost exclusively. In the meantime he can practice the cutting and shearing techniques.

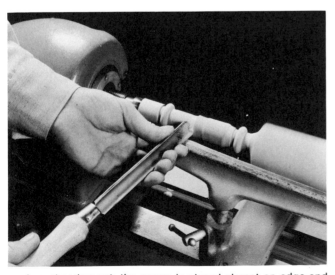

In a shearing cut, the gouge is placed almost on edge and moved parallel to the work. Don't try to cut too deeply, or feed too fast.

a roughing operation. Here, the tool is held almost on edge with your thumb behind it to keep it steady and to feed.

While each lathe chisel will do a category of jobs best, the overlap is so great that it's foolish to try to establish hard-and-fast rules. The tools work differently but the action you use, the feed angle, the cut direction, etc. are what influence the shape you get. A squarenose chisel or a spear point can produce a quality bead even though the skew might be the best tool to use for the job. The parting tool is basically for dimensional cuts, yet it is also very fine for shoulders, cleaning out corners and the like.

Practice a bit with each chisel trying to duplicate the shapes that will be described. Get the "feel" of each tool. Don't be surprised if you develop handling techniques that are "you," a kind of trademark.

APPLICATIONS

The gouge. This is a very versatile tool and may be

used in any one of the three positions. Actually, in some applications, all three of the cutting actions come into play. It's the best tool to use for roughing operations. The scraping action works well enough, but you should try to graduate to the shearing action quickly. Here, the tool is held almost on its side and moved parallel to the work. The depth of cut is maintained by the index finger of the left hand as it rests on the ledge of the tool rest.

Start roughing cuts somewhere along the length of the stock and direct feed toward an end. Move the tool rest laterally until you've done the same cut along the full length of the stock. Then readjust it to bring it closer to the work and repeat the procedure until you have the diameter you need.

This is approximately the routine to follow when you wish to reduce stock in a limited area. Just use the gouge between sizing cuts made with the parting tool.

Overall, the gouge is probably the best tool to use when you need to remove a lot of material. It is not a good tool to use on faceplate work.

The skew. The skew can be used in any one of the three actions. Typically, to scrape, place the tool on a side while you hold it at right angles to the work and then move it directly forward. The result will be a half-V. Flip the chisel and repeat, and you will get a full-V.

You can demonstrate a typical cutting action by holding the tool on its edge and then moving it forward. In this position the tool presents a sharp point to the work. It cuts fast and will leave a smooth finish. When you do this on the end of a cylinder or to square a shoulder, it's best to hold the chisel at a slight angle so that one of the bevels on the cutting edge will be flush against the work. When you work in this manner, you'll be using more than the point of the cutting edge.

Probably the smoothest cut you can make in lathe work is with the skew in a shearing action, but it's one of the toughest to master. Overall, you should picture the cutting point as being near the center of the edge of the chisel and high on the work. You can start by placing a bevel of the cutting edge flat on the work so no cutting occurs; tilt slightly until the edge begins to penetrate. Then move the tool in parallel fashion. Don't try to cut too deeply or to feed too fast.

The skew is often used to do ball shapes and beads. This advanced technique is best started by resting the heel of the cutting edge on the center line of the form and then rotating the chisel in a 45° arc. Since you won't be able to achieve the full shape in one pass, you must imagine the final shape and direct the chisel along lines that, when repeated enough times, will result in the form you want.

The skew is not the tool to use on faceplate work unless you limit it to a scraping action.

The roundnose. This is a very easy chisel to use simply because it is always used in a scraping action. To do a cove, just move the chisel directly forward. To enlarge the cove, combine a pivoting action with the forward feed. The sharper the tool, the faster you will cut and the smoother the results will be.

The roundnose is a very fine tool for faceplate work,

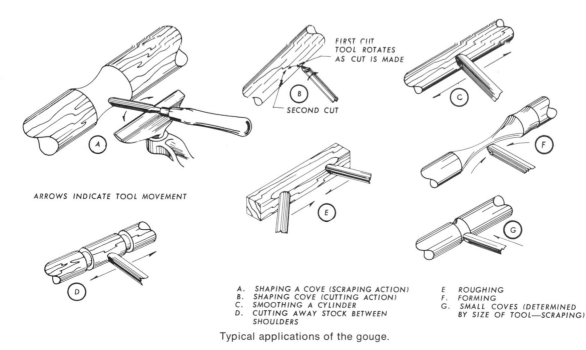

ARROWS INDICATE TOOL MOVEMENT

A. SHAPING A COVE (SCRAPING ACTION)
B. SHAPING COVE (CUTTING ACTION)
C. SMOOTHING A CYLINDER
D. CUTTING AWAY STOCK BETWEEN SHOULDERS

E. ROUGHING
F. FORMING
G. SMALL COVES (DETERMINED BY SIZE OF TOOL—SCRAPING)

Typical applications of the gouge.

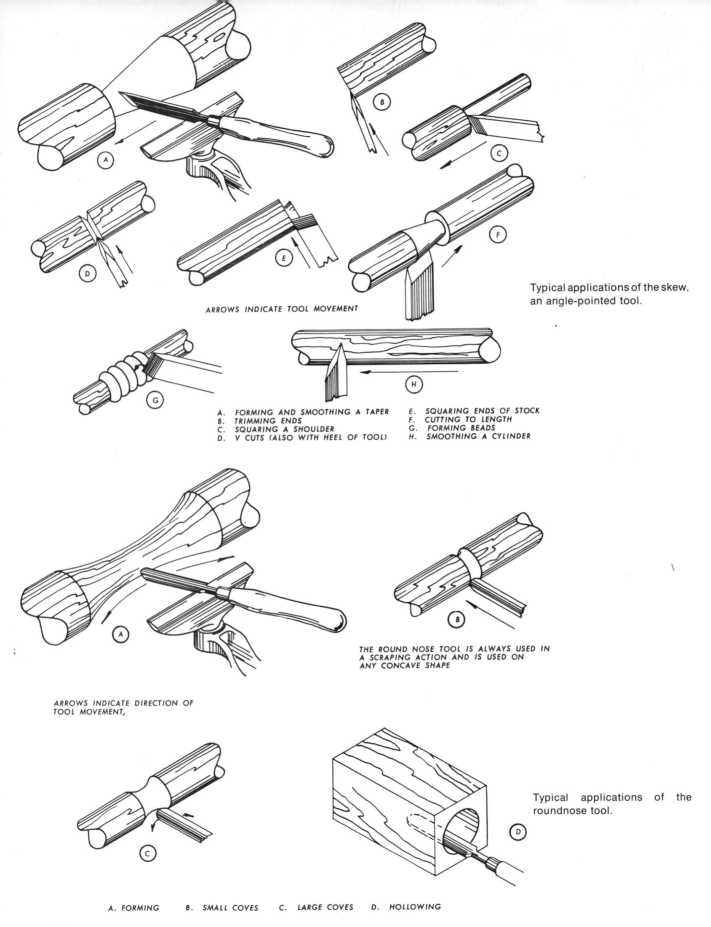

ARROWS INDICATE TOOL MOVEMENT

Typical applications of the skew, an angle-pointed tool.

A. FORMING AND SMOOTHING A TAPER
B. TRIMMING ENDS
C. SQUARING A SHOULDER
D. V CUTS (ALSO WITH HEEL OF TOOL)
E. SQUARING ENDS OF STOCK
F. CUTTING TO LENGTH
G. FORMING BEADS
H. SMOOTHING A CYLINDER

THE ROUND NOSE TOOL IS ALWAYS USED IN A SCRAPING ACTION AND IS USED ON ANY CONCAVE SHAPE

ARROWS INDICATE DIRECTION OF TOOL MOVEMENT,

Typical applications of the roundnose tool.

A. FORMING   B. SMALL COVES   C. LARGE COVES   D. HOLLOWING

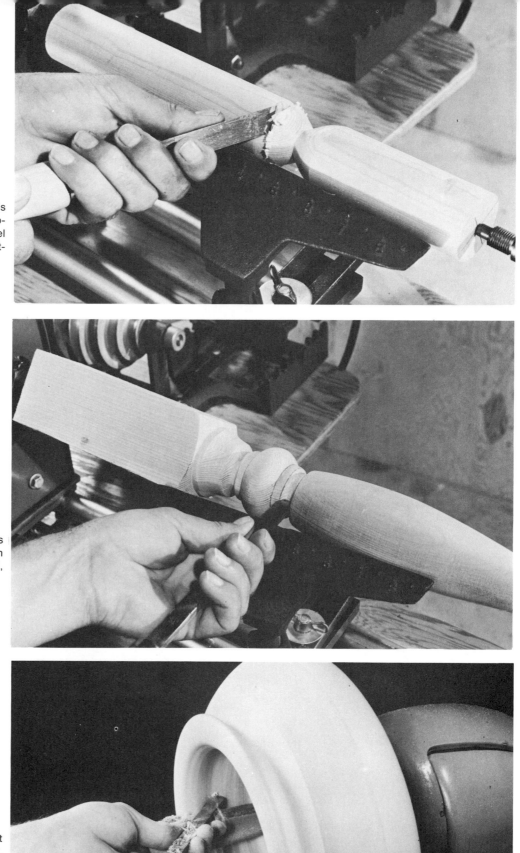

The pro way to use the skew is in a shearing cut. This is probably the toughest lathe-chisel technique so take your time getting into it.

The roundnose tool is always used in a scraping action. When you move it directly forward, you form a cove.

The roundnose is an excellent chisel to use on faceplate work. Note how the tool rest is positioned inside the project to get maximum support for the chisel near the cut area.

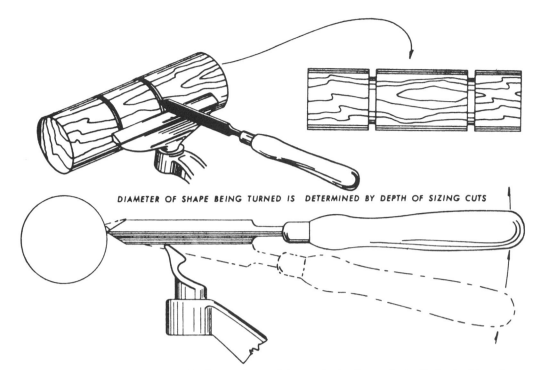

DIAMETER OF SHAPE BEING TURNED IS DETERMINED BY DEPTH OF SIZING CUTS

How to do sizing cuts with the parting tool. It goes faster if you start with the tool handle below the tool rest and swing up slowly as you cut.

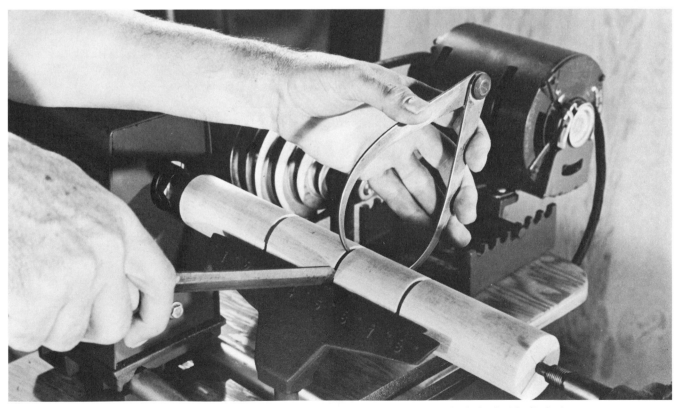

Dimensioning cut with the parting tool and outside calipers. Looks hairy but isn't. Just don't force the cut or the calipers.

especially when you are doing a hollowing operation. This occurs when you are forming a bowl or doing a round box. The point to remember is to situate the tool rest to provide maximum support for the chisel near the cutting edge even if it means the rest has to be situated inside the hollow being formed.

The parting tool. The parting tool is always used in a scraping action with the blade resting on an edge and with the feed action directly forward. The operation will go faster if you start with the handle a bit below the tool rest and raise it gradually as the cutting edge penetrates. You can also do it the other way: start with the handle on the high side and lower it as you go.

Quite often, the parting tool is held in one hand while the other hand grips outside calipers that ride the groove being formed. In this way, you'll know when you have reached the penetration you want on dimensional cuts.

When the cut is very deep, make slight clearance cuts on each side of the main groove to provide room for the body of the blade and thus prevent burning.

The squarenose. Beginners will find the squarenose

a very easy tool to handle. Keep it sharp, use it in a scraping action and feed it slowly, but steadily. When you move it directly forward, you form a fillet that matches the width of the chisel. Move it parallel to the work and you get a smoothing action. Feed it at an angle and you can form V's. Also, it's a very practical touchup tool for such operations as cleaning shoulders and smoothing convex forms.

Ordinary butt chisels can be used in place of the squarenose. If you are equipped with a set, you'll be well organized for this aspect of lathe work. You can choose a chisel width that is best for the job on hand. Use the widest chisel for smoothing jobs; use the narrowest one for touchup work such as cleaning shoulders.

The spear point. Often called a "diamond" point, the spear point is handy because its sharp point can produce clean lines, edges and corners. While it can be used to form V's and chamfers, mark dimensional lines, even do smoothing, it is most valuable for touchup applications. Your best bet is to limit its action strictly to scraping.

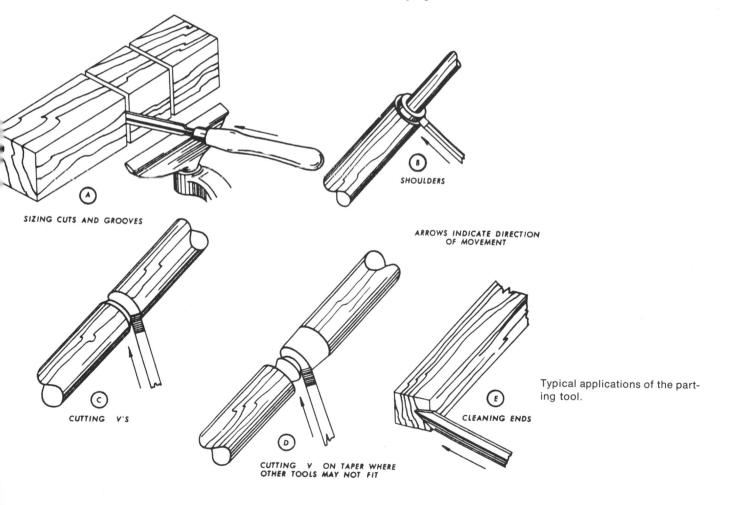

SIZING CUTS AND GROOVES

SHOULDERS

ARROWS INDICATE DIRECTION OF MOVEMENT

CUTTING V'S

CUTTING V ON TAPER WHERE OTHER TOOLS MAY NOT FIT

CLEANING ENDS

Typical applications of the parting tool.

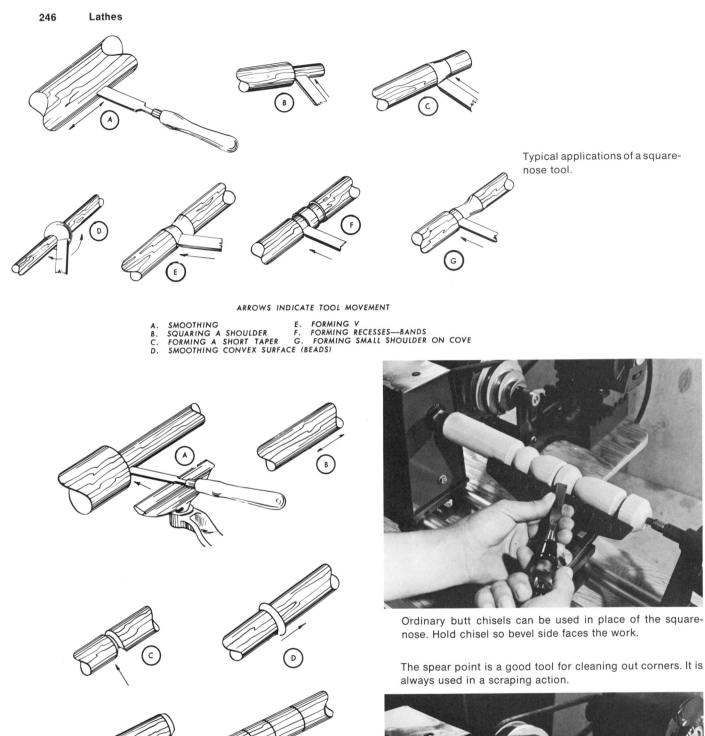

Typical applications of a square-nose tool.

ARROWS INDICATE TOOL MOVEMENT

A. SMOOTHING   E. FORMING V
B. SQUARING A SHOULDER   F. FORMING RECESSES—BANDS
C. FORMING A SHORT TAPER   G. FORMING SMALL SHOULDER ON COVE
D. SMOOTHING CONVEX SURFACE (BEADS)

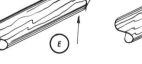

Ordinary butt chisels can be used in place of the square-nose. Hold chisel so bevel side faces the work.

The spear point is a good tool for cleaning out corners. It is always used in a scraping action.

ARROWS INDICATE DIRECTION OF TOOL MOVEMENT

A. SQUARING (TRIM CUTS ONLY)   D. CLEANING CORNERS
B. SMOOTHING   E. SLIGHT CHAMFERING
C. FORMING V's   F. MARKING DIMENSION POINTS

Typical applications of the spear point.

The carbides. Carbide-tipped chisels, while they can be used on wood, are nice to have mostly because they allow you to work on materials like metal and plastics at woodworking-lathe speeds. Most times, slow speeds are best, especially on hard materials. Waste should come off cleanly. Should the work begin to chatter or if you find you are getting a ridged surface instead of a smooth cut, it's a pretty good indication that the work is turning too fast, that you are feeding the tool too fast, or that you are trying to remove too much material in one bite.

The angle of the tool can help you do a better job with carbides. For wood and plastics, the tool handle should be slightly below the tool rest. For steel, keep it about level; for non-ferrous metals, raise it.

Tungsten carbide is very hard and will hold a keen edge for a long time, but it is quite brittle. Be sure that the cutting edges are protected; avoid banging them against hard surfaces.

Molding knives as chisels. If you own a molding head and an assortment of knives, you can have a lot of practical fun and do some fine work simply by making a handle for the knives so they can be used like lathe chisels. In fact, the technique is so intriguing that it pays to buy a few molding knives for the purpose even if you don't own a table saw.

The knives are always used in a scraping action and with minimum feed. In some cases, where the shape you want is large, it pays to remove the bulk of the waste with a conventional chisel and then finish with a knife.

The idea will work on softwoods or hardwoods, but be especially careful on soft species. You will not get good results by forcing the cuts. The wood should scrape away in a fine dust. Working so fast that you lift chips is not good practice; in fact, you will ruin fine detail.

It's a good idea to practice a bit on a scrap turning. Use a slow speed to start and move the knife directly forward. As it begins to cut, add a slight up-and-down

action to the handle as you continue to penetrate. As you can see in the accompanying photographs, you can accomplish some fairly professional detail work in this fashion.

Designing ideas. The worst thing you can do, unless you are just experimenting with chisels, is to start work on a lathe turning without any idea of what the result will be. Like the sculptor and his stone, you must visualize what is in the wood. Your best bet is to do this on paper by first drawing a center line and then combining classic forms to produce a good design.

Those same molding knives previously suggested for cutting are ready-made patterns for layout work. All you have to do is trace around them. If you don't own molding knives, you can probably find full-size profiles in tool manufacturers' catalogs. You can cut these out and mount them on cardboard. Study the classic forms shown in the accompanying sketch. No matter what turning you study, you'll find that these forms supply the bulk of the design.

Another good idea is to study the profiles of standard moldings. These too are based on classic forms. It's not a bad idea to amass an assortment of slim cross-sections cut from moldings you can buy in any lumber-yard. The catalog of a picture frame supply house will include such profiles in sketch form. So equipped, you will have no problem designing the project before you mount the stock in the machine. If the design looks good on paper, so will the final product. Remember that just covering the full length of a turning with detail after detail seldom results in an item you will want to live with

SPINDLE TURNING

Mounting the work. Before you mount the work in the lathe, you must find the center of the stock at each end. If the stock is square, all you have to do is draw inter-

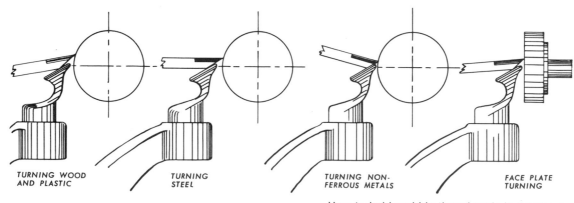

TURNING WOOD AND PLASTIC   TURNING STEEL   TURNING NON-FERROUS METALS   FACE PLATE TURNING

How to hold carbide-tipped tools in relation to the kind of material you are cutting. Your best guide is how the tool is cutting. Slow speeds are best, especially on hard materials.

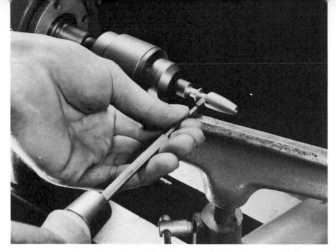

Carbide-tipped tools make it possible to shape metals and plastics at woodworking-lathe speeds. They are very fine tools for small jobs, even in wood.

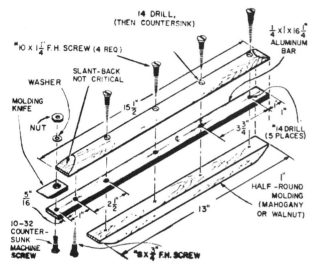

How to make a holder for the molding knives.

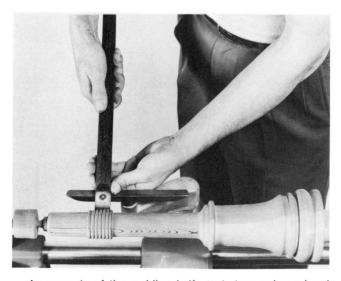

An example of the molding knife technique using a bead cutter. These small forms would be very difficult, and in some cases, impossible, with regular chisels.

Molding knives are excellent, readymade patterns for doing lathe design work.

secting diagonals at each end. The point at which they cross gives you the center. When the work is not square, use the following trick. With a pair of dividers or a compass, draw lines parallel to each edge of the material. Then, the center will be confined to an area small enough so that you can judge its location with reasonable accuracy.

A center-finder does an accurate job of locating the centers on round stock. It's possible you may already have on hand a V-shaped attachment that fits the blade of a combination square. If not, make a special tool like the one shown in the accompanying sketch and make it accurately. To use it, place the stock in the V and draw a line along the edge of the guide. Turn the stock about 45° and draw a second line. The center is where the lines intersect. Note that the center-finder is usable on square stock as well as round.

When the wood is soft, you can use an awl to indent points for the centers. This is all you need at the tailstock end. The spur center in the headstock must be seated firmly. You can accomplish this by removing the spur center from the lathe and tapping it in place in the work with a mallet. Don't use a steel hammer. If the wood is quite hard, take the time to make shallow saw kerfs on the lines you have drawn to find the center.

To situate the work in the lathe, place it firmly against the spur center and lock the tailstock in place about 1″ away from the opposite end. Then use the tailstock ram

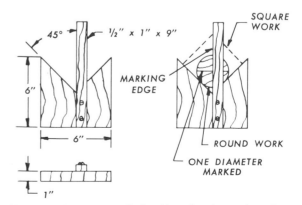

How to make a center-finder. Note that the tool can be used for square as well as round stock.

Assembling the molding knife: After you have drilled the holes through the aluminum bar stock (see drawing on opposite page), clamp the parts together and secure with woodscrews.

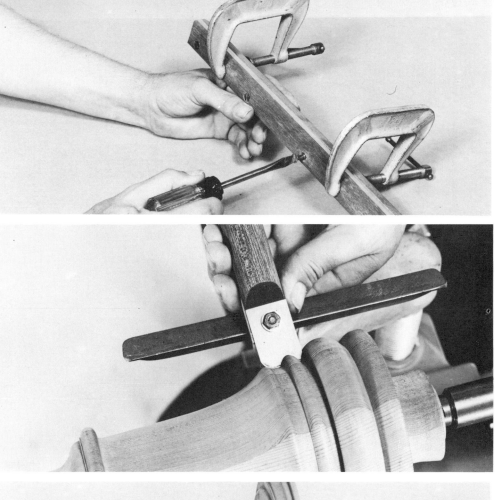

The larger the knife you use, or the larger the shape you are making, the slower the feed. Always use a scraping action with a slight up-and-down motion to speed the cutting.

The molding knife idea is as usable on faceplate work as it is on spindles.

Another way to make a holder for the knives is to weld a piece of flat steel to a length of steel tube. This way, you can add more weight to the tool.

DESIGNING AND TURNING SPINDLES

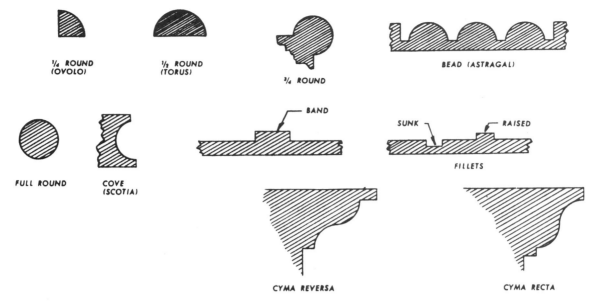

¼ ROUND (OVOLO)

½ ROUND (TORUS)

¾ ROUND

BEAD (ASTRAGAL)

FULL ROUND

COVE (SCOTIA)

BAND

SUNK   RAISED

FILLETS

CYMA REVERSA

CYMA RECTA

Some of the classic forms you can use when designing lathe projects.

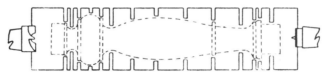

Try to visualize the finished turning *inside* the wood blank. Not knowing what you wish to end up with is a bad way to go.

Spindle turning is easier to do when you are careful about locating the centers at each end of the stock before you place the wood in the machine. Accurate placement at each end cuts down on initial vibration.

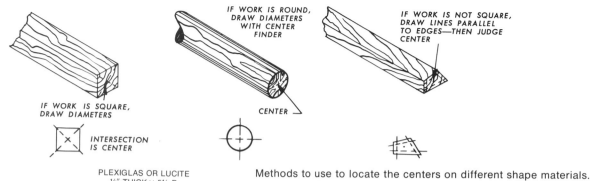

IF WORK IS ROUND, DRAW DIAMETERS WITH CENTER FINDER

IF WORK IS NOT SQUARE, DRAW LINES PARALLEL TO EDGES—THEN JUDGE CENTER

IF WORK IS SQUARE, DRAW DIAMETERS

INTERSECTION IS CENTER

CENTER

Methods to use to locate the centers on different shape materials.

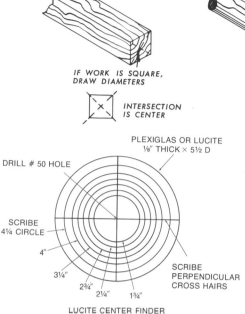

PLEXIGLAS OR LUCITE ⅛" THICK × 5½ D

DRILL # 50 HOLE

SCRIBE 4¼ CIRCLE

4"

3¼"

2¾"

2¼"

1¾"

SCRIBE PERPENDICULAR CROSS HAIRS

LUCITE CENTER FINDER

Another type of center-finder is made of clear plastic. Work is placed within the closest matching circle and a mark made through the tool's center-hole.

to bring the dead center into position. Don't bear too heavily, just enough to make good contact. Often, this setting will loosen, so it should be checked frequently as you are doing the turning. A drop of oil or a spot of wax on the dead center will help. When the wood is very soft and you have much turning to do, it may pay to use a furniture glide at the dead-center end. The indent for the point on the center can be accomplished with a prick punch. Another idea is to nail a small block of hardwood on that end of the work.

Layout. After the stock has been turned down to the point where you are ready for actual forming, it should be marked to define particular areas. A simple way to do this is to use a ruler on the tool rest with the work turning at slow speed. Mark the dimension points with a pencil.

You can work in similar fashion with a flexible tape but with the work stationary. Make your dimension points about ½" long. When you turn on the machine, the marks will be visible enough so you can hold a pencil against the turning stock to complete the line.

When you have duplicate pieces to form, it pays to make a marking gauge like the one shown in the accompanying sketch. This gauge is a piece of wood with brads driven into one edge. You hold it against the turning stock and the brads mark the dimension points. This method is good to use for simple turnings.

For more complex turnings, you should make a full-size cardboard template of the project. The template, as shown in the accompanying sketch, provides a profile for checking the shape of the work as you go. The center-line, straight edge can be used for marking dimension points.

A trick you can use to make a turning to replace a broken part is to use the part itself as a template. Slice the part down the center on a band saw or with a hand-saw to give you an accurate profile of the part you must shape. Place this on the stock and trace around it. Then, as shown in the accompanying photo, use a saw to cut into an adjacent side for dimension lines that match the profile. Cut to the full depth of each design feature; make kerfs on outer sides of all beads and other raised elements. You can then proceed with the turning, working first to clean out stock between designs and then to shape the details.

Slender work. Long, slender spindles require the support of a steady rest to keep the work from whipping and to avoid deflection under cutting pressure. Accessories to provide this support are available, but you can make a suitable one for yourself. This support is a V-block mounted on a platform that you can clamp to the lathe bed. Size the vertical block so the center of the V is on the work center line. Situate it as you go so the work is supported near the area where you are cutting.

Long work. No matter what the capacity of your machine, there is a limit to spindle lengths you can mount. For pieces longer than this limit, you simply turn separate parts and then join them. You can do this by drilling holes in the mating ends and then using a dowel between them. Or you can form a tenon right in the lathe on the end of one of the pieces and drill a hole in the other. More about how to drill the holes will be given later.

Sanding. Final finishing is done by using sandpaper while the part is turning in the lathe. The normal sand-

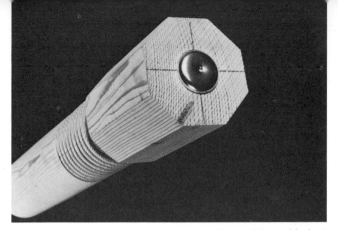

When wood is very soft, tap on a furniture glide and indent the center with a punch, or tack on a hardwood block, but only for placing in a dead center. This is not necessary on a live center.

A section cut lengthwise from a part you must replace can be used as a readymade pattern. Place it on the stock and trace around it as shown.

Marking dimension lines on the work with a flex rule. Make the marks about $\frac{1}{2}''$ long. They will be visible when the work is turning on the machine.

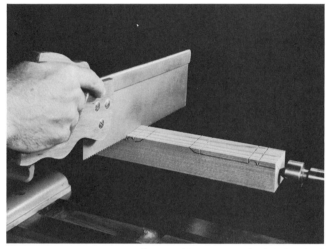

Use a handsaw on an adjacent side to cut to the full depth of the markings. These cuts will be visible when the spindle is turning on the machine.

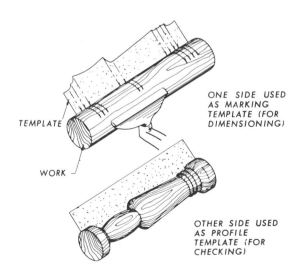

ONE SIDE USED AS MARKING TEMPLATE (FOR DIMENSIONING)

TEMPLATE

WORK

OTHER SIDE USED AS PROFILE TEMPLATE (FOR CHECKING)

A profile template with one straight side can be used for checking the work as you go and for the initial marking as well. It is merely turned over as needed.

ing procedure which calls for a progression through finer grits should not be regarded as a hard-and-fast rule. There is no point starting with a very coarse paper if the turning is quite smooth to begin with. In most cases, a medium-grit paper will do, and even this should be used cautiously around small details.

For straight cylinders, long tapers and similar areas, the sandpaper can be wrapped around a smooth piece of wood. Another way is to hold a strip of sandpaper between your hands and to use it like a shoe-polishing cloth.

A good way to get an extremely fine finish is to work with sandpaper until you are satisfied. Then, dampen the work with water but don't soak it. After it has dried, use fine steel wool to do the final smoothing.

Imaginative techniques. As it was suggested with using molding knives for shaping work, there is no law that says you must limit yourself to lathe chisels. As demonstrated in the accompanying photos, shaping

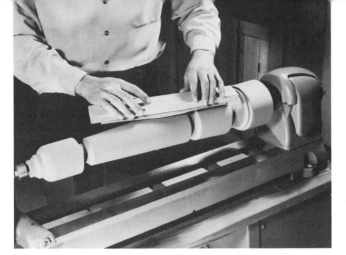

Sandpaper is a good lathe tool but be careful how you use it. For "flat" areas, tape or tack-nail the abrasive to a flat-surfaced wood block.

The shoe-polishing-cloth does a very good job. Keep the sandpaper moving and do not apply too much pressure.

A round file may be used to cut details into lathe work. Use heavy-cut files; the fine ones will clog too quickly. Move the file back and forth across the work.

A rotary file in a portable drill is also a good lathe tool. Hold the drill rock-steady.

"Surform" rasp cuts away material in quick order. Finish is not too smooth, but sandpaper takes care of that.

operations can be done with wood rasps or files, rotary rasps in an electric drill, a hand plane, Surform tools, etc. Don't be a purist and shy away from this aspect of lathe work. In the final analysis, it's what you produce that counts.

FACEPLATE WORK

Mounting the work. Draw lines from corner to corner on the square stock and from the intersection scribe a circle that is just a fraction larger than the diameter of the faceplate. After that, draw a second circle as a guide for rough cutting the blank stock to round on the band saw or jigsaw. The least you should do is remove as much of the waste as possible with straight saw cuts.

Use screws to fasten the faceplate to the turning block, but be sure to choose a size that will not interfere with chisel work. The general rule is to use the longest, heaviest screw. This you must do in line with the base thickness of the finished project.

After you have mounted the work in the machine, spin it by hand to be sure you have clearance between the blank and the lathe bed.

Templates and marking. To find the center, turn the work slowly with a pencil resting on the tool rest. Touch the work lightly with the point and then move

Faceplate turning is the way to go when you need trays, bowls and the like. The roundnose tool is an excellent choice for such jobs. Parting tool is being used here to form groove.

Scribe a circle that is a fraction larger than the diameter of the faceplate. This makes it easier when you center the faceplate on the work.

Use screws to attach the faceplate. These should be as heavy and as long as you can use without creating interference for lathe-chisel cuts. Remove as much waste stock as you can before mounting in the lathe.

slowly toward the center. This will quickly reveal the midpoint of the mounted work.

To scribe a circular dimension line, you can use dividers or a compass. Don't dig the dividers in either the center point or where you are scribing; a light touch is sufficient. To mark the perimeter after you have turned the work to full-round, you can use an ordinary marking gauge; or you can do the job simply with your fingers holding a pencil. In this case, your fingers would act as an edge gauge. This kind of marking can be done while you are turning the work by hand.

Templates, like those described for spindle turning, are just as useful on faceplate work, especially if you must turn out more than one piece of the same design. Make the template so it has a profile side and a straight edge. Carry the main detail points of the design across to the straight edge, and you will have a single template that will serve for marking dimension lines and for checking the shape as you work.

Depth gauge. You can easily make the depth gauge shown in the bottom sketch on page 255. It's nothing but a hardwood block through which you pass a dowel. The lockscrew will work if you just drill an undersize hole for the screw to be used. Put a drop of oil on the screw and drive it home so it will form its own threads. This

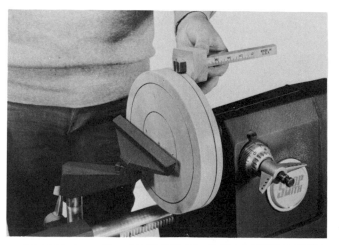

An ordinary marking gauge may be used to mark lines on the perimeter. Turn the work at very slow speed.

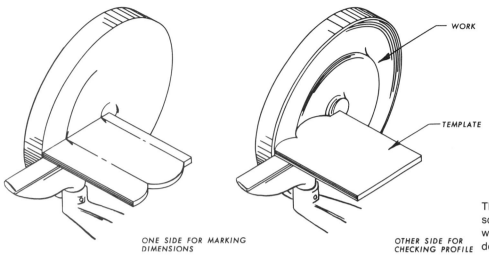

ONE SIDE FOR MARKING
DIMENSIONS

OTHER SIDE FOR
CHECKING PROFILE

WORK

TEMPLATE

The combination template described on page 252 for spindle work is just as useful when doing a faceplate job.

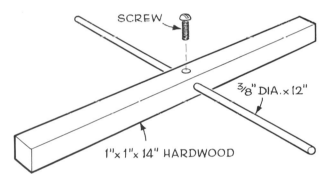

SCREW

3/8" DIA. x 12"

1" x 1" x 14" HARDWOOD

Easy-to-make gauge will let you judge the depth of faceplate turnings. It's especially useful for deep boring jobs — a round box being a typical example.

gauge is useful for checking the depth of items such as bowls and round boxes.

Chisel technique. This technique doesn't differ too much from spindle turning, but you should use a scraping action exclusively. The tool rest may be situated in front of the work, at the edge, behind it, even inside it. Be sure at all times that the tool-rest-to-work relationship provides maximum support for the chisel close to where you are cutting.

You'll find the roundnose a very useful tool, especially for the bulk of the waste-removal chore. Work will go faster if you set the tool rest for the point of the chisel that is on the work center line and if you drop the handle a little below the tool rest. Don't use the gouge or the skew, although it is not out of line to work with the

latter if you limit the application, for example, to cutting lines with the point or cleaning out shoulders.

A faceplate-mounted, heavy block of wood can cause considerable vibration so start at lowest speeds. Speed up only as you lighten the load by removing waste and only as long as you don't cause excessive vibration. Typical faceplate turnings require more time than spindle work simply because a lot of material must be removed before you get to the actual shaping. Therefore, patience is in order. Rushing the job can cause you to jab in the chisels, which can only do more harm than good.

Joining work. Quite often, it's necessary to join a spindle turning to a base that you form on the faceplate. Your best bet here is to plan on drilling a center hole in the base and form an integral tenon on the spindle. Actually, you can drill a hole in each part and join them with a dowel. More about drilling will be given later.

Thin work. When work is too thin to mount on a faceplate, you can often get the job done by putting the blank on a nut and bolt that you then grip in a lathe-mounted chuck. When this procedure is not practical, glue the work to a piece of scrap that is thick enough to be faceplate-mounted. If you use ordinary newspaper between the pieces, you'll find they are not too difficult to split apart after you have done the forming. This method will also work when you don't want screw holes to show in the bottom of the project.

Another idea, if a couple of screw holes in the part you need are acceptable, is to simply screw-attach the piece you will work on to a faceplate-mounted piece of scrap.

SPECIAL TECHNIQUES

The drinking cup trick. You can make a deep bowl

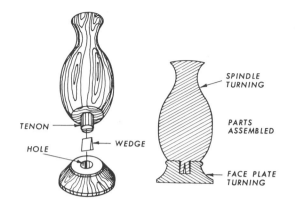

The tenon idea is good when you must join a spindle turning to a base made on the faceplate. The wedge is optional but can provide a lot of strength.

When joining parts you can form the tenon as an integral feature. Size it correctly to match the hole. A fit that requires banging with a hammer *is not* the way to go.

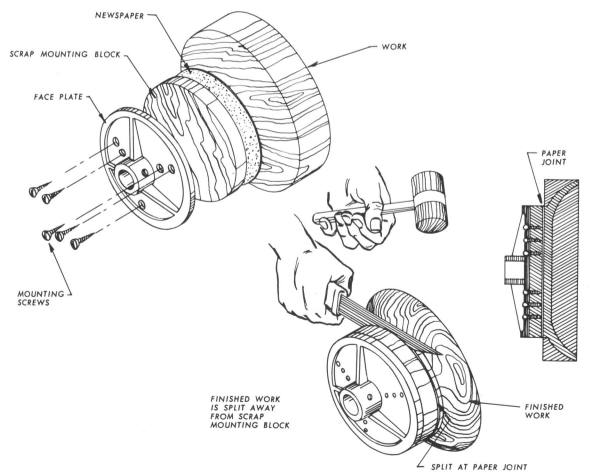

The technique of mounting faceplate work when you can't or do not wish to use screws in the base of the project.

from a thin board by using the old idea of the collapsible drinking cup. If you jigsaw a disc in the center of a board, the disc will drop through when you have finished cutting. However, if you do the same thing but with the machine table tilted about five degrees, the cut will be a bevel and the disc will fall only part way. If you do this with a series of concentric cuts, each ring will jam into the next one and the end result will be a cone shape. The more rings, the deeper the cone will be. When these are glued together, you mount them like any piece of faceplate work and then do the turning. The turning, of course, is lathe work; check the jigsaw chapter for a detailed explanation of how the beveling is done.

The screw-center. Jobs that are too small for spindle turning and not practical for mounting on a faceplate can often be done on a screw-center. This is the method to use for finials, round drawer pulls, and the like.

The screw-center is a special accessory that mounts on the spindle like any other attachment. Find the center of the work as you would for any other job. Use an awl in softwood or drill in hardwood so you can seat the screw. The screw should fit tightly, especially if the part will require considerable turning. One trick is to cement a piece of sandpaper to the face of the screw-center to increase the grip.

Outboard turning. This technique is possible on some machines to do jobs that are too large to mount conventionally. It is straightforward faceplace turning except, because of the work size, you must restrict yourself to minimum speeds. Manufacturers of machines that permit this operation usually list outboard turning stands as accessories. These are no more than supports for the tool rest. If you anticipate doing outboard turning occasionally, you can improvise a stand like the one shown in the accompanying sketch. Be sure the top-to-floor distance lets you place the chisel on the work center line. Don't push this kind of thing when cutting. Don't try to mount work so large that the tool motor must strain to turn it. If you wish to experiment with this technique, do so with softwoods. Let the heavier, harder woods come later.

Built-up sections. There are many lathe jobs that require a large diameter in a limited area of the work. Aside from using a large enough blank to begin with, which really produces a lot of waste, there are two methods you can use to facilitate such work. In one, you can use another woodworking tool such as the band saw or the jointer to reduce the stock in particular areas. In the other, you can add wood by gluing in those areas that require it.

The glue-on chore must be done with some precision.

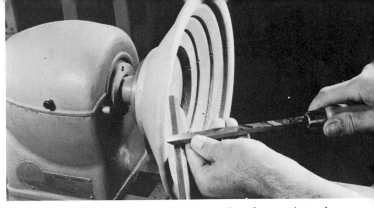

This deep bowl is the result of bevel-cut rings from a piece of ¾″ stock. The idea is very practical for lathe work but the actual cutting is a jigsaw operation. See that chapter for details, on page 156.

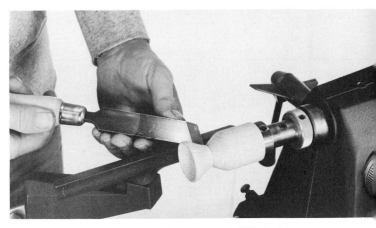

Lathe-chisel handling techniques do not differ just because the work is small and mounted on a screwcenter. Be sure that the screw has a tight grip in the work.

Outboard turning can be accomplished on some lathes but you must buy or make a special stand for use as a tool rest. Slow speeds and light cuts are in order.

The joint should be invisible after the turning is complete. Unless you deliberately plan otherwise, the grain pattern and direction should be compatible. Getting these results calls for discernment, as well as a good glue job. Be sure that mating surfaces are flat and true before you apply the glue and the clamps. Don't rush; let the glue dry thoroughly before you mount the work in the machine.

This kind of thinking applies to faceplate work as well as spindles. To build up a thick blank, you can glue thin pieces together. To facilitate the removal of waste in the lathe, the glued-on pieces can be rings that you precut on a jigsaw or even with a saber saw. If the project is to have sloping sides, play along with it by cutting rings of increasingly smaller diameter.

An interesting lathe procedure is to glue together blanks of contrasting woods. These can be simple or complex. They don't look like much in the rough form following the glue job, but after the turning they become intriguing inlaid projects.

Select wood for this technique to produce good contrast and, less importantly, similarity in degree of hardness. To experiment, try combining rosewood and maple, redwood and pine, birch and cherry, holly and walnut. Once you've tried it, you'll realize the technique's po-

tential. Often, the preliminary gluing job to build up the blank can take up more time than the actual turning.

Split turnings. A common split turning is one that is halved after the piece is shaped to produce two identical half-columns. This can be accomplished with solid stock by cutting on the band saw after the turning is complete, or you can work with the paper-glue joint that has already been described.

Another way is to make the blank by joining two similar pieces without using glue. This you can do by nailing the parts together at the extreme ends in areas that you know will be waste, even by using corrugated fasteners at each end of the pieces.

Needless to say, the mating surfaces of the joint, whether you use glue or not, must be flat and true. If you check over the sketches, you'll discover that the idea can be used not only for quarter-round molding, but also for half-moldings.

This is not the method to use every time you need a short piece of molding, but it's a fine procedure when you need something special.

Drilling. There are several ways to do drilling in the lathe. In one, the chuck and bit are mounted in the tailstock. The bit is still and the work turns. Feed is ac-

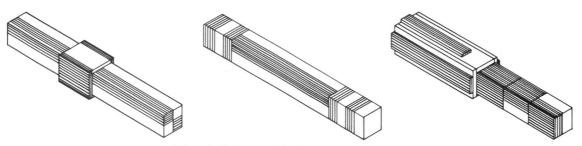

When building up blocks you can get fascinating results, by combining contrasting woods. A good glue job is essential.

These identical half-columns were two pieces to begin with —they were joined temporarily just for the lathe work.

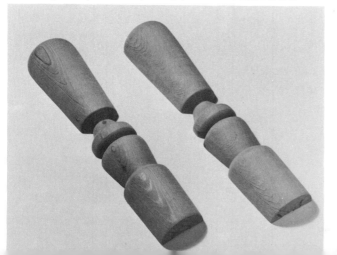

A simple way to do the temporary joining is to use corrugated fasteners as shown here. We left it projecting here—be sure to drive them flush when *you* do it.

complished by moving the tailstock forward or by using the tailstock ram. Such jobs are easier to do when the work is on a faceplate. In the second method, the drilling tool is in the headstock; the work is held against the center in the tailstock. Here, of course, the bit is turning and the work is still. The first method is preferred for faceplate work, the second method for spindles. Whatever way you work, standard drilling rules apply. Use slow speeds for large holes; increase speed only for small holes.

Quite often when you need a center hole all the way through a project for an item such as a lampbase, it's better to prepare for it before you turn the work. For this, you can use a kind of split-turning technique, running small center dadoes in each piece before you bond them with glue. Fill the hole at each end with a "key" so you'll have a solid area for the centers. After turning, you can hand drill through the keys to reach the square hole you have formed with the dadoes. If you do a good gluing job, it will be difficult to discover that the project is not a solid piece.

When the project length permits, you can lathe-drill through center holes by working from both ends of the stock.

Drilling can also be done on the perimeter of pieces; and if your lathe is equipped with an indexing device, you have a means for automatically gauging the spacing of such holes.

Your best bet is to make a drill guide that you use in place of the tool rest. As shown in the photos on page 260, there are several ways to accomplish this. In one, a steel bar or tube is fitted with a bushing for the drill you will use. In the other, you can get by with a simple wood block. When using them, be sure that the guide hole is on the work center line. It isn't necessary to make provision for drilling different size holes. If you provide, for example, a $\frac{1}{8}''$ or a $\frac{1}{4}''$ hole through the guide, you can accept it to use as is if that hole size is what you want or as a pilot hole that you can then enlarge to the size you require.

Spiral work. The forming of spirals is usually classified as lathe work, but truthfully it's mostly a hand job with the lathe used as a holding device after the stock has been turned to full-round.

The layout can be done precisely by dividing the total length of the spiral into equal spaces, each one about the diameter of the stock. The next step is to draw four lines along the length of the stock. These should run from common perpendicular diameters at each end. What these lines do is divide the cylinder into four equal $\frac{1}{4}$ rounds. Next divide each of the spaces into four equal

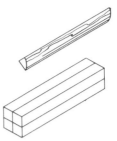

Gluing together four similar pieces and then separating them after turning will produce $\frac{1}{4}$ round moldings.

On a ShopSmith, you can drill by feeding the spindle forward when chuck and bit are mounted in the tailstock. On a conventional lathe, move the tailstock or feed with the tailstock ram. In either case, the bit is still, the work revolves. Obey usual drilling rules—slow speed for large holes, rev up only for small holes.

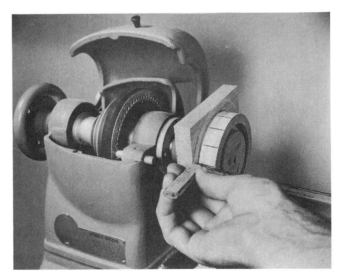

The holes in the pulley are spaced symmetrically about a circle. This enables you to space hole locations on a project without layout computation.

To drill horizontally on the perimeter of a job, make a guide like this. See text on page 259.

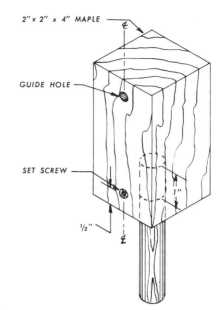

2" x 2" x 4" MAPLE

GUIDE HOLE

SET SCREW

1"

½"

Or make this more simple version. The reason for either is to have a mechanical means of positioning the drill. The guide hole must be on the horizontal centerline of the work.

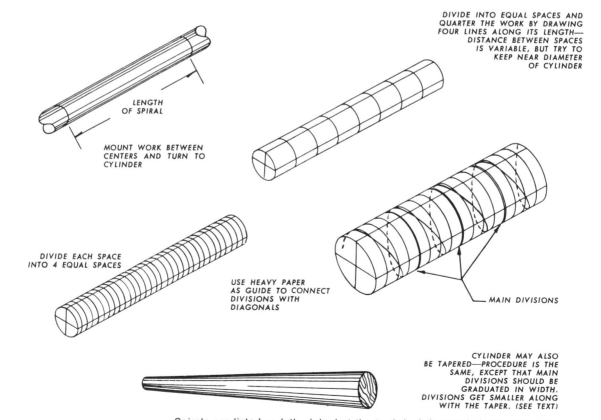

LENGTH OF SPIRAL

MOUNT WORK BETWEEN CENTERS AND TURN TO CYLINDER

DIVIDE INTO EQUAL SPACES AND QUARTER THE WORK BY DRAWING FOUR LINES ALONG ITS LENGTH— DISTANCE BETWEEN SPACES IS VARIABLE, BUT TRY TO KEEP NEAR DIAMETER OF CYLINDER

DIVIDE EACH SPACE INTO 4 EQUAL SPACES

USE HEAVY PAPER AS GUIDE TO CONNECT DIVISIONS WITH DIAGONALS

MAIN DIVISIONS

CYLINDER MAY ALSO BE TAPERED—PROCEDURE IS THE SAME, EXCEPT THAT MAIN DIVISIONS SHOULD BE GRADUATED IN WIDTH. DIVISIONS GET SMALLER ALONG WITH THE TAPER. (SEE TEXT)

Spirals are listed as lathe jobs but the truth is, it is mostly hand work. The lathe is not much more than a holding device. Follow these instructions to do precise spiral-layout work on true cylinders and on tapered ones.

parts and, using a heavy piece of paper as a guide, mark diagonals across each of the small spaces.

You can also work in fairly good fashion without all the layout by using a long strip of paper immediately. The paper can have parallel sides or be tapered. This paper is wrapped around the cylinder in spiral fashion, and the spiral line is marked by following the edge of the paper with a pencil.

Actual work is started by using a handsaw to cut the spiral line to the depth you want. As a depth gauge, you can make a mark on the saw or clamp a wood block to it. Work on the cut line with a round or square file, depending on how you visualize the final product. In essence, the initial file work opens up the groove you cut with the saw.

Then you can work with a flat file to shape the sections between the grooves. A rasp will speed up the job, but it's best followed by a smoother cut file before you get to the sandpaper chore, which is the final step. It's possible to have the work turning as you do the sanding, but you must be very careful to follow the spiral as you hold the sandpaper in shoe-polishing-cloth fashion. Start the spiral at slow speeds; increase the speed as you become confident.

Working with chucks. Sometimes it's not possible to hold work between centers, mount it on a faceplate, or secure it to a screw-center. At such times, it's good to know the technique of making wooden chucks.

A chuck doesn't have to be more than a tenon affair that you put on a screw-center. The tenon is designed to be a snug fit in a center hole that is in the work. This makes sense simply because, many times, it's better to drill a needed hole in the work before it is turned. Then it can't be mounted on a screw-center unless you provide the tenon-chuck.

Another way to proceed is to make a split chuck. A tenon on the work is gripped by the "jaws" of the chuck because of the ring that forces them together.

The whole chuck area should be viewed as a means of getting a job done when it can't be accomplished in the usual fashion. There is no point in trying to be prepared for such eventualities except to know the techniques to use. Wait for them to occur before you make tools.

A box with fitted cover. This box also uses a kind of chuck technique. What you do is mount the body of the box on a faceplate and turn it to the shape you want both inside and outside. Mount the stock for the lid on a second faceplate and form a recess in it that will fit the opening of the box's body. Return the body to the lathe and use it as a chuck to finish turning the lid. When the

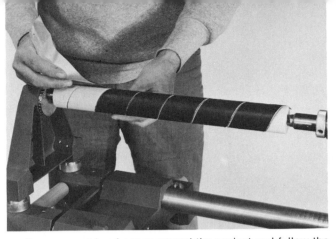

Or, wrap a strip of paper around the project and follow the edge with a pencil. Width of paper and how you wrap it determine spacing and "pitch."

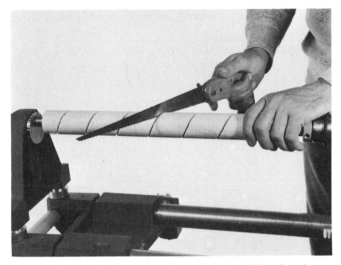

Start the job by following the layout line with a hand saw. To gauge depth-of-cut, you can clamp a block to the saw or make a mark on it.

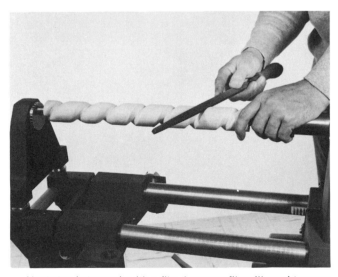

Next step is to work with a file. A square file will produce one shape, a round file another.

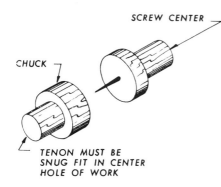

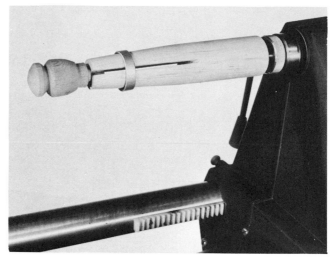

A simple chuck is a tenon design that is mounted on a screw center. Used if more conventional methods fail.

A split chuck is a good idea for work that has a tenon. Pushing up on the ring causes the "jaws" to grip the work.

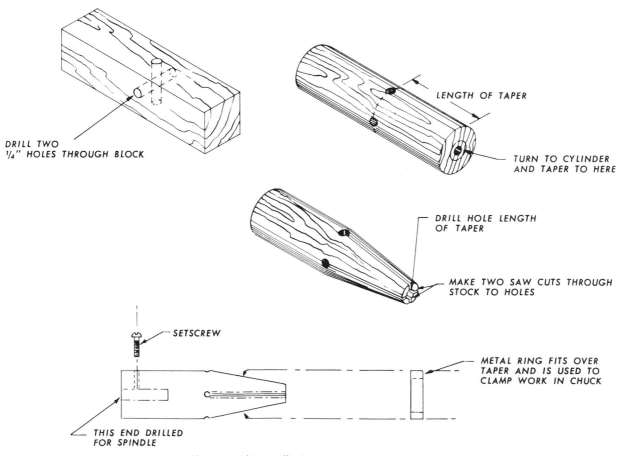

How to make a split chuck. Use maple stock.

The body of the box is used as a chuck for the lid (see text about box beginning on page 261).

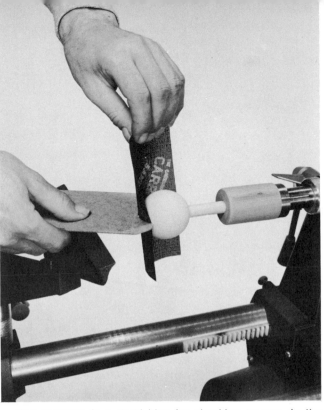

The template is a good idea for checking as you do the shaping, but also for the final sanding operation. Be sure the abrasive you use is flexible. Don't apply a lot of pressure.

body of the box is used as a chuck, the fit between it and the stock lid should be fairly tight. After the lid is formed, touch up the body lip with sandpaper so the lid will be a slip fit.

A ball shape. To make a ball shape, mount a blank between centers and turn it to remove most of the waste material. What you can do to begin is create a square with a tenon at each end. The square becomes the ball; the tenons are simply holding sections. It's wise to make a template that is half the ball shape. Use this template as a guide for a shaping and smoothing device.

The next step is to mount the work on only one tenon. You can do this with a conventional three-jaw chuck or by making a special wooden one. Now you can cut off the outboard tenon and work to achieve the final shape of the ball. The last step is to use the template as a touch-up device by placing fine sandpaper between it and the ball shape. Use a light touch and do the final finishing by hand holding the sandpaper.

After you are satisfied with the shape, separate the ball by using a parting tool or a skew in a cutting action and touch up the cut end by hand with sandpaper.

Ring work. There are a variety of techniques you can use to do ring work, and a choice will usually depend on the cross-section profile you want. For example, for a ring with a square cross-section, mount a blank on a face-plate and turn it to full-round with the diameter to match the O.D. of the ring. Make one cut with a parting tool on the edge of the turning. Its depth should be a bit deeper than the cross-section of the ring when viewed from the front. Make a second cut, again with the parting tool, on the face of the stock. Make the second cut to meet the first one; and when the two cuts meet, the ring will fall off onto the shaft of the chisel. The rim of the ring can be shaped before you separate it from the body of the faceplate-mounted stock. Essentially, these are the basics of forming rings.

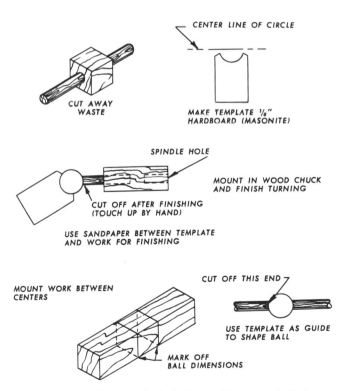

CENTER LINE OF CIRCLE

CUT AWAY WASTE

MAKE TEMPLATE ⅛" HARDBOARD (MASONITE)

SPINDLE HOLE

MOUNT IN WOOD CHUCK AND FINISH TURNING

CUT OFF AFTER FINISHING (TOUCH UP BY HAND)

USE SANDPAPER BETWEEN TEMPLATE AND WORK FOR FINISHING

MOUNT WORK BETWEEN CENTERS

CUT OFF THIS END

USE TEMPLATE AS GUIDE TO SHAPE BALL

MARK OFF BALL DIMENSIONS

Step-by-step through the technique of turning a ball-shape. Here, a wooden chuck is used for the final steps but a conventional chuck may be used.

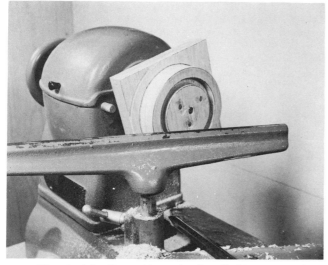

The stock for the making a ring is nailed to a scrap piece mounted on the faceplate. The face cut is done first. The separation cut will be done on the perimeter.

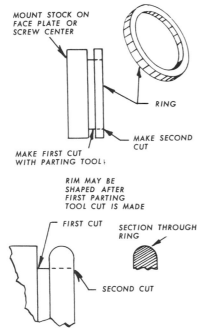

The two steps required for a simple ring cut.

If the cross-section of the ring is to be a true circle, then you must use a combination of faceplate turning and chuck turning. Start the job with faceplate-mounted stock and turn half of the ring shape. Make a chuck with a recess that will provide a snug fit for what you have done. This can then be pressed into the chuck, and the final half circle of the ring can be formed.

All chuck work of this type requires an accurate dimension in the cavity that holds the work. If you make a

mistake, it's often possible to compensate by wrapping a strip of masking tape around the ring to make it fit snugly.

A project like a circular picture frame or a one-piece circular molding that may be used to edge a flat tray can be done in this fashion. Mount the work on a faceplate and recess it to form a rabbet. Shape the perimeter as you wish. Then make a chuck to fit the rabbet diameter and shape the work on the opposite side. View the original rabbet cut, in the case of a picture frame, as the recess that holds the glass. If you are making a tray, simply cut a disc that fits inside the turning.

Ovals. The major factor in this process is a layout that you do on the ends of the stock after you have turned it to true round. Your best approach is to make a template that locates the true center plus two "off centers" that are on a common diameter. Note in the accompanying sketch that it's a good idea to draw a "ridge" line on the work. Once you have this line, it's easy to position the template to mark the common off centers.

Mount the work on one of the off centers and turn it as you would normally until the cut nears the ridge line. Be careful when positioning the tool rest. One side of the work will come closer to you than the other; the off center makes it possible to cut on just one side of the diameter. You'll find after this operation that one side of the stock is oval while the other side remains round. Shift to the second off center and repeat the operation. The final step is to use sandpaper to remove the ridge line.

Some jobs, a round picture frame being typical, can be done this way. The technique is to first form a circular rabbet, then the work is mounted on a chuck so the face can be shaped on the lathe.

Offset work. In this type of work, parts have a projection that is not uniform about a center line. You can find this on leg designs that end in a right angle departure from the "spindle." The cabriole leg is another good example. The idea here is that lathe turning can be applied to part of the project either before or after the overall shape is established. As you can see in the accompanying sketches and photographs, the turning is done on the true-center portion of the work—either in an overall or limited area. In the case of the cabriole leg, you can turn a round foot after the part has been bandsawed to shape.

This is not a difficult chore, but you must be aware that the off-center portion of the project can be a hazard. Always be sure, after you have set the tool rest, that you hand turn the work to check clearance. When you start cutting, keep your hand clear of the projection area. As far as lathe mounting is concerned, the work is unbalanced, so you are bound to get more vibration than you would from a symmetrical piece. Start at very low speeds. Increase the speed only if results indicate that you can do so without danger to yourself or to the work.

Finishing. To get to a final smoothness, work through progressively finer grits of sandpaper. The grit you start with must be judged on how smooth the project is to begin with. A very coarse paper may be completely out of line since all you will be doing is creating scratches you will have to remove with other paper. On lathe work, it's often possible to start immediately with a fine paper. Whatever you do, be careful around fine details since excessive sandpapering can destroy them.

When you are satisfied that the wood is smooth enough, dampen it slightly with water. Don't soak it. Let it dry and then do a final smoothing with fine steel wool. Some craftsmen use a handful of fine shavings to do this. It does bring out a degree of shine; but whether you use chips or steel wool, this is just a step before application of color or clear finish.

A simple finish can consist of plain wax. You pick up some wax on a cloth pad and apply it to the turning work. A slow speed is best, and you can apply as many coats as you wish as long as you allow sufficient drying time between the applications. After you are sure the part is evenly coated, do the final polishing with a clean, lint-free cloth.

Apply stain in similar fashion. Just be sure you don't saturate the cloth, or you will be spraying yourself as you color the wood. Remember when you do this kind of thing in the lathe that finishing materials require just as much drying time as they do when they are applied with a brush. Rushing the procedure will do more harm than good. Overall, it's best to apply any finish

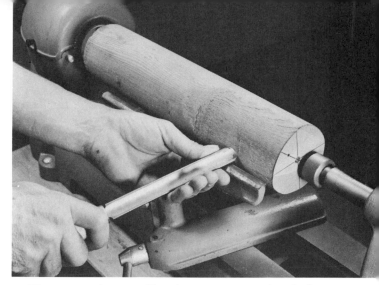

When you work on an off-center, you are removing stock on one side of the diameter. Cautious chisel handling is in order. Finish off the job with sandpaper. This will smooth the work and also "destroy" the ridge line.

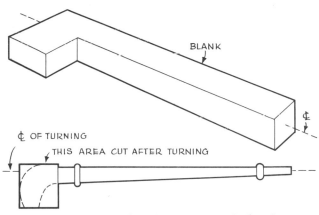

Typical part that calls for offset turning. Note that the center for lathe mounting ignores the projection of the work.

Turn in usual fashion but be very much aware of the off-center end. Keep your hands well away from it.

You can use the offset turning technique if you wish to turn one or both ends of a cabriole leg design. Slow speeds and caution are a must. See text on page 265.

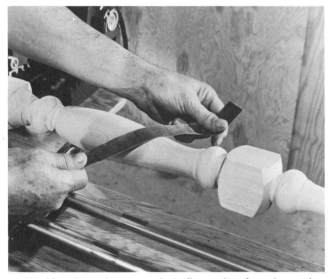

Working through progressively finer grits of sandpaper is a good idea, but it doesn't mean you must start with the coarsest paper.

in a diluted state; and the heavier the material you are using, the slower the speed should be.

Shaping attachment. With a lathe, you have the makings of a shaper. With a chuck spindle for mounting a shaper adapter, plus one or two easily made jigs, you have an efficient setup for producing decorative edges or doing such functional chores as forming tongue-and-groove joints. There is little a conventional shaper will do that can't be done here. Actually, you can even set up for horizontal drilling and routing.

You need a chuck spindle and a shaper adapter. The type of spindle depends on your lathe. If it has a straight, unthreaded spindle, you can use a shaper adapter that mounts directly on the spindle. If the lathe has a tapered hole, then you will need a tapered spindle chuck.

Most lathes will provide a high speed of about 5,000 rpm's. This speed level will do for shaping even though a higher speed is better. Don't use special pulleys to provide higher speeds unless you are sure the lathe is built for it. To compensate for speed that is less than ideal, you can slow up on feed rates and take small cuts.

The vertical jig is essentially a shaper table that stands on edge. The fences do the same job as a regular shaper fence but, in this case, they also support the work. On long jobs, stand at the side of the table and feed the work across. On small work, position your hands so they are never directly over the cutter.

The fulcrum pins in the vertical table make it possible to shape freehand against collars. There are limitations here because of the lathe bed and the fence slide bars but not enough to restrict most common jobs. If you wish, you can attach the slide bars with screws instead of glue. Then they can be removed if this would facilitate a particular operation.

With the horizontal jig, you can handle larger work more easily. Also, it changes the work position in relation to the cutter, and this feature increases the variety of shapes you can get from a single cutter. More important, perhaps, is that you can use a miter gauge to move work across the cutters, facilitating some kinds of cross-grain edge cuts. By working with router bits, you can use this table for special types of routing and for horizontal drilling.

Follow the construction details carefully. The jigs shown were made and sized for a 12″ lathe. Unless you have something similar, check the dimensions in the drawings against your own equipment. Be very careful when making the sliding bases: you can use a lot of rigidity here. If dimension changes are required to suit your tool, work from intersecting lines that represent the vertical and horizontal center lines of the lathe spindle.

A sanding table. Since it is possible to mount a disc in the lathe, the little table shown in the accompanying photograph lets you use the tool as a fairly efficient disc sander. The table can be as small or as large as you wish; however, even for the biggest machines, it shouldn't be much over about 14″ square. The table understructure sits on the lathe bed and is located with a block that fits between the ways. Organize table height so it is a bit above the horizontal center line of the disc.

Be sure that you use the safe speed for the disc you will mount. Note that the table has a miter-gauge groove so you can do end sanding accurately. For the techniques of disc sanding, see the chapter that deals with that particular tool.

When you apply the finish, do not saturate the cloth or you will be spraying yourself as well as coloring the project.

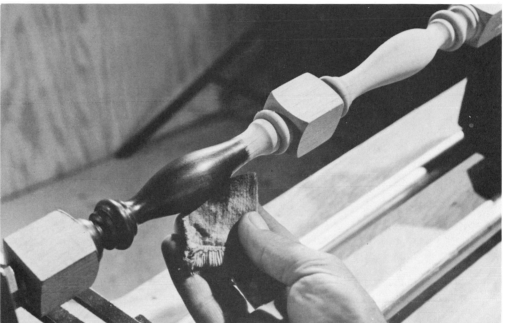

There are finishes available such as "Rub-n-Buff" that are quick and easy to do. You apply the finish from a tube and then buff with a soft cloth while the work turns on the lathe.

The vertical jig. For construction details, see following page.

Clamp the fence in place for edge-shaping big work. The fence must be parallel with the front edge of the table — check by measuring from each end of the fence to the front of the table.

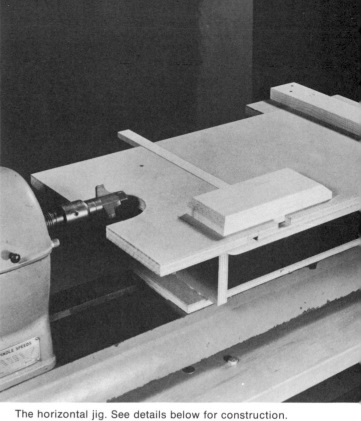

The horizontal jig. See details below for construction.

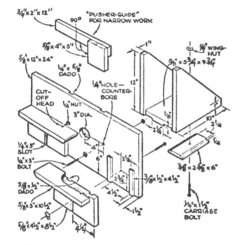

Construction details of the vertical jig.

Here is the relationship between the lathe-mounted cutter and the vertical jig. The fulcrum pins are for freehand shaping.

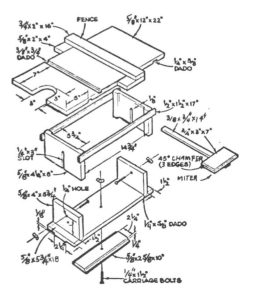

Construction details of the horizontal jig.

ROUTING ON THE LATHE

For routing, use a router chuck that locks on the spindle like the shaper-adapter. You can rout grooves, rabbets, round-end mortises, etc. Keep speed as high as possible.

Rout circular edges by using the pivot method. The pivot, a nail driven through the work into the table, should be on the spindle centerline. Position the work, move the jig to engage the cutter, lock the jig, turn the work to complete the cut.

Position of the work, with the vertical jig, makes a big difference. For partial cuts, like this one, the fences are on the same plane. When the entire edge of the stock will be removed, raise the outfeed fence to compensate.

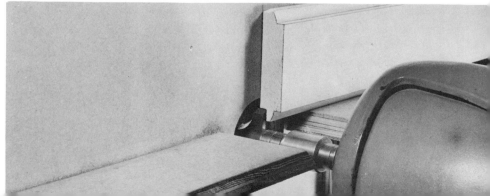

By moving the jig toward the headstock, you can use the back edge of the cutter, getting more from a single shape. Provide depth-of-cut adjustment by lateral movement of the jig on the ways.

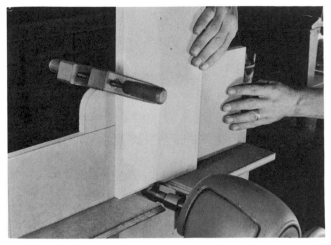

Clamping the work to an L-shaped guide makes cross-grain cuts safer and easier to do. The guide's long leg rides the table edge; the short one (90° to the first one) supports the work vertically.

Shape circular edges by pivoting the work on a nail driven into the table. For large discs "enlarge" the table by clamping an extra board to it. Position the work first, then move the jig in to engage the cutter.

SANDING ON THE LATHE

Drum sanding can be done on the lathe, using a speed of about 2,500 rpm for fine work. Reduce the speed as you go to coarser abrasive. When you make the jig, be sure to cut the hole just large enough to suit the drum you will use.

A table like this turns the lathe into a pretty efficient disc sander. Make it as described in the text. To lock it to the lathe use the same system described for the shaper jig. Be sure you use a speed that is safe for the disc you will mount.

7 | JOINTERS

The jointer is a powered planer designed to remove a predetermined amount of material from stock edges while leaving them square and smooth enough for assembly. Essentially, it does in seconds what requires much time and energy to do with a hand plane. More importantly, it provides accuracy in mechanical fashion by minimizing the possibility of human error.

Jointers are often organized for one-motor operation with a table saw. This is not essential as jointers can be and often are set up independently, but the combination affair does demonstrate the basic jointer function of smoothing edges after sizing cuts on the saw. The workpieces are overcut an amount to match the depth-of-cut setting on the jointer.

A jointer can be used for light surfacing operations, but this function does not put it in the "thickness planer" category. A jointer which removes thick amounts of material is a much heavier machine with features that include automatic feed, greater capacity, and a pretty good guarantee that, depending on your craftsmanship, the opposite surfaces of the work will be parallel after the cut.

A jointer will also do a variety of other operations well. It's really much more than a planer and, if used correctly, will do a fine job of forming rabbets and tenons, tapers and bevels, and many other practical chores.

PARTS OF A JOINTER

A three-knife cutterhead rotates between infeed and outfeed tables. The infeed table where you place the work to start the cut is adjustable to determine the amount of material you wish to remove. The outfeed table may or may not be fixed, which is a design feature that doesn't have too much effect on the range of the work you can do with this tool.

It's best for the infeed table to have a healthy rabbeting ledge, a positive depth-of-cut adjustment and a lock to hold the setting. The fence is usually a heavy affair that is adjustable angularly and laterally to the horizontal plane of the tables.

All jointers have spring-loaded guards designed to move aside during the pass and to come back quickly to cover the cutterhead after the cut. The guards are designed to be used. Doing without them, if you feel they are a nuisance on some jobs, is a poor excuse for taking big chances. Some of the accompanying illustrations show jointers being operated without the guard in place for photographic reasons only. It has nothing to

6″ Deluxe jointer for the homeworkshop has overall table size of 7″ × 42½″. ½″ depth-of-cut is good for rabbeting and similar chores. On this example, both the infeed and outfeed tables are adjustable. Fence has auto-stops at 90° and at 45° on both the right- and left-hand sides.

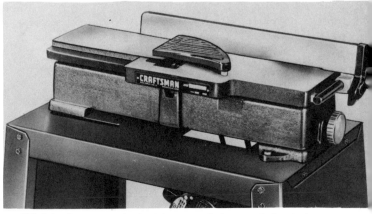

4″ jointer is a more typical homeworkshop tool simply because it is cheaper. Depth-of-cut is ⅜″, still pretty good for rabbeting work. Outfeed table is fixed; fence has a full tilt-range. Overall capacities are not impractical for general work that would be done by the home woodworker.

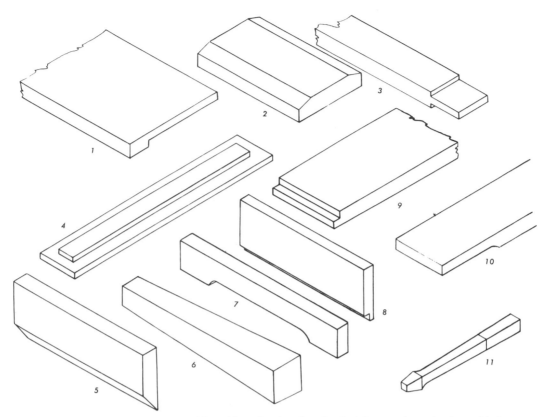

Typical jointer cuts: 1. wide rabbet; 2. chamfer; 3. stud tenon; 4. perimeter rabbets (raising); 5. bevel; 6. taper; 7. recess; 8. edge rabbet; 9. end rabbet; 10. surfacing (planing); 11. leg shapes.

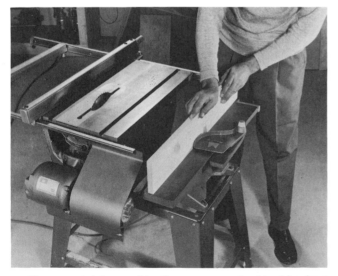

Many saw-jointer combinations are organized to drive from one motor. Thus you can quickly smooth edges. Each tool, of course, can have its own motor, which may be a better idea from a safety viewpoint. Use all guards—even though we may not show them for photo purposes.

The thickness planer is a heavy-duty machine with a self-feed mechanism. It is great for planing boards and for reducing thicknesses. On this machine, you know that opposite planed surfaces will be parallel. On a jointer, more skill is required to accomplish this.

do with good, safe shop practice. Use all guards available.

ADJUSTMENT FACTORS

The horizontal plane of the outfeed table must be tangent to the cutting circle of the knives. All jointers provide for accomplishing and maintaining this critical relationship. To check, set a straightedge on the outfeed table so it juts out over the cutterhead and then rotate the cutterhead by hand. Each knife should just barely scrape the straightedge. If the straightedge is lifted or if the knife doesn't touch at all, adjustment is required.

When this chore is accomplished, set the infeed table to match the plane of the outfeed table and adjust the depth gauge to read "0."

Normal fence position (with quadrant reading "0") forms a 90° angle with the tables. If the fence is not in this exact position, you cannot consistently joint edges that are square to adjacent surfaces. Most jointers provide stops for common fence-tilt settings. Set these carefully so that correct angles are provided.

Study the accompanying illustrations carefully, for they will demonstrate critical adjustment factors as well as warning signals that tell you a check is in order.

EDGE JOINTING

The general rule is to make all jointing cuts so the knives are cutting with the grain of the wood. It isn't always possible to follow this rule, but it does produce the most satisfactory results and also reduces the danger of kickback and splintering. When you do work against the grain or across it, reduce feed speed to a minimum and keep cuts very light.

On normal work, depth-of-cut settings should not exceed $\frac{1}{8}''$. A $\frac{1}{16}''$, even a $\frac{1}{32}''$, setting is better if it gets the job done since it requires less power and wastes less wood. Often, on hardwoods or on large pieces, the job is done best by making a couple of light passes as opposed to a single heavy one. This is especially true with against-the-grain cuts and surfacing operations.

The jointing pass should be a smooth action from start to finish. Place the work edge firmly down on the infeed table with the adjacent surface snug against the fence. Use your left hand to maintain this work position and your right hand to feed. Move the work at reasonable speed and don't stop until you are well clear of the cutterhead. Such advice is sound only because it establishes a jump-off point. Work size, hardness of the wood, and the operation itself will also bear on how you hold the work and how fast you should feed.

Some operators feel the hands should never pass over the cutterhead. But if the guard is there and you are as alert as you should always be, this point isn't always

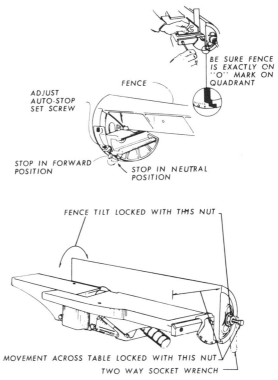

Typical jointer nomenclature. When auto-stops are provided, use great care in setting them up and check them periodically. Only so can you be sure that you will get maximum accuracy from the tool.

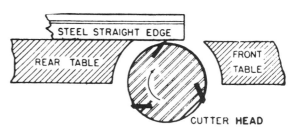

A straightedge, placed on the outfeed table, must be tangent to the cutting circle of the knives. This is essential for good jointer operation. Depending on the design of the machine, you adjust the table to the knives or the knives to the table.

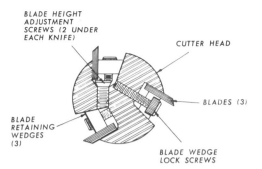

Method of knife-locking and adjustment in the cutterhead will differ from tool to tool but all jointers have three knives and a husky cutterhead. Check your Owner's Manual for specifics about your machine.

A good way to adjust the infeed table is to draw a dimension line on the work and adjust the infeed table until the cut is exact. Then set the scale pointer.

"Normal" position for the fence is at "0". Check this position and adjust the auto-stop if necessary while using a square as shown.

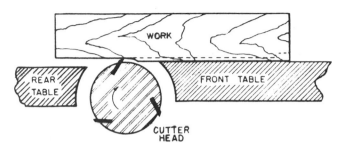

When the rear table is too low, the work will drop and be gouged.

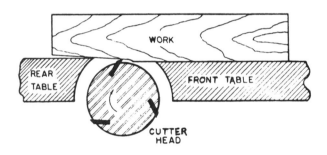

When it is too high you'll have difficulty passing smoothly over the knives.

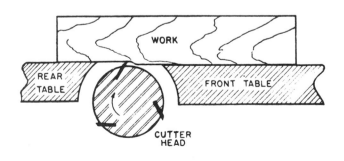

When rear table and knives are in correct alignment, work passes smoothly over the cutterhead and rests securely on the tables *before* and *after* the cut.

During jointer cuts, hand position should be such that the work is held firmly down on the tables and snug against the fence through the pass. Good idea to keep hands on top and back edges of the wood.

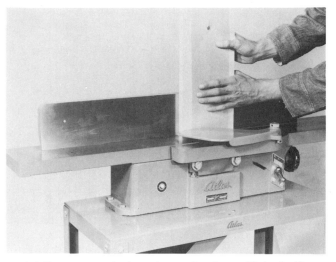

Jointing across stock ends can be done efficiently if you minimize depth-of-cut and use the two-pass technique described in the text.

valid unless the work size brings your hands too close to the cutters. In such a case, you probably shouldn't be working without special precautions anyway.

JOINTING END GRAIN

If you do such jobs in one continuous pass, it's inevitable that the knives will split off a portion of wood at the very end of the pass. To avoid this problem, use a double-pass technique. Advance the work over the cutterhead only enough to joint an inch or two. Then lift the work, reverse its position and complete the job with a second pass. With plywood, judge the grain direction of the surface veneer as if you were working with solid stock.

When jointing four edges on a piece of work, do the end-grain cuts first in single passes. The third and fourth passes, made with the grain, will remove the imperfections left by the first two cuts. This method does not apply to plywood. On such material always use the double-pass method.

SURFACING

Surfacing is almost the same as making a jointing pass except that the work is placed flat rather than on edge. Keep depth of cut to a minimum and use a very slow feed. It's very important to maintain uniform contact with the tables throughout the pass to avoid tapered cuts, gouges, and generally unsatisfactory results. That's why, in most cases, it's a good idea to work with a pusher-holddown tool.

Such an accessory, which you can make yourself, does more than help to do a good job. It provides a good

If you try to do the job in one pass, tearing will result at the end of the cut. This applies to cross-grain cuts on solid stock and to plywood.

The first partial pass is shown here. At this point, lift the stock from the machine, reverse its position and complete the cut.

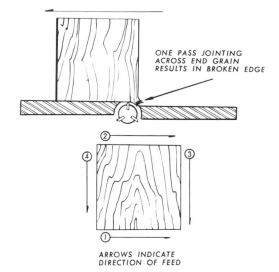

ONE PASS JOINTING ACROSS END GRAIN RESULTS IN BROKEN EDGE

ARROWS INDICATE DIRECTION OF FEED

When you are jointing four edges use a pass sequence as shown by the numbers. Cuts 3 and 4 will remove the imperfections at the ends of cuts 1 and 2.

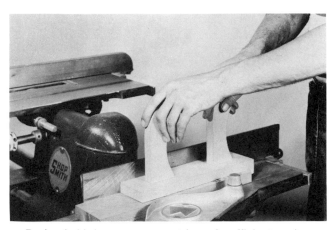

Pusher-hold downs are a must for safe, efficient work on a jointer. With this design you can use one or both hands depending on the size of the stock you are working.

A fine way to organize for good pusher-hold down action on long stock is to make both the tools shown here.

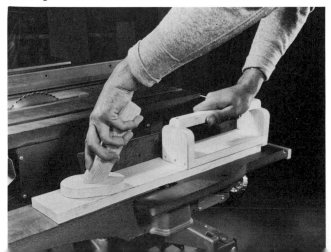

degree of safety, especially when working with stock that could bring your hands too close to the knives.

Often, it's possible to do a surfacing cut with just one hand on a pusher-holddown tool. At other times it may be necessary to use your left hand to hold down the front edge of the stock while your right hand guides the holddown device at the rear. The whole matter is mostly a question of adjusting your position in relation to the length of the stock to make sure that the workpiece's contact with the table is continuous throughout the pass.

DISTORTED STOCK

"Dished" (hollowed or rounded inward) stock, even in some extreme cases, can be jointed if you work on the dished side first, making as many passes as you need to create a straight edge. If the opposite edge is also distorted, you can then do a rip cut to straighten that edge and end up with a second jointer pass.

Extra care is required if you are going to joint a curved edge since you'll have little bearing surface on the first pass or two. After these are accomplished, the job gets easier.

This kind of situation should be avoided, for example, on stock that has one straight edge. It would be better to use the one straight edge to ride the rip fence on a table saw to remove the distortion. Then you can do the jointer cuts.

Warped boards are dished across the width. With most jobs, the high points provide a pretty good bearing surface for the initial passes if you work with the concave side down. If the warp is uneven, set the board so it bears on the three highest points and keep it so placed through all the passes needed to remove the flaw.

The convex side is more difficult to do since you must be concerned with keeping the surfaced side parallel to the tables if the board is to end up with parallel surfaces. In fact, it's usually wiser to use a table saw to remove the convex side after you have jointed away the concave side.

Boards in "wind," which is a full-length twist, are a different case. A very small amount of such material can be handled successfully if you work as you do with a simple warp. In extreme cases, don't even attempt it. Or, if you want to salvage as much as you can, cut the board into shorter lengths and see what you can then accomplish.

RABBETS AND TENONS

The jointer is an excellent rabbeting machine as long as its maximum depth of cut is sufficient for your needs. Since most home workshop jointers will cut ½" deep and

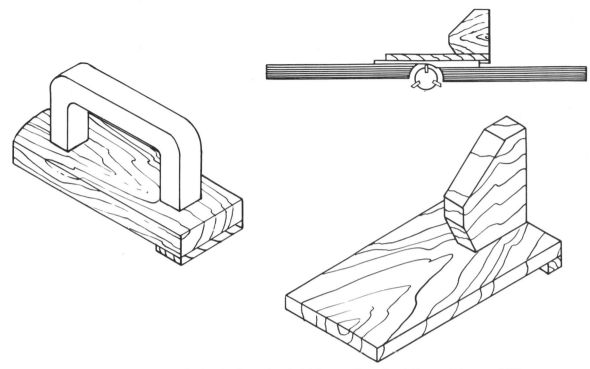

Construction details of a few basic pusher-hold downs. They should be a minimum of 12″ long by 4″ wide. The back ledge should be $\frac{1}{4}$″ thick.

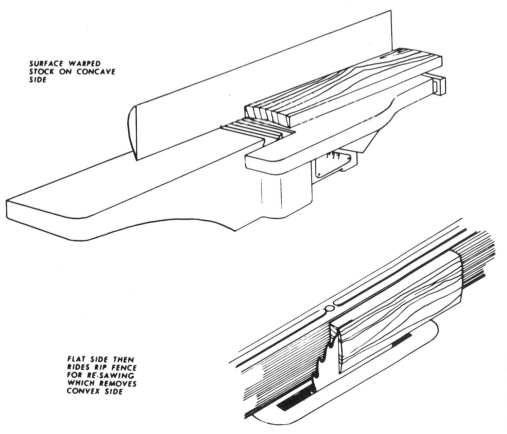

SURFACE WARPED
STOCK ON CONCAVE
SIDE

FLAT SIDE THEN
RIDES RIP FENCE
FOR RE-SAWING
WHICH REMOVES
CONVEX SIDE

Narrow, warped stock can be surfaced by using the jointer to flatten the concave side and then the saw to rip off the convex side. This is feasible within the capacities of the tools you own.

HANDLING WARPED BOARDS

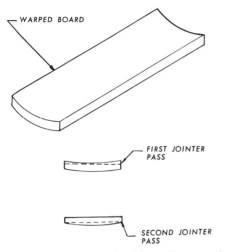

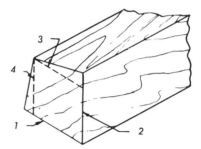

Stock that is distorted like this should be jointed on the dished side first.

You can do both sides on the jointer but guard against rocking when you do the convex surface.

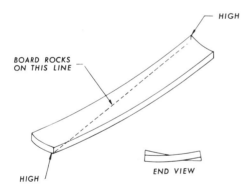

Boards in wind can be rough. If the distortion is extreme, forget it! Sometimes you can salvage some of the wood by cutting the board into shorter pieces.

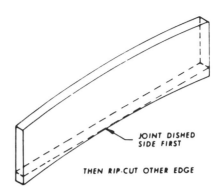

Rough stock to be squared can be done as shown. Make one cut to smooth a side and then cut # 2 to smooth and square the adjacent edge. Make cuts 3 and 4 on the saw a bit oversize and then return to the jointer to smooth them.

the thicknesses of the wood you will be working with most often are 1″ or under, there really isn't much of a restriction here.

To organize for a rabbet, lock the fence from the front edge of the knives a distance equal to the rabbet-cut width. Set the infeed table to the rabbet depth. Place the work on the infeed table, snug against the fence, and advance over the knives as you would for any other job. When you need a deep cut on tough wood, it's wiser to make a couple of passes, adjusting for more depth of cut after each pass.

To create a tenon or a tongue, flip the stock and repeat the procedure.

Such cuts on the end of stock are a little more difficult because you are working across the grain. It may be necessary to make the cuts more shallow and to reduce the rate of feed, not only to make the cut smoother but to reduce the feathering and splintering that can

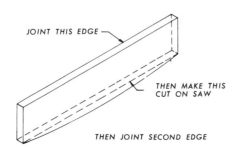

Work sequence when the stock is distorted on one edge only.

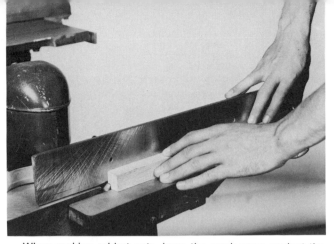

When making rabbet cuts, keep the work snug against the fence and down on the table through the pass. You can't use the guard on such applications but most jointers provide for covering the cutterhead behind the fence. Don't work on pieces so small you can't hold them safely.

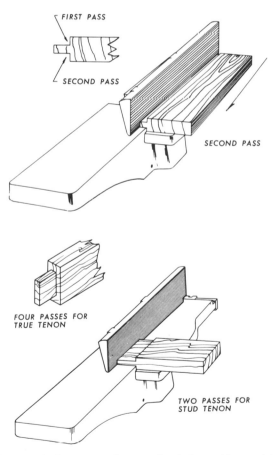

You can do tongues or tenons simply by making matching cuts on opposite edges. The tenon passes are harder to do because you don't have much stock bearing against the fence. Its a good idea on such jobs to use a pusher-hold down.

occur at the end of the cut.

It's good practice to work with stock that has an overwidth of about $\frac{1}{16}''$. Then, after the cross-grain rabbet or tenon cut, you can do a jointer pass to remove any imperfection.

In most situations where rabbets and tenons are cut across stock ends, it's a good idea to use a pusher-hold-down device to do the feeding. Remember, too, on such jobs it's not possible to use the guard so you have an exposed cutterhead until the work itself covers the gap. Keep your hands well away from that area and be extra alert.

CYLINDER WORK

Rabbeting. Cutting a rabbet in a cylinder is entirely possible, but the initial problem that will be encountered shouldn't be minimized. You must hold the work firmly enough to guide it past the knives until the flat surface that is formed by the cut rests solidly on the outfeed table. At this point, the procedure is no different than the same job on flat stock.

Don't do this kind of cut on small dowels or on any piece too short to be held safely. Should you need to shape a short piece in such a manner, do it on the end of a long piece and then cut off what you require.

As shown in the accompanying photo, there is a simple way to guide the stock when such cuts must be repeated oppositely with similar dimensions or with variations.

The method does provide a means to create, for example, T-shaped joiners between panels or corner finishers on case work, even though adjacent panels may have different thicknesses.

Tenoning. The jointer can form tenons on cylinders and will guarantee similarity when the same shape is required on multiple pieces. A couple of methods are shown in the accompanying sketches, but the basic idea is to be able to rotate the stock against the direction of rotation of the cutterhead. The jointer fence may be used as a stop to gauge the length of the tenon, or you can use an L-shaped guide to do the job.

If the jointer knives are shaped at the ends to cut, as they are along the normal cutting edge, then you can rest the work on the rabbeting ledge and go directly forward to start the cut. If the knives are not so shaped, then you must brace the work against the guide above the cutting circle and lower it slowly to make contact. Then you rotate the work to form the tenon.

CHAMFERS AND BEVELS

A chamfer and a bevel are similar and are made in

about the same way. The chamfer does not remove the entire edge of the stock.

The best way to work is to tilt the fence so it forms a closed angle with the tables. This provides a tight nook to snug the work and keep it steady during the pass. If you work with the fence tilted in the opposite direction, you must be very careful to keep the work from sliding out from under you. Chamfers can often be accomplished in a single pass. Bevels usually require repeat passes.

V-BLOCK WORK

For a large percentage of routine shop work, the V-block jig provides greater convenience and more accuracy when you have to do the same job on many pieces.

The jig is but a V-block with an offset that matches

the tool's maximum depth of cut. It has its own fence, but this is just a means of attachment to the regular jointer fence. Attaching this and similar items to the jointer should not be a problem since all jointers usually have holes through the fence for just such purposes.

On maximum cuts, the forward end of the jig rests solidly on the outfeed table, but this changes as you reduce the cut. Therefore, don't bear down too heavily as you pass the knives. It's also possible, when necessary, to use a wooden shim between the jig and the table.

This jig can be used to create a flat on a cylinder, but don't use it for the same purpose on small dowels or on any piece that is too small to be held safely.

OCTAGONAL SHAPES

Making octagonal shapes with a jointer is a question of making similar bevel cuts on all four edges of a piece

It is okay to rabbet a cylinder so long as you realize that *you* are the *only* control until you have enough flat to ride the outfeed table. Don't do this on pieces too small to handle safely.

A second cut in the cylinder is guided by a block that is clamped to the rabbeting ledge or to the fence. With such a setup, the second cut is as easy as working on flat stock.

An L-shaped guide block clamped to the infeed table positions the work for forming tenons on round stock. Guide position and depth-of-cut setting determine tenon diameter. Fence position determines its length. Turn work very slowly, keep hands clear of the knives.

This is a similar jig but shaped so the jig itself gauges the tenon length. Work is rotated very slowly against the direction-of-rotation of the cutterhead.

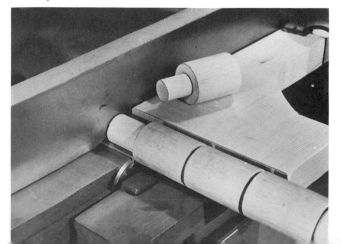

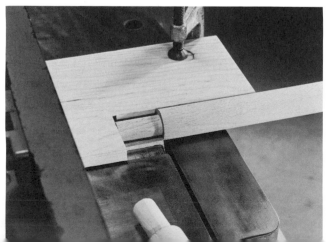

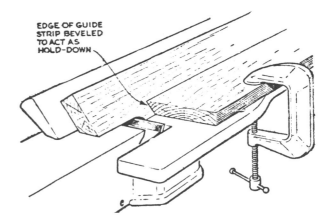

On open-angle bevel work, the guide block makes very good sense. It is even better when you shape its edge on the saw to conform to the jointer-cut angle.

Here is another way to make tenons in round stock. The block is shaped—either by drilling or making a V-cut—to accept the work size. It can be used only when the ends of the knives are shaped to cut.

A V-jig makes it easy to chamfer or bevel, especially when the cut is required on many pieces. Situate the jig so the knives clear the shoulder of the offset. Secure it with wood screws through the fence.

Bevels or chamfers are accomplished by tilting the fence to the angle desired. A closed angle is best since it creates a nook for the work. Even so, a clamped guide block keeps the work in just-so position.

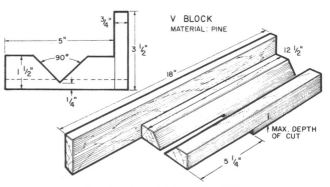

Construction details of the V-jig.

To use the jig, hold the work firmly in the "V" and pass slowly over the knives. The jig was designed for a 6" jointer but it will work as well on a 4" design. The width of the V-block should cover the full width of the tables.

You can approach or accomplish octagonal shapes by making cuts on all four edges of a piece of square stock.

of stock that has been accurately squared. Set the fence at 45° and make the pass on each edge. Repeat passes are often required before the job can be considered finished.

TAPERING

You can do a simple taper by setting the infeed table to the depth of cut you want and then positioning the work so the starting point of the taper rests on the forward edge of the outfeed table. For a 12" × 3/8" taper, mark the work 12" in from one end and set the infeed table for the 3/8" cut. Rest the work as described, pull it toward you, and you will achieve the taper.

When the cut must be duplicated on other sides or when you need the same cut on different pieces, it's a good idea to clamp stop blocks to the jointer fence so you will have positive positions for both the start and finish of the pass. Tapers in excess of the machine's maximum depth of cut can be accomplished with repeat passes.

Tapers that are longer than the infeed table must be handled differently. For example, with a 24" × 3/8" taper, mark the stock into two 12" divisions and set the depth of cut for 3/64". Make the first pass from the first 12" mark and a second one from the second 12" mark, and you will have the required taper.

Approximately the same procedures apply when you wish to limit the length of the taper while confining it to some midpoint. The idea is simply to clamp stop blocks to the fence on both infeed and outfeed sides of the cutterhead. These control the start and finish of the cut.

Variations of these techniques can be utilized extensively to produce legs, rails and similar parts for chairs, tables and such projects, or merely to add a design element to a component for any project.

RECESSING

The recessing cut is often referred to as a "stopped

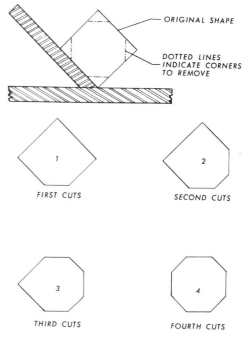

Working without the V-jig you can accomplish octagons on any pieces regardless of size because now you can do repeat passes.

CUTTING TAPERS

Doing a taper is a question of holding the work as shown and then pulling it across the knives. Hold the work firmly down on the table. Employ a stop when you must repeat the cut on other sides or when doing similar pieces.

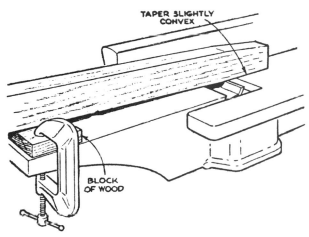

TAPER SLIGHTLY CONVEX

BLOCK OF WOOD

A block of wood can be used as shown when doing short end-tapers. The cut will be slightly convex. To eliminate the convex factor, tack-nail the height block to the work instead of clamping it to the table.

Start a mid-way taper by holding the stock firmly against the stop block clamped to the infeed end of the fence. Hold the stock down firmly and pull it slowly across the knives until it hits the stop block clamped to the outfeed end of the fence.

chamfer." It's often seen on base members and bottoms of table and stand legs. When you have a jointer with a fixed outfeed table, the cut is made in two passes with stop blocks on the fence to gauge pass length. This still leaves a raised area in the center of the cut since all you've done is form opposite tapers. You can leave it, since it's quite decorative in itself, or remove it by cutting on another tool.

When the outfeed table is adjustable, you can do the cut in one pass merely by lowering both tables an equal amount. Whether you make the cut in one pass or two, you can't cut any deeper than the maximum setting of the jointer.

COVING

If you accept depth-of-cut limitations, you can do some respectable coving work on a jointer. The process involves passing work diagonally across the knives so the knife end produces the cove arc. When the knife ends are not shaped to cut, the work must be moved toward the end of the knife rather than into the end of the knives. When the knife ends are shaped to cut, then you can move work directly across them, parallel to the cutterhead, and get a cove cut.

Remember that the cove arc is limited by the tool's maximum setting. Because of this, you should not plan to produce an item such as a wooden rain gutter. However, the jointer as a coving tool can be utilized for moldings or molding details, for panel-edge shapes, or for stock reduction that ends in a curve rather than a square corner.

THE PIVOT JIG

With the pivot jig, you can rotate stock as the knives cut and produce a perfect disc with a fine, ready-to-use edge. This jig provides a means of positioning work so it can be turned on a vertical plane. The center line of the pivot should be just forward of the center line of the cutterhead. There is a small arc of the cutting circle that can be used here, but it doesn't impose any critical limitation on depth of cut. Actually, if you wish to be a bit more flexible in the setup of the jig, you can slot the holes through which you bolt the jig to the jointer fence.

To work with the pivot jig, mount the rough cut work on the pivot but clear of the knives. Hold the work firmly and lower it slowly to make contact. Then turn the screw that locks the slide and rotate the work very slowly against the direction of rotation of the cutterhead. A slow, firm feed with a reasonable depth of cut will give you a perfect edge even though you will be cutting cross-grain in some areas. In this fashion you can even do

Upper line on the work shows how a recess cut is formed in one pass when both tables of the jointer are adjustable. Bottom line and the cut itself show it when done on a jointer with one adjustable table

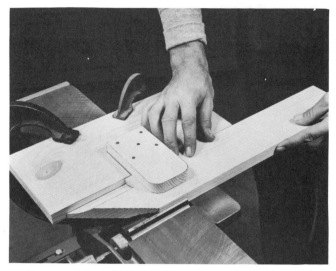

Coving job is being done here with a jig that provides a gauge and a hold-down. Since these knives are end-shaped to cut, the work can be moved directly into them. This is a good setup when same cut is required on many pieces.

FIRST PASS

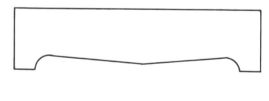

SECOND PASS

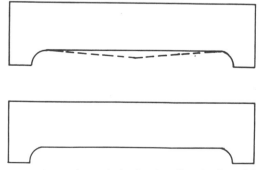

the second pass is made by turning the stock end-for-end. The center point (dotted line) can be removed or left as a decorative detail.

Here the work is aimed toward the outboard edge of the knives. This time the guide is clamped to the outfeed table. This and the preceding photo show how to do some coving when the knife-ends are *not* shaped to cut.

Cove cut on stock edge with the work being moved diagonally toward the inboard end of the knives. Limitations are imposed by height of drive pulley. Work direction is guided by a block clamped to the infeed table.

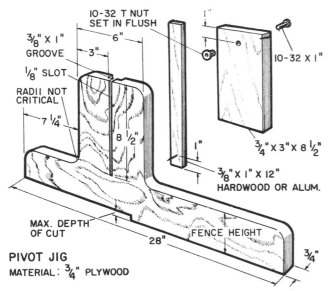

10-32 T NUT SET IN FLUSH

6"

3"

3⁄8" X 1" GROOVE

1⁄8" SLOT

RADII NOT CRITICAL

7 1⁄4"

8 1⁄2"

1"

10-32 X 1"

3⁄4" X 3" X 8 1⁄2"

3⁄8" X 1" X 12" HARDWOOD OR ALUM.

MAX. DEPTH OF CUT

FENCE HEIGHT

28"

3⁄4"

PIVOT JIG
MATERIAL: 3⁄4" PLYWOOD

The pivot jig is a means of holding and turning work on a vertical plane. You can reduce the length of the jig if necessary but don't reduce its height. The pivot point is a heavy roofing nail.

Rough-cut work is mounted on the pivot and then slowly turned against the direction-of-rotation of the cutterhead. For precise duplicates, make a mark on the slide after forming the first piece. Use the guard even though we don't show it here.

circular recess cuts by making a full-circle cut the first time and then limiting the pass the second time.

THE UNIPLANE

This brand new tool is not a jointer or a planer, yet it can do many of the functions of either. Because of its cost (over $400.00), it will probably not become a common workshop tool, yet it is interesting enough to take a look at.

In essence, the uniplane is a highly sophisticated rotary planer mounted in a heavy-duty structure similar in appearance to a jointer. The cutting action is on a vertical plane, and it's so smooth and fast (better than 30,000 cuts per minute) that very little pressure is required to feed the work or keep the work in contact with the fence. There is no tendency for the work to be lifted or kicked back.

To use the machine correctly, you must make a pass that takes the work completely across the cutterhead area. Of the eight cutters in the head, four project .002″ farther than the others. They are the "finishers" and do their job on the "up" side of the disc. The uniplane really makes a double cut, one when you enter the cut zone and a shave touch when you leave it.

Maximum depth of cut is only $\frac{1}{8}″$, but you will be more impressed by how little you can remove. Shaving off $\frac{1}{64}″$ is a routine chore. Grain direction, in relation to the pass, has no effect on the finish you get as the finish will always be smooth.

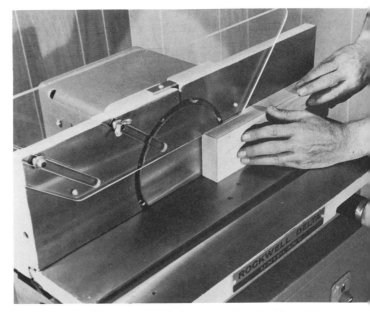

Uniplane's eight cutters revolve around outer rim of the visible disc. Machine cuts smoothly across end grain, produces perfectly smooth miters, chamfers and bevels.

8 SHAPERS

In most home shops, shaping operations are usually done on a drill press, radial arm saw, or table saw with a molding head. Quite often, homecraftsmen use a router mounted under a table setup or work with a hand-held router. Such applications can result in very acceptable shaping jobs.

While you need not feel impoverished if you make do with shaping accessories for the other tools mentioned, the individual shaping machine is a tool specifically designed to provide optimum shaping results. Since basic shaping techniques are constant regardless of the tool being used, all of the shaping procedures shown in other sections of this book apply to the shaper as well.

GENERAL FEATURES

Cutter mounting on the shaper is by means of a vertical spindle, but it differs from the drill press, for example, in that it is mounted under the work table and is designed to withstand considerable side thrust and speed. Since the drive mechanism is below, there are no top side obstructions (such as a drill-press column) to interfere with work size and work handling.

A good shaper will have a hollow spindle so designed that it will accept auxiliary spindles such as a "stub" for doing cope-type cuts. Built-in adjustments permit raising or lowering the spindle so you can position the cutter; positive locks let you secure it at the desired height.

The usual spindle diameter is $\frac{1}{2}''$, and this goes along with the common $\frac{1}{2}''$ hole size of popular three-lip shaper cutters. Other spindle diameters can be $\frac{5}{16}''$ or $\frac{3}{4}''$, but the latter is pretty much a commercial concept for constant, superduty functions. The spindles are fitted with a tie-rod or stud that passes through the main, hollow spindle and is secured at the free end with a nut.

A good home-size shaper—one that will handle three-lip shaper cutters with a $\frac{1}{2}''$ hole efficiently—can be driven with a $\frac{1}{2}$ HP motor. If you plan to expand the use of the tool by using some of the other types of cutters that will be shown in this chapter, then a $\frac{3}{4}$ or 1 HP motor will not be out of line.

It is important to be able to reverse the motor's direction of rotation. Being able to work in two directions is part and parcel of shaper technique. Sometimes a switch, in addition to the on-off switch, is provided for motor direction changes. Other times a lever is provided as part of the main switch to accomplish the same thing.

Motor speed and pulley relationship should be organized for a spindle speed of about 10,000 rpm's. Some shapers might be designed for more speed, some for less, so be sure to read the owner's manual that comes with the tool you buy and obey the speed recommendations.

The shaper fence is basically a two-part deal that locks securely to the shaper table. Either half of the

The individual shaper has its mechanism mounted under the table. It has adequate speed for the job, the right power, and a control that lets you change direction of cutter rotation.

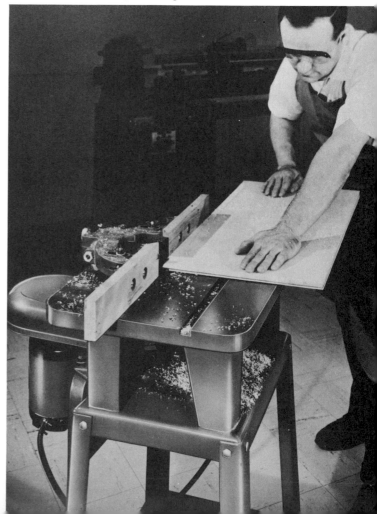

This shaper kit is available from AM&T Tool company. It provides all the necessary hardware. You add the assembly work and the wood materials to make a shaper that looks like the machine at left below.

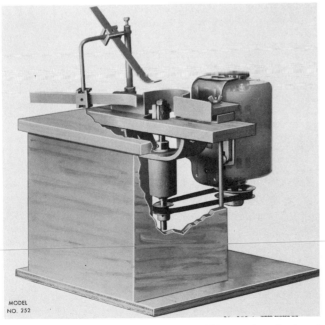

The recommended speed is about 5,800 rpm. An adjustment wheel on the spindle provides for cutter height adjustments. A reversing switch for the motor may be installed.

Many craftsmen mount a portable router as shown for use as a shaper. The fence in the drill press chapter for use with shaper work can be used as part of a router-shaper design.

fence is adjustable, and the entire unit is removable for freehand shaping against fulcrum pins and collars. Fence adjustment is exactly the same as for shaping operations on other tools. When the cut removes part of the work edge, the fences are set in line. When the cut removes the entire work edge, then the outfeed fence is brought forward an amount that equals the depth of the cut so the work will have support after it has passed the cutter.

CUTTERS

Cutters mount on the spindle as they do on a shaper adapter used in the drill press. Again, the difference here is that the spindle is under the table instead of over it. Collars are used in freehand work to control the depth of the cut, but they are also used when working with a fence to take up spindle length that is not occupied by the cutter.

Collars made for the shaper are available in thicknesses ranging from $\frac{1}{8}''$ up to $\frac{1}{2}''$ and in various diameters. Many shaper craftsmen will make up special collars to suit a particular application. You can even buy ball-bearing collars. The advantage of this feature is that the collar will not turn with the spindle, thus eliminating scoring and burning that can occur with solid collars. The most you can do with solid collars is to keep them clean and polished.

You can buy cutters, such as the *glue joint* or the *tongue-and-groove*, that are designed to do a specific job; or you can buy combination cutters, such as the *bead and quarter round*. The latter types are designed for partial cuts; you use that portion of the profile that suits a particular job. The others are designed for full profile cuts.

A three-knife cutterhead is often used on a shaper. This is like a small-size table-saw molding head, and there are a variety of ready-shaped knives that can be used with it. Since they come with a $\frac{3}{4}''$ center hole, they are pretty much a heavy-duty tool. But they can be used on a $\frac{1}{2}''$ spindle by mounting them with a bushing.

Another type of cutter consists of open-face knives that are locked between slotted collars. They have an advantage in that you can buy blank knives and grind them to any shape you wish. Actually, you can grind a different shape at each end of the knife. You must be extremely careful when mounting such knives. If the collars do not bear equally and tightly on both knives, the less secure one could fly out when you flick the switch. This can happen because you have done a poor job of securing the knives to begin with or because somehow you have installed knives of unequal width. This would cause one knife to be gripped, the other

Spindles thread on to one end of a stud or "tierod" that slips through the hollow, main spindle and is secured with a lock nut at the opposite end. This arrangement permits the use of different spindle designs.

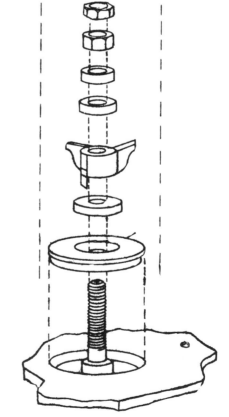

Three-lip shaper cutters mount on the spindle as they do on a shaper adapter that you would use in the drill press. Collars are used for freehand work, but also to take up unused spindle length when you are working against a fence.

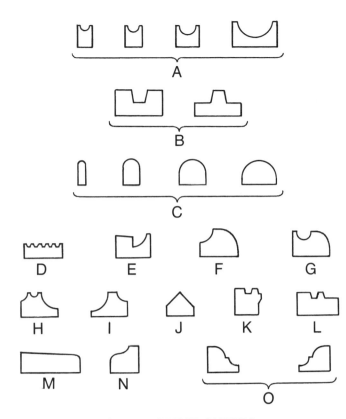

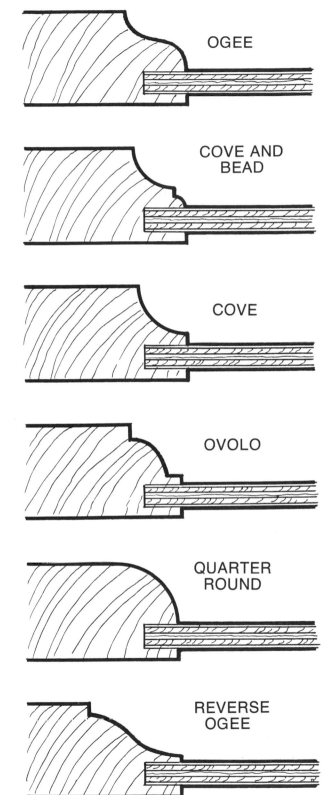

OGEE

COVE AND BEAD

COVE

OVOLO

QUARTER ROUND

REVERSE OGEE

EXAMPLES OF 3-LIP SHAPER CUTTERS

A $\frac{1}{4}''$, $\frac{3}{8}''$, $\frac{1}{2}''$, 1" bead cutters
B   wedge-type tongue-and-groove sets
C $\frac{1}{4}''$, $\frac{1}{2}''$, $\frac{3}{4}''$, 1" flute cutters
D   multi-bead cutter
E   door lip (cabinet)
F   combination cove and quarter round
G   "   bead and cove
H   "   bead and quarter round
I   "   quarter rounds
J   diamond flute
K   special drawer joint cutter
L   "   glue joint cutter
M   panel raiser
N   ogee molding
O   Right- and left-hand bead-and-cove molding cutter

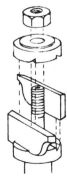

Open face knives are mounted between slotted collars. Use special care to lock them in securely. Blank knives may be ground to any profile.

Examples of classic molding forms, shown with inserted panel sections.

to be loose. Should you check out this type of cutter, be sure to read carefully the accompanying instructions.

SAFETY

Use all the guards that come with the machine or buy them if they are sold as accessories. The guard that is used for freehand shaping is a ring affair that is held over the spindle. It offers good protection and even does some hold-down work if you set it so it rests on the work's surface.

Never try to freehand shape anything that is too small or too narrow to provide adequate hand room. If you must shape a narrow piece, do it on the end of a wide board and then slice off the part you require. This practice holds for even curves, varying curves or straight pieces. When feeding, keep fingers hooked over work edges. This will guard against your hands slipping to where they should not be. When working against collars, be sure that there is sufficient bearing surface against the collar. As stated before, keep the collars clean and polished. Soiled or scarred collars will not only harm the work, they will make it harder to feed.

Whenever possible, set up so that the cutter is under the work. This positioning will put the work between you and the cutters and eliminate the possibility of damaging the work should you accidentally lift it during a pass.

Many of the illustrations show cutters at the top edge of the work and do not show guards. However, this is only so the operation can be seen more clearly.

OPERATIONAL TECHNIQUES

Regardless of which way the cutter turns, the work must always be fed against the direction of rotation. When the cutter is turning in counterclockwise fashion, the work is fed from the right to the left. When the cutter turns clockwise, work is fed from left to right. This method applies whether you are working against a fence or doing freehand feeding against collars.

Work may be placed flat on the table or on edge. Since there is nothing above the cutter (like the drill-press spindle), you can handle any work width when doing an on-edge pass.

Try to feed so you are cutting with the grain, which will always produce the smoothest cuts. When conditions demand otherwise, slow up on the pass. Many times in such circumstances, it's wise to do the job in repeat passes; simply increase depth of cut after each pass until you have the shape you want.

Cross-grain cuts will usually result in some slight imperfections at the end of the pass. You can minimize these by being very cautious at the end and finishing with minimum feed speed. You can eliminate them by shaping a piece that is a bit oversize and then doing a jointer cut or a slight rip cut with a hollowground blade on the edges after the shaping operation. The idea is to remove any imperfections by making a second cut.

The ring above the table is a guard that is used when doing freehand work against collars.

This model has an open-grid table. Hold-downs (on the left) help keep work flat on the table and snug against the fence. Some units provide them as standard equipment. With others they are available as accessories.

When you must shape all edges or adjacent edges of a workpiece, do the cross-grain cuts first. The final with-the-grain cuts will remove the imperfections left by the previous passes.

Most shapers provide for the use of a miter gauge. It's a good idea to use it on all cross-grain work, but it's very important to use it when you are shaping an end on narrow stock. If you don't have a miter gauge, make a right-angle backup block to use in its place. Such precautions will keep the work square to the cutter and will prevent rocking of the work.

When you are doing a full cut, the outfeed fence must be advanced to support the work after it has passed the cutter. The best way to do this is to start with the outfeed fence retracted. Then adjust the infeed fence for the depth of cut you wish. Make a partial pass—that is, hold the work against the infeed fence and feed until an inch or so of the work edge has passed the cutter. Turn off the machine and then adjust the outfeed fence until it bears lightly against the shaped edge.

Feed speed, regardless of the power and rpm's of your machine, should always be slow and steady. Make wise judgments in relation to the results you are getting and in tune with how the machine is reacting. It's never wise to cut so deep or so fast that there is an obvious decrease in rpm's or a noticeable objection in terms of motor sound. The harder the wood, the deeper the bite, the more cautious you must be. You will find when you force the cut that you will get obvious burn marks. Some of these will be difficult to remove, so it makes sense not to create them at all by working with sharp tools, sensible feed, and reasonable depth-of-cut settings.

SPECIAL FENCES

Almost any type of fence can be secured to the shaper table in place of the regular fence by organizing the item to use the same hardware employed with the standard fence or simply by using clamps.

A long fence can be handy for work that requires more support than you can get from the regular shaper table. It's also good to have when you wish to use stop blocks to control the length of a cut. Regular shaper fences are seldom long enough to permit much flexibility in this area. This type of fence is usable for many jobs such as shaping, narrowing, and precutting strips. Cut a work-size rabbet in a block that you then clamp or nail over the cutter. The narrow work can then be fed through the block in complete safety.

Since the regular shaper fence is quite low, you can provide more support for wide work that must be shaped with on-edge passes simply by making an extra-high auxiliary fence. Be sure that the vertical member is

HANDLING THE WORK

The work may be placed flat on the table, or fed on edge. Either way, always try to work so you are cutting *with* the grain. This will produce the smoothest cuts possible.

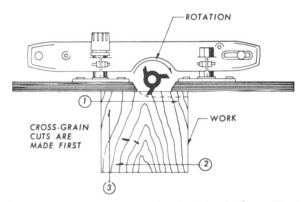

When you must cut crossgrain, do it slowly. On multi-edge work, do the crossgrain passes first. The last passes should be on with-the-grain edges.

A miter gauge is a big help on all crossgrain work. It is a *must* when the work is narrow. If you don't own one, make a special right-angle backup block and use it like a miter gauge.

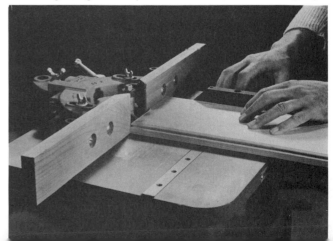

square to the table and that it is adequately braced to provide rigidity.

A miter fence, when used with blank knives, will let you do bevel-type operations on the shaper. It will also let you do shaping cuts on edges that are already beveled, as well as form tongue-and-groove joints on miters. You can make the jig adjustable simply by using hinges to attach the table to the fence. An assortment of angle braces that you use under the table will let you organize for different bevel settings. Attach the angle braces with screws driven through the top of the table. Thus, you can change quickly from one set of braces to another. The braces you make, at least to start, should include 45°, 30° and maybe 15° settings.

You can do some fairly decorative edge work by making a special fence that permits you to move work directly into the cutter without any normal feed action. The fence is a straight board with a series of equally spaced holes drilled along the bottom edge. A pin in the holes acts as a stop for the work. To do the job, you brace one edge of the work against the pin and then move directly forward to make the cut. Pull the work back, set the pin in the next hole, and then make the next cut. Just keep repeating the same procedure. Spacing of the cuts will depend on how you place the stop pin. Be sure to use at least $\frac{3}{4}''$ stock for the fence. Quarter-inch holes, spaced an inch apart, will do to start. You can always add more holes if you wish. Use a short length of $\frac{1}{4}''$ drill rod as the stop pin.

PIVOT WORK

You can do pivot work by using a hardwood bar in the miter-gauge slot. A nail driven through the end of the bar serves as a pivot point. This operation should not

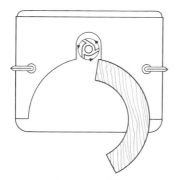

Segment jig for outside curves. When you do work like this, be sure that the curve of the jig and of the work are perfect matches. Both the jig-edge and the work-edge must be even and smooth.

FREEHAND SHAPING

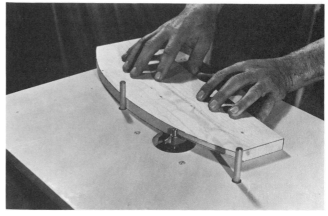

Freehand work is braced firmly against the infeed fulcrum pin until it contacts the cutter. At the end of the cut, use the outfeed pin for support.

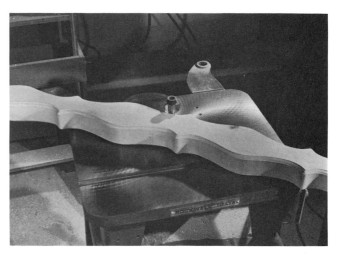

Unobstructed table surface of the individual shaper is an advantage when doing freehand work. You can work on any side of the table that is convenient in relation to the size and shape of the work piece.

To do inside work, you merely situate the work so the cutter is inside the opening. Shown in process is leg structure for a coffee table.

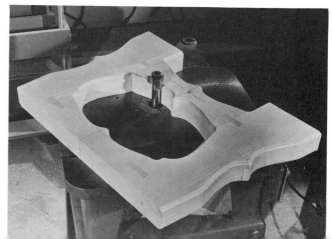

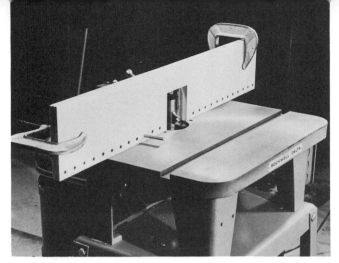

The fence for decorative edges is simply a flat board that is clamped to the regular fence. On all special fences, size the opening to reveal as little of the cutter as possible.

You can do pivot work by using a hardwood strip in the table slot. Here, the pivot pin is extra long just so it can be seen; best to keep it as short as possible. Read the text before trying this technique.

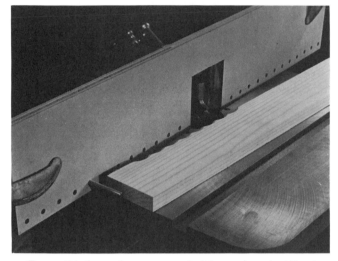

To use this fence, brace one end of the work against the stop pin and then move the work directly forward into the cutter. Pull the work back, re-situate the pin and repeat.

be approached carelessly. Place the work over the pin and leave the hardwood bar loose as you hand feed to get the depth of cut you want. Then, turn off the machine and use a clamp to secure the bar position. Hold the work firmly, turn on the machine, and rotate the stock against the direction of rotation of the cutter. If you neglect to use a positive grip, the cutter can take over and spin the work out of control. Keep the depth of cut light and feed slowly.

SEGMENT JIGS

The examples of segment jigs that are shown are much the same as those shown for shaping operations on other tools. The jigs can be organized for inside or outside cuts. It is important for the bearing edge of both the jig and the work to be true and smooth.

These jigs are designed for mass production use. When you have a few pieces to do, it's probably faster to handle them as freehand cuts against collars. An advantage of a segment jig is that it provides a little more safety than a similar freehand operation on narrow work.

If you check the shaping sections of the radial-arm-saw and the drill-press chapters, you'll find a V-jig that is recommended for shaping the edge of circular stock. The same thing can be done on the shaper. The advantage of the V-jig lies in its being able to handle any diameter work within its capacity.

STATIONARY BELT AND DISC SANDERS

Belt and disc sanders on stands have become standard finishing tools in the home woodworking shop. Often, the enterprising craftsman will rig up his own disc sander by mounting a suitable plate directly to the shaft of a properly powered motor and then adding a table for work support. It has already been discussed how tools like the lathe and the radial arm saw can be used efficiently as disc sanders.

In concept, the disc sander is a fairly simple tool. The belt sander is a bit more complicated since it requires two drums and built-in adjustments so the belt may be positioned correctly.

The tools may be purchased individually or as a combination. The combination unit is perhaps the better choice for the homecraftsman. It provides both items mounted on a single stand and powered by one motor. So mounted, they do not impose any operational restrictions. Anything you can do on either as individual tools may be accomplished when they are combined.

If a choice had to be made between the individual tools, it would probably be wise to decide in favor of the belt sander because you can improvise on other tools for disc-sander chores.

You can spend a lot of money for a combination unit, especially if you are attracted by a heavy-duty model that's powered by a plus 1 HP motor and runs on 220V. But good homecraftsman designs are also available. You can even buy a belt sander in kit form or an unadorned type that provides function without frills. Whichever model you choose, remember that sanding operations, especially when you are trying to remove a lot of material, require considerable power. Generally, a $\frac{1}{2}$ HP to $\frac{3}{4}$ HP motor is not out of line. When you shop, check the motor size recommended by the manufacturer. Never use less.

Disc sizes can range from 6″ up to 12″, belt widths from 4″ to 6.″ Two common belt sizes for home shops are 4″ × 36″ and 6″ × 48″. The latter dimension in each size (36″, 48″) indicates the full length of the belt; the larger the belt (or the disc), the more abrasive surface you have to work with.

These abrasive tools are among the best finishing aids you can have in the shop. They do not replace portable

versions, but they will substantially reduce the amount of postconstruction finishing that remains to be done. You can finish project components as you go so they are fairly well organized for final coats before you even assemble them. Also, many sanding jobs are much easier to do when you can apply the work to the tool, such as a final touch on the end of a 2×4 or the precise finished sanding of a picture-frame miter.

In addition, keep a few general safety rules in mind when using belt and disc sanders. Whenever possible, feed work so your fingers are hooked over the edge of the stock to guard against sanding your fingers instead of the work. Don't, without special precautions, work pieces so small that they can be drawn in between the abrasive surface and the edge of the table. Remember that metal

Heavy-duty belt-disc combination is driven by a plus 1 HP motor and sits on a totally enclosed stand. The belt is 6″ × 48″ and the disc is 12″ in diameter. Note that each unit has its own separate tilting table.

Another combo unit, more in the homecraftsman's area, has a 6″ × 48″ belt and a 9″ disc. The disc sander has a table, the belt has a "stop". A minimum of ½ HP is recommended for driving such tools.

You can mke your own 6″ × 48″ belt sander by working from a kit that costs about $24.00 (Gilliom Manufacturing Co.). All necessary metal parts are included. You supply the wood and the motor.

"Unadorned" economy model 4″ × 36″ belt sander (AMCO) costs about $20.00 plus motor. The disc sander and its table are accessories that run another $8.00 or so. It also has facilities for drum sanding and grinding (top).

sanding causes sparks which might contact an accumulation of wood dust and easily cause a fire. When you change from wood to metal sanding, be sure that you first clean the tools.

THE BELT SANDER

This tool uses an endless abrasive belt that rotates over two drums. The bottom drum is powered; the other is an idler. Since the abrasive moves in a straight line, the belt sander is an especially good tool for doing sanding that is parallel to the wood grain.

The width of the belt does not indicate a limit on the width of the stock you can sand. By making repeat passes and adjusting the work position after each, you can sand boards that are wider than the belt itself.

Cross-grain work is also permissible but done mostly when you wish to remove a lot of material quickly. It should always be followed by with-the-grain sanding to remove scratches that remain after the cross-grain work.

All belt sanders can be used in either a vertical or horizontal position. This is possible because they tilt back from the bottom end. In general, use the vertical position for any kind of end sanding; use the horizontal position for surfacing and sanding of edges on long pieces.

Adjustments. The back of the belt is marked with an arrow to indicate the correct direction of rotation. When you view the drums, you'll note that they turn "down" or in a clockwise direction. Point the arrow on the belt so it will follow the same route.

To mount a belt, lower the upper drum. This decreases the distance between the drums and permits the belt to slide into place easily. Then, raise the drum until there is no visible slackness in the belt. Don't overdo this *tensioning* adjustment. The second adjustment is *tracking*, which is centering the belt over the drums and keeping it moving in the same line. Tracking is accomplished with a tilt action in the upper drum. Tilt one way and the belt will move to the left; tilt the other way and the belt will move to the right. The idea is to adjust so the belt does neither. Your best bet is to sight the upper drum and make an as-close-as-possible arbitrary adjustment. Then turn the motor switch quickly on and off. If the belt moves one way or the other, make an adjustment to compensate.

When the belt is tracking correctly, you may use the machine. After a short period of work, increase the tension a slight amount. You may find that slight tracking readjustments may become necessary as you work. At such times, you may work the adjustment knob as the belt is turning.

The methods of accomplishing tensioning and tracking may vary from machine to machine, so read your owner's manual carefully for specifics in relation to the tool you own.

Edge sanding. Use the machine in the vertical position with the table adjusted to form a right angle with the abrasive surface. Rest the work solidly on the table and advance it slowly to make contact. When the work is curved, make the pass in a sweeping motion; remember that the belt cuts quickly, so allowing the

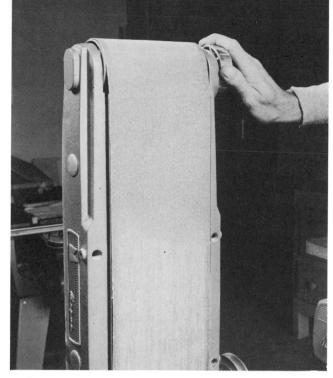

Belts are marked with an arrow. When placing the belt over the drums, be sure the arrow points in the direction of rotation of the drums. *Tensioning* of the belt is done by raising or lowering the upper drum. *Tracking* is done by tilting the upper drum.

work to sit too long in one position will produce too flat a surface.

If you are going from a flat edge to a round edge, approach the job with the flat edge parallel to the belt and swing gently into the curve. In essence, the surface of the belt should be tangent to the curve at point of contact at all times. Usually, you should do preliminary cutting with other tools so the amount of material to be removed by sanding will be minimal. In any case, excessive pressure against the abrasive is poor practice. Better to make two or three light-pressure passes than a single heavy one.

Try to work so you will be using the entire width of the belt. Keeping the work still will clog the belt in one area and may very well stretch it out of shape.

For square ends, move the work directly forward into the belt. When possible, use a miter gauge to assure squareness. Here too, it's a good idea to move the work across the belt as you move it forward. This can be done whether you are working freehand or with a miter gauge. Another reason to keep the work moving is to avoid obvious striations that can result when you do nothing but feed directly ahead. This factor is more critical with coarse papers than with fine.

How you do inside corners will depend on the design of the machine. If there is an outboard guard, it must be

Always keep the work moving. Gentle pressure and smooth sweeps always result in better work. Several passes to get a job done are better than a single heavy thrust.

Do end sanding by moving directly forward into the belt. When possible, use a miter gauge as a guide. When you are removing a lot of material, move the work laterally as well as forward. Overworking one area of the belt can lead to clogging or even cause the belt to stretch.

removed. You must adjust tracking so the edge of the belt moves right on line with the outboard edge of the backup plate. Then the job becomes pretty straightforward end sanding. Do one side of the corner; then flip the stock and do the other.

Angles. Simple bevels are done by tilting the table; the job is fairly much an end-sanding chore. You will be more accurate if you work with a guide. The guide can be the miter gauge or, lacking one, a piece of wood that you clamp in place after checking its position with a square. If the edge is compound, then you must set both the table and the miter gauge. The angles you use must be compatible with the miter-gauge and saw-blade settings you organized for the original cut. Remember that sanding removes material, so original cuts should be made a fraction oversize.

To do chamfers or to *break* edges (which simply means destroying a sharp corner), adjust the table to the angle you want and then move the stock directly forward. If you have a lot of chamfering to do on many similar pieces, it will pay to make a trough jig like the one shown in the sketch on page 298. The angle of the slanting pieces is organized to suit the chamfer you require. This jig is best used with the machine in its horizontal position.

When the bevel you are doing is on stock that is not longer than the belt is wide, then, as previously mentioned, the operation is pretty much an end-sanding chore. For longer work, you will have to sweep across the belt and the results will depend on how skillfully you do it. Start close to an end, apply very light pressure and maintain it as constantly as possible as you feed across. Excessive pressure can cause the belt to dig in at one edge or the other.

You can, if you wish, clamp a straight piece of wood to the table parallel to the belt. Then you can pass the work between the guide and the abrasive. This procedure must be a light-touch operation.

Surface work. Surfacing, or sanding of long edges, is best done with the machine in a horizontal position and with a fence set up as a guide. How you organize for the fence will depend on the design of your machine. In some cases, it's possible to use the one table in both its normal belt-upright position and as a fence when the tool is tilted horizontally. With other machines you can buy an accessory that is used as a fence. Many times you can make a simple L-shaped affair that you can bolt to the machine for fence use.

Don't feed the work in the same direction that the belt is traveling; you may well end up with no work between yourself and the belt. Always feed the stock against the direction of rotation of the belt unless you provide a stop to keep the work from being thrown by the belt. Again, some machines provide such a stop with the tool or as an accessory that you can buy. Another solution is to make your own or to use the regular table in its normal position even though the machine is horizontal. The latter idea or using a stop you make yourself works when stock length is not greater than the work surface of the belt. When the work is longer, then you must use the side fence idea and feed the material against the belt's rotation.

When you angle the fence to the belt, you can feed stock diagonally at times when you wish to remove a lot of material quickly. This results in cross-grain scratches, and the operation must always be followed by with-the-grain sanding in order to get an acceptable finish.

To do bevel work, just tilt the table to the angle you require. Here, both the miter gauge and the table are adjusted to match original sawing angles of a compound cut.

A fence is a good accessory when the tool is used horizontally. Sometimes the table or the stop may be used as one. This simple L-shaped fence is bolted in place using holes that are provided for other accessories.

You can work freehand to do small chamfers or to "break" edges. If the work is critical, use a miter gauge or clamp a right-angle piece of wood to the table or stop.

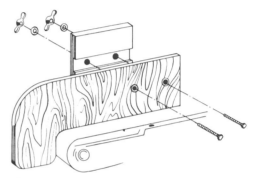

Even when you can use the table or a stop as a fence, it pays to make an auxiliary addition that will run the full length of the belt and curl over the top drum. Bolts go through holes in the table or stop. If necessary, drill them.

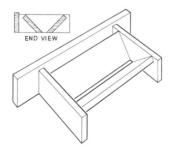

END VIEW

A trough jig will let you do production work when you need the same chamfer on many pieces. The angle of the side pieces determines the angle of the chamfer. This jig is used with the tool in horizontal position.

DON'T WORK THIS WAY! We're showing a how-not-to-do-it photo simply because the mistake is so common. Action of the belt can throw out the work and leave nothing between your fingers and the abrasive. Always feed *against* the belt's rotation and hold the work firmly.

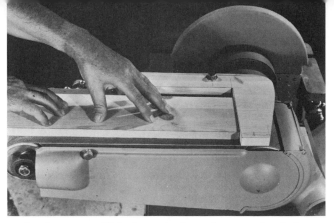

A safer, more efficient way to do surface sanding is to use the table or a stop as a brace for the work. This L-shaped jig does a good job. It attaches to the sander just like the fence we described earlier.

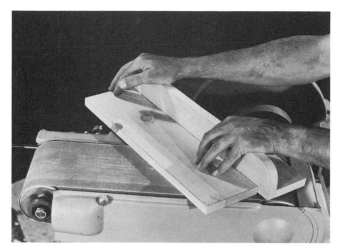

Do "crossgrain" sanding like this when you wish to remove a lot of material quickly. Usually, its done with a coarse abrasive and the understanding that with-the-grain sanding must follow in order to get a good finish.

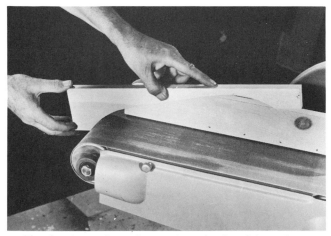

It's okay to work on the top drum freehand, but when you want the sanded edge to be square to adjacent surfaces, it's best to use the fence as a guide.

Inside curves. All machines permit the use of the top drum as a "drum sander." If there is a guard, it must be removed. The job can be done freehand, especially if you are smoothing something like a cabriole leg or doing irregular edge scalloping for an antique effect. When you want the sanded edge to be square to adjacent surfaces, then it's good practice to use a fence as a guide for the work.

Odd jobs. The belt sander is constructed so there is a backup plate behind the belt only at the front of the machine. This feature allows you to use the backside of the belt for such jobs as sanding knobs, round edges, and ball shapes. If you ease off on belt tension a bit, you'll get more slack in the belt which will help in these types of jobs. It's also possible to buy slashed belts for rounding-off operations although such items are not easily found in stores that deal mostly with the homecraftsman.

You can try slashing your own belt. Choose a fine-grit belt and use a sharp knife to cut slits on the back side of the belt that are about 5″ or 6″ long and from $\frac{3}{16}$″ to $\frac{1}{4}$″ apart. Do this across the width of the belt but leave about $\frac{1}{2}$″ of solid belt along each edge. Slit the length of the belt but leave about $\frac{1}{2}$″ of solid belt between groups of slits.

THE DISC SANDER

How to mount paper. There are many ways to mount paper on a disc sander, and everyone usually ends up with one method that he finds preferable. One

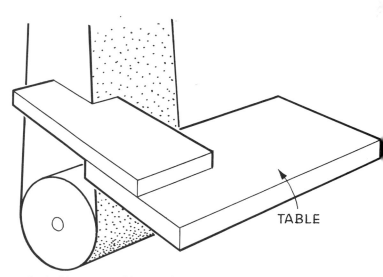

Do inside corners this way. On some tools it may be necessary to remove an outboard guard. Be sure to track the belt so its edge is in line with the outboard edge of the back-up plate. Again, be careful of your hand positions.

older method is the use of a disc stick that is almost like a stick shellac wrapped in a cardboard tube. You peel back the paper and apply the exposed sticky material to the revolving disc until the disc is fairly evenly coated. Then you press the abrasive sheet against the disc. This method works best when you "warm" the disc by holding a block of wood against it while it is turning.

Another method involves the use of a special rubber cement that is applied with a brush to both the disc and the paper. When the cement dries enough to be tacky to the touch, you press the sheet and disc together.

You can also buy abrasive sheets with self-adhesive backings which work well. However, with long-period storage the paper backing that protects the adhesive sometimes sticks too well and comes off in pieces.

Another material that can be used is a spray mounting adhesive that is available in art supply stores. Even though it isn't made for the purpose, it seems to work well and is very easy to use. Simply spray the back of the sheet, and when the application is dry enough to be tacky, press the sheet onto the disc.

Whatever method you use, always be sure to clean the old adhesive from the disc before applying a new coating. If there are sticky areas, use a solvent to soften the adhesive and then rub off with fine steel wool. Always be sure to apply the adhesive evenly in order to get the sandpaper flat on the disc; any bumps will result in imperfections on the sanded surface.

Incidentally, when you are doing a job that can be accomplished best by working through two grits of paper, you can organize a "double-sanding" disc. This is simply a matter of cutting a circle from the center of the coarser paper and then cutting a disc from the finer paper to fit it. Both pieces of paper are mounted on the sanding disc so you can work on the outer portion for one grit and the inner portion for the second grit.

After mounting a new disc, run the machine freely for a minute or so and stand away from the edge. This procedure tests whether the bond between the disc and sheet of abrasive is good enough to be safe.

Direction of rotation. Most discs will turn in a counterclockwise direction, which means you should place the work on the table on the left so you will be using the "down" side. Using the "up" side will cause the disc to lift the work and will throw grit into your face. Even so, sometimes it's necessary to use the "up" side, such as in sanding a long edge freehand and sweeping across the full diameter of the disc. When you have to use the "up" side, keep a firm grip on the work, hold it snug to the table and wear goggles.

To some extent, you can choose the abrasive-surface speed at which you wish to work. The slowest speed is at

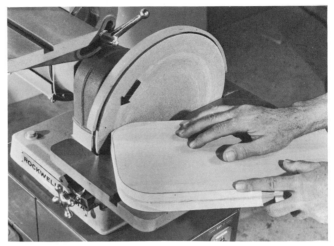

The disc rotates counter-clockwise (see arrow) so always place work on the left side of the table. This is the "down" side of the disc. Working on the right side will lift the work from the table and throw grit into your face. Keep the work moving and try to feed laterally as well as forward. Staying too long in one position on curved work will create flats.

Be very careful when sanding material that is longer than the disc diameter. For one thing, you will be using the "up" side of the disc as well as the down. For another, it's easy for the edge of the disc to dig into the work and cause gouging.

the center of the disc; it increases as you approach the outer edge. Remember this is surface speed, not rpm's. Also, if you held a piece of wood directly against the midpoint of the disc, you would create circular marks but do no sanding.

General operational procedures. Remember that the disc rotates. Therefore, it can't be used to do with-the-grain sanding. It is possible to surface cut by feeding with the stock on edge and its surface against the disc, but you will have arc marks that will have to be removed later by sanding with the grain. The depth of the arc marks will, of course, depend on the grit of the paper you are using.

It is always best to work with a light, smooth feed. Pressure should never be excessive even when you must remove a lot of material. A few light touches do a better job than a single heavy push. This approach is better for the work, and it will help prevent clogging the paper quickly. The no-force rule is especially true when you are working on material that is longer than the disc diameter. Forcing against the edge of the disc can cause gouging. Also, since disc speed is high, too much pressure can cause excessive heat which can burn the wood and the paper.

Keep the work moving. If you hesitate in one spot when sanding a curve, you will create a flat surface in that area. If you are doing end sanding, move the work directly forward into the disc but add a lateral feed after you make contact. The length of the lateral stroke can be from the outer edge of the disc to somewhere close to the center.

Although the disc can't get completely inside the corner of a right-angle cut, you can get close enough so that only a little extra hand work will be required to complete the job. It is best to sand one leg of the work by moving it across the abrasive until the edge of the disc almost touches the adjacent side. Then, flip the stock and sand the second edge by moving directly forward. When both legs of the cut are long, then it might be best to do each by moving across the face of the disc. In either case, don't force when you approach the inside corner. The exposed edge of the disc can mar the work.

Round off corners by using a gentle, sweeping motion. Start by holding the flat of the work parallel to the disc

and then moving in to make light contact. Once you touch, start the sweeping motion. The plane of the disc must be tangent to the arc at all times.

Square ends and miters can be guided with a miter gauge. In either case, the work and the miter gauge may be moved laterally after the initial contact is made. When you have many similar jobs to do and the material to be removed by sanding is minimal, it's a good idea to clamp the miter gauge in position so all you have to do is move the stock directly forward. If you don't have a miter gauge, simply substitute a straight piece of wood for the gauge. The angle between the wood guide and the disc can be established with a protractor.

Chamfer jig. Chamfering can be done freehand; but when a groove is required on more than one edge of the stock or when it must be repeated on similar pieces, it's wise to make a simple jig as a guide. A chamfering jig is no more than a notched board that is clamped to the disc sander table. The long leg of the notch holds the work in position for the correct chamfer angle; the short leg limits the amount of material that can be removed. Thus, whether you are doing two pieces or a hundred pieces, you'll know that all the chamfers will be uniform.

Pivot sanding. This type of sanding is a fine way to sand perfect circles or arcs. The setup for the work doesn't have to be much more than a piece of plywood through which you have driven a nail for use as a pivot. When you clamp the plywood to the table, the nail should be about center on the down side of the disc, and the distance from the nail to the abrasive should equal the radius of the work.

An adjustable jig for pivot sanding is another possibility. The platform is a piece of $\frac{3}{4}''$ plywood that is dadoed to receive a sliding, hardwood bar. If you make the sliding bar to fit tightly in the dado, you won't have to worry about clamping it in place for various radii settings. Drive a small roofing nail through one end of the bar. Make another bar to match the groove in the sander table and assemble the platform and the bar so there is about a $\frac{1}{8}''$ gap between the front edge of the platform and the disc. Clamp the platform to the table so the sliding bar is about centered on the down side of the disc. This position is variable. When you have many pieces to do, it makes sense to shift occasionally so you will be using the full width of the down side.

To use the jig, set the pivot point away from the disc a bit more than you actually need for the work. Place the work in position on the point and tap the sliding bar forward until the disc contacts the work line. Then, slowly rotate the disc to sand the full circle. It doesn't matter whether you turn the work left or right.

When possible, use a miter gauge as a guide for sanding miter cuts. Work is moved directly forward while it is held snugly against the miter-gauge head. Make initial sawing cuts in such a way that you can keep to a minimum the material that must be removed by sanding.

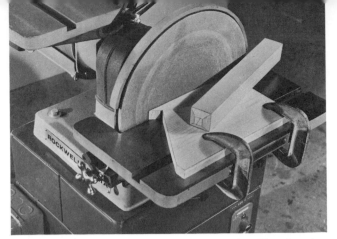

Typical jig setup for such jobs as chamfering. The short leg on the jig assures that exactly the right amount of wood will be removed from the work.

The work is held against the long leg of the jig and then moved directly forward.

In pivot cutting, it's assumed that you have bandsawed, jigsawed or somehow prepared the work so that the bulk of the waste has been removed before you go to the final sanding.

Sanding to width. You can sand straight or curved edges to exact width if you clamp a guide to the sander table so you can pass the work between the guide and the abrasive.

For straight edges, use an offset fence as a guide. This fence can be a straight piece of wood clamped to the sander table so the distance from its inside edge to the down side of the disc is a bit less than the width of the workpiece. The guide is angled just a bit so that when the pass is made, the work will contact the disc on the down side only.

To do the sanding, place the forward edge of the work on the up side of the table. Then move it forward in a steady, smooth manner. Don't take too deep a bite, and remember that since the abrasive does remove material, the original saw cut on the stock should be a bit oversize.

Both this idea and the pivot circle-cutting technique can be used to do beveling simply by tilting the sander table.

There are two ways to sand curves to width. With one, you install a dowel guide in a platform that you clamp to the sander table. The distance between the dowel and the disc equals the thickness of the work. You

The adjustable jig for pivot sanding. The arrow indicates the pivot point which is only a short roofing nail driven through the end of the sliding bar. The center of the work is pressed down over the pivot point.

Then the work is rotated in a full circle. When you have much of this to do, reposition the platform frequently to avoid working on just one area of the disc.

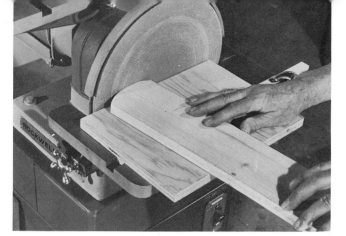

The pivot jig may also be used to round off ends. Be sure the pivot point is on the centerline of the work.

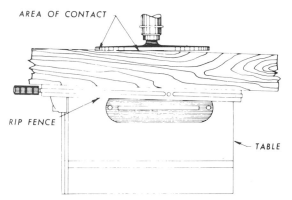

On a ShopSmith, you can do sanding-to-width by off-setting the fence. The work is moved at an angle against the disc, contacting it from edge to about center. This technique is good with lumber and ideal with plywood.

You can accomplish the sanding-to-width job by using a straight piece of wood as a guide. Feed is from right to left. The guide angle here is exaggerated just so you can see it. In use, it should be minimal so as to use as much of the disc, from the outboard edge to the center, as possible.

pass the work between the dowel and the disc, turning the work as you go to maintain the point of tangency.

Another way is simply to clamp a pointed stick to the sander table. The work is passed between the point on the stick and the disc.

In either case, it's assumed that the stock has been bandsawed or jigsawed so that a minimum of material remains to be removed. Also, the inside edge (the one that will ride the dowel guide or the point on the stick) must be sanded smooth before you do the outside edge. The inside surface can be done on a drum sander or by using the top drum of the belt sander.

Pattern sanding. Pattern sanding calls for an auxiliary table that is clamped to the regular table. A rigid, metal guide strip is attached with screws to the front edge of the auxiliary table. Size the guide strip so its length is a bit less than the radius of the disc and its width is $\frac{1}{4}''$ or so

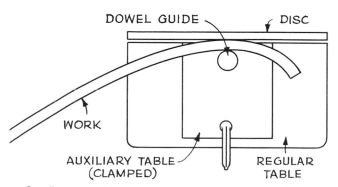

Sanding curved work to width using a dowel guide. The dowel is placed to allow just enough space to apply the work against the disc. The guide is clamped to the table.

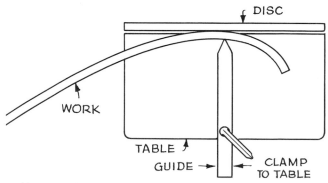

You can also use a pointed guide. In either case, the inside curve of the work must be sanded smooth to begin with. That can be done on a drum sander or by using the top drum of the belt sander.

more than the platform's thickness. The pattern, which is the shape of the work you want but undersized to compensate for the guide thickness and some clearance between the guide and the disc, rides the guide. The work, cut slightly oversize to begin with, is tack-nailed to the pattern. As you move the pattern while keeping it in contact with the guide, the work is sanded and matches the shape of the pattern. A simple way to secure work to the pattern instead of tack-nailing is to drive nails through the pattern so the points project on the top side. Then the work is simply pressed down on the points.

This method is not efficient when you need only one piece, but it is a very fine technique to use when you require many similar pieces.

Pointing dowels or other round stock. This process may be done freehand, but it's better to work with a guide. Simply drill a hole through a piece of wood with the size of the hole to match the size of the work. Clamp the guide block to the sander table at the required angle and then pass the work through the hole to make contact with the disc. Rotate the work to do either pointing or chamfering. To get a flat surface, move the work directly forward; don't allow it to rotate at all.

Metal work. Sanding metals (or plastics) doesn't differ too much from sanding wood materials on either the belt sander or the disc sander. Use the correct abrasive and when working with hard materials, use less feed pressure. It's important to wear goggles on all abrasive operations but especially critical when abrading metals. Remember what was said about the possibility of fire when changing from wood sanding to metal sanding.

You'll find that many of the ideas described for woodworking will do for metal. For example, if you needed a perfect circle in sheet metal, you could use the pivot sanding technique on the disc sander exactly as described for wood. When the metal is very thin and you have done the original cutting by supporting the sheet metal on scrap wood, do the pivot sanding with the sheet metal still on the scrap backup.

Metals do get hot. When doing work on small pieces, it's better to grip them with pliers instead of your fingers.

The setup for pattern sanding. The pattern is kept in contact with the guide strip. The work, tack-nailed to the pattern, gets sanded. The pattern must be smaller by the thickness of the guide strip *plus* the clearance between the guide strip and the disc.

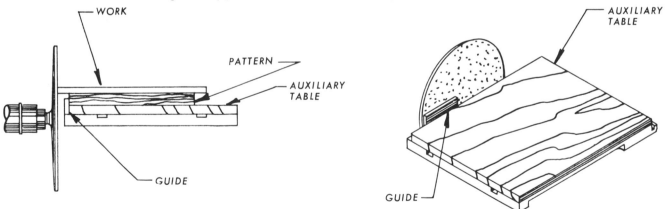

While the bench grinder can be a very versatile tool, its main function in a woodworking shop is to renew the worn edges and maintain the sharp edges of cutting tools. These cutting tools may be hand tools such as butt wood chisels or power-driven cutters such as jointer knives and twist drills.

The function of the grinder as a safety tool is often overlooked. With a grinder, you are more likely to keep tools sharp, and sharp tools mean better and safer work. In addition, you are more likely to remove, for example, burrs from the head of a cold chisel or even a nail hammer before they can become dangerous projectiles.

It's true that you can drive grinding wheels on other tools such as the drill press, the radial arm saw, the lathe, or even the table saw. With proper precautions these temporary setups can be used efficiently. But a good grinder is the one tool that is specifically designed for the job, and for optimum results there really is no substitute.

GENERAL CHARACTERISTICS

The most popular grinder is a self-contained unit that resembles a double-shaft motor quite a bit. However, it is so encased with covers, guards and shields that the only areas exposed are those parts of the grinding wheels that you need to see in order to work.

The bench grinder is a plug-in-and-use unit that you bolt down to an existing bench or mount on a special bench that you make or buy as an accessory. The word "pedestal" in the name of the tool merely indicates a particular design of floor stand (usually heavy-duty) on which the grinder rests.

Some grinders are belt driven. A pulley is mounted on the shaft that drives the wheels. This pulley, by means of a V-belt, connects to another pulley that is on a separate motor shaft. Such units are cheaper than the self-contained ones, but they require more mounting room. In addition, by the time you add a motor, extra

Five-inch bench grinder drives two vitrified aluminum oxide grinding wheels at about 3,400 rpm. Main purpose of the grinder in the home woodworking shop is to keep tools sharp, but you can also use it to drive wire brushes and buffing wheels.

pulley and V-belt, you're really not much ahead financially.

A grinder is often thought of in relation to its polishing head. This polishing head unit does have a horizontal shaft and you can mount grinding wheels on it, but it does not approach being a safe grinder. Many manufacturers will tell you specifically that the polishing head they show in a catalog is not for grinding.

The size of a grinder is listed in terms of wheel diameter. For example, if it's called a 7″ grinder, you know it is designed to turn 7″ grinding wheels. Home shop sizes run from 5″ to 7″ with motor horsepower ranging from $\frac{1}{4}$ to $\frac{1}{2}$. When you get into 8″ wheels and motor horsepower $\frac{3}{4}$ or more, you are entering the heavy-duty area where the tool is designed for continuous production work in places such as machine shops and garages.

Regardless of the size of the tool, it should be equipped with strong wheel covers, eye shields (preferably adjustable) and adjustable tool rests. If it has a water tray and a flexible gooseneck lamp, so much the better. Such extras as spark arresters, exhaust outlets and adjustable spark deflectors are good to have and will be found on the higher priced units.

When you situate any grinder, be sure to bolt it solidly to a good, strong support. The less vibration you have, the easier it will be to do work well.

WHEELS

A grinding wheel is made of abrasive grains that are bonded together by means of a special material. Each of the grains is a cutting tool that becomes dull as it does its job and finally tears loose so another sharp grain can take over. The makeup of any wheel involves five factors: the abrasive, the grain, the grade, the structure, and the bond.

The abrasive is the material that does the cutting. Most of the wheels supplied with home-type grinders are of aluminum oxide. This is good for grinding all materials that have a high tensile strength such as high speed steel and carbon steels. Silicon carbide is good for working on low tensile strength materials like brass, bronze, gray iron, aluminum, and copper.

The grain has to do with abrasive grit size, and there are as many categories here as you will find in common sandpaper. "Coarse" grits will run from #12 to #24. "Medium" grits will run from #30 to #60. "Fine" grits will run from #70 to #120. Even finer grits in the "very fine" and "flour size" categories can run from #150 to #600.

Wheels supplied as standard equipment with the grinder you buy usually fall into the general medium category, even when they are listed as "coarse." The

Grinding wheels may be shaped, or purchased pre-shaped to do special jobs. This one renews the serrations in pliers' jaw. More common wheels are square- or round-edged. Cup wheels, if your machine can handle them, are good for sharpening tools like gouges and roundnose lathe chisels.

coarse (sometimes called out as a "medium coarse") will be about a #36, and the medium (sometimes called out as a "medium fine") will be about a #60. These grit sizes in aluminum oxide are very good for all-purpose wood-shop work.

The grade of a wheel has to do with the bond, which can run from "very soft" to "very hard." Hard wheels hold abrasives together even under extreme pressure while soft wheels permit them to loosen easily. In general, hard wheels are used for grinding soft materials while the soft wheels are used on hard materials. Between the two extremes, a medium-hard grade, is best for average work.

In essence, structure refers to the spacing of the grains throughout the wheel. Hard, brittle materials are handled best on wheels with abrasive grains that are closely spaced. Wheels with widely spaced grains do better with soft materials that tend to clog the abrasive.

The bond refers to the material that is used to hold the abrasive grains together. For our purposes, we are concerned with a vitrified bond which consists of special clays and other ceramic materials. The bond material and the abrasive grains are fused at high temperatures to form a glasslike mass. The result is a high-strength, porous wheel with a cool cutting action. The vitrified bond is excellent for general-purpose grinding.

SAFETY AND CARE OF WHEELS

Never run a grinding wheel faster than the speed that is listed on the flange. Excessive speed will generate destructive heat and will also subject the wheel to centrifugal force that it may not be able to withstand. Both conditions can result in wheel breakage.

Test a wheel for cracks before you mount it. Do a visual check for chipped edges and cracks that you can see, then mount the wheel on a rod that you pass through the arbor hole and tap the wheel gently on the side with a piece of wood. The wheel will ring clear if it is in good condition. A dull thud may indicate the presence of a crack that can't be seen by eye. If it happens, don't take any chances; discard the wheel.

Good grinding wheels have metal bushings and are fit tightly on the spindle. However, they must not be so tight that you have to hammer them on or so loose that they will not run true. Washers made of blotting paper should be placed on each side between the wheel and the flanges. Be sure the diameter of the paper washers is not less than the diameter of the flanges. The purpose of the paper washers is to equalize the pressure on the sides of the wheel.

Tighten lock nuts only as tight as they have to be to secure the wheel. Excessive pressure can cause the wheel to break. After the wheel is mounted and all guards replaced, let the wheel run idle for a minute or so as you stand to one side.

Always adjust the tool rests so they are within $\frac{1}{8}''$ of the wheel. This will reduce the possibility of getting the work wedged between the rest and the wheel. Whenever possible, work on the face of the wheel. Working

When you must point or bevel or just chamfer an end on bar stock, do it this way if the work-size permits. Both the drill and the wheel are turning.

The same technique can be used when you wish to reduce diameter. Keep pressure very light. Be sure to provide for minimum clearance between tool rest and face of the wheel.

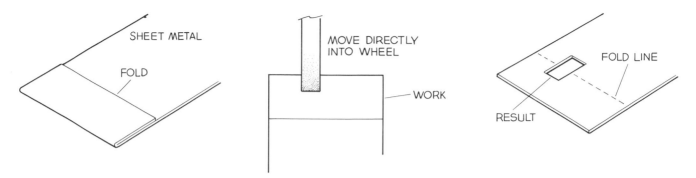

The technique to use to create a square hole in sheet metal. Don't make the fold too sharp or the sheet metal may crack when you unfold it after grinding.

on the side of the wheel is necessary for many jobs but inspect frequently to be sure you do not reduce wheel thickness to the point where further use becomes hazardous.

Wear safety goggles or a good face mask on all grinding operations even if the job is simple such as touching up a screwdriver tip. Metal grinding creates sparks so keep the area around the grinder clean. Let the wheel come up to full speed before you apply the work.

TO DRESS A WHEEL

"Dressing" a wheel can be done to renew sharpness or to true up the face of the wheel. The most common type of dresser is a mechanical one with star wheels that revolve as the tool is pressed against the wheel. To use it, set the tool rest so the gap between it and the face of the grinding wheel is just enough so the heel of the dresser can brace against the forward edge of the tool rest. Tilt the handle of the dresser up at a slight angle but do not make contact with the grinding wheel until after you have turned on the motor. Press the dresser easily against the turning wheel until you get a bite; then move slowly from side to side across the wheel. A small bite and many passes is better than a big bite and one pass.

It takes a little experience to do this job. Work cautiously, hold the dresser with force on the tool rest, do not use excessive pressure against the grinding wheel, and you'll soon master the technique.

JOB POSSIBILITIES

If you have to remove metal from metal, the job can probably be done on the grinder as long as it's feasible to apply the work to the tool. Welded joints can be smoothed; round or square bar stock can be scored on an edge of the wheel as a preliminary step to hack-sawing or cutting with a chisel. Burrs that form on the hammer end of cold chisels can be ground away. You can even do such jobs as forming a square opening in metal tubing simply by moving the tube directly into the face of the wheel. A similar job can be done on sheet metals if you fold the metal as shown in the accompanying sketch and then, with the fold line forward, move the work straight into the wheel. When you unfold the metal, you have a square opening. Of course the thickness of the wheel dictates the minimum cut. You can do wider cuts by making more than one pass, but you can't make narrower ones.

Working with a portable drill facilitates pointing rods and even reducing end diameters. Chuck the rod in the drill and let it spin as you apply it to the turning wheel. It isn't necessary to apply a lot of pressure, but it is a good idea to avoid using just one spot on the wheel. Working in this manner will usually produce more accurate results than if you tried to do it freehand.

HOLLOW-GROUND EDGES

Creating a hollow-ground edge is easy to do on the face of the wheel simply because the wheel shape produces the hollow-ground form automatically. The tool must be held at an angle with the work edge against the upper part of the wheel. The more acute the angle, the longer the cutting edge will be. Many times, it's possible to rest the blade of whatever you are sharpening against the rear edge of the tool rest and to use this contact as a pivot to bring the cutting edge of the tool forward. Take light touches until the grinding is complete.

Flat bevels are best done on the side of the wheel. In all cases, keep the metal cool. Have water on hand so you can quench the item frequently. Allowing the metal to get too hot can destroy the temper of the tool.

but it takes a considerable amount of experience to do the job professionally. Creating holders for tools will help eliminate human error. Quite a few jigs are sold as accessories for the grinder. Some are simple and hold only a few tools; some are complex and make it possible to hold objects that range from plane blades to scissors. Special ones are sold for sharpening twist drills. Anytime you can make a job easier or better by buying or making a jig, do so.

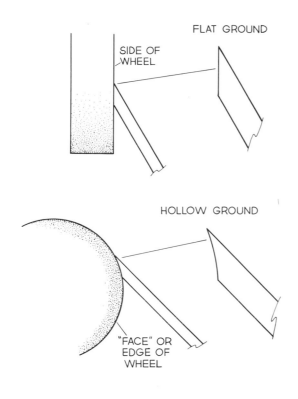

Hollow-grinding is done on the face of the wheel—flat-grinding on the side. In each case, the more acute the angle between tool and wheel, the longer the bevel will be. See text for cautions about wheel-side use.

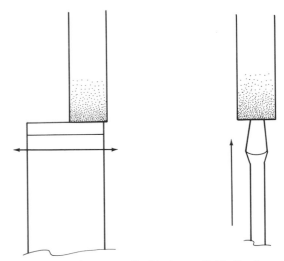

To square an edge, move the blade parallel to the face of the wheel. When the edge is narrow, such as the tip of a screwdriver, you can move directly forward into the wheel. Remove the least amount that will do the job.

WORKING ACROSS THE WHEEL FACE

To renew a straight edge, work on the face of the wheel. If the work is wider than the wheel thickness, then you must pass laterally while keeping the work edge parallel to the face of the wheel. If the work edge is narrow, you can move the work directly forward.

To do this kind of work with more accuracy than you might be able to achieve freehand, make the miter-gauge jig shown in the accompanying sketch. This jig is no more than a platform with a groove cut to receive the bar of a right-angle guide. You can make it for one wheel or long enough to span across both tool rests. Attach it with clamps or drill a few holes through the tool rests so you can secure this jig and others like it with wood screws driven up through the bottom.

Using jigs with the grinder is very important. Anything that can be sharpened can be sharpened freehand,

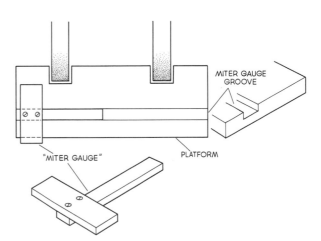

The miter-gauge jig will prove very useful for many grinding jobs. When you set it up, be sure the groove is parallel to the wheel faces and that the head of the "miter gauge" is square to the bar. Make the jig for one wheel or to span across both.

TIPS ON SHARPENING

Twist drills. Twist drills can be sharpened freehand, but it's a tricky job that even some experienced mechanics never master. To get some idea of the proper technique, choose a new, $\frac{1}{2}''$ twist drill and go through the following procedure with the grinding wheel still.

Hold the drill near the cutting edge between the thumb and index finger of your left hand. Hold the shank end of the drill between the thumb and index finger of your right hand. Place the drill on the tool rest so its center line makes the required angle with the face of the wheel, and then slightly lower the shank end. Since you are working with a new drill, it will be easy to gauge the angle simply by placing the cutting edge of the drill flat against the face of the wheel.

Advance the drill to place its heel against the grinding wheel and then, in a combination action, slowly raise the shank end of the drill while you use your left-hand fingers to twist the drill in a counterclockwise direction until the grinding approaches the cutting edge. Don't exert a lot of pressure; don't try to work too fast. After you have gone through this procedure a dozen times or so with a new drill, test your skill by sharpening an old one.

Another possibility is to make the jig shown in the accompanying sketch and work against the side of the wheel. To use the jig, place the drill so the cutting lip is against the side of the wheel and the body of the drill is against the guide block. To do the sharpening, the drill is rotated as it is swung to a position that is parallel to the pencil line. Here too, in order to do a good job, it's wise to go through the procedure with a brand new, large size drill and with the wheel stationary. Doing this a few times will give you the feel of what is involved. Naturally, the angle of the guide must be changed if the point angle of the drill is not 59°.

Wood chisels. These tools cut best when they are square across the cutting edge and have a hollow-ground bevel. Squaring the edge is necessary only after the chisel has seen considerable use and knicks appear. It is done by placing the chisel flat on the tool rest and moving it parallel to the face of the grinding wheel. This can be done freehand or by using the miter-gauge jig described previously. Remove only as much material as you have to.

To do the bevel, tilt the tool rest to the required angle and again move the chisel across the face of the wheel. If the chisel is narrow enough, the lateral motion may not be necessary. Another method is to make a special guide block that provides the necessary bevel angle. The length of the bevel should be about twice the thickness of the chisel; this usually produces about a 30° angle.

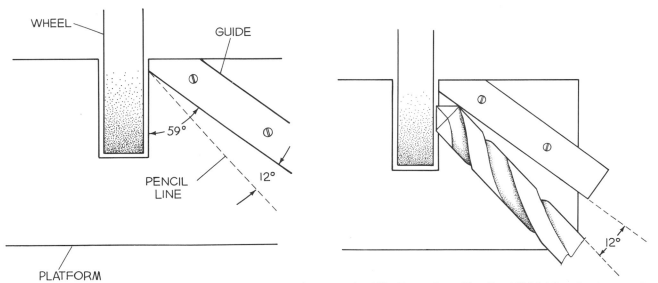

This simple jig (*left*) will provide a lot of help when you must sharpen twist drills. To use it, position the drill (*right*) and make a small clockwise turn as you move the drill away from the guide block and bring it parallel to the pencil mark. Try this with a new drill and the wheel still a few times to get the feel of it.

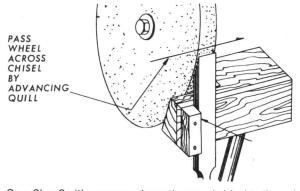

PASS
WHEEL
ACROSS
CHISEL
BY
ADVANCING
QUILL

On a ShopSmith, you can clamp the wood chisel to the guide and do the grinding by advancing the quill. On a conventional grinder, you pass the chisel back and forth across the face of the wheel.

Special twist drills holders are available as accessories. These are adjustable for many styles and sizes of drills and come with specific instructions for their use.

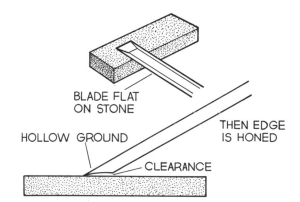

BLADE FLAT ON STONE

HOLLOW GROUND

THEN EDGE IS HONED

CLEARANCE

After grinding, hone as shown here. Be sure to maintain the slight clearance between the heel of the cutting edge and the stone when you are honing the bevel.

Some amount of burr will be left on the cutting edge, so the grinding operation should be followed by honing the chisel by hand on a flat stone. This should be done with the chisel tilted on its bevel but with a little extra tilt to get some clearance between the heel of the cutting edge and the stone. The chisel should also be level but resting on the back surface of the blade. Alternate between the two positions until all the burrs are gone and the edge is keen enough to cut a hair.

The honing operation actually produces a secondary bevel that does a beautiful cutting job. When you use chisels with care, the honing can be repeated quite a few times before it becomes necessary to go through the grinding procedure again.

All of the information in this section applies to hand-plane blades and similar items, as well as to wood butt chisels.

Jointer knives. Jointer knives are done much like chisels, but it's not recommended that you try to do them freehand. Instead, work with one of the two jigs shown in the illustrations on page 312. One jig spans across both wheels of the grinder and offers the advantage of being able to go from coarse grinding to fine grinding

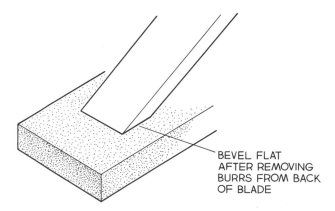

BEVEL FLAT AFTER REMOVING BURRS FROM BACK OF BLADE

A flat-ground edge is honed in similar fashion after it has been shaped on the flat side of the grinding wheel.

without a jig change. Of course, if the knife is in fairly good shape to begin with, you can confine the grinding to the less coarse wheel.

The second jig employs a sliding block that has been kerfed at the correct knife angle. The knife must fit snugly in the kerf before you do the grinding. This is especially important because three knives are involved. If you don't grind them carefully, the knives will be of different width and, because of the knife-adjustment method employed by some jointers, you will end up cutting with just one or two of the knives.

When you use the jigs, be sure that you go through each grinding procedure on each knife before you make any jig change. This assumes that more than one pass will be required to create a new edge. No matter what, keep the cuts extremely light and do not permit the knives to become overheated. You can do honing on the knives after grinding or between grindings as described for wood chisels but don't overdo the secondary bevel since this will weaken the cutting edge. Also, check the jointer chapter to see how knives may be honed while they are mounted in the machine.

This jointer-knife jig spans across both wheels so you can use both or either of the grits. The bevel on the guide must be shaped to provide the correct angle on the knife. Check this with a protractor.

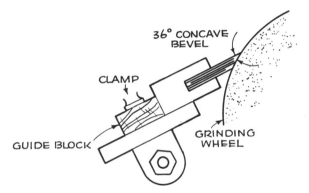

This jointer-knife jig employs a sliding hardwood holder that grips the knife securely. When you must make a second pass, do not change the position of the guide block. Instead, place a piece of paper between guide block and knife holder.

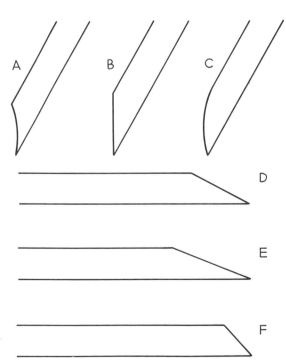

A-(hollow ground) and B-(flat ground) show good ways to shape a cutting edge. It must never be rounded as in-C. This can result from poor grinding. The bevel length should be about 2× the chisel thickness (D). A longer bevel (E) might work better on softwoods but it will knick and dull easily. The edge should never be blunt as in (F).

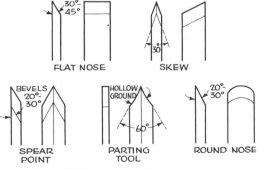

Wood-turning chisels are ground to angles shown here. All bevels are ground flat except for that of the parting tool, which always has a hollow-ground bevel.

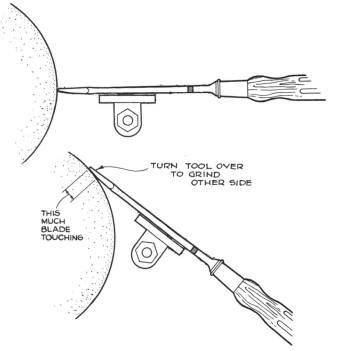

Remove nicks from a screwdriver tip by moving it directly forward into the face of the wheel. It may be flat-ground on the side of the wheel but a small amount of hollow-grinding is better. You'll find that the tool will not lift easily when you twist the screw. Be sure the sides of the tip are parallel.

A parting tool is easy to do by just renewing the "V" on the side of the wheel. Keep the tool level and be sure to grind an equal amount on both edges. Hone after grinding.

To do a punch, adjust the tool rest to the correct angle (the *original* angle on the punch) and then simply rotate it against the turning wheel to make the end symmetrical. Grind away only as much as you have to. Avoid overheating.

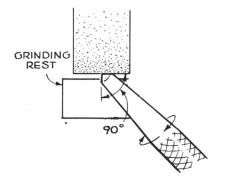

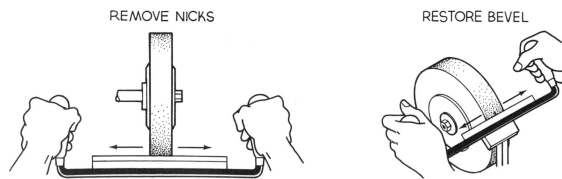

REMOVE NICKS RESTORE BEVEL

A draw knife can be ground with a single or a double bevel. It will be easy to maintain the original bevel since there are sure to be unworn portions at each end of the blade. Use light pressure in this operation.

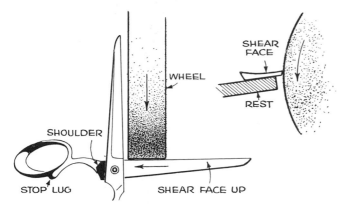

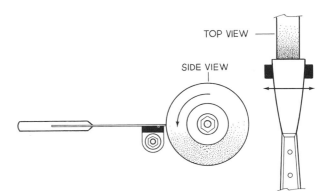

Do scissors and shears on a fine grit wheel that is square across the face. Make very light passes and keep the motion uniform to guarantee a straight cutting edge. Such tools should be honed after grinding.

All you want to do with a putty knife is square off the edge— then remove burrs and smooth the end by working on an oilstone. Thin materials like this overheat easily, so use a delicate touch.

PART II

PORTABLE TOOLS

PORTABLE CIRCULAR SAWS

Many years ago the Skil people made power tool history by introducing the portable circular saw. Today there are dozens of models available made by many different manufacturers, yet it is not unusual to hear a portable circular saw referred to as a "Skil-saw," which has almost become a generic term for this power tool. It's also common to hear such names as "cutoff saw," "utility saw" and "builder's saw." All these descriptive titles fit, but it's an error to limit this saw's applications to just the one type of work implied by each of these names.

The portable circular saw was developed originally as an aid to construction men so house framing timbers could be sized right on the job without the time and effort previously required by the handsaw. Just the time saved is impressive. It might take you as much as a minute to cut through a 2 x 4 with a handsaw. The powered tool will do it in seconds.

With some know-how and a few jigs, you can broaden a portable circular saw's applications until it comes close to matching the performance of a table saw or radial arm saw. You can use it to cut rabbets or dadoes, bevels and miters, as well as to size identical pieces. It will not replace the stationary tools, but in some areas it has advantages over them. Its greatest advantage is its portability: you can tote the tool in your hand and apply it to the work whether you are doing preliminary cuts on a large plywood panel in the shop or trimming roof or deck boards at the actual work site.

Saw size is indicated by the diameter of the blade. This is important but should not be the sole factor in choosing a portable circular saw. Also consider the depth of cut—the thickness of material the blade can get through on both straight cuts and on 45° bevels. If all you plan to use it on is $\frac{3}{4}''$ stock, then there really is no problem. But it's more realistic to think in terms of material up to 2″ thick. Even here, consider the difference between *dressed* lumber and *rough* lumber. There can be a $\frac{3}{8}''$ difference in thickness between the two. So, if lumber in the rough is in your picture, you may need more depth of cut than the fellow who works on dressed stock only.

Since saw sharpenings reduce the diameter of the blade, getting a blade that is just big enough for the

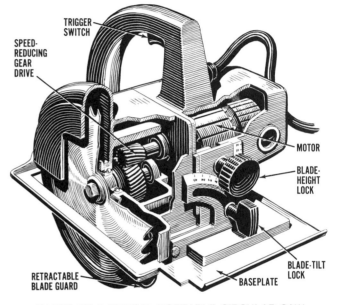

PARTS OF A TYPICAL PORTABLE CIRCULAR SAW

piece of work when the blade is new may not be wise. Also, a blade that is constantly buried in the cut will not function as efficiently as it should. All of this seems to indicate that it's better to overestimate when judging the tool's capacity.

Models that are most available to homecraftsmen range from about $6\frac{1}{2}''$ up to $7\frac{1}{2}''$. Most of these will pass the basic depth-of-cut test. Generally, the larger the size, the more powerful, heavier and more expensive the tool will be. Getting the biggest size just because you can afford it isn't good practice. You might be better off choosing a smaller size as long as the tool performs as you demand, simply because it may be more comfortable to handle.

Blade speed is called out in rpm's when the blade is running free. This number indicates the cutting speed only when the tool is sufficiently powered to stay close to the same number of rpm's when you are cutting. It's obvious that a fast turning saw that slows down considerably when cutting isn't really going to be faster than a slower tool that does not bog down.

If you can possibly arrange it, it's a good idea to actually test a sample of the tool you are interested in or have the salesman do it for you with a demonstrator model. Be sure to "heft" it yourself. When all other factors are satisfactory, how the tool feels in your hands can logically determine which saw you choose from a variety of units. Weight and ease of handling can also be important safety factors. A tool that is too heavy for you or that feels awkward when you grip it can be hazardous.

GENERAL CHARACTERISTICS

Once you have purchased a portable circular saw, you should spend more than a few minutes in your workshop becoming familiar with the tool and how it handles. Make test cuts on some $\frac{3}{4}''$ plywood clamped securely to a bench and on a length of 2 x 4 supported on sawhorses or some other platform. Set the blade projection so it is about $\frac{1}{4}''$ more than the thickness of the material you are working on. A greater projection is actually more efficient, but for safety's sake keep it to a minimum. Place your right hand on the handle with a finger on the trigger and your left hand on the knob. Position yourself so you are out of the line of cut. Work so the weight of the saw is supported by the bulk of the stock, not the cutoff portion.

The upper portion of the saw blade is guarded by a fixed housing. The lower portion is covered by a guard that should automatically telescope into the top housing as you move the tool forward to make the cut. Be aware, therefore, that the portion of the saw blade in the cut and the amount of the saw blade that extends below the stock are not covered by the guard as you are cutting. At the end of the cut, the lower guard will swing down to encase the saw blade.

When you face the blade, it is turning in a counterclockwise direction. This means it is cutting on the "up" stroke and suggests that the good face of the stock should be "down" when you cut. This factor is critical only when the material you are cutting deserves such consideration.

Feed speed should be judged by how the saw is cutting. The thickness of the stock, whether you are cutting with or across the grain, and the hardness of the material are factors that should help you determine how fast you can cut. Most importantly, keep the blade cutting steadily without undue strain on the motor and keep the blade cutting on a straight line. Portable circular saws will kick back easily if you bind the blade by going off the line. Binding can also happen on green wood when the kerf closes. When your first cut indicates that this is likely to happen on subsequent cuts, it's wise to be cautious by tapping a shim in the kerf to keep it open. Do this only

Blade projection can be seen by setting the saw over the edge of the stock to be cut. Minimum projection is the safest method, but not necessarily the most efficient.

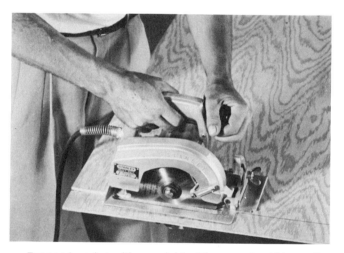

For good work position, weight of the saw should be on the bulk of the work, not the cutoff portion. The tool should be gripped firmly, with both hands when possible.

when the cut is long enough to permit doing it and only after the saw blade has stopped turning.

Some saws are equipped with a "riving" knife. This accessory is the equivalent of a splitter on the table saw, and it doesn't hurt to keep the knife on the circular saw for general use. It can interfere with plunge cuts but at such times can easily be removed.

Many tools are equipped with a "slip clutch." Its job is to allow the saw blade to slip when the blade is confronted with an adverse situation, such as a knot in the wood, even though the motor continues to turn. Such a device is a tricky mechanism simply because its efficiency depends on how it is adjusted. The instructions you get with your tool will tell you how to properly adjust it.

"Riving" knife (where arrow points) attaches to upper housing and sits in the kerf to act as a splitter which helps to keep the kerf from closing and thus binding the blade.

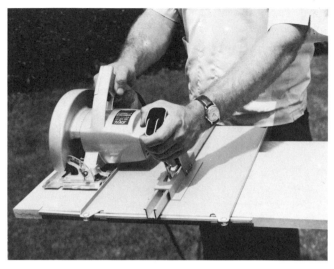

Commercial jig is adjustable for various stock widths. Pressing trigger handle causes the jig to grip the stock between back and front flanges. The saw rides edge of the jig.

In most cases it's simply a question of tightening the retaining nut on the arbor just so. However, if you tighten this nut too much, the clutch won't work. If you loosen it too much, you may get slippage to the point where the saw loses efficiency. When the situation is optimum, the slip clutch will protect the motor and help avoid kickback. If you have a slip clutch, it can improve the safe operation of your circular saw but remember that the most dependable safety devices are a sharp blade and a feed speed that lets you cut through the wood quickly and smoothly.

Another safety factor in some portable circular saws is an electronic brake. No extra buttons to push or procedures to go through are required to operate this brake. When you release the trigger, the brake automatically works; the blade says "whoosh" and stops—just like that!

CUTTING TECHNIQUES

Straight cuts. Crosscutting is a job frequently done with the portable circular saw. Whenever possible, whether you are working in the shop or on location, it makes sense to clamp a guide strip to the work to keep the tool on a straight line. You should establish the distance from the edge of the baseplate to the cut line by test cuts. Thus, you will always know how far from the cut the guide strip should be clamped. This dimension can vary depending on the style of saw blade you are using, so you must check it each time you change blades. As a matter of fact, it should also be checked after you have a blade sharpened.

On narrow cuts, it's often more convenient to use a

COMMON PORTABLE CIRCULAR SAW BLADES

A. Combination blade, for all-round work, does ripping, crosscutting, and mitering.

B. Planer does three kinds of cutting, too, but leaves smooth edge that requires no sanding.

C. Flooring blade, of special steel to withstand contact with nails, is for cutting up used lumber.

D. Plywood blade produces smooth, splinter-free cuts in any direction relative to surface veneer.

E. Cut-off blade is used in crosscut squaring and trimming to size. It holds keen edge over long period.

F. Ripping blade resembles combination blade except that backs of teeth are not beveled.

guide that you can hold to the work by hand. For example, you can use a common shop square as a guide or you can make a guide with more capacity merely by nailing two pieces of wood together in an "L" shape. The short leg should bear against the edge of the work, and the long leg should act as a guide for the saw.

Of course, you can do such work freehand by relying on yourself to keep the blade on the cut line. In any case, to start the operation, place the front edge of the baseplate on the work so the guide notch is in line with the cut mark. Start the saw; after the blade has revved up to full speed, move the tool forward to start the actual cutting. Remember that the saw kerf has width, so the actual cut must be made on the waste side.

When you approach the end of the cut, the guide-notch area of the baseplate will be off the work, so you'll have to watch the blade itself. This is more pertinent on freehand cutting than when you are working against a guide. In the latter case you shouldn't have to watch the cut line at all. Just be sure to keep the baseplate snug against the guide strip throughout the pass.

Working with both hands on the saw is a good idea but not always possible. You may need one hand to hold a guide, support the work, or even brace yourself.

On this model, pressing down a button keeps the shaft from turning. The button is spring-loaded and only works when depressed manually.

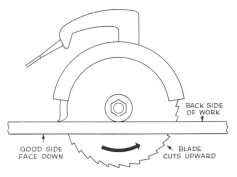

Saw blades turn in a counterclockwise direction which means they cut on the "up" stroke. Therefore, the good face of the work should be down since most splintering will occur when the teeth leave the cut.

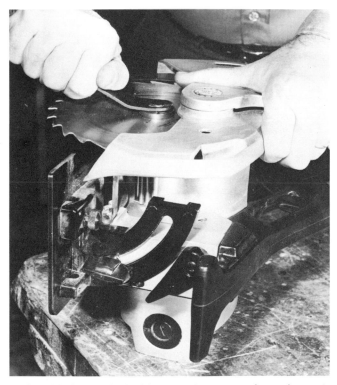

Saw blades are locked in place by means of an arbor nut. How you accomplish this while keeping the motor shaft stationary depends on the design of the tool you own.

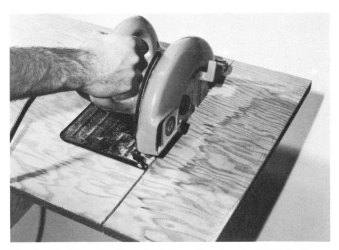

One-hand operation is safe if the other hand, presumably holding the work, is well away from the cut area. Keep your body to the left of the cut line.

The last should be avoided if possible. Just be aware that both you and the tool should be in stable positions. When in doubt, step back and reconsider. It is always important to be aware of the situation and what it demands of you.

Try to keep the saw on the bulk of the work. This isn't always possible, especially on out-of-the-shop jobs, but many times you can make a choice. For example, let's assume that you are trimming off the end of a long 2 x 4. Whether the saw will rest on the waste portion of the 2 x 4 or on the body of the work depends on which side of the 2 x 4 you stand. Apply this thinking also if the cutoff portion is the part you need. The only extra thinking you have to do is determining which side of the cut mark you want the kerf to be on.

Cutting thick stock beyond the maximum depth of cut of the saw can be accomplished by making matching cuts from opposite sides. In such a case, layout and correct positioning of the saw are of primary importance if the two cuts are to meet exactly. When you have many such cuts to do on similar materials, it will pay to make a special U-shaped guide that can be clamped to the work so the two saw cuts will mate. Another way is to make a setup so the work can be flipped in correct position for the second cut after the first one has been accomplished.

Butt cuts. The following little trick will help when you must trim the ends of boards to make a matching joint. Just overlap the board ends and cut through both of them at the same time. Thus, even a slight error in cutting will not affect how the two ends join together. This method works whether you are making a straight, angular, long or short cut in ripping or cross-cutting.

You can get through extra-thick stock by making matching cuts from opposite sides. Good layout and accurate placement of the saw for each cut are important.

On soft materials like this roof-deck insulation, you can make a maximum cut on one surface and then snap the material to break uncut section. If appearance of the cut is important, then, of course, you must cut from both sides.

When you can, use a two-hand grip. Also, be sure to weight or clamp down the work when it isn't heavy enough to sit on its own. Seat front edge of shoe solidly on work before you make contact with the blade.

CUTTING MULTIPLE PIECES TO LENGTH

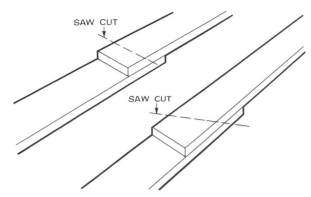

Straight or angular butt cuts can be done by overlapping the pieces and cutting through both of them at the same time to assure a perfect joint between the cut edges.

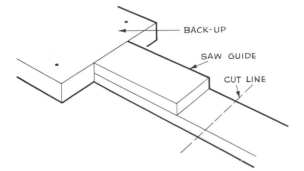

One way to cut many pieces of similar length. The saw guide equals the length of the workpiece you want less the distance from the edge of the saw's baseplate to the cut line.

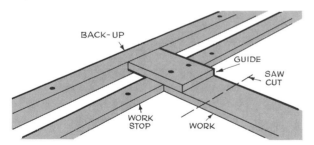

To cut many pieces of similar length when the pieces you need are short, use method shown. Guide, work stop, and backup should be clamped or nailed securely to the work platform.

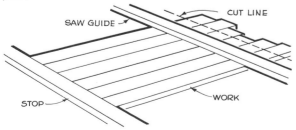

One pass trimming of multiple pieces can be done as shown. Nail the saw guide to the first and last workpieces.

Cutting to length. In using a portable saw to cut similar pieces, whether you are working in the shop or on the job, usually the easiest technique is to nail down a backup board and then cut a guide block that will determine the length of the pieces you will produce. The guide block is the length of the part you want less the distance from baseplate edge to saw blade. The work and the guide are butted against the backup, and the saw is moved along the guide to make the cut. In this example, the guide and work are hand held for the cut.

In a second example (see accompanying sketch), the setup involves a work stop in addition to the backup and the guide. Since all three of these items are nailed down, you can be concerned with just holding the work and making the cut.

Another possibility, when you need to trim many pieces to the same length, is to butt the pieces edge-to-edge and cut across all of them at the same time. Many professionals do this kind of thing freehand, but accuracy is easier if you use a stop against which you can butt the ends of the pieces, plus a saw guide. It isn't necessary to do more than tack-nail the guide to the first and the last piece in the set you are cutting.

As shown in the accompanying sketch, it's also possible to make a bed jig so you can do accurate cutting of any material that fits between the bed sides, whether it's a piece of plywood or a set of individual pieces. The depth of the bed determines the thickness of the material you can so handle. As shown, a bed jig is good for anything up to dressed 2x stock. The saw blade rides the slot cut in the platform; the saw-blade edge of the baseplate rides against the outboard frame member of the platform. This kind of jig can be made small or large,

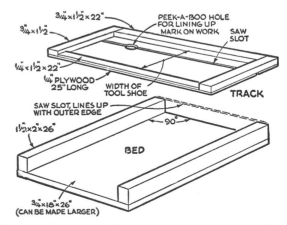

Jig setup for crosscutting involves a bed and a track. Work is positioned in the bed; the tool rides the track above to make the cut.

depending on the kind of work you plan to do. It can even be large enough to handle a 4′ x 8′ plywood panel.

Ripping. A good deal of what has been said so far applies to rip cuts as well as crosscuts. The primary distinction—whether you are cutting with the grain or across it—doesn't seem nearly as important as the length of the cut. Even the importance of choosing the right saw blade is minimized since in so much portable saw work the supersmoothness of the cut edge is not so critical.

As in crosscutting, use a clamped-on guide or an edge guide to help produce a straight cut. A commercial edge guide is fine to use when the width of the cut permits. Remember, however, that it's not as easy to be accurate with such an edge guide as you can be with a wood strip simply because it does not prevent you from being wobbly with the saw.

Most saws are designed so the guide may be used on either side of the blade. To choose which side to place the guide, just consider which position involves the least extension of the guide and which provides the most saw support. Sometimes your decision has to be based on which end of the board you are going to start from, especially if the board is part of a fixed assembly and you don't have much choice in determining operator position.

With some edge guides you can create a setup by using both a clamped-on strip and the guide. This combination can be useful when you need to cut a number of long pieces of equal width. In this situation, the edge guide rides against the clamped-on strip, and you adjust the guide after each cut you make, using the calibrations on the edge-guide bar if they are provided. Similarity in width will depend on how accurately you adjust the edge guide after each of the cuts.

When material thickness allows it and you must cut the same amount from a number of pieces, you can do the job by stacking the parts and cutting through them all at the same time. This method is very feasible, regardless of the maximum depth of cut of your tool, when you are working with $\frac{1}{8}$″ and up to $\frac{1}{4}$″ paneling. Of course, the thicker the material, the fewer the number of pieces you can stack for cutting.

Grooves and notches. You can form dadoes and grooves by setting the blade projection to the depth of cut you require and then making a series of overlapping cuts. Your best bet is to use a guide strip for the outline cuts. Then you can work freehand to remove the waste material between them. It's also possible to make a series of parallel cuts that do not overlap and then rely on a hand chisel and mallet to remove the waste. This tech-

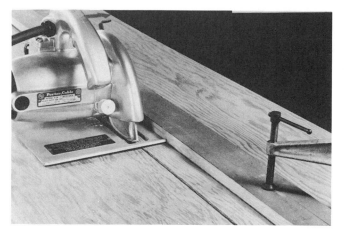
A guide strip is nothing more than a straight piece of wood. It can be clamped in some mid-way area or . . .

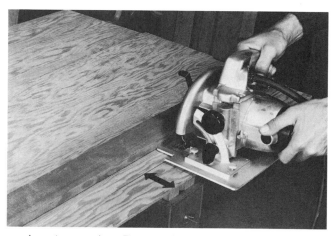
close to an edge. Be sure that you maintain full contact between baseplate edge and the guide strip throughout pass.

An edge guide is very convenient for ripping to width. The guide may be positioned so its guide-flange is either on the left or right-hand side of the blade.

Some guides are calibrated but be sure to check how accurate they are before you rely on them.

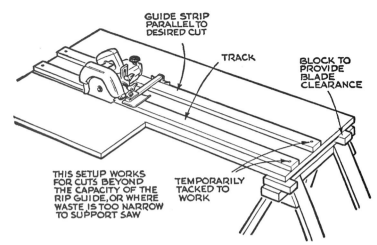

Rip cuts beyond reach of the standard guide can be accurately made if you ride the shoe against a fence tacked or clamped to the face of the stock. If your saw's shoe doesn't project outside the blade, and its motor housing is too low to clear a fence, use the setup shown.

The greater the width of cut, the more difficult it is to use edge guides because the more extension you have, the easier it is to wobble as you cut. In such situations, a clamped-on guide strip is better to use.

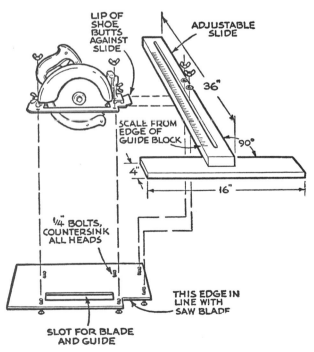

Jig shown is designed so the guide and the saw move together in making extra-wide rip cuts. The position of the saw on the guide arm determines the width of the cut.

Edge guides are often used as shown. In this case, the saw has a two-way blade and is cutting backwards.

Cutting close to a vertical can be a problem. How tight you can get depends on the design of the tool, but no circular saw will cut flush in such a situation.

This model has a two-piece base. The saw-side section of the plate is removable which makes it possible to move in close to a vertical.

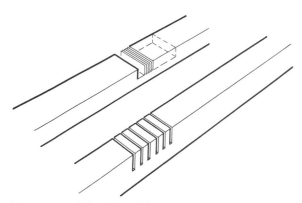

You can cut dadoes by making a series of overlapping, parallel cuts to remove waste stock completely (top), or you can space the cuts and remove the remaining wood between the cuts with a chisel (bottom).

nique might be more applicable to short dadoes and notches than to long grooves.

To cut notches, such as the ones you need in a stairway stringer, make two cuts that meet at the base of the angle. In order to clean out the corner, you must make the cuts a bit longer than is needed to form the notch. To minimize this extra cutting, use maximum blade projection. If this is not acceptable for appearance, cut just to the line and then finish up with a handsaw or a saber saw.

Angular cuts. To do cross or rip bevels, tilt the circular saw to the angle you require. Most machines have tilt scales, but when the accuracy of the cut is critical, it's best to use the scale setting as a guide only. Check the test cut with a protractor before you proceed with the job. Also, check to see if the cut-line edge on the base plate is a good indicator for bevel cuts, as well as for square cuts. Be sure the tilt lock is firm and the leading edge of the base plate is seated firmly on the wood before you make contact with the blade.

The general rules for tool handling and feeding apply in making angular cuts. You'll do better if you work against a clamped-on guide strip or with an edge guide. It makes sense to check the real distance from the cut to the side of the base plate on any angle setting that you use frequently. Do this by actually making a short cut in a board and then measuring from the cut to the edge of the plate. Thereafter you will know, whether you require one cut or many, just where to clamp the guide strip.

Handle a simple miter pretty much as you would a crosscut by guiding the saw freehand along a line or by using a guide. Accuracy will depend on how careful you are when doing the layout. Since miter cuts are made most often across narrow widths, you can use an adjustable protractor as a guide. Protractors are available as accessories, or you can make one yourself.

To cut many pieces of molding or very narrow pieces, you can work with a kind of miter box ordinarily used with a handsaw. The basic design, a U-shaped trough with cuts across it, is the same, but for the portable saw you add a saw guide and a ledge for saw support. The box you make for a portable saw also has to be longer than one designed for a handsaw. Provide for left- and right-hand miter cuts with a saw guide and support ledge for each. The depth of the box can't be greater than the maximum blade projection on your saw. It will pay to nail the box to a solid surface. Keep your hands well away from the cut area.

Special mitering setups are available commercially. Some provide for swiveling tracks so the saw can be set on either side of a center line. Others are made strictly

Bevel cuts are accomplished by tilting the tool to the angle you need. On short cuts you can work with a protractor. On long cuts, use a clamped-on guide.

for molding and narrow stock. The saw is mounted on a pivot so it can be swung up or down. If the saw projection on your tool is controlled by pivot action, then you can make yourself a similar unit by following the accompanying construction details of a "swing saw table."

Plunge cuts. Cuts within a panel are easily made no matter what the design of the portable circular saw. The basic approach to making plunge cuts is to support the saw on the work with the blade clear and the guard retracted. Then, with the blade turning, lower the tool slowly until it seats firmly on the base plate.

If the blade projection on your saw is handled by pivot action, it's best to hold the saw so it is tilted on the front edge of the baseplate. Then turn the saw on and slowly

Circular saws will tilt to 45°. When the tool is tilted and you make a miter cut, the result is a compound angle. Depth of cut at 45° should be enough to get through 2x stock.

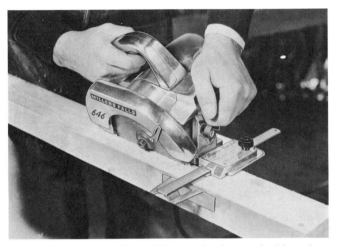

On long cuts, an edge guide can also be used, although a clamped-on guide is usually more effective.

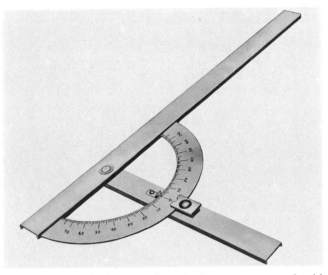

A protractor is the most important accessory you should have. With it, you can set up quickly to guide the saw for square or angular cuts.

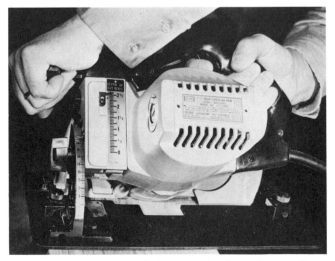

Most tools are equipped with tilt scales (as well as depth-of-cut scales), but it's best to use them as guides only. Trust the cut only after you have checked the angle of the blade with a protractor.

MITERING

Miter cuts can be done freehand, but accuracy is easier to achieve when you take the time to clamp on or tack-nail a guide strip.

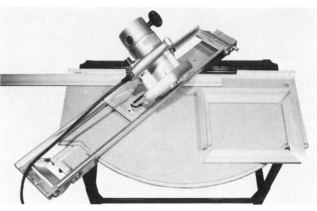

Table and track arrangement for mitering is a commercial item. The track swivels for the cut angle you want. When the track is set at an angle and the tool is tilted, you get compound angle cuts.

This is an adjustable version of a crosscut jig so you can set it for angular cuts. Size the length of the slot so its extremes will be stop-points for 90° and 45° settings.

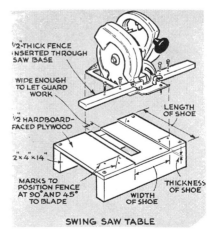

Motorized miter box is basically a cutoff saw, pivoted at the rear end so it can be brought down to make the cuts. It's especially useful for moldings.

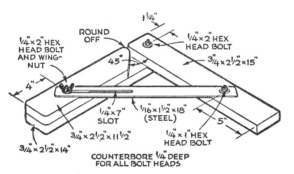

You can make a special miter box for use with a portable circular saw. Make guides and saw-support ledges for both left-hand and right-hand miter cuts.

Here's a special mitering setup you can make yourself. It will work only with saw designs that provide a pivot action to achieve depth of cut.

bring it level to the piece of work. If you have an elevator-type depth adjustment, line the retracted blade up with the layout mark and then sink it into the work while the blade is turning.

In order to clean out corners, you must saw a bit beyond the line. Maximum blade projection will minimize this. If you wish to avoid overcutting entirely, saw just to the line from both directions and then clean out the corners with a handsaw or saber saw.

It's sometimes advisable, after you have made two or three of the cuts, to nail or clamp a support across the pocket. Securing a support will keep the waste from binding the blade as well as prevent the waste from falling out when the cuts are complete.

Rabbet cutting. Cutting rabbets is mostly a question of setting up the work so the saw may be positioned for the related cuts. When you make overlapping, parallel cuts, the job is done with repeat passes. Your best bet is to use a clamped-on guide for the shoulder cut. Then

you can make a series of freehand passes to remove the waste.

For a two-pass rabbet, proceed with the clamped-on guide to do the shoulder cut. Then stand the stock on edge for the second cut. This, as shown in the accompanying drawing, takes a little more organization since stock edges are rarely wide enough to provide good support for the saw.

When you need just one rabbet, use the repeat pass procedure. When you need the same job on many pieces, it will probably pay to set up the two-pass technique.

For example, let's assume that you need 6 or 8 pieces of plywood 1' wide and 4' long with a rabbet cut along the ends. A good way to do this is to cut the rabbets on a full sheet of plywood and then slice up the sheet into 1'-wide pieces.

Circular cuts. The portable circular saw really isn't designed for such work, but you can cut circles by using

PLUNGE CUTTING

To do plunge cutting, mark the cutout on the work and situate the saw blade to cut on a line. Initially, the blade is above the work. Cutting starts as you lower the blade to make contact. You can work freehand or . . .

against a guide strip. Start each cut as close to the beginning of the line as you can get, but you will probably have to backtrack the saw a little bit to catch the corner.

When the tool is seated solidly on the baseplate, feed it forward to the next line. The guard will have to be held in a retracted position as you start each plunge cut.

When you get to the third or fourth cut, clamp or tack-nail a support strip across the waste to keep it from twisting and possibly binding the blade.

RABBETTING

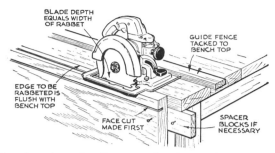

How to set up for the second cut on a two-pass rabbet operation. Note that you can operate in this way on the edge of your workbench.

First cut of a two-pass rabbet. Cut shown is the shoulder cut, guided by a strip that is tack-nailed to the work. Saw projection equals the depth of the rabbet.

A standard rip guide is all you need to rabbet a timber like the one shown. Hold the tool level throughout the pass, supporting it firmly when you come to the end of the cut.

Second cut is made by clamping the stock in a vertical position. It's important to design the setup to provide good support for the saw. Saw projection equals the width of the rabbet.

Don't force the cut when you use the pivot method to cut a circle. Be sure to get through the stock by cutting in stages, cutting about $\frac{1}{16}''$ deeper on each pass.

a pivot-guiding system and being very patient about getting through the stock. The radius gauge is a strip of wood or metal fastened in the rip-guide slot and pivoting on a nail. The kerf you cut will really be a cove so feed very slowly and don't attempt very small circles.

The cut has to be made in stages. The first stage of the cut should be just enough to break the surface of the wood. Thereafter, increase depth of cut about $\frac{1}{16}''$ for each pass. Feed the saw slowly and stay on the motor side. These steps are more applicable when you're working on thin panels, but be sure that you supply good support for any piece of work in which you're making a circular cut.

A PANEL SAW

You've probably seen an apparatus like the one shown in a lumber yard, so you know how convenient it can be for initial sizing cuts on large panels. This mounted portable circular saw is designed for vertical use so the project takes up very little room. You can, if you wish, add braces to the back so the unit can be freestanding, or you can just lean it against a wall.

The device is basically a frame with a track-mounted portable circular saw. The work is placed in the frame and crosscut by moving the saw vertically. Cables from sliding-door closers (or you can use spring-type sash balances) connect to the carriage to counterbalance the weight of the saw and carriage. Actually, the same result could be accomplished by using a steel weight. The steel weight could be attached by cable to the carriage with the cable running over a wheel at the top of the frame.

Since the saw can be turned 90° and the carriage can be locked, the setup is fine for rip cuts too. In this situation, the saw sits still and the work is moved.

One-inch OD pipe is used for the tracks. Black-iron pipe ($\frac{3}{4}''$) works well, or you can use something larger if you wish. Just be sure you have the track material on hand before you make the related parts. The reason for the two-piece, bottom track support is to provide adjustment so the tracks can be set parallel.

The carriage holds the cutoff saw securely and permits its vertical action. The saw is bolted to a plywood plate that fits the cutout in the carrier. Both the plate and the cutout are square. This feature permits the saw to be turned so it can be used for either crosscutting or ripping. Accuracy in construction is very critical here.

Check over all the details in the accompanying drawings before you start construction. Most of the material is construction grade fir, but you must be selective and choose straight stock. It might pay to spend a little more and buy a similar kiln-dried material. Green lumber can dry out and cause distortion that will destroy the accuracy you build into the tool.

Incidentally, no matter how you go about counterbalancing the weight of the saw and carriage, don't set things up so the saw will be snapped back at the end of a cut. The whole idea is to relieve the weight so you can move it easily up or down.

HOW TO BUILD A PANEL SAW

It's easy to cut full-size sheets when you have a panel saw to use. All you have to do is guide the tool up and down the tracks. Carriage and saw weight are counterbalanced as described in text.

Since the carriage is designed to permit turning the saw 90°, the panel saw can be used for ripping operations. In this situation, the saw is locked in position; the work is moved for the cut.

HOW TO BUILD A PANEL SAW (CONT.)

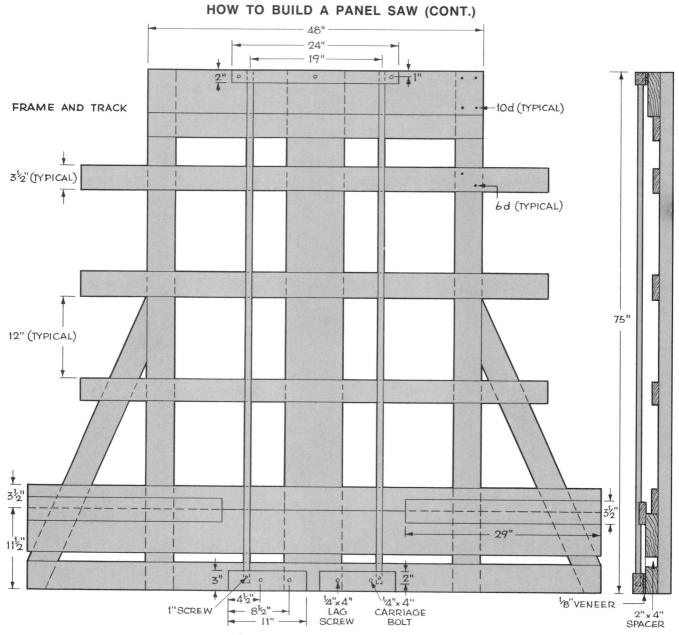

Construction details of panel saw frame.

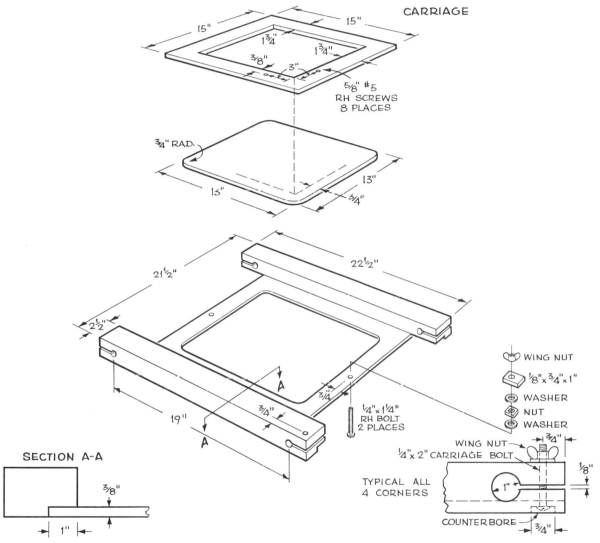

Construction details of carriage and saw mounting arrangement.

12 | SABER SAWS AND RECIPROCATING SAWS

Not too many years ago, the saber saw made as big a splash on the power tool market as the portable cutoff saw did when it first appeared. The enthusiasm hasn't waned, and it is completely justifiable because with a saber saw you can do many on-location jobs that you would do on the band saw or the jigsaw in the shop. Even with stationary tools on hand, work size often makes it more convenient to do a chore with a tool that you apply to the work.

The saber saw makes neither of the previously mentioned stationary tools obsolete. In the case of the band saw, the saber saw can't compete in cut speed, nor can it rival the big tool in jobs like resawing, pad cutting, or making compound cuts. The concept of the saber saw demands a stiff, relatively wide blade, so it's not about to challenge the jigsaw in terms of fine, tight-radius fretwork. Its greatest advantage lies in its small, palm-grip size and in its portability.

And it can do piercing without the need of a starting hole. Since the blade is chucked at one end only, it's possible to so angle the tool by resting it on the front edge of the base plate that the blade teeth begin to cut as you bring the tool to a vertical position. This permits cutting into the material's surface and, finally, as you approach normal operating position, to penetrate through the stock.

What makes the tool even more exciting today is the great variety of blades available and the fact that modern versions provide different speeds, even variable speeds. Thus, you can choose a good combination of blade and speed for cutting anything from leather to steel. With the right blade, you can do heavy-duty work like notching studs or stringers and merely by changing to another blade design (and maybe another speed), go immediately to inside work on cabinets and paneling.

You'll find that stroke length, the up-and-down action of the blade, and available speed or speeds will vary from model to model. Of course, the more you pay for a unit, the more you get. Stroke length, power, speeds, and versatility increase with price. For not much more than $10.00, you can buy a $\frac{1}{6}$ HP model with a $\frac{1}{2}''$ stroke and one speed of 3,200 spm. Even in this price range, the tool may have a tilting base as well as a built-in sawdust

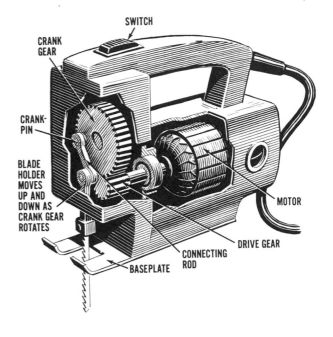

PARTS OF A TYPICAL SABER SAW

The tool greatest advantage is its small size and portability. Here it is used to cut out a window opening in paneling that has already been installed, eliminating the necessity of pre-cutting the material.

Even low-cost units provide such features as double insulation, a selection of speeds, and a full tilting baseplate. The last feature is important if you plan any kind of bevel cutting.

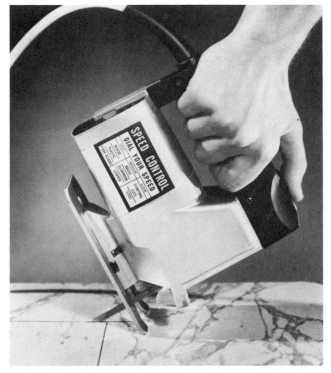

A great asset of the saber saw is being able to make plunge cuts, permitting you to cut through stock without a blade insertion hole.

With the correct blade and the right speed, you can get smooth cuts in sheet metal and other materials that include fiberglass paneling (shown), wood and wood compositions, pipe, hard metals, plastics, tile, and plaster.

blower. The "middle" price range may get you a $\frac{1}{4}$ HP machine with a $\frac{3}{4}''$ stroke and a special switch that lets you select between two speeds, for example, 3,400 spm or 2,700 spm. Get into the top price range, and you can have a full $1''$ stroke and a hearty $\frac{1}{2}$ HP with a selection of speeds that runs from about 1,300 spm up to 3,200 spm.

The smaller, short-stroke units do not have tremendous cut speed, but many of them have good capacity. There aren't any that won't cut at least $1\frac{1}{2}''$ softwood. It's a good idea to check the capacity factor in terms of the work you plan. Usually this is listed as so many inches in hardwood and so many inches in softwood. Many times you will even be told the capacity in aluminum and in steel.

Some units provide a straight up-and-down blade action while others have a canted blade or one that moves in a small orbit. The last two back the blade away on the downstroke and move it forward on the up or cutting stroke. The idea is to reduce power-wasting drag on the downstroke and to free the kerf of waste. This can reduce friction and heat and prolong blade life.

To get the most from a saber saw, you should be able to tilt it from zero to 45°. This tilting allows you to make bevels, cross-bevels, and even compound cuts. Check this feature when you view an "economy" unit. Some models provide special inserts. These attach to the base plate and minimize the opening around the blade to eliminate or at least lessen the amount of chipping that occurs as the blade teeth leave the stock.

Importance of blades. A close study of the blades that are available for the saber saw is almost a course in the use of the tool. In most cases, one blade is supplied with the tool when you buy it. It will be a general-purpose blade, like a combination blade generally supplied with a table saw. To use this single blade for all jobs, however, will impose limitations and restrictions that will reduce the quality of your output and even increase your shop chores.

For example, by using a special blade that is designed to cut plywood, you can reduce considerably, and sometimes even eliminate, the follow-through sanding needed to get a good edge. By using a blade with wave-set teeth, like those you find on a common hacksaw blade, you can use the saber saw like a power hacksaw. For jobs in leather, rubber, cardboard and the like, there is a toothless blade that fits the tool like any other blade but cuts like a knife.

If you are involved in remodeling work, there are blades that can slice through an occasional nail without damage and others that are shaped so that it's possible to cut through moldings and baseboards flush up against a wall. Saber saw blades are not so expensive that you can't have an all-inclusive assortment to be pre-

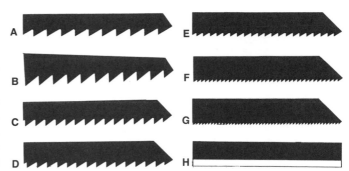

A sampling of the many saber saw blades available: (A) 7-tooth blade for fast, rough cuts in thick wood and plasterboard. (B) 7-tooth extra long, for sawing logs and timbers up to 4″ thick. Usually 6″ long. (C) 10-tooth, for all-around use on hardwood, softwood, composition board, plastics. (D) 10-tooth taper-ground, for cuts in plywood, veneer, plastic laminates. (E) 14-tooth, for soft, nonferrous metals (aluminum, copper, brass) up to $\frac{1}{4}$″ thick. (F) 24-tooth, for fine cuts in thin sheet metal and tubing, either ferrous or nonferrous. (G) 32-tooth, for ferrous metals (iron and steal), pipe, and solid rod and bar stock. (H) Knife blade, for rubber, leather, wallboard, cloth, resilient floor tiles.

Some models are called "scroller saws." A scroller saw is basically a saber saw but includes a feature that enables you to turn the blade independent of the feed direction of the tool. This feature can be a great convenience when doing intricate cuts.

Wise choice of blades can make a big difference in the quality of the cut. Cut on the bottom piece was made with a coarse, few-teeth-per-inch blade. A small-toothed, taper-back blade made the cut on the top piece.

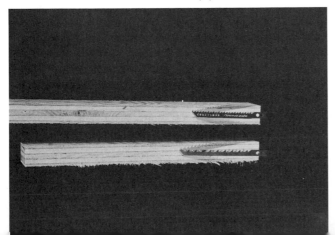

pared to cut anything from a sheet of paper to $\frac{1}{2}$″ steel. Such an assortment can prove the most economical in the long run since you will be less likely to abuse blades on jobs those blades were never meant to do.

Two or three dollars will buy blades to set you up for most wood cutting; another dollar or two will start you on metal cutting. These same blades can also be used on other materials such as hardboard, wallboard, insulation sheeting, and floor tiles.

The accompanying selection chart does not list the blade width, length, or the tooth form simply because such details would lead to repeating blade-use descriptions and would make the chart difficult to use. Actually, the number of teeth per inch is probably the single most important factor except in sawing plywood. In this case, to get the smoothest cut possible, a hollow-ground or taper-back blade design is ideal.

Normally, you should choose a wide blade ($\frac{3}{8}$″ or $\frac{1}{2}$″) for straight cuts and a narrow one ($\frac{1}{4}$″) for doing curves. The thickness of the material should also influence your choice in blade length. Blade lengths can be short (from $2\frac{1}{2}$″ to 3″) or long (from 4″ to 6″). Lengths can vary according to tool brand, but most manufacturers do supply both long and short blades.

Always choose the shortest blade that will do the job. The big 6″ varieties are not usually recommended for tools that have less than a full 1″ stroke.

Of two similar blades, the one that is taper-ground or hollow-ground will produce the smoothest cut, just as a hollow-ground circular saw cuts smoother than a combination blade. A very important point to remember is

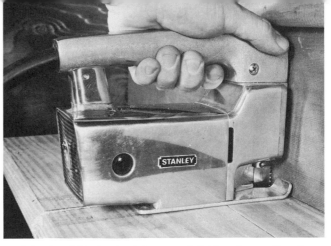

Special flush-cut blade (also called "offset") puts the teeth of the blade at the toe of the baseplate to let you cut through a section of attached molding or baseplate.

A flush-cut blade also lets you cut right up to a wall and can cut surfaces that are difficult to get to. In this respect, it is more useful in some instances than a hand saw.

WOOD

TEETH PER INCH	MATERIAL	RECOMMENDATIONS
3	Lumber, logs	Fast cuts in heavy lumber (up to 6″ thick) or logs to 5″ dia.
5	Lumber (nailfree)	Fast but rough general cutting; good for ripping stock $\frac{1}{2}$″ to 2″ thick.
6	Lumber	As above, but produces cuts a bit smoother.
7 or 8	Lumber, insulation board	Good general-purpose blade, especially for construction work; medium-smooth cuts.
10	Lumber (especially hardwood) under $\frac{1}{2}$″ thick, wallboard	Smoother cuts, but slower on heavy work; for scrollwork; also good for composition board, plastics. (Some saw makers recommend for general-purpose cutting; others offer special taper-back or hollow-ground version to reduce chipping of plywood, laminates.)
12 or 14	Plywood	Smoothest cuts in plywood and fine scrollwork; also good for materials such as linoleum or rubber tile, hardboards, nylon, Plexiglas, and fiberglass. Also for plastic laminates, though some makers recommend use of 14 (or even 18) t.p.i. metal-cutting blade.
10 (H.S.S.)	Wood with occasional nail	Special steel will stand up under nail-cutting; also good for materials such as asbestos, laminates, etc.
7 (flush cut or offset)	Lumber	For cutting flush to a wall, as with baseboards and moldings.
SPECIAL-PURPOSE KNIFE EDGE	Leather, cork, cloth, paper, cardboard, rubber, Styrofoam	Material being cut must be firmly held and supported.

METAL

TEETH PER INCH	MATERIAL	RECOMMENDATIONS
6 (H.S.S.)	Aluminum, copper, brass, laminates, compositions	Heavy cutting in plate or tubing; sample maximum cut: $\frac{1}{2}$″ in aluminum plate.
10 (H.S.S.)	Same as above	General cutting with smoother finish than above.
14 (H.S.S.)	Aluminum, brass, bronze, copper, laminates, hardboard, mild steel, pipe	General cutting with smooth finish; maximum in steel: $\frac{1}{4}$″-$\frac{1}{2}$″ depending on manufacturers' specifications.
18 (H.S.S.)	Same as above	For lighter materials; maximum cuts about $\frac{1}{8}$″.
24 (H.S.S.)	Sheet metal, light-gauge steel, thin-wall tubing, Bakelite, tile, etc.	Finest-tooth blade offered by some makers; wave-set.
32 (H.S.S.)	Thin-gauge sheet metals, thinwall tubing, metal trim	Wave-set blade cuts fine kerf; maximum in steel: $\frac{1}{16}$″. For typical hacksaw jobs.

NOTE: For information on length and width of blades, see text.

that a wide blade with few, heavy-set teeth per inch will often turn as tight a radius as a narrow blade with many teeth per inch and little set. It's even possible that the heavy blade might make a tighter turn than the other because the big blade forms a wider kerf and thus the body of the blade has more room to turn.

Bear in mind when the chart recommends a blade for scrollwork that the narrowest, finest-toothed blade you can buy for a saber saw can't begin to match the fretwork designs you can cut on a jigsaw when it is fitted with a fine jeweler's blade.

Some manufacturers make blades that are intended to fit only their saws. When you are in doubt about which blade to buy for your tool, take the old blade with you and be sure to match the shank end. Though the trend is toward standardization, there is some discrepancy in the combinations of teeth per inch, set, lengths, and widths the makers offer. Be sure to study the owner's manual that comes with the tool you buy for any specifics concerning the tool-blade relationship.

All blades, stiff as they are, can still bend, twist, or arc in the cut. The main cause of such evils is forcing the cut, trying to get the teeth to chew out more material than they were designed to handle. You can easily tell when you are guilty of this by sound and feel. If the cut isn't progressing steadily without excessive feed pressure, the blade is being overworked, it's dull, or you may be using the wrong one.

Do not use woodworking blades to cut any metal except do-it-yourself materials, such as aluminum, that can be worked with ordinary woodworking tools. In a pinch, however, you can use metal-cutting blades to cut wood, hardboards and similar materials.

As far as speeds are concerned, use low speeds for tough jobs and high speeds for the easy ones, but always remember that choosing the right blade for the job you are doing is your best assurance of good work quality and long blade life. An advantage of speed control, regardless of the blade, is that you can alter speed in the middle of a job. For example, slow down a bit when you hit a particularly dense grain area or a knot in a piece of wood.

Consider Teflon-coated blades, even though they are more expensive, if you plan to do much work with green, damp, or pitchy lumber. When doing such work, select a blade with few teeth per inch and lots of set. When you are working on heavy stock but want a nice finish, it's all right to go to a smoother-cutting blade, but you must work much slower than you would with the recommended blade.

"Toothless" blades. These are new tungsten-carbide blades, first introduced for industry but now avail-

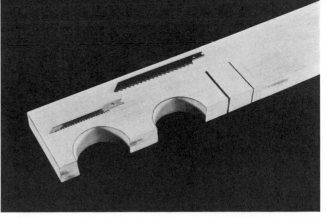

Both the narrow blade and the wide blade made the tight turns. Fewer and heavier-set teeth of the latter cut a wider kerf and thus provide more room for the blade to turn.

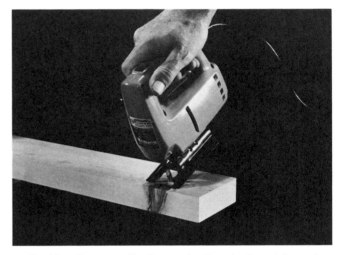

Rocking the saw will often make it easier to get through a knotty area. Combine the technique with a slower speed.

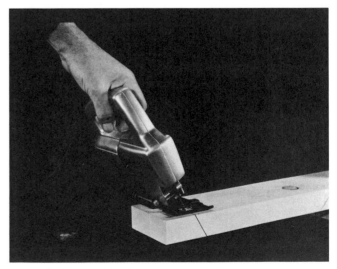

Do bevel cuts by tilting the base to the angle you require. Remember, this increases the thickness of the cut so a slow speed is required.

NEW "TOOTHLESS" TUNGSTEN-CARBIDE SABER SAW BLADES

Tungsten-carbide saber saw blades include (from left to right) fine, medium, and coarse grits, and flush-cut type. They can cost as much as $2.50 but can outlast regular toothed blades as much as 10 to one.

Toothless, tungsten-carbide blades do jobs, such as cutting through nailed down flooring, that would ruin an ordinary blade. Coarse grits work best for such applications.

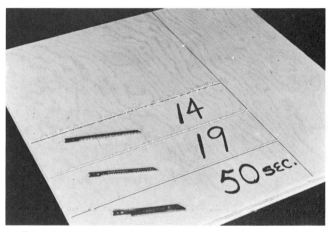

Even though toothless blades cut on both the "up" and the "down" stroke, they are not speed demons. It took 50 seconds for one to make a cut in this wood while regular toothed blades did it in 14 and 19 seconds. However, note obvious difference in splintering at the surface.

With a toothless, tungsten-carbide blade, you can easily cut materials like ceramic tile. The work must be firmly supported to avoid cracking the material.

able to home workshoppers. These blades cut almost anything and have a very long life. While a circular blade has teeth, these new saber saw blades do not. Instead, the cutting edges consist of hundreds of particles of tungsten-carbide granules fused to the blade material.

Cutting speed is not a strong point of the new blades. A group of teeth will chew out more material than a line of grit and generally do it faster. Judged under home workshop conditions, this suggests that the toothless blades do not—and probably aren't meant to—replace comparable toothed ones. But they do provide a valuable supplement, since no conventional blade can cut easily through ceramic tile or slate or through unsandwiched sheet metal without excessive burring and edge lifting.

The blades will work on wood, and they leave an impressive, almost sanded edge with minimal splintering and feathering. But they do not cut as fast as conventional blades.

Under test conditions, a medium-grit tungsten saber-saw blade took about 50 seconds to make a 10″ cut through ¾″ DF plywood. A 10-tooth-per-inch, taper-back blade made it in about 19 seconds. A 7-tooth-per-inch blade with set teeth ran the 10″ in about 14 seconds. There was, however, a big difference in the cut quality. Although the taper-back blade (designed for the purpose) left a respectable edge, the tungsten blade came out on top.

Tungsten-carbide blades are also a good choice when cutting hard metals. Testing again showed that it took about 92 seconds to go through a 1¼″ OD, heavy-walled steel tube with a 32-tooth, wave-set saber-saw blade. With a coarse-grit tungsten blade, it took about 80 seconds. This is not a great difference in time, but the results were startling as far as durability was concerned. The conventional blade was obviously tired after the job, while the toothless blade was ready to repeat the chore many times over.

The durability factor applies to the toothless blades generally. There is no question that they will outlast conventional blades by a most impressive margin.

In some cases in the home workshop, there is no basis for comparison with conventional blades. The toothless ones will cut ceramic tile, slate, asbestos cement, clay pipe, brick, stainless steel, countertop material, and many other similar problem materials.

The accompanying chart suggests grit selection for various materials. All of the grit types cut comparatively smooth edges with little feathering and chipping. The fine grit works best in thin, hard materials when cut quality is important and when chipping or delamination might be a problem. Medium-grit blades can be used if you wish the job to go faster or if you find that the material you are cutting is packing between the tungsten-carbide particles.

Coarse-grit blades cut the fastest and, since they form a wider kerf, will make smaller radius cuts than blades with finer grits. This feature is comparable to being able to make a tighter turn with a wide, heavy-set blade than

a no-set, narrow blade. There is simply more room to maneuver.

Tool speed can be a factor in working most efficiently with the toothless blades. Slower speeds work best on such materials as stainless steel and countertop laminates. In all cases, tests indicate that it's wise to start at slow speeds and build up spm to the point where the blade is cutting most efficiently. Do this, at least for the first time, on each new material you tackle.

The plunge cut. With a saber saw, you can do internal cutting without a lead-in cut from an edge of the stock, and you can get started without even having to drill a blade insertion hole.

Angle the tool so it rests on the forward edge of the baseplate. This angle must be such that you are presenting the teeth of the blade to the surface of the stock. A snug grip and a firm contact between the work and the baseplate are in order. Turn on the motor and very slowly tilt the machine back to make contact. You must avoid causing the initial contact to be between the point of the blade and the work. If you don't, you might as well have placed your hand on a pogo stick. The tool will do nothing but hop.

The initial cut is a groove. As you continue to tilt the tool back, the groove lengthens and deepens and finally penetrates. Keep the contact between the baseplate and the work very firm. If you allow the tool to move back, you'll bounce off the back end of the groove. Also, let-

MATERIAL TO BE CUT	FINE GRIT	MEDIUM GRIT	COARSE GRIT
Fiber Glass (Polyesters, Epoxies, Malamines, Silicones).	✔	✔	X
Ceramic Tile, Slate, Cast Stone.	X	✔	
Asbestos Cement, Nail Embedded Wood, Plaster with Nails.			X*
Chalkboard, Carbon/Graphite, Clay Pipe, Brick.	✔	X	
Stainless Steel Trim, Sheet Metal to 18 Ga., Ducting. Counter Top Materials, Tempered Hardboard.	X*		
Plywood, Hardwood Veneer Plywood.	✔	X	

*Use slower speeds with variable speed saws.   "X" boxes show most popular grit size.

Select **fine grit** when a smooth cut is desired in thin, hard materials where precision is important, particularly where splitting, chipping, or delamination is a problem. Use **medium-grit** blades where faster cutting is needed or when loading of fine-grit blades occurs. The **coarse-grit** blades cut faster in thick or softer materials where a rougher finish is acceptable. **Coarser grit** saws will permit up to a 30% smaller radius cut.

Courtesy of Remington Arms Co. Inc.

HOW TO PLUNGE CUT

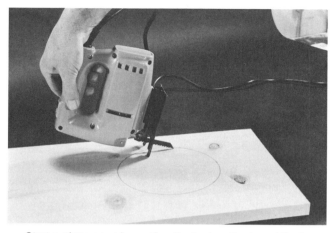

Start a plunge cut by resting the tool on the toe of the base-plate. Angle must be such that you are presenting the teeth, not the point of the blade, to the surface of the work.

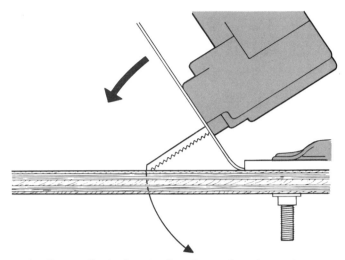

Another method of protecting the surface is to clamp a piece of wood to the work and brace the toe of the baseplate against the edge of the clamped-down piece.

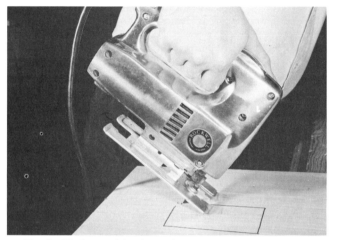

Slowly tilt the tool back so the teeth start to cut a groove. The more you tilt, the deeper the groove gets until you finally penetrate.

As a precaution against marring fancy-surfaced materials like hardwood paneling, you can rest the toe of the base-plate on a small piece of scrap stock.

Do the plunge cut until the tool is resting firmly on the base-plate and then proceed to cut in normal fashion.

The amount of relief material you must remove to do corners will depend on the width of the blade and, to some extent, the thickness of the stock. Sharp corners must be approached from two directions.

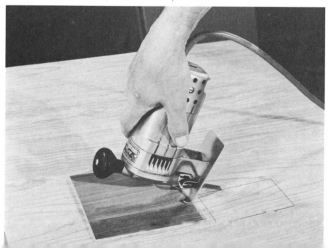

You can make a right-angle guide block for all square corners. The guide can serve as a brace for the plunge cut as well as a guide for cutting the lines.

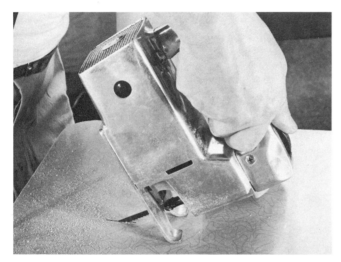

The plunge cut can be accomplished through many types of material. On countertop material, use a firm grip because the slippery surface makes the tool a little harder to control.

ting the tool jiggle as you penetrate can mar the surface of the stock. To minimize this possibility, there is no law that says you can't place a thin piece of scrap between the baseplate and the work—even heavy cardboard will do. Another way to provide firm support until penetration occurs is to clamp a piece of scrap to the work. Then you can brace the toe of the baseplate against the edge of the scrap.

When you try the plunge cut for the first time, do it in a waste area. After some practice you'll be able to accomplish it directly on a cut line. Before feeding to cut further, be sure you have penetrated sufficiently to seat the tool solidly in its normal, fully flat baseplate position. If the cutout is circular, then you just proceed in one direction to complete the operation. When square corners are involved, slant toward a line and then to a corner. Back out and then slant to an adjacent line so

you can make a second cut at right angles to the first one. This will have to be repeated for each corner. If the corners are rounded, then, of course, you can just make a turn. In such situations, it often pays to drill holes at the corners. This provides the shape you want and also eliminates the need for plunging. Incidentally, the plunging process can be overdone. It's nice to know you can do it when necessary, but if you are doing some complicated piercing work that would call for many plunge cuts or if you are involved with some delicate material and it is possible to do blade insertion holes, be safer and do that instead.

Many of the ideas given in the jigsaw chapter in relation to piercing, backtracking, etc. can also apply to saber-saw work.

Freehand cutting. The one thing you should avoid is vibration either in the tool or the work. Therefore, work that is not large enough to sit solidly on its own should be clamped or weighted down. To keep the tool still, apply firm pressure both down and forward. Avoid sideways pressure on the blade. Remember that the blade is chucked at one end only; lateral force can cause problems, damage to the blade and substandard cut quality being the most obvious.

Be sure that the baseplate is in firm contact with the work at all times. The only exception to this rule might occur when you hit a knot in the wood. Here, rocking the tool might help the blade get through more easily. The idea is to pivot up on the toe and thus decrease the contact area between the blade and the work. Coming back down does the same thing. In effect, you are concentrating the cutting power.

Saber-saw blades cut on the "up" stroke so splintering

Remember that the blade cuts on the "up" stroke. Bottom and top views of a cut made with the same blade are shown. Clean cut on the left (bottom of work) suggests that all materials should be cut with the good side down.

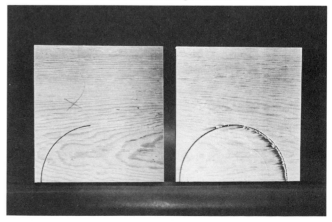

and feathering will occur on the surface of the work that is in contact with the baseplate. This suggests that any-time the finish cut is important that you work with the good side of the stock down. This is not always possible. You may, for example, need a hole through installed wall paneling. In such cases, work with a blade designed to produce a smooth cut even though cut speed might be reduced. A little trick that may come in handy is to place a strip of transparent tape over the cut line before you saw. This does the job of holding the wood fibers still regardless of the blade action. Another solution, if your saw is so equipped, is to use the special insert mentioned earlier.

Visualize the cut before you start working. Some-times preliminary incuts will save you considerable backtracking. Don't force blades around turns they are obviously struggling to make. In some cases, radial cuts, such as those described for band saw and jigsaw opera-tions in their respective chapters, can be used with the

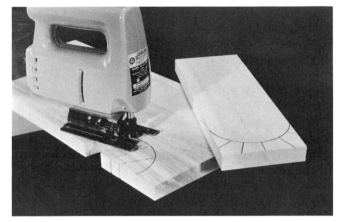

In many cases, you can get around a difficult arc by first making the kind of radial cuts shown here. Waste that falls off as you proceed with the cut gives the blade more room to swing outward as it goes around.

Visualize the cut before you start. In situation shown, it would be wise to make the short, shoulder cut first.

The radius you can turn will depend on the width of the blade you select for the job.

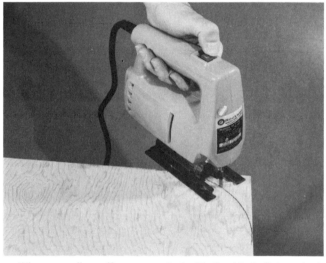

When rounding off corners, start with the blade flat against one edge of the stock. Use a very slow feed as you go off the tangent to enter the arc.

Full-curve scallops can be done in one continuous pass. When the arcs meet at a point, first make cuts from the edge to the point.

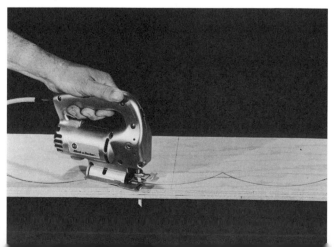

saber saw. For example, if you need to cut a small half circle in the edge of a piece of stock, you could facilitate things by making a series of cuts from the board edge to the line before you start to saw the arc. This would cause pieces of stock to fall away as you cut and provide more room for the blade to maneuver.

Guided cuts. While it isn't difficult to do freehand straight cuts, you can relieve yourself of some of the strain by using a guide to gain better accuracy. The most common guide is a rip guide. This is very similar to those supplied for portable circular saws. Sometimes, one is supplied with the tool when you buy it. If not, you can buy one as an accessory. The guide is inserted through slots (or some similar arrangement) in the baseplate and is secured with screws. To use it, you measure from the fence on the guide to a tooth that is set in the guide's direction. As you cut, the fence rides the edge of the

MAKING GUIDED CUTS

Some tools come equipped with a rip guide. If yours doesn't, you can buy one as an accessory.

When a cut is beyond the capacity of the rip guide, you can tack-nail or clamp down a straight piece of wood for a guide. Be sure that the edge of the baseplate is in constant contact with the edge of the guide.

While it is not difficult to follow a straight line freehand with the saber saw, you can use a rip guide as an aid to accuracy. The fence on the guide must ride the edge of the stock throughout the pass.

Most rip guides are designed so you can use them for pivot-cutting circles. For jobs beyond a guide's capacity, you can substitute a straight piece of wood, feed, and let the pivot do the guiding.

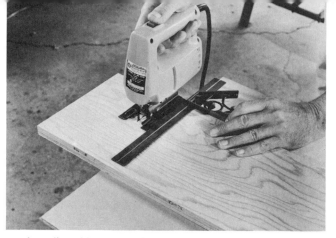

An adjustable square (shown) can be used as a crosscut guide. (For wider work, use a carpenter's square.)

Gentle curves can be accomplished by using a clamped-down guide strip. This method is good to use when you need many similar pieces.

It is not difficult to follow a pattern with the saber saw. The pattern can be heavy cardboard for a few pieces or hardboard when you require many parts.

stock and maintains a uniform cut width. The guide may be used with almost any blade, but you will be most successful, especially on heavy stock, if you work with a wide blade. Although the accessory is called a rip guide, there is no reason why you can't use it on cross-cuts as well.

When the cut you are making is too far from the stock edge to use the rip guide (or maybe it's at an angle to the edge), you can use a straight piece of wood in its place. Tack-nail or clamp the "straightedge" to the work. Position it away from the line of cut a distance that will be equal to the measurement from the edge of the base-plate to a tooth set in its direction. To make the cut, you keep the edge of the baseplate in constant contact with the guide.

In most cases, the rip guide will serve to do pivot cutting of circles. Adjust the guide so the distance from the pivot point to a tooth set in its direction is equal to the radius of the circle you require. Follow that rule if the disc you are cutting out is the part you want. If the circle in the work is what you want, then measure from a tooth on the opposite side of the blade. Your best bet is to make a plunge cut before you set the pivot point. Then, holding the pivot point firmly, feed the tool slowly; let the pivot device do the guiding.

When the circle you require is beyond the capacity of the rip guide, you can substitute a straight piece of wood that is sized to fit the baseplate slots. A nail driven through the strip of wood serves as the pivot.

A good guide for crosscutting, when work width permits, can be an ordinary adjustable square or, for larger work, a carpenter's square. Hand hold such guides firmly as you move the tool along the blade. Any of the guides shown for use with a portable cutoff saw, including some of the homemade ones, can be used with a saber saw as well.

You can also shape guides for doing curve cuts, although the technique is most applicable when the curve is not too extreme. Using such guides is a good way to cut delicate curved pieces. The important thing is to maintain a constant tangent contact between the guide and the edge of the baseplate.

Cutting metal. With the right metal-cutting blade mounted and a suitable speed, you can cut any metal that can be touched with a hacksaw blade. You can also do it faster and with much less effort. Actually, you increase capacity since you are not hindered by the yoke shape on the conventional hacksaw.

Regardless of the material, be sure at least two teeth are in contact with the edge of the stock. Thin material can sit between the teeth of a coarse blade, and this can result in stripping the teeth, bending the blade, or break-

CUTTING METALS WITH A SABER SAW

It's acceptable to work on a heavy metal sheet without support other than what you supply to keep it firm.

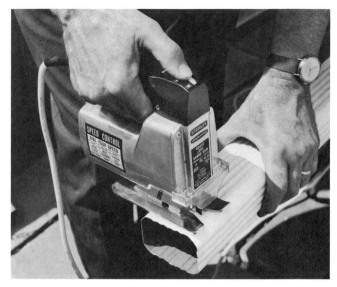

Galvanized material like gutters and downspouts can be cut pretty cleanly with a fine-tooth, wave-set blade or a tungsten-carbide, toothless blade.

On thin sheets of metal, you will always get a better cut if you tape the work to a backup sheet of scrap wood.

THICKNESS OF METAL — TWO TEETH OR MORE CONTACTING METAL — A

COARSE TEETH STRADDLING METAL RESULTS IN STRIPPED TEETH — B

BLADE TOOTH SIZE FOR METAL CUTTING

When cutting thin materials, be sure that at least two teeth of the blade contact the edge. Coarse teeth that straddle the material can be stripped.

You can do plunge cutting on metal, but it's not easy. It's better to work by doing a lead-in cut as shown.

ing the blade. Of course, this does not apply to tungsten-carbide toothless blades.

As the material gets thicker, you can use coarser blades. In fact, it often pays to do this since very small teeth can clog quickly.

All work must be firmly supported. When possible, if it is small, grip the workpiece in a vise. Other items can be clamped to or weighted down on a bench top. Very heavy sheet metals do not require any special consideration other than wise blade choice and good speed. Thin sheet metals should either be supported on the underside with scrap wood or sandwiched between covers of thin plywood or hardboard. Set up in this way, even intricate shapes can be cut from thin sheets, and the parts will have smooth edges and little burr.

When working with heavy nonferrous metals, it pays to apply a grease stick lubricant to the blade as you work. This will help keep the teeth from becoming clogged with waste metal.

RECIPROCATING SAWS

It's difficult to select a name for this tool. They are called "reciprocating" saws, "bayonet" saws, and "all-purpose" saws. Some manufacturers have a pet name like Rockwell's "Tiger" saw, Shopmate's "Blitz," Skil's "Recipro," Millers Falls "Super Saw," and Powr-Kraft's "Recip."

What emerges from the names, descriptive titles, and uses is a heavy-duty, all-purpose sawing tool that works something like a saber saw but is far from it. Reciprocating saws drive a blade to-and-fro on a horizontal plane as opposed to the vertical action of its little brother.

Reciprocating saws are often described as the "you name it, they'll cut it" tool. From 12″ diameter logs to steel pipe and bar stock, woods and plastics and other materials, this saw will do things you should not attempt with other, portable sawing tools.

Reciprocating saws can drive blades as long as 12″, although 6″ is more commonly used, and stroke length may be well over an inch. Most of them will supply more than one speed, while some have a built-in variable speed control mechanism. Because the saw is designed for a multitude of uses on various materials, being able to select a speed for the job and a blade to go with it is almost a necessity.

Most of these saws permit adjustment so you can cut close to walls and into corners. Prices start at about $40.00 and go up to considerably more depending on whether the tool is designed for commercial use or for home use. It's hard to find one tool in the category that is delicate in any way. The big ones can pull as many as 8.0 amps; I don't think I've seen any that pulls less than 4.0.

If a plumber, electrician, carpenter, installation man, or remodeler had to choose between a saber saw and a reciprocating saw, chances are he would choose the latter. And this is a good clue to the tool's capabilities.

For average in-shop and on-location chores, the home-craftsman will be quite content with a good saber saw. For those times when you might be building a carport or deck, cutting up firewood, building a fence, making a retaining wall, doing a major house remodeling job, cutting through a wall to install a new window or door, or doing other jobs of that nature, the reciprocating saw can be a fine tool to have.

USING A RECIPROCATING SAW

Cutting through a full-thickness wall is no hardship for a reciprocating saw. The blades cut on the back stroke so all tools provide a shoe for adequate bracing.

Because the reciprocating saw is so rugged, it is a fine unit to have for remodeling jobs. Always use the shortest blade that is adequate for the job.

The reciprocating saw can do many jobs you might ordinarily do with a saber saw, but that does not make it a complete substitute for the saber saw.

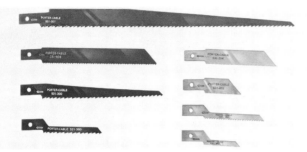

Different lengths and widths of blades are available for reciprocating saws. Some are designed especially for cutting metals, others for wood.

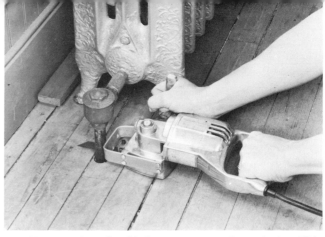

With a metal-cutting blade, you can saw through pipe. This model allows you to cut almost flush with the floor.

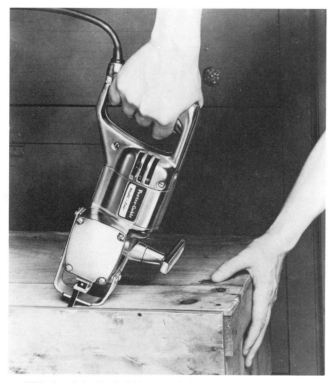

With the right kind of blade and the correct speed, it doesn't matter whether you are cutting through an occasional nail . . .

. . . or through a stucco wall. Make sure there are no live electrical wires in the wall before you begin to cut.

Like the saber saw, the reciprocating saw can be used to do plunge cuts. Since the blade is at the front of the machine, the pivot action to get the blade started is reversed.

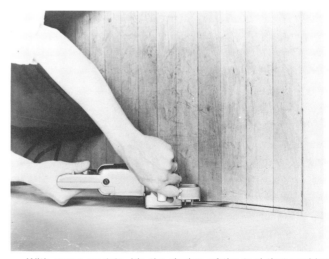

With some models, it's the design of the tool that enables you to cut close to an adjacent surface.

Statistics indicate, as far as sales are concerned, that portable drills are the most popular power tools. The reason is simple: the portable drill is an excellent, basic tool-kit accessory even if the owner's involvement in do-it-yourself activities is limited to an occasional cut with a handsaw. What has also helped is that the modern drill, especially in the light-duty, small capacity range, has become more and more inexpensive while, at the same time, it has been improved to offer additional, practical features.

On the other hand, you can view the electric drill as a power source to drive a wide variety of accessories with activity ranges from polishing shoes to sawing wood. Therefore, the power drill can become the basis of a fairly efficient power tool shop. Ironically, the total cost of the attachments will usually far outweigh the original cost of the drill!

If you plan to use a power drill only occasionally, undoubtedly you would be wise to select a low-cost, light-duty unit. So equipped, you can do a variety of jobs, such as drilling holes for screws or drilling through a wall and into a stud, or drilling holes in masonry. However, it would not be reasonable to expect a less than ten dollar, ¼″ tool to do everything a house builder requires and to do it often. The final choice of a drill must be based on what you need it for. Price can't be the sole factor.

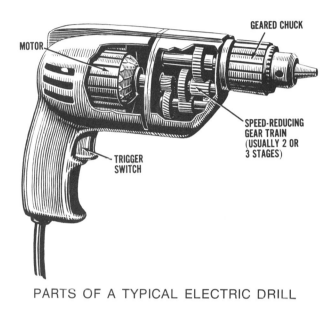

PARTS OF A TYPICAL ELECTRIC DRILL

Quite often you can save money by purchasing a kit with drill, useful accessories, and a tote-about case. Be certain the drill is the right size for the jobs you will do.

A ¼″ electric drill that is priced under $10.00. It is rated at ⅐ HP with 1.9 amps and has a single speed of 2,250 rpm's. A similar ⅜″ model, also under $10.00, is rated at ⅐ HP with 2.2 amps and runs at 1,000 rpm's.

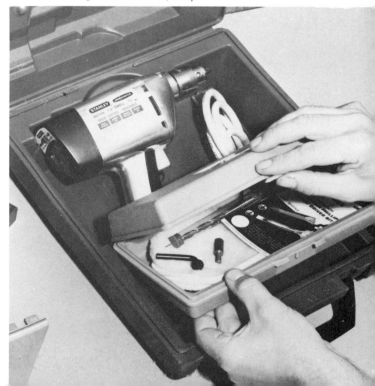

SIZES

Common sizes of electric drills are ¼″, ⅜″, and ½″. The size indicates the maximum shank diameter that can be gripped in the chuck—not the drilling capacity. Many cutting tools, like spade bits that go up to 1½″, have shanks turned down to ¼″. Circle cutters, fly cutters and the like form holes well over ¼″, but many of them have ¼″ shanks and can be gripped in a small capacity drill. However, complete freedom to do this is another matter. The drill may not have the power for the job, especially over an extended period of time.

Generally, the user can quickly judge if he is overtaxing the tool. It will get warm quickly, it will stall, or the speed may decrease to the point where the bit isn't cutting. Heed such warning signs to avoid abuse.

Your expectations of any drill must, first of all, be based on the size of the drill. Larger drills, of course, have more power. Secondly, judge a drill on how the manufacturer lists the tool. You'll find different "ratings" even in a given same-size category. If the maker lists one for "commercial duty" and another for "light duty," you can expect to find differences in the two that go beyond price. In addition, terms like "good," "better," and "best" that are used in the manufacturer's literature about the tool are clear indicators of the drill's quality. Another signal to look for is the length of the guarantee. In the manufacturer's catalog, one ¼″ drill might be guaranteed for 90 days, another for a full year.

SPEEDS

There was a time when you did not have a choice concerning the speed of the drill. In essence, you bought a drill for its power or its chuck capacity, and you got one compatible speed. The combination of size-power-speed made the unit ideal for a particular category of work. You can still do this, and it might even be a wise basis for selection if you wanted exceptional performance in a limited area. However, the tool would be a compromise if you checked it out for general-purpose applications.

The major drill feature today is built-in variable speed, and you can get it in any drill size. An interesting factor here, which points up the logic of lower speeds being more compatible with greater capacities, is that even with variable speeds the range decreases as the drill size increases. A ¼″ drill may go from zero to 2,000 rpm's or more, a ⅜″ drill may have a top speed of 1,000 rpm's, and a big ½″ tool may be limited to a maximum of 700 rpm's.

In the final analysis, no one drill will be ideal for every application you can think of. This point is made be-

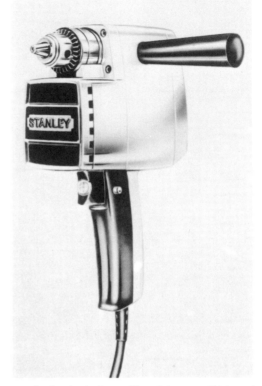

Recessed chuck design with minimum offset makes this model usable in very tight places. It pulls 3.5 amps, has ½″ chuck capacity and operates at 400 rpm's.

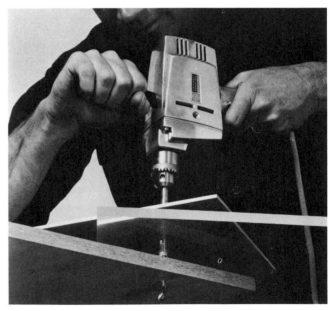

A great advantage of the variable speed drill, regardless of its size, is the fact that you can choose a good speed for the material you are working on and the size of the hole you are forming. Bigger drill sizes often take lower speeds.

cause portable drills are the most abused of power tools. The best choice for anyone must be in line with how the tool will be used.

Variable speed will make any drill more flexible, but it doesn't change some basic concepts. A ¼″ drill, even at the right speed, isn't likely to hold up too long forming oversize holes in masonry or steel. A ½″ unit might be awkward to handle on small drilling jobs. When you think in terms of some accessories, you'll find that light-duty units may have a nice speed range for broad application but lack power for the more demanding chores.

FEATURES TO LOOK FOR

The prices of portable drills are not so far out of line that a fellow can't think in terms of having more than one. A ⅜″ unit with variable speed might be the best first choice simply because it can accomplish more than a ¼″ model but also do the jobs of smaller units.

An adjustable speed control knob is a good feature. It is set to provide a predetermined speed. Thus, you can do any number of similar operations that require a particular rpm without reliance on finger control.

The purpose of double insulation is to provide a safety barrier between possible electric leaks and your hand. Disassembling such tools yourself is not recommended.

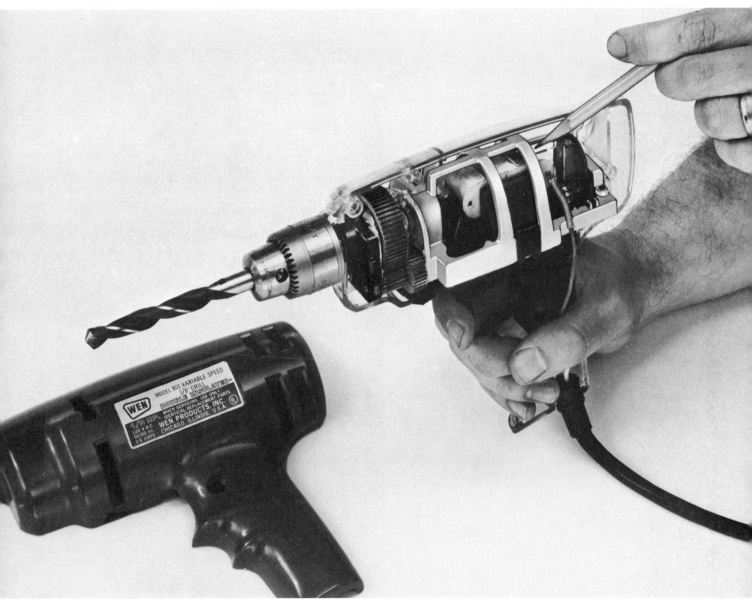

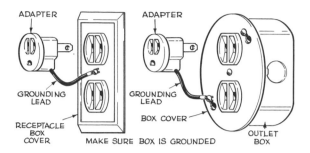

Most tools that are not double insulated come with an adapter plug so you can work with two-hole outlets. Be sure to follow instructions for attaching grounding lead that is part of the adapter.

Cordless drill is a boon to the do-it-yourselfer as it may be used anywhere, especially where electricity may be a hazard. The drill has a built-in power source that may be fully recharged in 10 hours. A ¼″ model that operates at 800 rpm's is shown.

Double insulation is a good feature to look for simply because it eliminates the need to follow through on the 3-wire system that is a part of conventional units. In essence, double insulation provides safety barriers between a possible electric leak and your hand.

A reversing switch is recommendable since it will permit you to loosen things as well as tighten them. Also, you can do a better job with such accessories as sanding drums, wire brushes, and buffing wheels when you can change from one direction of rotation to another. It will also help these accessories last longer.

How the tool "feels" in your hand can be important. Some handles are placed centrally; others are more like a pistol grip. Centered handles might provide better balance. Most of the drills of interest to the do-it-yourselfer start at about 2 lbs and run close to 5 lbs. The more power the tool has, the greater its capacity and the more it will weigh. Assuming all other critical factors among an assortment of tools are similar, then it's sound to base your choice on how the tool feels in your hand.

OPERATING TECHNIQUES

Since drill handling and scope of application relate more to what you grip in the chuck than to the tool itself, a minimum of text is used to point out general operating techniques while the accompanying illustrations and captions are used to point out operating details.

The more powerful the drill, the more torque there will be at the cutting end. Heavy, ½″ drills are strong enough so that, should the cutter jam in the hole, the drill will spin and take you with it. To a lesser extent, this is also true of small units. To avoid such problems, always maintain a firm grip. You can do this with one hand or with two. Often, when the work is small and the drilling is light, you can hold the work in one hand,

the drill in the other if hand pressure is sufficient to keep the work firmly down on a workbench or sawhorse. Holding the job in midair and then applying the drill is not good practice. When necessary, secure the work to a bench with clamps or in a vise.

Many jobs call for drilling on a well fastened item. You might be forming access holes through studs for wiring or plumbing or maybe cutting into masonry. In such cases, grip the drill with both hands, using any auxiliary handle that may be provided with the drill.

Be sure to use the chuck key at all times and be certain you have removed it before pressing the switch. Otherwise, it might fly out. Before you work, also check to be sure the shank of the tool is centered in the chuck. It is possible to grip it off-center.

When working with a single speed model, it's a good idea to make a dent with a center punch at the point the bit should enter. This method will keep the bit from "walking." Using a center punch is very important on hard materials but a good precaution on soft materials as well.

If you wish, you can do without the center-punch chore when working with a variable speed model. Just place the tip of the bit where you wish to drill and start at minimum speed. Apply pressure and stay at slow speed until you have formed a pilot cut; then you will not have to worry about the bit moving off. Gradually increase the speed until the bit is cutting efficiently.

Many tables could be made of optimal speeds for every bit size and for every material that can be drilled. Such tabulations might be essential in industry but difficult to compile at home using a portable drill. First of all, while you might be able to control speed, there is no gauge to pinpoint all the speeds throughout the range. Secondly, the free-running speed of the drill is not the load speed. Lastly, it isn't critical that you use the optimal speed for all jobs. Getting close enough to it to do a good job without damage either to the work or to the tool is not all that difficult.

Use this general rule as a guide: high speeds for small holes, low speeds for big holes. This rule does not apply to spade bits where speeds between 1,000 and 2,000 rpm's should be used. In fact, you don't have to worry about speeds at all if you remember that the correct combination of feed pressure and speed will keep the tool cutting constantly and without stalling. If you are not making chips or dust, you are just burnishing.

When drilling holes, use a piece of scrap as a backup to minimize splintering on breakthrough. This also applies to sheet metals to eliminate buckling that can occur under drill pressure. When using twist drills, especially in metal, it's a good idea to drill "up" to the size you want. This method applies to any hole size above $\frac{1}{8}''$ and simply means that you start with a small pilot hole and enlarge it by stages. Here too, remember that as the hole gets larger, the speed should be reduced gradually.

When working with materials such as glass, slate and ceramics, the drilling should be done at slow speeds and, generally, with special carbide-tipped tools. These are specially made for such drilling and do a fine job. You'll get nowhere with conventional bits. Start the drill at minimum speed while exerting a firm, steady pressure. Once you have formed a pilot cut, apply some water or a special coolant that has been compounded for the purpose. At this point, you can pick up on speed until you get steady results.

Most accessories designed to be powered by an electric drill come with literature that tells you a good operating speed. In many cases, the best speed must be a compromise. For example, consider shaping accessories for power drills. Shaping is best done at high speeds—as high as 30,000 rpm's. However, you can't even approach this rate with a portable drill. Even so, you can do an acceptable job. The best procedure is to slow up on feed while you use the highest speed available. Slow feed lets more teeth pass over a given area of the work and this is approximately equal to the combination of fast speed and normal feed.

There are also safety considerations in judging the speed to use. For example, some cutting discs might be dangerous if turned at higher speeds than they were designed for. Buy yourself a pair of safety goggles for general shop use as well as portable drill applications. These goggles are essential for any job that throws off chips, dust, or splinters.

Most of the drill accessories shown in this chapter are available in large hardware stores, home handyman supply centers, and large department stores.

When you are drilling into or through a wall, be aware of what you might hit. Spaces between studs often contain electric wiring, plumbing, or insulation.

Drilling after parts have been tack-nailed together often makes it easier to form accurate dowel holes.

When drilling holes that go completely through the material and the appearance of the rear side counts, use backup blocks. These will minimize or eliminate the splintering that occurs on breakthrough.

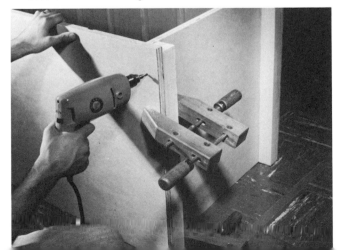

DRILLING TOOLS

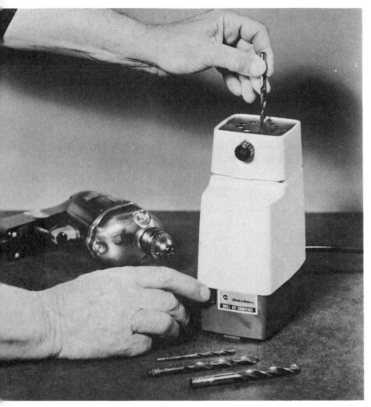

Sharpen bits to retain the original keenness and angles on the tips. Although sharpening can be done by hand, it takes considerable practice to acquire the knack. The new gadget shown works like a pencil sharpener.

When a good job of drilling in metals is done, waste curls out of the hole as shown. A good idea is to start at a slow speed and rev up gradually to optimum cutting efficiency.

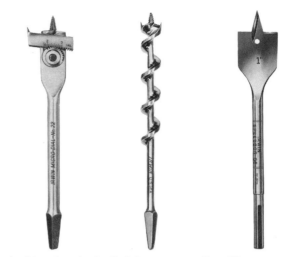

Avoid using tools that have screw tips. These are best handled in a bit-and-brace setup. Spur bits form exceptionally clean holes because the spurs cut even before waste removal begins. Spade bits are very fine, all-around, wood-drilling tools.

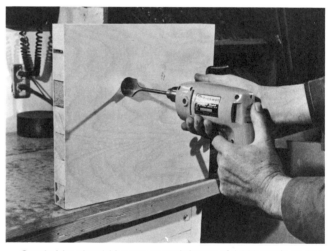

Spade bits should be run at a minimum of 1,000 rpm's and as high as 2,000 rpm's. Hold the drill firmly and apply enough pressure so the bit keeps working.

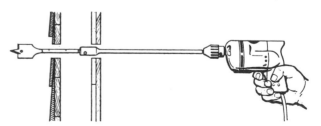

Extensions are available for use with spade bits and other drilling tools. Combining extensions can give you a good reach but pose the problem of whip. Be sure the bit point is firmly seated before you start the motor.

A long point on a drill bit is advantageous when an angled hole is required. The point of the bit can be firmly seated before cutting begins.

KEEPING THE DRILL LEVEL

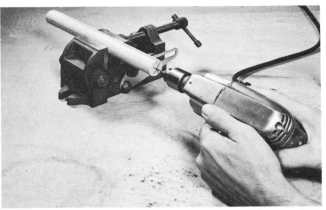

Apply pressure on the drill so force is exerted in a straight line with its axis to gain accuracy as well as to avoid bending or break of the bit if it is small. When possible, brace your hands and the drill as shown.

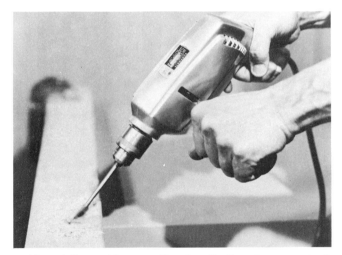

Many drills provide an auxiliary handle. If you have one, don't store it away and never use it. On some jobs, it can provide a lot of needed rigidity.

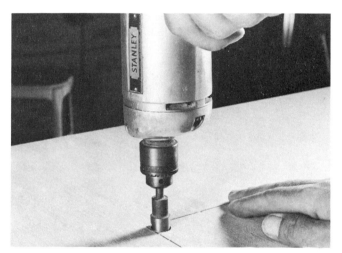

For vertical cuts, be sure the tool is perpendicular before you turn it on. If accuracy is critical, use a square as a guide.

"Power-Bore" bits (Stanley) are fast and clean-cutting. All sizes, from $\frac{3}{8}''$ up to 1'', have $\frac{1}{4}''$ shanks and long brad points. Overall length is $5\frac{1}{2}''$ so that, as with spade bits, you can drill fairly deep holes.

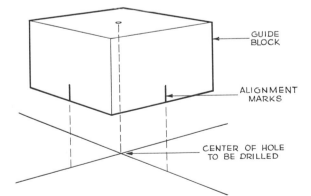

Guide block to keep drill vertical. Alignment marks on the block can be set on intersecting lines on work that determine the hole location. Keep the hole in the guide block small. Use a hardwood for the guide block.

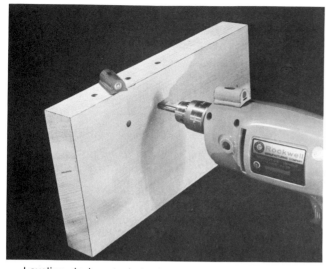

Leveling devices to help you gain accuracy when drilling freehand are available for permanent attachment to your drill. One shown on top of drill is for horizontal alignment only. A second version has an extra bull's-eye for vertical alignment also.

DRILLING TO DEPTH

Plastic device, which locks on to a drill bit at any point so you can limit penetration into the work, comes in two sizes.

Some drills are designed so that a stop rod may be used to limit penetration.

DRIVING SCREWS

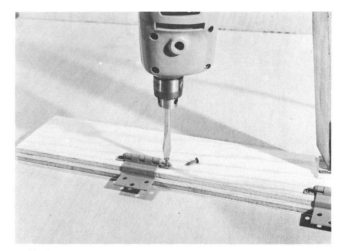

Variable speed drill is very handy to drive screws. If drill has a reversing switch, you can also remove screws. Bit should fit the screw-head slot, and a slow speed should be used.

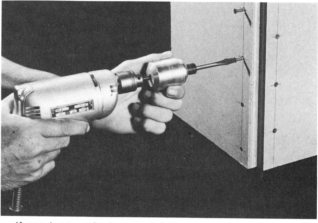

If you have a single-speed drill, you can buy an accessory that permits efficient screw driving. Some of these devices have a clutch so revolution stops as soon as the screw is seated firmly.

A sleeve (called a "finder") is often part of a screwdriver bit designed for power use. It slips over the screw head, automatically positions the driver in the slot, and makes it difficult for the driver to slip off the screw. It also acts as a stop to help prevent overdriving.

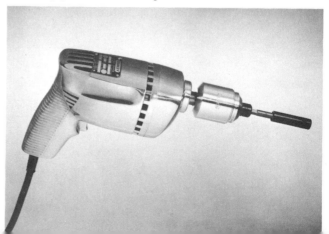

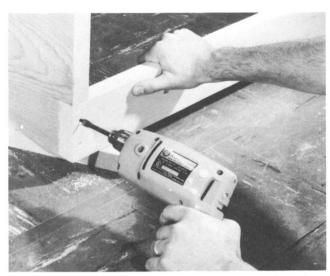

Screws driven into end grain do not hold as strongly as those that penetrate cross grain. In such situations, use a heavier, longer screw than you would normally.

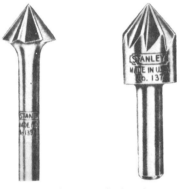

Countersinks are used to seat flathead screws flush to the work surface. They may not be necessary with very small screws in softwoods but are a necessity with hardwoods, plastics, and metals.

Combination bits are available that form pilot hole, body hole and even a countersink or counterbore in one operation. The counterbore section forms a seat for wooden plugs that can be glued in to hide the screws.

Screw No.	Shank Diam.	Lengths Available	Lead Holes	
			Hardwood	Softwood
0	.060″	$\frac{1}{4}″-\frac{3}{8}″$	$70(\frac{1}{32})$	$75(\frac{1}{64})$
1	.073″	$\frac{1}{4}″-\frac{1}{2}″$	$66(\frac{1}{32})$	$71(\frac{1}{32})$
2	.086″	$\frac{1}{4}″-\frac{3}{4}″$	$56(\frac{3}{64})$	$65(\frac{1}{32})$
3	.099″	$\frac{1}{4}″-1″$	$54(\frac{1}{16})$	$58(\frac{3}{64})$
4	.112″	$\frac{1}{4}″-1\frac{1}{2}″$	$52(\frac{1}{16})$	$55(\frac{3}{64})$
5	.125″	$\frac{3}{8}″-1\frac{1}{2}″$	$49(\frac{5}{64})$	$53(\frac{1}{16})$
6	.138″	$\frac{3}{8}″-2\frac{1}{2}″$	$47(\frac{5}{64})$	$52(\frac{1}{16})$
7	.151″	$\frac{3}{8}″-2\frac{1}{2}″$	$44(\frac{3}{32})$	$51(\frac{1}{16})$
8	.164″	$\frac{3}{8}″-3″$	$40(\frac{3}{32})$	$48(\frac{5}{64})$
9	.177″	$\frac{1}{2}″-3″$	$37(\frac{7}{64})$	$45(\frac{3}{64})$
10	.190″	$\frac{1}{2}″-3\frac{1}{2}″$	$33(\frac{7}{64})$	$43(\frac{3}{32})$
11	.203″	$\frac{5}{8}″-3\frac{1}{2}″$	$29(\frac{1}{8})$	$40(\frac{3}{32})$
12	.216″	$\frac{5}{8}″-4″$	$25(\frac{1}{8})$	$38(\frac{7}{64})$
14	.242″	$\frac{3}{4}″-5″$	$14(\frac{3}{16})$	$32(\frac{7}{64})$
16	.268″	$1″-5″$	$10(\frac{3}{16})$	$29(\frac{9}{64})$
18	.294″	$1\frac{1}{4}″-5″$	$6(\frac{13}{64})$	$26(\frac{9}{64})$
20	.320″	$1\frac{1}{2}″-5″$	$3(\frac{7}{32})$	$19(\frac{11}{64})$
24	.372″	$3″-5″$	$1(\frac{1}{4})$	$15(\frac{3}{16})$

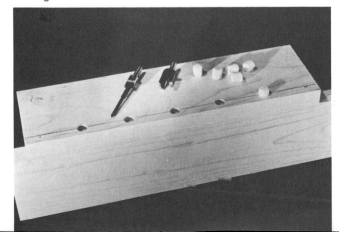

Plugs are cut with plug cutters which come in different sizes and form plugs up to about $\frac{3}{4}″$ long. Since you can use them across the grain, it is easy to match the grain pattern of the plug and the work.

ABRADING OPERATIONS

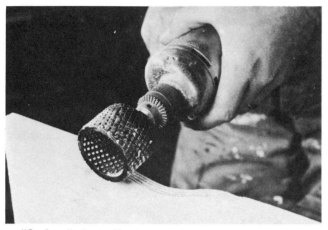

"Surform" drum (Stanley) works like a drum sander but removes material more quickly. In general, it should be the tool to use before you go to a conventional drum sander.

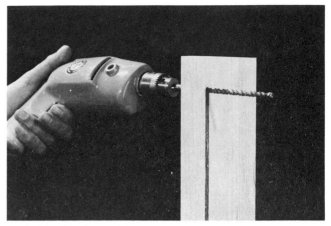

A sickle bar is good for touching up or enlarging an opening already made by other means. These accessories will cut in any direction and are end-shaped so they can bore their own starting hole.

Cheese-grater-type disk rasp is a good tool for doing rough "sanding." Keep rasp level with the work to prevent making concentric rings in the surface.

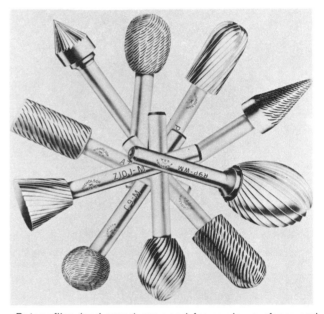

Rotary files (and rasps) are good for carving surfaces and edges into various shapes. They work best at high speeds.

The Surform has dozens of holes, each of which has a sharp cutting edge to cut away the wood. When working with it, use both hands to hold the drill against the cutting actions.

Most useful disc sander is a flexible rubber backup disc faced with an abrasive sheet that is secured with a center screw. One shown is a swivel type being driven with a right-angle drive.

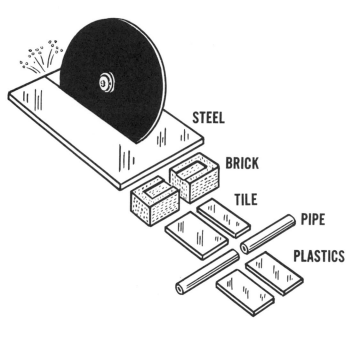

STEEL

BRICK

TILE

PIPE

PLASTICS

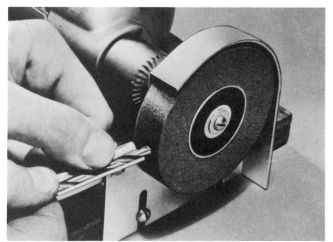

Here's an attachment that turns your drill into a "grinder". Use it for sharpening drill bits and other shop tools. Speed must be in line with the kind of wheel you mount.

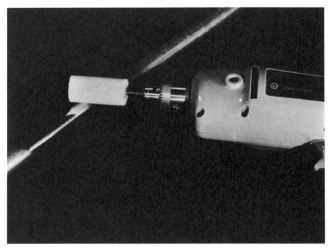

Hard felt polishing wheels come in various shapes and sizes. They may be used dry or with polishing compounds and are hard enough so you can shape them with a file to make a sharp or rounded point.

An ordinary pencil eraser makes a fairly good tool for polishing small pieces of jewelry. The average pencil is easily gripped in the chuck jaws of a $\frac{1}{4}$" drill.

The "Whizz-Disc" (Arco) is a tough, bonded abrasive that lets you cut through a variety of materials.

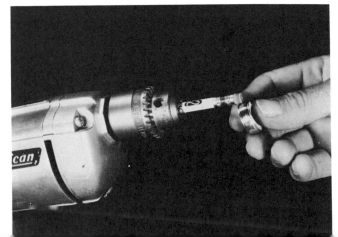

STANDS

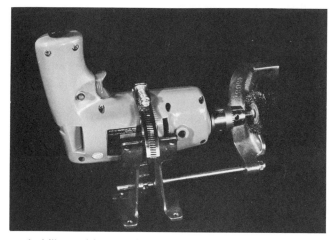

A drill stand is good for wire-brushing, grinding, polishing and similar jobs. This economical version locks the drill to a base with an adjustable clamp and also provides a guard. You can screw the base to a bench or to a block in a vise.

This type of stand lets you use a portable drill in stationary drill-press fashion. The designs are not universal enough to permit the use of any drill in any stand. Check to see if the manufacturer of your drill also provides a stand for it.

Drill stand that you make yourself. For details on how to construct it, check chapter on the all-purpose portable tool table described at the end of this book.

DRILLING FOR DOWELS

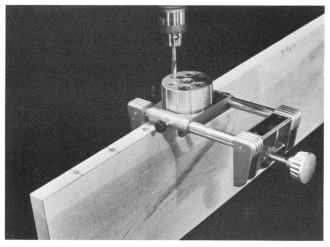

This doweling jig (Sears-Roebuck) has a revolving turret that moves on parallel arms. Its capacity is up to 4″, and it provides six hole-guide sizes from $\frac{3}{16}$″ to $\frac{1}{2}$″. You can clamp it to a single board as shown or to several when you wish to match holes.

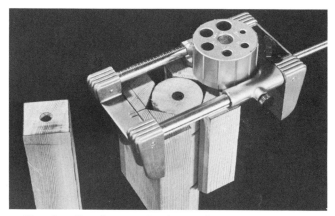

The doweling jig can also be used as a tool for accurate concentric drilling if you cut a pair of V-blocks to use with it. The V-blocks can also be used to center a hole in the end of square stock as well as to mark center points on blanks for spindle mounting in the lathe.

Another doweling jig locks mating pieces of wood together for the drilling of matching holes. A clamp and a thickness block is used beyond the jig. The center arm of the tool swings from side to side to drill pairs of holes.

SHAPING

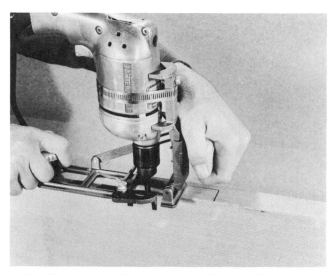

The "Routermatic" is an attachment that can fit any portable drill so it may be used as a portable "shaper." Here, it is used with a flat-bottom bit to make the mortise for a door hinge. It may also be used with conventional, piloted router bits for doing edge shaping and the like. Knobs allow handling like a hand plane.

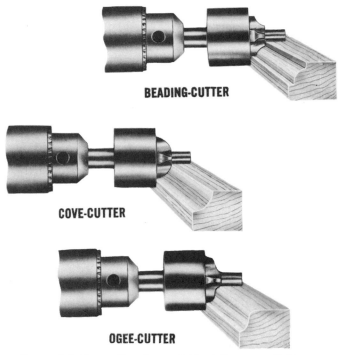

BEADING-CUTTER

COVE-CUTTER

OGEE-CUTTER

Corner finishing cutters for portable drills are available.

MASONRY DRILLING

Drilling in masonry calls for power, special carbide-tipped bits and a slow speed. Keep a firm grip on the tool and apply enough pressure so the bit will be cutting constantly.

You can do any occasional hole in masonry even with a small-size drill, but you must be careful to avoid damage to the tool or the bit.

Tile is brittle and you must exercise care, especially when starting the hole. Use minimum speed until you have formed a pilot cut. Dab on some water and increase the speed a little.

For better holding power, position the hole in a brick wall for an anchor bolt in a mortar joint rather than the brick itself.

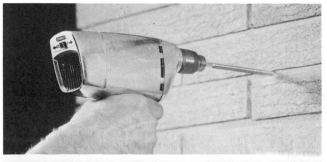

CIRCLE CUTTERS

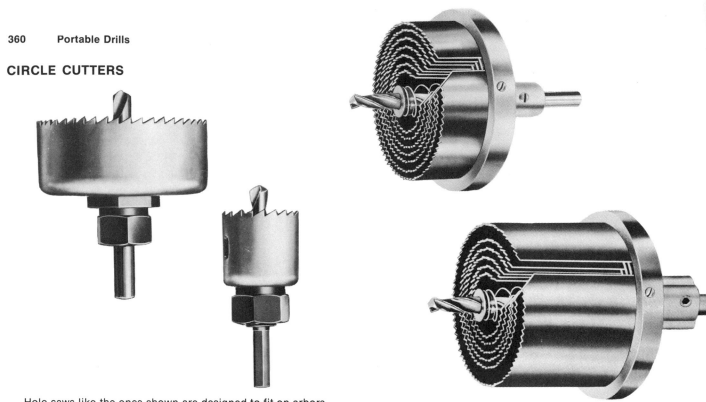

Hole saws like the ones shown are designed to fit on arbors that are gripped in the drill. Each hole saw is good for a specific size hole. Sizes range from ⅝" to 6". The larger sizes are difficult to handle with any home workshop drill.

Types of hole saws shown provide different "saw blades" for various size holes. They also include a slug-ejector, a spring-loaded device that pushes out the cut disc. In addition, they can cut different hole depths as well as different diameters.

MULTI-TOOL ACCESSORIES

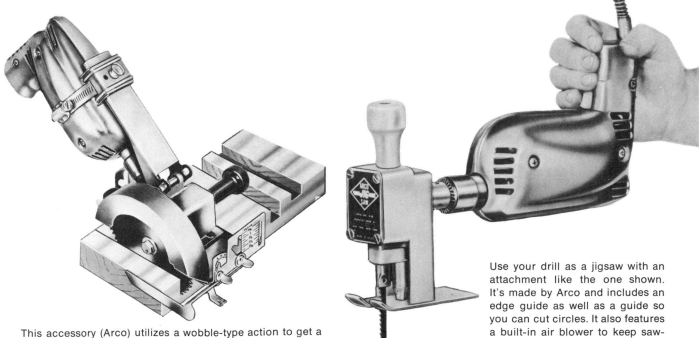

This accessory (Arco) utilizes a wobble-type action to get a wide cut from a straight saw blade.

Use your drill as a jigsaw with an attachment like the one shown. It's made by Arco and includes an edge guide as well as a guide so you can cut circles. It also features a built-in air blower to keep sawdust away from the cut line.

OTHER USES

For a good many accessories such as wire brushes and grinding wheels, arbors like the ones shown are a must. Common sizes have $\frac{1}{4}''$ or $\frac{3}{8}''$ shanks and can grip accessories with center holes ranging from $\frac{1}{4}''$ up to $\frac{1}{2}''$.

Want to use your drill as a pump? Black & Decker's new accessory makes it possible. It can be used with any common garden hose to move 200 gallons per hour.

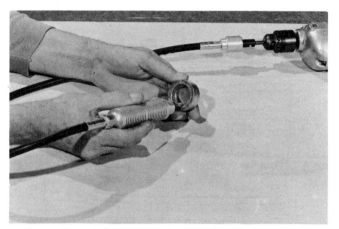

"Torque-on" (Craftsman) is a fine impact tool that will work in any drill with a $\frac{3}{8}''$ or larger chuck. It is adjustable so you can use it on $\frac{1}{2}''$ nuts or even small wood screws.

Some flex shafts are made especially for portable-drill applications. If so, follow the instructions concerning speeds and direction of rotation.

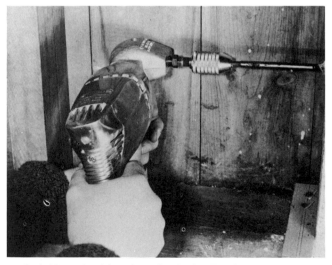

A right angle drive that chucks in the drill like any other cutter makes it possible to work in confined places.

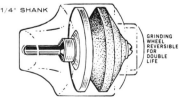

Special grinding wheel accessories let you sharpen such items as lawn mower blades, knives and scissors.

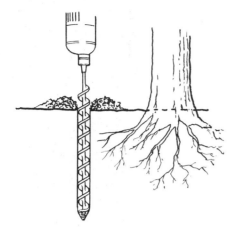

For drilling holes in soil to water or fertilize trees around the drip line, there are special bits available. These bits come in different sizes so you can work around small shrubs as well.

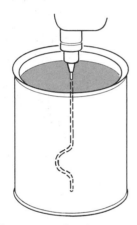

For mixing paint, you can bend up a rod yourself to insert in your portable drill or buy a commercial accessory made for the purpose.

There are many types of wire brushes available. Most are shanked for gripping in a chuck. Others require an arbor. Use them (with goggles) for cleaning chores, for brushing wood, for putting a satin finish on soft metals, etc.

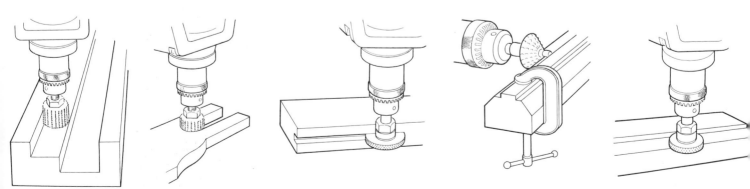

Rotary rasps come in different shapes and sizes and may be used for shaping, routine cuts, and milling jobs. They will cut plaster, plastics, aluminum and other materials as well as wood.

If you associate a saber saw with a jigsaw or band saw, a portable drill with a drill press, a cutoff saw with a table saw or radial arm machine, then the router must correspond to the shaper. With a router, you can form fancy edges on workpieces, but the uses of the router are broader than its purely decorative applications.

For example, with one accessory, the beginner can produce dovetail joints that look professionally done. It's also a fine tool for making dadoes, grooves and rabbets, and it can't be beat for trimming laminated countertops. With special template guides installed in the base, it will follow almost any pattern you care to design with speed and precision. It can incise or pierce, and if the model is really powered, it can cut through plies of material to produce duplicate pieces.

The router is basically a simple tool. Most models consist of a motor with a gripping device at one end and an encasing sleeve affair that has an attached base on which the whole unit rides. Speeds are high, anywhere between 18,000 and 35,000 rpm's, and this feature is partially responsible for producing cuts smooth enough to require little further attention.

Router prices vary considerably. Generally speaking, the more you pay, the more power you get. This factor, however, shouldn't discourage anyone who is on a limited budget. All of the models offered by manufacturers can be considered either light-duty ($\frac{1}{3}$HP to $\frac{1}{2}$HP) or heavy-duty ($\frac{3}{4}$HP and above). The difference in the two types is not in the scope of their applications but in the speed with which a job can be accomplished. A job done in one pass with a big machine may require two, or even three, passes with a lighter model, but the end result will be the same.

The router is an uncomplicated machine, but this fact shouldn't cause you to be casual when using it; it does turn bits that can slice through hardwoods. So respect for this tool is as necessary as with any power tool. Use only those accessories specifically designed for operation in a high speed tool. Be sure the accessories you buy are mountable in the machine you own. Check and recheck for bit security before you turn on the motor. When you flick the switch, be sure the cutter is not in contact with the work. Keep a firm grip on the router since it has

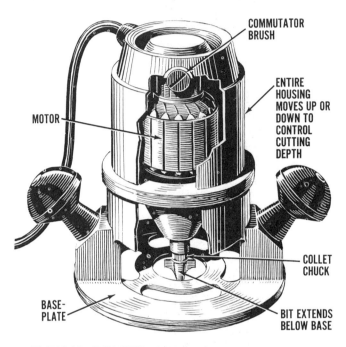

TYPICAL ROUTER AND ITS MAJOR PARTS

considerable starting torque. Obey all the safety procedures that are printed in the literature that comes with the tool and, as always, do not wear loose clothing that can be snagged by revolving bits and cutters.

CUTTERS

Cutters are mounted in a gripping device that is on the free end of the motor shaft. How a cutter is securely attached relates to the particular tool's design. Some models require one wrench, some two to lock the cutter in place, but whichever is the case, the cutting tool must be locked firmly. It's never a good idea to minimize the amount of tool shank gripped in the chuck in order to achieve more depth of cut. A $\frac{1}{2}''$ insertion is minimal, $\frac{3}{4}''$ even better. Some routers have a button device to secure the shaft as you lock on the bit. Others have flats on the shaft so you use one wrench there and a second one to tighten the chuck.

A good deal of router versatility is due to the vast assortment of cutters and bits that can be mounted in its

363

gripping device. Shank sizes can run from $\frac{1}{4}''$ up to $\frac{1}{2}''$, but you'll find the greatest variety in the $\frac{1}{4}''$ size simply because any router on the market is designed to grip that diameter. Even the big units that can grip $\frac{1}{2}''$ shanks are usually designed to take interchangeable chucks so that they can also accommodate the smaller bits.

Cutters can be one-piece units or screw-on types. With the latter, you can employ one shaft to mount various profiles. Many designs are pilot-tipped: the area below the profile is a smooth shank, and this rides against the work edge as a guide for the cut. There isn't much control in this situation for the width of the cut, but the depth of cut relates to how much the bit extends below the baseplate. It's important that the pilot has substantial bearing surface against the work edge. Also, it is important for the pilot area to be as smooth as possible. It rotates at router speed as it rides the work edge. Therefore, maximum performance can be achieved only if the area is free of dirt and gummy deposits that can accumulate.

Piloted cutters can be used in a freehand manner. Other types, like the dovetail, sash cope, or even straight bits, can be more easily controlled when the router is guided by mechanical means. These guides are special accessories that you can buy or make. For example, the dovetail cutter—when used for multiple, mating cuts—is best guided by a dovetail jig. This jig provides for precise fitting of "male" and "female" forms and, in most cases, the two can be accomplished in one operation. At the other extreme concerning guides is the simple, clamped strip of wood that lets you accurately cut a dado, a rabbet, a groove, or whatever. In addition, a pivot arrangement allows you to rout a perfect circle or arc.

Buying anything less than bits of high speed steel is a waste of money since they just won't hold up. For special applications or particular jobs that you will repeat very often, purchasing long-wearing, carbide-tipped cutters makes a lot of sense. If you are going to do a great deal of router work on laminates, plastics or plywood, seriously consider buying the carbides. Laminated material has a lot of abrasives in it and so contributes more to dulling than solid wood materials.

Router prices increase with size and horsepower. These models bring the versatility of the tool within reach of all homecraftsmen. ½HP tool on the left sells for approximately $40.00. The other ¼HP model sells for under $35.00.

TYPES OF ROUTER CUTTERS

Bits are locked into the chuck end of the spindle. Always insert the bits a minimum of ½″ into the chuck. Doing otherwise simply to achieve more depth of cut is poor practice.

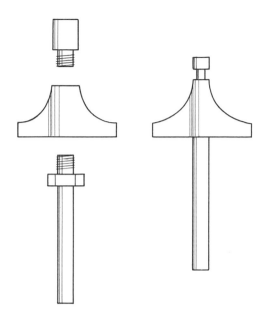

A conventional one-piece, pilot-tipped bit (top). The other is a screw-on type, which also ends in a pilot but allows different cutters to be mounted on the one shaft.

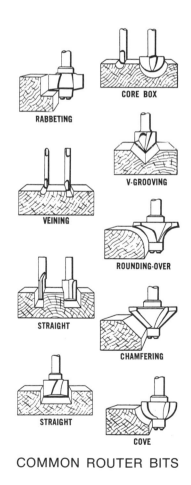

RABBETING
CORE BOX
V-GROOVING
VEINING
ROUNDING-OVER
STRAIGHT
CHAMFERING
STRAIGHT
COVE

COMMON ROUTER BITS

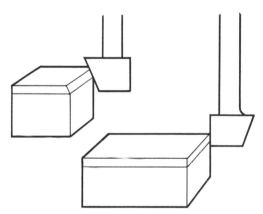

Combination trimming bit for laminates can be used to produce a square edge or a beveled edge.

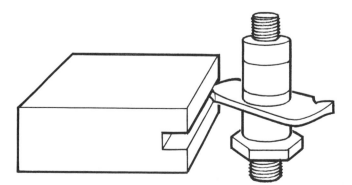

Slotting cutter is used mostly to form a spline groove to install "T" moldings on counter edges.

⅞HP model sells for about $70.00. It has some extra features such as a see-through window for depth-of-cut settings.

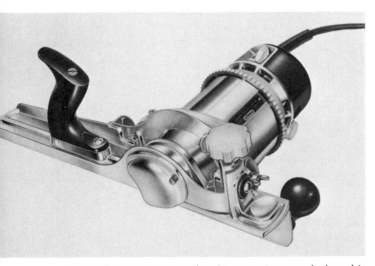

Quite often, even conventional type routers are designed to take accessories that increase the basic unit's flexibility. Here, the accessory turns the router into a powered plane.

OPERATING THE ROUTER

If you take a bird's eye view of the router, you will see that the motor rotation, and thus the direction of cut, is in a clockwise direction. The router should be used, whenever possible, so that the cutter tends to pull itself into the work. If, for example, you are using a clamped strip as a guide to cut a groove, you should feed from left to right. Working from the other direction gives the router freedom to run along the edge of the wood, and the whole operation will require more control in order to produce the smooth cut you want.

There are times, however, when this rule must be broken or when it's more convenient to use several feed directions. You'll encounter the necessity for this type of approach quite a bit in freehand routing. Most importantly, grip the router firmly at all times so that you have control. A firm grip is necessary for guided cuts as well as freehand work.

Feed speed and depth of cut go hand in hand, even though it's not farfetched to say that the slower the feed, the smoother the cut will be regardless of the cut depth. But you must keep the cutter working. Generally, the more wood you are cutting away, the slower the feed should be. If you feed too fast, you will reduce the efficiency of the motor. This will be apparent from the sound of the motor, if nothing else. If you feed too slowly, you will accomplish nothing worthwhile, and you may hold contact between the bit and a part of the wood long enough to generate excessive heat. This will definitely burn the wood and may even draw the temper from the cutting tool. At the correct "load," which has to be a combination of feed and cut, the tool will operate at constant speed without overheating: the cut will be smooth, and there will be no burning. Be sure, after turning on the switch, that you allow the tool to reach full speed before coming in to make contact with the work.

The more powerful the tool you own, the faster you can feed and the deeper you can cut. Final judgments have to be made by the individual in line with the equipment he is working with. If it's obvious that the tool is struggling to make a particular cut, decrease the depth of cut for the first pass and then make a second one after adjusting the bit to get the full cut you want.

Work security is important. If you secure the project well so that it remains still, you automatically eliminate one factor that can produce rough cuts. On large parts or on complete assemblies, this movement problem is minimized. But many times you might do routing work on small components prior to final assembly. In my own shop, I keep a heavy piece of steel on the workbench for just such applications. When the component is small, I

The router works well on plywood, but on deep cuts it's best to do the first cut just deep enough to get through the surface veneer. This approach will help appearance of the finished job.

A clamped-on guide strip is a very common method of guiding the router for straight cuts. The router can be pushed away from the operator or, as shown, pulled toward the operator. Either way is fine as long as the router is moving from left to right, and there is enough lateral force to keep the router in constant contact with the guide strip.

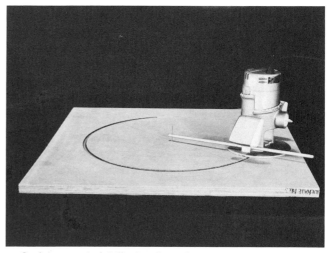

Grainless material like hardboards rout very smoothly. However, they are hard and quite abrasive so repeat passes should be used to achieve a deep cut.

A router can be applied to work even after all the parts have been assembled. For example, this applies to framing jobs, whether they are for pictures or for panels.

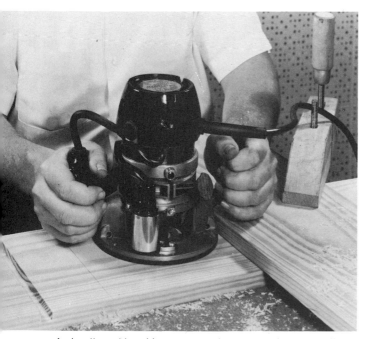

As in all woodworking, crossgrain cuts are the most difficult to do, especially when the wood has very prominent grain. Keep feed slow and depth of cut reasonable.

place the steel piece on it as a weight to hold it down while I apply the router. If this proves impractical, then I use thin strips of wood applied as a "frame" around the workpiece. The idea is to make an immovable object out of what you are working on. Clamps, of course, can also be used to fasten a workpiece in place.

SIMPLE CUTTING

The most common method of guiding the router for straight cuts is to work along the edge of a board that is clamped to the work. The guide board must have a smooth edge and should be fairly stiff, especially if the cut is a long one.

Direction of feed is from left to right, and you may either push or pull the tool—a decision based mostly on operational convenience. Whichever you do, it pays to exert some lateral force as well. The object is to keep the router base snug against the board as you are feeding for the cut.

When possible, work with a cutter that matches the dado width you need. When this isn't practical, accomplish the job by making several passes. On extra wide cuts, it's a good idea to use two guide boards. Place the two boards in such a manner that the router will be guided for the outline cuts. The waste between the initial cuts can be removed freehand.

When this kind of setup is wise and you need many similar cuts, join the two guide boards with a nailed-on crosspiece at each end. These crosspieces will hold the distance between the two boards no matter where you use them on the project.

The edge guide that comes with the tool or that you buy as an accessory is very useful for straight cuts, especially when the cuts are close to an edge. An edge guide is also good to use when the router itself must be placed on the edge of the stock. If the edge is narrow, which means very little support for the tool, clamp

pieces of wood against both sides of the stock. The purpose is to expand the work edge to gain a better bearing surface for the tool.

Decorative trim cuts on edges may also be guided by clamped-on boards, or you can work with pilot-tipped cutters. There are times when a guide board or a commercial edge guide is good to use even when the cutter has a pilot. You may find the use of a guide board or edge guide especially practical on hardwoods, allowing you to minimize the pressure you must exert to keep the pilot in contact with the work edge and thereby reducing the possibility of burning the workpiece.

Remember, when using profile cutters, that it is often possible to vary the results you can get from one cutter simply by experimenting with the depth-of-cut setting.

CIRCLES AND CURVES

Cutting circles or curves with the router is primarily a matter of good layout followed by techniques that enable you to accurately guide the tool along the lines. Anyone with a compass and a straightedge can quickly make a variety of frivolous designs, but it seems more sensible to use these tools so they produce practical solutions to workshop problems. Such a problem might involve no more than the need to round off the corner of a board or sheet of plywood—a problem that might be solved merely by tracing around a handy paint can.

There is nothing wrong with that method if the paint can happens to be close to the desired diameter. But what if you want to rout a decorative matching groove inside the curved edge? The same paint can won't do. Since you are forming arcs of concentric circles, the second radius must be just so. The "points of tangency" (where the curve blends into the straight line or edge) can't be haphazard. And it isn't likely that you will have a second paint can that has just the right dimensions for the job.

A tangent is a straight line that touches the circumference of a circle at one fixed point. The transition from curve to straight line is perfect at that point. To locate it, construct a radius that is square to the line at that point. This important layout trick remains constant no matter what scale you work in.

When you construct four tangents that are square to each other, you automatically have a perfect square. Divide that square into four equal squares, and you come up with two perpendicular diameters of the circle. The points where the diameters meet the sides of the square are points of tangency.

Tangency also occurs where two circumferences touch. For a design involving reverse (S) curves, one arc should move away from the other at the exact point

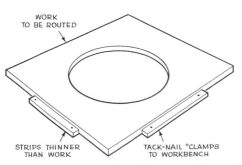

WORK TO BE ROUTED

STRIPS THINNER THAN WORK

TACK-NAIL "CLAMPS" TO WORKBENCH

It's important to secure all work by clamping or by using weights. On small jobs, you can use thin strips as shown to frame the work and thus hold it steady for the cuts.

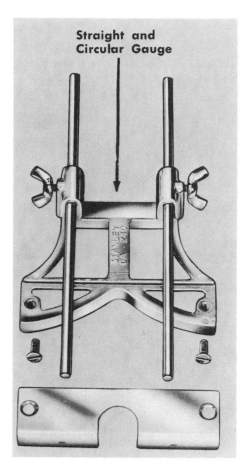

Straight and Circular Gauge

The router edge guide is a very practical accessory. With it you can maintain edge distance on straight and, sometimes, circular cuts. Some tools come equipped with this item; with others you buy the guide as an accessory.

A triangular piece, screwed to the bearing ledge on an edge guide, lets you work very close in corners. This technique is a good way to form a glass rabbet after the frame pieces have been joined.

The edge guide is very good to use when cuts are close to an edge and when the same cut must be repeated on many edges. Once the guide is organized, you can work completely around the work piece.

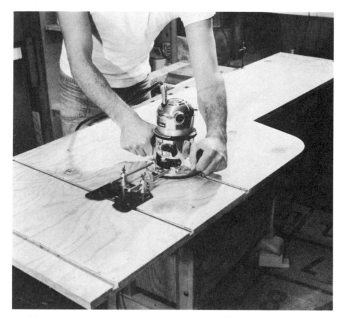

Here's a way you can use an edge guide to space distance between cuts. This method will work best when the edge guide is sturdy, and you don't overextend it so that it becomes unwieldy.

To do angle cuts, simply adjust your guide strip accordingly. Cut shown is a stopped cut so the feed is from right to left.

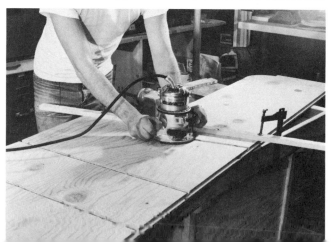

Curved grooves can be formed by using a pattern. The guide is clamped or tack-nailed to the work and the router is fed around it for the cut. It's all right to rotate the router body, but you'll spoil the cut if you pivot at point of contact between the base and the pattern.

Wave-type lines are no more than arcs of circles smoothly connected. Here, the arcs were laid out on a piece of hardboard and cut out as a pattern. Direction of feed is indicated by the arrow.

where the curves touch—even if the circles are of different size.

The circle is the "womb" within which any multisided shape can be formed. The simplest example is the square you construct by connecting the tangency points of perpendicular diameters. The five-pointed star, or an octagon, are easy to create when you construct them inside a circle.

All the constructions discussed here are based on geometrical facts. If you strike the arcs and make the connections as indicated, the results will be perfect whatever the size of the project.

Carelessness in layout will destroy the whole pattern. It's quite easy to be precise enough so that your construction of a perpendicular can be used to check the accuracy of a carpenter's square. If the square doesn't fit the 90°

corner of the perpendicular you construct, the tool is wrong!

Any line you draw with a compass can be duplicated with the router, but you can't guide the router by eye and expect accurate results. Instead use a length of steel rod or a dowel with a hole near one end for a nail pivot to accurately guide the router through arcs or full circles. The diameter of the rod must fit the holes in the router base that are there for the edge guide.

The trammel design in the accompanying sketch is a worthwhile accessory to make because of its great flexibility. If you make the two heads for it, you can use it for design layout work beyond the capacity of conventional dividers. For decorative grooving or for such things as forming circular "dadoes," the trammel-router combination is ideal. It can also be used for cutting through the work material. On anything over $\frac{1}{4}''$ material, however, you'll probably have to make repeat passes before you pierce. On some such jobs, even though you might do the layout using the methods given, it might be wiser to do the cutting on a band saw or with a saber saw.

TEMPLATE WORK

To do template routing, you incorporate special guides in the router base. The guide provides what is essentially a sleeve through which the cutter passes. You use the router in a normal manner, making certain that the sleeve is in constant contact with the pattern or "template" that you have made. Since the sleeve on the guide has thickness, the cutter will be held away from the pattern by that amount. On some jobs this may not be at all critical. When it is, you simply compensate by making your pattern just that much larger for inside cuts or that much smaller for outside cuts. For example, the pattern for an inside circle would be the radius of the circle you need plus the thickness of the sleeve wall.

The pattern you make can be a full duplicate of what you wish to rout into the work, or it can be just a detail that you wish to repeat in various places. Quite often a simple pattern can be used in a repeat, overlapping fashion to create a very complicated design. Either way, be sure the pattern is attached firmly to the work by clamping or by tack-nailing.

JOINT IDEAS

The router is the most impressive when it is used to turn out dovetail joints. This type of very fine craftsmanship would be much too discouraging to accomplish by hand, but with a router you'll have no excuse for not using them on all your high quality furniture projects.

Making dovetail joints in fine style isn't even a question of skill but merely a question of acquiring a special

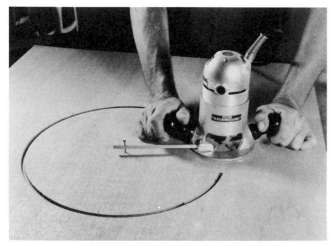

Pivot cutting is very simple whether you are doing an arc or a full circle. Use a length of steel rod or a wooden dowel as shown here. The nail is the center of the circle. Move the router in a counterclockwise direction.

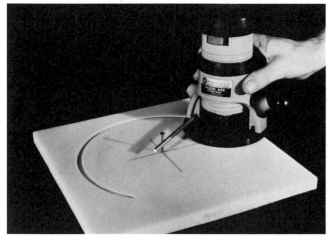

You can do pivot work regardless of the material, although you may have to drill in order to seat the nail. This material is Corian, a new plastic that routs almost like a hard maple.

Some edge guides are organized so they may be used as pivot guides. This guide has a hole in the center of the V-shaped part; through this hole you drive a nail to act as the center of the pivot point.

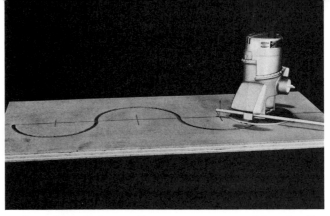

A good way to form uniform reverse curves while using the pivot system is to locate the new pivot point after each half-circle cut. Keep the router bit in the end of the cut already formed and tap down the pivot pin in its new location.

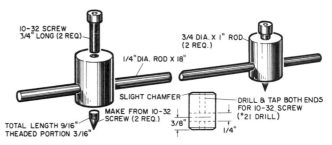

Construction details of a trammel tool you can make for layout work and for use as a router pivot guide. For layout work, you need two heads. As a pivot guide for the router, you only need one head.

jig and template that you use with the router and a dovetail bit. Once you are familiar with the jig, it shouldn't take much more than a minute to do each corner of an average-size drawer. The jig provides for holding two pieces of wood (for example, the front and the side of a drawer) in correct position. Since the shapes are cut simultaneously in both members, they fit exactly.

The dovetail jigs are very common. Most manufacturers who make routers list the jigs as accessories. Just be sure that you read the instructions that come with the jig very carefully and that you follow them to the letter. Go through the procedures on a couple of scrap pieces before you tackle an actual project.

You can also use the dovetail cutter in the router without the special jig to form single dovetails. These can be accomplished in stock edges or on surfaces to make permanent joints or interlocking, sliding parts. When you are making such a cut in the stock surface, it's a good idea to employ two guide strips. These form a track in which the router can fit snugly and thus assure a straight-line cut.

When doing the job on the edge of a board, secure the work in a vise or some other fastening device and clamp support pieces on each side of it to create a surface on which the router can rest solidly. Then you can work

371

USING TEMPLATES WITH A RULER

The router, equipped with a template guide and used with a pattern, is excellent for outlining duplicate pieces.

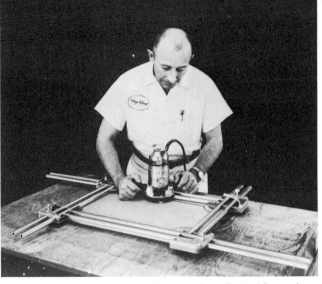

A commercial router template may be adjusted for various designs. It is used mostly for cutting door panels and is very good for production work.

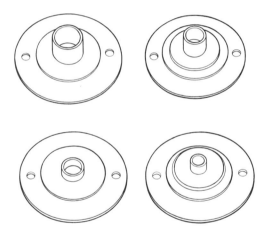

Various size template guides are available. Size difference is in the ID of the sleeve. Most common sizes are for router bits that range from $\frac{1}{8}''$ to $\frac{3}{8}''$.

You can easily do piercing work by using a template guide and a pattern. Be sure the work is elevated above the bench. On thick stock you may have to make repeat passes to get completely through the stock.

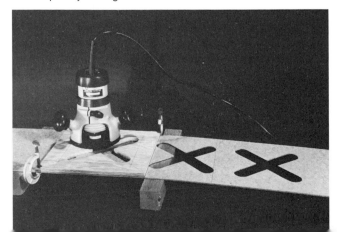

with the router edge guide to be sure the cut will be down the center of the workpiece. To do the tongue part, you follow the same procedure, but you must make two passes, one along each edge of the stock. It doesn't matter that you might also be cutting into the edge of the clamped-on support blocks. Here, you must work very carefully when setting the router guide to be sure the tongue fits the slot. Making the tongue just a fraction narrower than the slot is good practice. If you must hammer the two parts together, you are trying to be too precise.

A similar setup can be employed with straight bits to form mortises. These will have round ends so you must either square them with a chisel after the router work is done or use them as is and round off the edges of the tenon to match. When the mortise must be right in the center of an edge, set the edge guide so you can cut from both sides of the work. Thus, you will assure that the distance between the cavity and the work edge is the same on both sides. Always cut the mortises first; then size the tenons to fit.

LAMINATE TRIMMING

Trimming plastic laminate materials is a major use of the router; even special routerlike tools are made for that one specific purpose. However, these tools are commercial items, and you can do the same job in your own home by using a standard router and a special attachment.

In most cases, you replace the regular router base with a special veneer trim kit. In essence, these kits are assemblies that have a bearing or a pilot of some sort that is independent of the cutter. The bearing rides against the edge of the work, and this controls the amount of material that will be removed by the cutter. The arm

COMMON JOINTS YOU CAN DO WITH A ROUTER

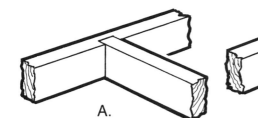

A.

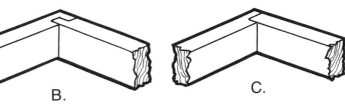

B.

C.

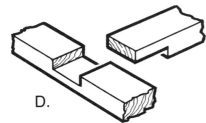

D.

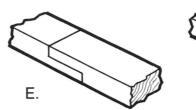

E.

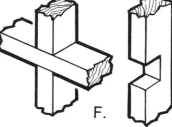

F.

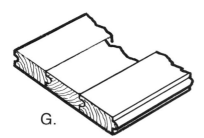

G.

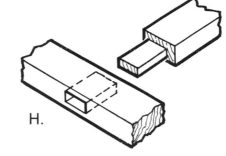

H.

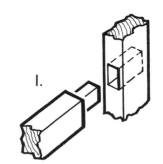

I.

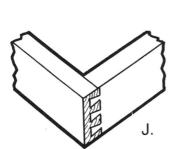

J.

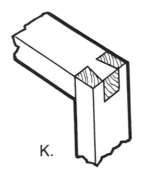

K.

L.

A. Dado
B. Dado rabbet
C. Rabbet
D. Middle lap
E. End lap
F. Cross lap

G. Tongue and groove
H. Mortise-tenon
I. Blind mortise-tenon
J. Blind dovetail
K. Single dovetail
L. Lap dovetail

MAKING DOVETAIL JOINTS

Single dovetails are done with the dovetail cutter but require more careful work to assure the parts will go together well.

The dovetail joint in its various forms used to be a sign of supercraftsmanship. Today, with a router, they can be turned out like any production-line item.

When cutting a dovetail in the surface of the stock, set up guides on each side of the tool so that the cut will be as straight as you can make it. Dovetail cuts have to be made in one pass.

When cutting in the edge of stock, clamp blocks to each side of the work so you will have a platform on which the router can ride. Use the edge guide to keep the cut centered.

Dovetail accessory is used with a router and a dovetail bit. Pieces to be joined are held by the fixture, and the mating cuts are formed at the same time.

MAKING MORTISE-AND-TENON JOINTS

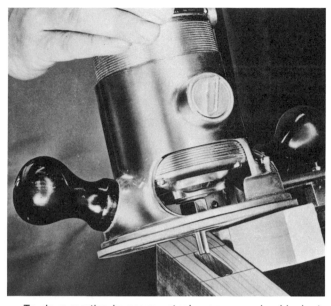

To do a mortise in narrow stock, use a wooden block attached to the edge guide to act as an edge-distance gauge.

To form tenons, clamp the workpieces together. In this way, you will be making the same cut on each of the pieces.

Provide bearing-surface blocks on each side of the work when forming tenons on the edge of stock. Tenons should be formed after the mortise cavities are shaped.

To do cross-lap joints, butt the pieces edge-to-edge so you can cut them at the same time. Depth of cut should equal ½ the stock thickness; width of cut should match the stock width.

You can use the edge guide to do rabbet cuts as long as there is enough bearing surface for the flange on the guide. Special rabbeting bits are available, but these are best used in a high-powered router.

You can also do rabbeting by working with a clamped-on guide strip. On wide rabbets, use the guide strip for the shoulder cut; then you can clean away the remainder freehand. Grasp the handles of the machine firmly.

LAMINATE TRIMMING WITH A ROUTER

Special accessory is mounted on the router for laminate trimming on countertops.

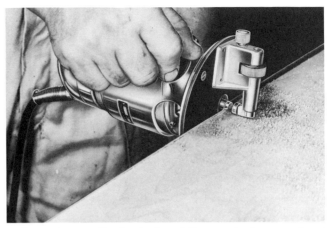

In most cases, the front edge of the counter is covered and trimmed. With correct setting of the laminate-trimming accessory, the cut edge will be flush with the counter surface.

After the surface is covered, the router is used as shown to trim the top layer so that its front edge will be flush with the edge covering.

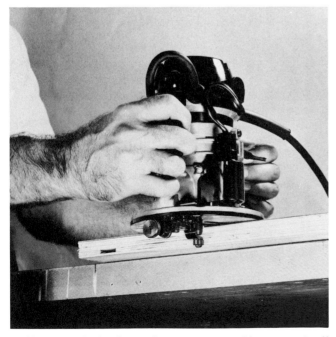

You can trim laminates for countertops with your router if you equip it with a special accessory. The unit provides for precision settings so the cutter will trim the laminate flush to the edge of the material it is mounted on.

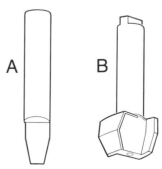

Typical bits you can use with the laminate trimmer accessory. "A" is solid carbide; "B" is carbide tipped. They can be used to make either bevel or flush cuts, depending on the depth at which they are set.

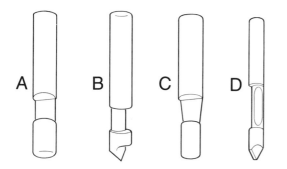

These bits can be used without an accessory guide. "A" trims flush. "B" trims flush but has a point so you can drill through the material before starting to cut. "C" works like "A" but produces a beveled edge. "D" works like "B" but is a longer design and is carbide-tipped.

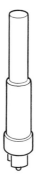

Another type of bit that is used quite often has a ball bearing fastened to the lower portion. This acts like a pilot, following the shape of the work while the cutting edge just above it does the trimming.

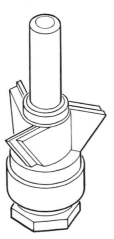

This type of cutter has a ball-bearing end for use as a pilot, but you can change the cutter to do either flush trimming or bevel trimming. You can even get different cutters to provide various bevel degrees.

that is part of the bearing is adjustable; therefore, you have very fine control over cut depth.

Different types of bits are available with the trimmer kits. Most times these bits are either solid carbide or carbide-tipped which is necessary to cut material that is so hard and abrasive.

It's also possible to get trimming bits that can be used without a special guide. These are designed so that just a small section of the bit actually does the cutting. The remainder of the bit is smooth and serves as a guide against the work edge.

Getting a good job done is more a question of being careful when setting the cutter than anything else. It is critical, of course, to hold the router in correct position throughout the pass. Any accidental tilting can cause the cutter to dig into the work. Effective slow passes are possible, but you shouldn't be so cautious that you end up doing more burnishing than cutting.

HINGE MORTISING

Professionals who do quite a bit of hinge mortising employ a special jamb and door butt template that is especially designed to do the job. These are completely adjustable so you can organize them for any size door, whether two or three hinges are involved. If you had a dozen doors to do, it might pay you to rent one of these, but for an occasional job you can get by in good fashion my making a pattern and working with a template guide. Door hinges are fairly standard in size, so once you have made the template, you can store it for future use.

Many hinges have square corners, and for these you must do some chisel work after recessing with the router. You can, on the other hand, buy hinges that are rounded off. The entire job of installing such hinges can be done with a router. Depth of cut is important, but there is a little trick you can use to assure precision. Set the cutter so its end is flush with the bottom of the router baseplate. Then use the hinge itself as a gauge to determine the cutter projection. When you are working with a template, use the template plus the hinge to establish cutter projection.

INLAY WORK

The router is a fine tool to use to create the recess into which you glue ready-made inlay. When the inlay is a strip, choose a straight cutter that matches its width and work with a clamped guide or the router edge guide to form a very shallow groove. The groove, or any other recess, must never be deeper than the thickness of the inlay, but it can be a bit less because the final sanding will bring the inlay flush to the adjacent surfaces.

With round, rectangular or odd-shaped inlays, it's

best to position the inlay and mark around it with a sharp knife. Then use the router freehand to remove the waste. If you are confident enough, you can work right up to the knife line. Otherwise, remove the bulk of the waste and finish off with a sharp chisel.

It's possible to work with a template and template guide. In this case, use the inlay itself to mark the cutout you need in the template and then increase the cutout size by the thickness of the wall of the template sleeve. This method is especially effective when you have many similar inlays to do.

A special recess and insert guide with a ring is available. This guide enables you to use one template to cut the inlay itself and then to rout out the recess into which it will be placed. What you do is rout out the recess with the special ring attached to the guide. Then you remove the ring and, using the same template, cut the inlay.

AS A SHAPER

The router can provide you with some of the advantages of a stationary shaper providing you either make or buy a special table for mounting it. Quite often, the router edge guide is clamped to the router in an inverted position. In effect, this position makes the edge guide a fixed shaper fence and can be quite practical for straight-line cuts that do not remove the entire edge of the stock.

If you make the simple table shown in the accompanying drawing, you can even incorporate fulcrum pins to

Easy way to set an inlay is to scribe around the inlay itself with a sharp knife. Then use the router freehand to remove the waste. Depth of cut should be a fraction less than the thickness of the inlay.

do some freehand routing on edges that can't be guided by a fence. Many manufacturers list "shaper" tables in their catalogs as accessories for the router. Whether you make such a table or buy it, it is a handy item to have for jobs where bringing the work to the tool is better than applying the tool to the work.

With a table, you can work with a fence or with fulcrum pins, or you can employ pilot-tipped cutters as you would in a normal manner. That is, the pilot rides the edge of the work to control the cut.

FREEHAND ROUTING

Freehand routing can be a lot of fun, but since you don't have a mechanical guide, the results depend on how you handle the tool. You can sketch any design on a board and follow the lines with a router bit or you can recess between them.

Freehand routing can be done on any wood—even non-wood materials—but you'll find it easiest to do on woods that have a minimum of grain. For example, the router will be easier to control on basswood than on fir because hard grain areas will tend to lead the bit.

Control of the router for such applications is mostly a matter of practice. Clamping a couple of pieces of wood (preferably different types) to your workbench and "carving" them with freehand application of the router is good training in this area.

Start with very light cuts since these will provide the least resistance to changes in feed direction. A firm grip is essential whether you are cutting with the grain, against the grain or across it.

V-bits and veining bits are commonly used for freehand work involving letters. Core box bits are very good for recessing. Even a pilot-tipped profile bit can be used to shape the edges of a recess you have formed with straight bits.

TAPERED FLUTES

If you cut a slot in a board that is shaped like a ramp, you can use it as a guide to form tapered cuts in another board. It is best to use a template guide in the base of the router and to form the slot in the board so its width matches the outside diameter of the sleeve on the guide.

The procedure to follow is simply to make straight cuts that are guided by the ramped slot. As you go down the ramp, the depth of cut of the bit gradually increases. This is done quite often in circular or half-circle fashion, but don't make a template that has a series of radial slots. Instead, make a template with a single slot and drive a nail through one end to serve as a simple central pivot. The degree of taper is determined by the slope of the

SHAPING WITH A ROUTER

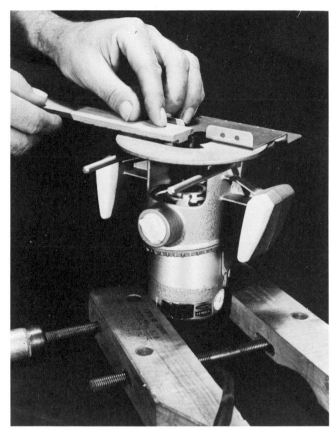

When the router is held securely, the edge guide can be utilized as a "shaper fence." This setup limits what you can accomplish but is practical when the work size permits.

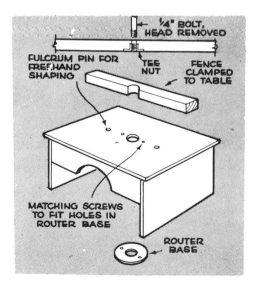

This simple table will let you mount your router so it can be used as a stationary shaper. If you include the fulcrum pins, you can even do freehand shaping on pieces that can't be fed by a fence.

Ready-made unit lets you mount your router so it can be used as a stationary shaper. However, be sure to check whether the router you own can be mounted on the table you are interested in.

With the shaper-table setup, operate as if you were working with a regular shaping machine. Hold the work firmly and adjust your feed pressure so the tool will be cutting steadily.

You are not limited to working on stock edges. Here, a countersink is used to form a V-groove.

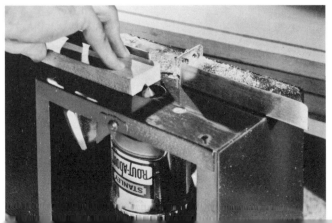

ramp on the template. The length of the cuts is unlimited: you can make the ramp template six feet long if you wish to.

AS A LATHE TOOL

Using the fast spinning cutter of a router instead of a wood-turning chisel opens up a whole new world of possibilities for turned-wood projects. The jig required is very simple, and once you have made it, you can use your router on the lathe to make any number of identical spindles or to "turn" sections that might be too slender and limber to do with a conventional chisel. True cylinders or cones can be done almost automatically, and you'll be able to do uniformly shaped and spaced flutes or facets.

Make the jig from $\frac{3}{4}''$ plywood with the parallel top rails about 4" wide and spaced about 3" apart. The top surfaces should be about $1\frac{1}{2}''$ above the lathe centers for most work. A core-box router bit will work best for most

To get tapered flutes, use a template that causes the router to move up (or down) a ramp. This, in effect, gradually changes the cut depth of the tool.

Freehand routing is fun to do but requires some practice to get to the point where you can follow a line accurately. A firm grip is necessary.

jobs, but ordinary countersinks and rotary-file burrs can also be used if they are especially right for the job you are doing. Straight router cutters should be used for turning straight cylinders and for fluting and grooving.

Be sure to clamp the jig firmly to the lathe bed. Adjust for depth of cut on the router so that the cutter will touch the stock about midway between the horizontal and vertical center line when the router base is resting on the top rails of the jig. This position seems to be best for good cutting action, but if experimentation with a particular cutter proves otherwise, don't hesitate to change a bit one way or the other.

With the lathe turning at about 1,000 rpm's, move the router slowly from left to right, removing no more than $\frac{1}{8}''$ of stock at a pass.

To mass produce duplicate spindles, cut a template from tempered hardboard. You can mount a sample between centers and then clamp a strip of hardboard to the jig's rear platform. Then use the router itself as a marking gauge by moving it along the spindle with the cutter held in contact with the work while you trace the contour on the hardboard with a pencil. Do this with neither the lathe or the router turning! After the contour is marked on the hardboard, remove it from the jig and saw it to shape. Sand the profile edge smooth and then replace the template on the jig's platform.

Now, for as many pieces as you care to make, the template will guide the router and assure accurate duplication.

Fluting cuts are done with the work in a locked position and with only the router working. For peripheral cuts, both the lathe and the router must be turning.

LATHE WORK WITH A ROUTER

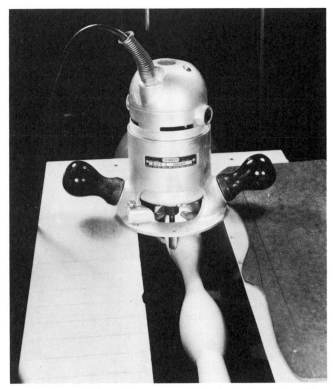

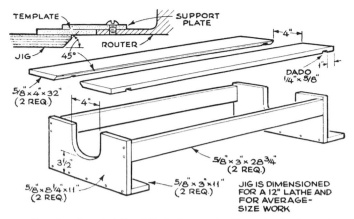

Construction details of jig to be used with router for turned-wood projects. Check the dimensions against your own equipment before cutting parts.

Shaping spindles with a router works best when the cutting tool contacts the work about 45° forward of the vertical center line. Cut the material away in easy stages until you can make one final, light sweep with the router base held in full contact with the template.

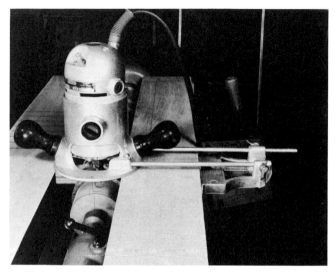

The router edge guide can be used as a gauge that rides that back edge of the platform. This setup is a good way to "turn" true cylinders or to reduce areas of cylinders.

You can increase the versatility of the router turning-jig by fastening a stiff sheet-metal auxiliary base to the router. Secure auxiliary base with flat-head screws.

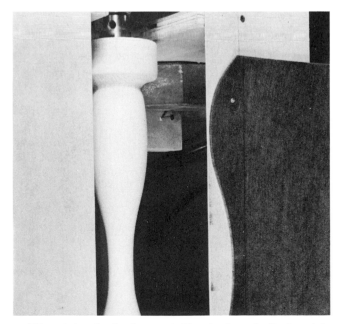

When doing duplicating work, it's wise to make the template after you have turned a spindle in the conventional manner.

With the auxiliary base and an L-shaped guide that is clamped to the jig, you can form perfect grooves or bands. For accurate spacing of cuts, mark lines on the jig for guide position.

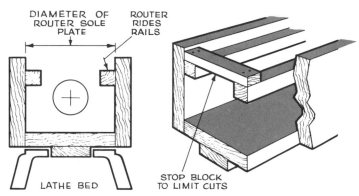

Trough jig is designed for the router you own. When it is clamped to the lathe bed, it provides a simple-to-use track to control router feed direction.

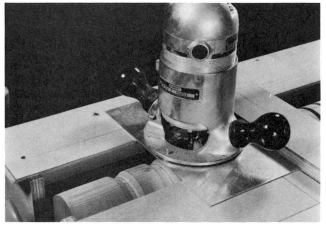

To make the cut, adjust the router for depth of cut and feed slowly from front to back. Both the lathe and the router are turning. You can get different kinds of cuts depending on the cutter you mount in the router. For cutters that are pilot-tipped, you must first form a groove.

By using the edge guide, you can move the router parallel to the spindle and accomplish fluting and similar jobs. Adjust the router so the cutter is exactly on the center line of the workpiece.

Track setup shown lets you feed the router directly down the center line of the spindle. Cutter projection controls depth of cut of, in this case, the flutes. Strip across the tracks controls length of cut.

If your lathe is equipped with an indexing head, you can use it to position the work for the cuts. If you don't have such a setup, then you must clamp or otherwise secure the stock while the router is cutting.

15 PORTABLE BELT AND PAD SANDERS

Whether you are finishing a newly assembled item or refinishing an old item, a powered sander is necessary to properly sand the raw wood before applying the finish or to remove the existing finish. For best results, the use of this power tool is also essential between and after applications of the finish, whether it is stain, varnish or enamel.

The two basic home workshop portable electric sanders are the belt sander and the pad sander. Despite the fact that there can be considerable overlap in function, neither tool is an acceptable substitute for what the other does best. The belt sander is a real workhorse. With a wise selection of abrasive material and grit size, you can quickly smooth down unplaned lumber, remove old finishes, polish metal, reduce stock thickness, even re-edge garden tools like shovels and hoes. In some homecraft areas, like boatbuilding, the belt sander is almost indispensable. It will also be extremely useful on such jobs as reducing a door's width or length to get a good fit, putting a bevel on a door's edge, working on slate or marble, and getting an even surface on 2 x 4's that you have laminated for a bench top.

The pad sander is also capable of some heavy-duty work, but it is essentially a tool for finer, lighter work. It is useful on fine furniture—coated or uncoated—where a belt or a disc might gouge dangerously. With a pad sander, you can also smooth down taped joints on sheetrock before sealing and painting, work on lacquer after it has dried to get a mirrorlike gleam, do smoothing between applications of shellac or varnish, and produce satin-smooth finishes on metals and plastics as well as wood.

THE BELT SANDER

Today's portable belt sanders are to older models what a new, compact cars are to military tanks. But there is an important exception: the compact, modern sander can do the same job as the old giant sanders. An old unit was heavy and cumbersome and could gouge up a board before the new owner mastered its use.

Units that are now available to the homecraftsman are smaller, lighter, easier-to-handle packages. Most of them have greater power, and many offer a larger, more effective abrasive surface than old models without neces-

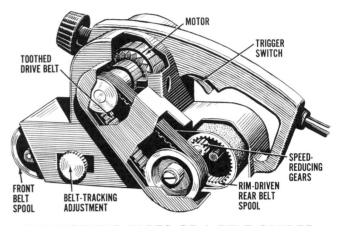

THE WORKING PARTS OF A BELT SANDER

sarily an increase in belt size; this may be achieved with a larger shoe, the platen that describes the area that makes contact with the work.

For example, compare a 4″ belt moving over a 4″ x 4″ shoe with a 3″ belt moving over a 3″ x 5″ shoe. Actual abrasive contact with the work is much the same so power requirements should be similar. The 4″ machine has to be bigger to enclose the wider belt, but even so, the weight increase is less than startling. For example, one manufacturer's 4″ sander is 3½ pounds heavier than their 3″ sander. In two other cases, the weight difference between 4″ models and 3″ models is only 2 pounds.

However, even such minimal increases in weight should be evaluated if you are going to do a lot of jobs that require extensive sanding on vertical or overhead surfaces. In such cases, the extra weight will seem to increase in proportion to the length of the work time.

Speeds. Available speeds (called out in surface feet per minute) range from about 750 to about 1,500. Higher speeds generally correspond to increases in power and price. You'll get a better sander at a higher price, but generally you'll be buying it for more productive sanding, not better sanding. A low speed sander can do the same job as a high speed sander, but it will take longer. A slow feed with a low speed sander will permit as much abrasive action over a given area of the work as a fast feed with a high speed tool.

Models that supply different speeds are available. The

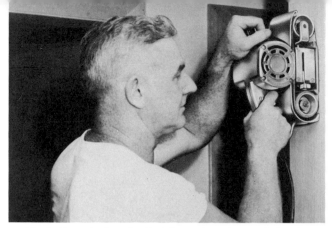

The belt sander is a fine tool for on-location work. Its chores can range from final smoothing of planed lumber to the removal of existing finishes when you wish to prepare a project for a new look. One of the major considerations is the careful choice of abrasive and grit in relation to the type of sanding job you are doing.

Belt sanders are generally made of fine-quality materials since they must be made right to stand up under some of the tough jobs they are designed to do.

Other features. On many jobs it will be convenient if you can work up against a vertical surface. For example, you might be sanding a floor or smoothing a shelf and wish to work flush to the wall. Most models are designed to provide for this kind of flush sanding. If this operation is important to you, then check for protrusions on the open side that might prevent such use.

Dust collectors are built into some units or may be purchased as accessories. They are efficient enough to make them worth considering, especially for in-the-house chores. The tools make a lot of dust quickly so when you have a collector mounted, be sure to empty it frequently. A stuffed bag will reduce sander efficiency. When you change from wood sanding to metal work, clean the bag. Metal sparks can cause fires in wood dust.

Many manufacturers list stands as accessories. These hold the belt sander so it can be used like a stationary tool. The stand may position it for horizontal and vertical use just like a stationary belt sander, or it may provide for the sander to be used flat. Check the chapter on the all-purpose portable tool table for suggestions on how you can use the portable belt sander in such fashion by making your own stand.

Adjustments. The belt sander uses a continuous belt of coated abrasive running over two drums, one at each end of the machine. The rear drum is powered by the motor, the front drum is an idler that is adjustable for both belt tension and tracking. All belts are marked with an arrow on the uncoated side to indicate correct direction of rotation, which is in a clockwise direction. When you mount the belt, be sure the arrow conforms correctly.

To mount a belt, you must decrease the distance between the drums. In most cases, this is accomplished

difference between a "high" and a "low" setting can be as little as 200 SFPM. That is not a startling difference but not to be discounted. There will be many times when you wish to move the tool faster without decreasing the amount of sanding done. Also, a coarse-grit belt moving at high speed will remove stock fastest. With a very fine grit belt, a slower speed will minimize the possibility of burning the work and clogging the abrasive. The slow speed is also better for many types of polishing jobs.

Sizes. The size of the belt sander is called out in terms of belt width. The most common sizes are 3″ and 4″ with a belt length of 21″ or 24″. An increase in length does not always mean an increase in width. There are 4″ x 24″ and 4″ x 21″ sizes as well as 3″ x 24″ and 3″ x 21″ sizes. Wider belts do make it easier to keep the tool flat and also help prevent wavy surfaces and gouging.

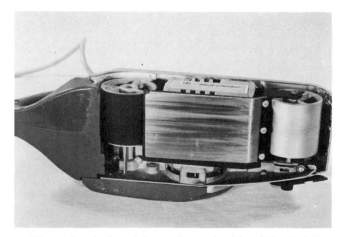

The platen is the plate on the underside of the tool that determines how much abrasive surface will contact the work. The "endless" belt rides the two drums.

Accessories, such as this built-in dust collector, can effect price of belt sander. Note that this model is organized for two-hand operation.

Even with a dust collector attached, this unit can sand flush to vertical walls. If this feature is important to you, check for protrusions on the free side of the belt that might interfere with this function.

Some units are made so you can use a regular vacuum cleaner as a dust collector. They work fine, but it does mean moving the cleaner around with the tool.

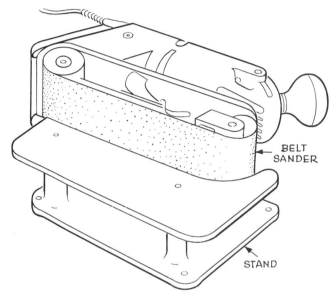

This accessory stand places the belt sander on its side. Be sure, if you are interested in obtaining this kind of stand, that the unit will fit the sander you own.

Kits which usually include a case, the sander, and an assortment of belts, are also available.

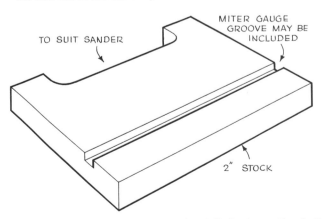

You can make an accessory stand that places the belt sander on its side simply by cutting a piece of heavy stock to fit the machine. Shims and clamps will have to be used to keep the sander in position.

by standing the tool on its front drum and pushing down firmly until the front drum is locked in a retracted position. Then the belt is slipped over the drums and a lever (or a similar device) is pressed to release the front drum. This mechanism is spring powered to provide the needed tension.

Tracking is done by aligning the belt perfectly so that it runs in a straight line over the two drums. No lateral motion can be allowed since that can cause the belt to move off the drums or move the other way to rub against the machine casing. A knob on the side of the tool is turned to alter the angle of the front drum. After the belt is mounted and tensioned, use the tracking knob until the front drum appears correct. Then, quickly turn the machine on and off and observe the results. If necessary, make a slight adjustment and then turn on the tool. Make the final adjustment as the belt is running. When it is tracking correctly, the outboard edge of the belt should run approximately along the outboard edge of the drums. Don't worry if the tracking isn't exactly correct after you have used the sander a bit. This usually happens and simply requires an additional touch with the adjustment knob.

On the other hand, if you must constantly make adjustments to keep the belt in proper alignment, then you should have the sander checked professionally.

Some tools have a belt guide or "traction block" mounted to the frame at the left and rear of the idler drum. This guide is to protect the frame of the machine against abrasive action due to poor tracking. The belt should run evenly across this block. The belt can very lightly touch the guide, but it must not rub against it. Such guides are usually replaceable; therefore, if it becomes worn and uneven, get a new one.

Operating techniques. If you set down a belt sander and then flip the switch, it will travel like a tractor on treads and will not do any sanding. So the first rule to learn is to start the tool before you make contact with the work. Then keep it moving. Holding it in one spot will create depressions that are difficult to smooth out.

Generally you should work in strokes that parallel the grain, going to and fro and adding a very short lateral motion so you will be overlapping the main strokes. If you feed laterally instead of using an in-line action, you will, in effect, be doing cross-grain sanding. The end result will not be acceptable and will show, especially after a stain application.

The major feature of the belt sander is that it has a straight-line action that permits you to sand parallel to the wood grain. This action always produces best finishing results. When you go against the grain with a belt sander, you can raise considerable nap which does not produce the smoothest surfaces. However, going against the grain can be used for faster stock removal.

Keep the platen flat on the work at all times and don't bear down on the tool more than you need to keep the sandpaper cutting. Many times the weight of the sander itself will provide adequate pressure. Turn the sander off after you have broken contact with the work and don't set it down on a bench or whatever until the belt has stopped running.

When you come off the end of the work, keep the sander on the same plane. Allowing it to tilt will round off the end of the workpiece.

Just as the belt sander can travel like a tractor and take off on its own unless you hold and guide it with firmness, it can grip pieces of wood and throw them back toward the operator. Anytime you are sanding material that is not heavy enough to sit on its own and is not attached to something solid, secure the job to a bench top

Belt changing is accomplished by decreasing the distance between the two drums. Usually, the front drum locks in a retracted position. After you mount the belt, pressing a lever causes the front drum to spring forward to provide correct belt tension.

Tracking is done by turning a knob on the side of the tool. This alters the angle of the front drum so you can cause the belt to move laterally and adjust for good in-line rotation.

HOW TO OPERATE A BELT SANDER

Start the sander before you make contact with the work. Keep a firm grip but do not attempt to weigh down the machine with your body.

Keep the tool level when you come off a stroke. Letting it tilt, as shown, will cause the end of the work to be rounded. Turn the machine off after you have broken contact with the surface of the work.

Whenever possible, especially on small pieces, use a backup strip to brace the work. The strip must be narrower than the stock thickness. It may be tack-nailed or clamped.

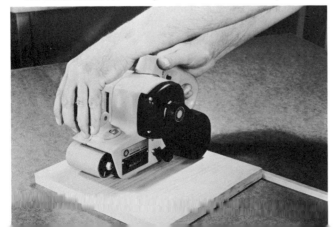

or across sawhorses by using clamps, weights, or even tack-nails in waste areas. When the part is small, brace it against a backup strip that is clamped or tack-nailed to the bench top. This, of course, should be thinner than the stock thickness. Don't try to hand hold small pieces while you control the sander with the other hand. You could lose a fingernail.

Remember that the belt sander, especially with coarser grit papers, removes material quickly. When you are sanding plywoods or veneers, be careful. It isn't difficult to sand right through the surface layer.

Do cross-grain sanding when you wish to remove material quickly. Going directly cross-grain removes material fastest, but you can also use an angular feed. These methods are best for jobs such as smoothing down stock that you have laminated for a bench top or for a table slab, removing the roughness from a tree slab that you might wish to use as a bench or coffee table, or eliminating the roughness from unplaned lumber. In all cases, the cross-grain work is an initial step. Follow with straight-line passes using finer grits of paper.

You can sand edges with a belt sander, but you must be very careful to keep the platen flat on the work. The narrower the work, the more difficult this is to do. You can add narrow strips of wood that you clamp to the work in order to broaden the edge you must work on. When you have two pieces to do, you can clamp them together with a spacer block between. With this setup the total width should not be more than the width of the tool's platen.

When you have many pieces to do, you can clamp them together as a pad. Then all the pieces may be done as if the assembly were a solid block of wood. This method is also applicable for curves. If, for example,

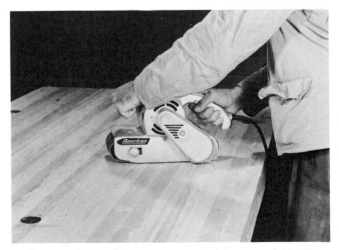

Cross-grain sanding removes material very quickly. Here, it is being done to smooth down 2 × 4's that were laminated for a bench top.

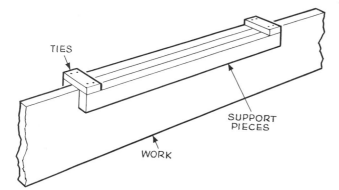

It is easier to sand edges square when you add support pieces to broaden the work surface. You can clamp these in place or, as shown, use ties.

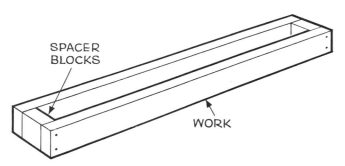

When you need one piece, add a support strip and clamp the two together with a spacer block between. Total width must not be greater than the belt width.

When you have many pieces to do, clamp them together to form a pad and then sand the assembly as if it were a solid block. Note the backup strip.

you wish to sand the curved ends of fence pickets, clamp a dozen or so into a pad and sand them all at the same time.

Removing old finishes. Make the first passes with an open-coat abrasive. Choose a grit in relation to the thickness of the finish. The thinner the coating, the less coarseness you need. Remember, however, that thick coatings of paint, some of which can soften under the belt action, will quickly clog even tough, open-coat abrasive belts. In such situations, you can save considerable effort and some money by removing the bulk of the finish with a solvent that is made for the purpose or with a scraper. Then you can use the belt sander.

Generally, it's best to work so you are pulling the sander toward you. Start the strokes from the end of the project that is farthest from you so you will be moving the sander from abraded areas back into painted ones. In

effect, you will be sanding with the rear of the machine. In most cases, you will discover that this helps to prevent belt clogging. Nevertheless, examine the belt frequently. Use a stiff brush on it to help keep it clean as you go. (For further information, see the chapter on abrasives.)

Metals. For smoothing and removing blemishes, the techniques to use do not differ from those for woodworking except that you select an abrasive that does a better job on hard materials. For final finishing, try to work with special belts and materials that are made for the purpose. Some such commercial items include "Lusterliquid" (Black & Decker), "Greastick," and "Stanbrite Belts" (Stanley). With all such materials, the manufacturer supplies detailed instructions for use so be sure to read the literature that comes in the package.

Quite often, you can polish or get a satin finish on metal simply by working with a very fine-grit paper. Another trick is to make a lubricant by mixing 3 parts of kerosene to 1 part of heavy oil. Stir the two materials and then apply the mixture to the work surface. Mount a fine belt (about 3/0 or 4/0) and work as if you were doing a sanding job. Be careful when working with such flammable mixtures. Provide good ventilation and clean the sander thoroughly after the job is done.

THE PAD SANDER

Many times pad sanders are called "finishing sanders," a good clue to the tool's application. The tool isn't built for heavy stock removal, but it can do some heavy work. However, its major use is for fine smoothing and for putting an elegant, mirrorlike gleam on lacquer, varnish, and even shellac. You can use it with a wider variety of abrasives than is feasible with other power sanders, but for the most part it actually does its best work with comparatively fine grits.

WORKING PARTS OF A PAD SANDER

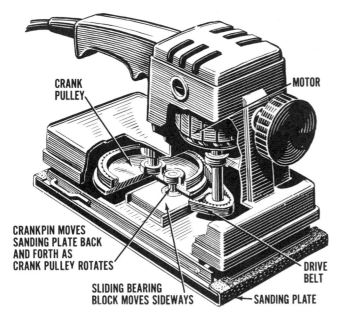

CRANK PULLEY

MOTOR

CRANKPIN MOVES SANDING PLATE BACK AND FORTH AS CRANK PULLEY ROTATES

DRIVE BELT

SLIDING BEARING BLOCK MOVES SIDEWAYS

SANDING PLATE

It's a mistake to assume that the pad sander is just a substitute for "elbow grease," even though fine finishes can be produced by hand. The broad, flat pad on the powered sander makes it possible to maintain an even, level, abrasive-to-work contact that is difficult to imitate with fingers.

Directions of movement. The pad sander comes with straight-line action, orbital action, or both. On the straight-line design, the pad moves to and fro. The orbital action is circular. Some tools are available so you can change from one action to the other. Many homecraftsmen prefer a minimal orbit, high speed machine. It does fast work and leaves "swirl" marks you'd need a microscope to find. The orbital action does cross-grain work, but obvious scratches will occur only with coarse papers or slow speeds.

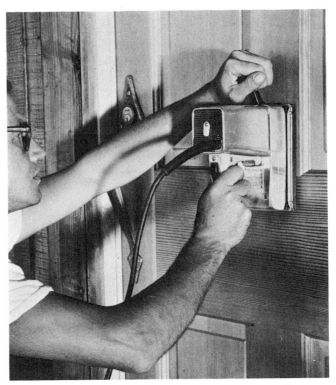

The pad sander is an easy on-location tool to use. It will do some rough work with coarse paper, but its forte is a final supersmooth touch that no other tool can accomplish.

With a pad sander, it's easy to work right into corners of assembled projects.

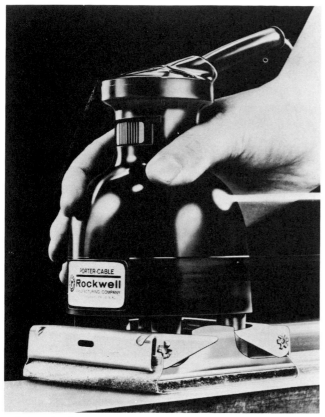

A favorite finishing tool of many homecraftsmen has a tiny orbit of $5/64''$ and a speed of 12,000 rpm's. Balance is excellent so even one-hand operation is not out of line.

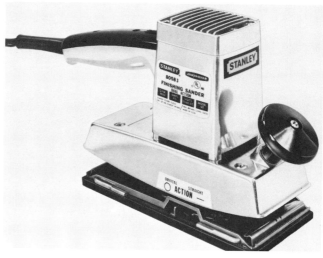

Typical dual-action finishing sander. Flicking a lever on the side of the tool will give you either straight-line or orbital sanding, a feature worth the additional cost.

With many sanders you can buy an accessory kit that will set you up for "dustless" sanding. The kit includes a skirt that encases the pad and a bag that collects the dust.

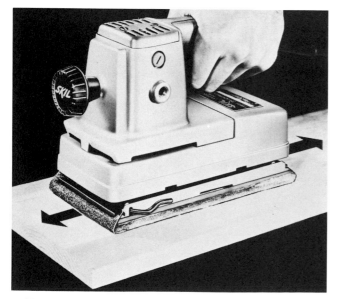

This model is a heavy-duty, straight-line machine that drives a big $4\frac{1}{2}'' \times 9''$ pad. A vacuum cleaner attachment is available for it if you wish to minimize dust.

This pad sander is organized so that you can buy attachments that let you use an ordinary vacuum cleaner for dust collection. Note how the add-on skirt covers the pad area.

Late model pad sanders usually provide double insulation. This model is a ½ HP, dual-action tool.

Pad sanders are available in kit form. This kit includes a can of wood putty.

Mounting paper. The design of the machine must provide for pulling and keeping the abrasive sheet taut across the pad. If the paper is loose so that it doesn't move as a unit with the pad, sanding efficiency will be impaired. Be sure to study carefully the literature that comes with the tool you buy so you will be able to achieve and maintain paper tightness across the pad.

Incidentally, most pads are sized so you can cut three sheets for the sander from a standard sheet of sandpaper. Special packs of precut sheets—some of one single type, some containing assortments—are also available. In either case, you have a broad selection of types and grits.

The pad. All sanders come with a soft felt pad that provides the right flexibility for average work. On some materials, like fir with its hard-and-soft-grain pattern, a hard shoe will provide a more efficient backing for the paper. You can create a hard shoe by using a sheet of thin hardboard between the regular pad and the paper.

Conversely, a softer shoe than that provided may be an advantage when smoothing down an existing finish or when working between applications of a finishing material. To improvise, you can use a section cut from an old rug or a piece of thin sponge or foam rubber. It's good to test the use of the extrasoft paper backing when you are working on convex or concave surfaces or on some molding designs, columns or spheres.

Using the tool. Many pad sanders are equipped with an extra knob that permits two-hand operation. This feature is mostly for guiding the machine, not a means of applying extra pressure. In some situations, like sanding vertical surfaces, the extra knob provides handling convenience. In most cases, when you are doing routine work on flat, horizontal surfaces, the weight of the tool is about all you need to provide sufficient abrasive bite. Too much pressure can actually produce scratches that you would then have to remove.

No matter what the action of the sander is, it's usually best to work in strokes that parallel the grain, using some slight lateral motion so that the main strokes are overlapped as much as 75%. Because of the variety of work that you will encounter, it's not always possible to work this way. When you must use a feed that is cross-grain, go slowly, let the abrasive work on given areas of the wood.

With a pad sander, it's possible to feed directly into a corner or flush to a vertical surface. This is true whether you are working horizontally or vertically. It's usually the "open" side of the sander that you should bring to bear against an obstruction. You'll know when you are wrong because contact between the tool and the obstruction will cause very obvious vibration.

Edge sanding. With edge sanding, a two-hand grip is a help in keeping the tool level so that you won't round off the edge. Edge sanding is not too bad a job to do freehand, but when squareness is critical, clamp pieces together into a pad so you can sand them as if they were a solid block. When you have one or two to do, use the extra support pieces described for use with the belt sander. The whole idea is to provide enough work surface so it becomes easy to keep the sander on a level plane. If you don't have enough pieces to make a pad, add extra support pieces so that you accomplish the same thing.

Changing the pad. In most cases, the original pad is held down with screws that secure it to a baseplate.

A regular pad can be replaced with a hard pad secured by using projecting brads.

With a hard pad and a fine emery paper, the pad sander makes an excellent honing tool for touching up lathe chisels, plane blades, knives and the like.

Most tools provide for two-hand use so you can guide the tool more accurately, not so you can apply more pressure.

When working against obstructions, you'll find that the open side of the tool creates less chatter. There is no abrasive or metal on the open side to bang against the wood.

Even thin edges can be sanded square and smooth if you pad the pieces as shown here. Straight-line sanders may be used in diagonal fashion for faster stock removal but should be used with the grain in the final stages of sanding.

When you wish to change to a softer or harder pad, use the original one as a pattern for the new one and attach in basic fashion. Another way to change a pad—and this works best with a hard pad—is to drive some small brads through the new pad and the pad that is on the machine. This is usually sufficient for the new pad to function efficiently.

Typical uses for a hard pad include sanding woods that have a very prominent hard-and-soft-grain pattern and using the sander as a honing tool.

Sanding finish coats. With a pad sander, you can sand a finish coat of lacquer, enamel, shellac, varnish, or whatever. How you work on the top coat will depend on the material involved and how much gloss you want. A basic procedure is to use a ready-made rubbing compound, which is a standard item that you can buy in hardware and auto-supply stores.

The compound is applied to the work surface and then gone over with the sander using a piece of carpeting in place of the regular pad and paper. You can also work with burlap, and often it's possible to agitate the burlap simply by gripping it tightly about the base of the machine with one hand as you do the feeding with the other hand.

For a superfine furniture finish, you can do wet sanding with a silicon-carbide, superfine-grit, waterproof paper mounted on the sander. There are many lubricants you can use for wet sanding, but many people still prefer the clean water and soap combination. This is done by rubbing the abrasive with ordinary hand soap and wet-ting down the work surface with a sponge. Always wear rubber gloves as well as insulated shop shoes.

There are also other techniques you can use. Various grades of pumice and rottenstone may be mixed with light or heavy oils. Sometimes just a light oil and a very fine emery paper will produce the finish you want.

You can also do wax finishes. Apply the wax to the work by hand. Then make a pad of cheesecloth or some similar material and place the sander in the center of it. Apply just enough pressure on the sander so that the sander pad will move the cloth pad.

Pad sanders are excellent tools for smoothing down between finishing coats and for a final touch on the last coat.

DISC SANDERS AND POLISHERS

Sander-polishers is a category of portable power tools that can be misunderstood and unappreciated. All too often sander-polishers are confused with pad sanders or even belt sanders.

Granted, both the pad sander and the belt sander may be used for some amount of polishing work, but it's incorrect to refer to them as sander-polishers. Inserting the word *disc* into the name lessens the confusion between a disc sander and a pad sander or a belt sander. This applies whether the disc sander is purchased as an individual tool or as one half of a combination tool that is also used as a polisher.

If you do become intrigued and decide to check out these specialty tools, you'll find that you have a basic choice to make. You can buy a separate disc sander, an individual polisher or a unit designed to do both jobs. Assuming all other factors are similar, the only difference between a portable disc sander and a portable polisher is speed. The disc sander works best at speeds that are too high for optimum results when polishing. Therefore, the combination sander-polisher should offer an adequate sander speed (between approximately 3,400 and 5,000 rpm's) and an adequate polisher speed (between 1,800 and 2,500 rpm's). Some single-speed units provide for doing both disc sanding and polishing at an "in-between" speed.

Some units are designed to take such accessories as drill chucks, wire wheels, and even grinding wheels; others require adapters in order that they can be so equipped. It is wise to consider such flexibility if you envision multipurpose application.

Another tool in this general area is often called a "sander-grinder." Speeds are generally high, running about 5,000 or 6,000 rpm's; better than 1 HP is not unusual. Quite a few of them are industrially rated; all of them are heavy-duty tools. Accessories for such units may include grinding wheels and discs, even cup grinding wheels and wire cup brushes. This is the kind of tool you will find in welding shops, auto-body repair and remodeling garages, and any place where heavy-duty sanding is the rule of the day.

OFFSET AND IN-LINE DESIGNS

The in-line design looks pretty much like a portable drill. The weight of the motor is directly over the pres-

Shockproof tool looks like a drill (it can be equipped as one) but is available as a 6″ portable disc sander (above) and as a 6″ polisher (below).

The tool has a speed of 3,200 rpm's and is actually the heart of a little power workshop.

sure area; the control handles are in positions that will be familiar to you if you have done any portable drill work at all.

A right-angle bend is the major feature of the offset design. Since such tools have a longer body, your hands will be more widely separated. They can provide a greater reach and are often handier for getting into tight places. For example, it's easier to reach the center line of an automobile roof with an offset polisher.

Considering the job these tools are designed specifically to do, the offset is often preferred, even though for average jobs the in-line design will probably feel more natural for most people. It seems easier to let the weight of the tool supply pressure to the pad. With an offset, a lot of the tool weight is between your right hand and the working end of the machine. This pretty much dictates that your left hand supply any pressure you need above what is there simply by resting the tool on the work. Controlling the offset isn't really difficult; you simply have to learn a new handling technique before you become at ease with the tool.

Sizes of these tools are listed in terms of disc diameter, the average being 7″.

USING THE DISC SANDER

In many situations, the portable disc sander will remove more stock faster than a belt sander. It will never do a final sanding as smoothly, but it just isn't designed for that purpose. It should be used for fast, preliminary smoothing of rough stock, for "taking down" and feathering fiberglass work and filled dents on automobile bodies, refinishing of metal surfaces, removing old paint and varnish and even, with the correct abrasive, smoothing down stone or concrete.

If you wish to get to fine finishing on rough stock, use the disc before you take over with a belt or a pad sander. Often, by working through progressively finer grits of paper, you can go directly from the disc sanding operation to pad sanding. Less critical surface preparation like exterior paint jobs may require nothing beyond the disc, especially if you use one of the new foam backup pads with a fine paper. Always remember that the disc has a rotary action which is essentially cross-grain sanding.

A particular handling technique is necessary for successful portable disc sanding. Never place the disc flat on the work. If you did so and kept the tool in one spot, you would do nothing but cut circular grooves. You would also clog the abrasive very quickly.

The first rule is to tilt the machine a bit and apply just enough pressure to bend the rubber backup pad. Quite often the weight of the tool itself is sufficient to

do the job. Apply additional pressure only if the job requires it but never so much pressure that the rpm's are drastically reduced.

The tilt of the machine should be such that about $\frac{1}{4}$ to $\frac{1}{3}$ of the abrasive surface comes in contact with the work.

Too much tilt is as bad as none since you will be using only the edge of the disc which can result in grooving the work. It certainly doesn't take maximum advantage of the abrasive disc.

The second rule is to turn on the motor before you make contact with the work and then to keep the tool moving constantly. A haphazard feed pattern is incorrect. Instead, use sweeping, straight-line, overlapping strokes. Even with the disc sander, try to work in line with the grain when you are doing the final strokes.

Open-coat paper is recommended for most sanding operations; it's essential when you are removing an existing finish. Coarser grades of paper will rough out material quickly. Finer grades won't cut as fast, but they will produce smoother finishes. Generally, coarser grades should be used on hardwoods, at least to start, while finer grades may be used on softwoods.

Replace the abrasive disc when it is dull or has become glazed, especially with paint. You can try to clean glazed discs (see the chapter on abrasives), but if you are unsuccessful, throw them away. You can, however, get more use out of dull discs by limiting their use to curved surfaces. Also, a dull disc will actually produce a finer finish than you can get by using a new disc of the same grit number.

Work surfaces should be cleaned with a brush or a

Other accessories include a bench stand and a bench-grinder attachment.

Disc sander-polisher kits are available. This kit includes a yoke and handle so the machine can be set up for doing floors.

The kit also includes a stand so the tool can be used on a workbench. Here a wire brush is turning.

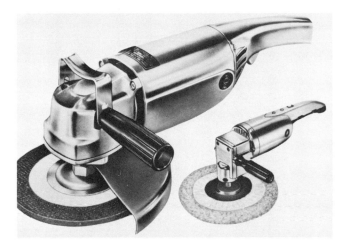

Note the difference between a home-style sander-grinder (left) and sander-polisher (right). The former is usually a heavier tool with a single speed. The sander-polisher shown here with a speed of 3,400 rpm's for sanding and a speed of 1,800 rpm's for polishing.

In-line design (right) has the same appearance as a portable drill. Offset version (left) has a right-angle bend and a much longer body.

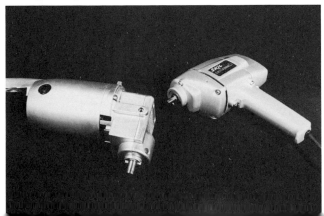

vacuum cleaner to remove loose grit, paint particles, and other loose material. This will lengthen the life of the abrasive and will prevent scratches caused by foreign material being stuck between abrasive grains.

When sanding existing finishes, you may find that the high sanding speed will soften paint and cause the disc to clog quickly. When this happens, switch to the lower polishing speed to reduce the heat that is softening the paint and keep the tool moving fast over the work.

STATIONARY MOUNTING

Some manufacturers supply a special stand as an accessory so the tool can be locked down for stationary use. If not, or if you wish to save some money by making your own, the accompanying sketches show you how to provide a table setup whether the tool you own is an offset or in-line design. Notice that the table surface is made in two pieces so that you can remove the forward section when you need more room for items like polishing bonnets.

POLISHING

As a polisher, the disc sander-polisher can be useful to either husband or wife. With proper instruction and an accessory or two, the lady of the house will use it as often as you do. Both of you will achieve glossy surfaces on your car, your furniture, your walls, and your floors that you couldn't get any other way.

Tool handling when polishing doesn't differ too much from disc sanding except that when you begin a polishing job, you can rest the bonnet flat on the work surface. Then you can finish up by tilting the tool and using a section of the bonnet in a sweeping motion as we described for disc sanding. If you have a two-speed tool, be sure to switch to the low polishing speed.

Hold the tool firmly but operate with an easy, free motion. Don't force the tool by applying unnecessary pressure. When you are doing a flat surface, the weight of the tool alone is usually enough to exert sufficient pressure for a good polishing job.

Keep the tool moving. Use long sweeping motions in a back-and-forth action that advances along the surface being polished. Don't work in a circular or spiral pattern because this will only create swirls in the finish.

Be sure to read the instructions that are printed on the container of wax or polish that you buy. Some materials must be buffed while in a damp state; others must be allowed to dry. Use polishes or compounds that are designed for machine work. Some that are intended for hand application will mat a powered polishing pad and can burn or smear the finish.

Do initial work with the bonnet resting flat on the

The portable disc sander removes material faster than any other workshop tool. It is a very fine tool for jobs like the one shown where initial sanding steps must bring the work to a reasonable stage for finishing touches.

The disc sander, with coarse, open-coat paper, may be used freehand to remove old, blistered paint. Special attachment shown for a Rockwell-Delta disc sander converts the tool into a "power paint remover." Vertical and horizontal adjustments let you work flush to overhangs or vertical walls without gouging or marring the work surface.

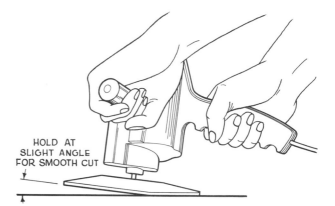

HOLD AT
SLIGHT ANGLE
FOR SMOOTH CUT

To use properly, tilt the machine so you make contact with about ¼ to ⅓ of the abrasive surface.

While in operation, resting the tool flat on the work will result in swirl marks, scored circles, and quickly clogged paper. Tilt the machine at a slight angle.

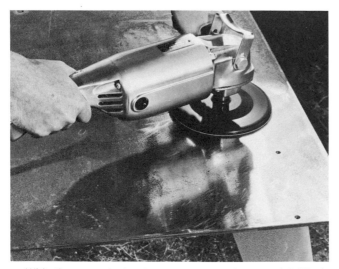

With the correct abrasive, you can work on metal. Work carefully and use parallel, overlapping strokes. Roughness of this much-used welding table is no match for the abrasive action of the disc.

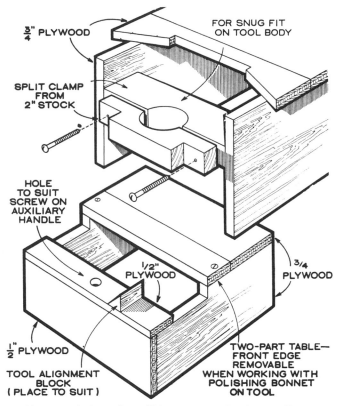

Here are designs that will let you organize for an offset tool (top) or an in-line tool (bottom). Use plywood for all parts except the split clamp. Make split clamp from 2″ solid stock, sizing it according to your machine.

surface. After most of the wax film or the polish has been removed, you can tilt the machine as described for disc sanding operations. The tilting enables you to bring a cleaner section of the bonnet into play.

When working on a vertical surface, start at the top and work down. This will keep dust and film from being deposited on completed sections. On flat surfaces, start at the point farthest away from you so that as you work, you won't be dragging the tool's power cord over finished areas.

Pads and buffs that you use on a machine polisher can become clogged or gummed up after they have been used a while. When this happens, wash them in soap and warm water and then rinse thoroughly. Shake off as much of the water as possible and then mount on the tool to "spin dry." A lamb's wool bonnet can be treated in similar fashion and left to dry completely while still on the rubber backup pad. This will minimize shrinkage of the bonnet.

Since disc sanding and machine polishing chores do spew out particles of waste and grit, it's wise to wear safety goggles when operating the tools.

TIPS ON CAR POLISHING

Work in an area that is out of the sun or choose an overcast day. Do a good wash job first to remove all dirt and grease. Very light deposits of road tar and oil can be removed with cleaners and polishes, but stubborn accumulations should be worked on with special solvents that are sold for the purpose. Do this by hand with a clean cloth.

A liquid, combination cleaner-polish will do a good job

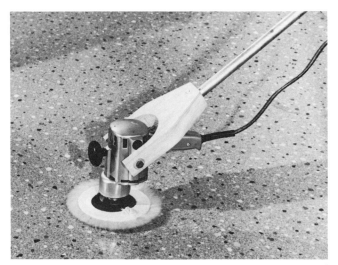

For floor polishing, you can make a pivoting yoke out of 2″ stock that lets you attach an extension handle. The handle can be a 4′ length of aluminum tube. Use bolts through holes in the yoke and into the tool's side-handle holes. Size the yoke opening to fit the tool.

When doing vertical surfaces, start at the top and work down. Always read the instructions on the container of the cleaner, wax or polish that you buy. Power polishers will do a good job on furniture and countertops as well as walls.

but check to be sure that it does not contain abrasives; it must be a type that can be used with a power tool. Read the instructions on the container and apply the liquid as recommended. Heavy-duty polishes are available for use on old cars or cars that have badly dulled or oxidized surfaces.

Apply the liquid from the top of the car down and let dry. Remember that drying will occur more slowly in cold weather. The liquids will often form a white film when they are dry.

Start with a pile fabric pad which is available as an accessory that you attach directly to the standard rubber backup pad. Begin at the top of the car and work down, using long slow strokes and allowing the weight of the tool to supply pressure. It is not important to remove all of the cleaner in this operation. What you miss in corners or around edges will be eliminated by the last buffing.

Replace the fabric pad with a lamb's wool bonnet. Be sure to center the bonnet on the pad and to tie it as tightly as possible. A taut buff is essential for smooth operation and good balance. After tying, tuck in the ends of the lacing so they will not fly out when you are working.

Go over the entire car again to buff the finish to a high luster. If your car has not had this kind of attention for a while, you may have to repeat the entire procedure in order to get a new-car sheen. After that, occasional touches with the bonnet will keep the finish looking good until another full job is in order. When you use the bonnet between complete jobs, be sure that the car is free of dust.

After you are through with the machine operation, you may notice a slight haze and some swirl marks. A few swipes by hand with a clean cloth will remove them quickly and leave a high luster.

17 ABRASIVES

The most commonly found abrasives for use in the home workshop are such *natural* ones as garnet, flint (quartz), and emery, and such *artificial* ones as aluminum oxide and silicon carbide. The natural ones are mined like any mineral while the artificial ones are essentially products of an electric furnace. The aluminum oxide is fused bauxite; the silicon carbide results from a sand-coke fusion.

Each of the abrasives is especially good for a particular application, but in practice overlaps do exist. A particular grit in one abrasive will often do the job when the best abrasive is not available. It is a good idea to know the abrasives and what they are best used for. Then, when you must, you can improvise, but wisely.

TYPES OF ABRASIVES

Aluminum oxide is available with either paper or cloth backing. The cloth backing is always stronger and more flexible. It can be used dry or with a lubricant; is excellent for machine sanding of wood, plastics and metal; and can take a lot of abuse. The paper backing can be used on machines but is generally recommended for hand work. Aluminum oxide is probably the most popular abrasive today for all-around shop use.

Silicon carbide is excellent for wet sanding either by hand or machine. You can use it on undercoats and primers as well as on uncoated surfaces. You'll find in most cases that it is the best abrasive to use on metals. It comes with a paper backing but is waterproof. It's ideal for very fine work such as the final sanding of an auto-body repair job to get a glass-smooth finish.

Emery is another good metal abrasive that is fine for polishing jobs and even for initial steps like removing rust and scale. It may be used either dry or with a lubricant.

Garnet is very good for wood sanding, is available with a paper backing, and is used dry. It's a fairly good all-purpose shop paper even though aluminum oxide is favored over it for power tool use.

Flint is the least durable of the abrasives and comes with a paper backing. It is cheap and, therefore, often used on preliminary work when you know the job will result in quick clogging. Although it is not made for power sanding, you can cut up standard sheets for use with a pad sander. It is never used for wet sanding.

In order of hardness, the abrasives can be listed as follows: silicon carbide, aluminum oxide, emery, garnet and flint.

The least expensive abrasives are the natural ones. The synthetics cost more but they last longer.

SIZES

The grit number of an abrasive is actually a *mesh number* indicating the particular size wire or silk screen that was used to filter the abrasive material during the manufacturing process. For example, particles that pass through a number twelve screen would total twelve to the inch if they were lined up. When the screen control becomes impractical because of the size of the particles,

The grit of the abrasive paper has to do with the size of the abrasive particles. "Coarse," "medium," and "fine" are general classifications. Within each, there is an assortment of grit sizes. See charts on next pages.

then fairly complex flotation systems are used to accomplish the same thing. Grit sizes can go from the #12, which is the coarsest, to #600, which is the finest.

The resulting smoothness of a project depends on the grit you use. The #12 would produce results similar to what you would get by rubbing wood with tiny, sharp stones. Using #600 is almost like rubbing with flour. The usual recommendation of working through progressively finer grits of paper until you achieve the smoothness you want is good, but the critical factor is the choice

ABRASIVE	USE	GRIT			REMARKS
		ROUGH	MEDIUM	FINE	
aluminum oxide	hardwood aluminum copper steel ivory plastic	2½-1½ 40 40-50 24-30 60-80 50-80	1/2-1/0 60-80 80-100 60-80 100-120 120-180	2/0-3/0 100 100-120 100 120-280 240	Manufactured, brown color, bauxite base, more costly than garnet but usually cheaper to use per unit of work
garnet	hardwood softwood composition board plastic horn	2½-1½ 1½-1 1½-1 50-80 1½	1/2-1/0 1/0 1/2 120-180 1/2-1/0	2/0-3/0 2/0 1/0 240 2/0-3/0	Natural mineral, red color, harder and sharper than flint
silicon carbide	glass cast iron	50-60 24-30	100-120 60-80	12-320 100	Manufactured, harder but more brittle than aluminum oxide, very fast cutting
flint	removing paint, old finishes	3-1½	1/2-1/0		Natural hard form of quartz, low cost, use on jobs that clog the paper quickly

Here are suggestions that will help you select a type and a grit for a particular material and finish. Which grit you start with has much to do with the original state of the surface you work on.

New tungsten-carbide sheets are very durable; but since they are actually thin sheets of metal, they are not as flexible as regular paper. They are best used for flat sanding jobs.

Typical materials that are used for polishing. Note the special belts that are designed for portable belt sander use. With all such products, carefully study the literature that is supplied with them.

TYPE	VERY FINE	FINE	MEDIUM	COARSE	VERY COARSE
flint	4/0	2/0-3/0	1/0-½	1-2	2½-3½
garnet	6/0-10/0	3/0-5/0	1/0-2/0	1/2-1½	2-3
aluminum oxide and silicon carbide	220-360	120-180	80-100	40-60	24-36

This chart groups different abrasives into five classes of word grit-descriptions and indicates the numbers of the grits that fall in each.

of the grit you start with. Many manufacturers of abrasive materials simplify the grading system by using words instead of, or in addition to, mesh sizes. The words can go from "extra coarse" to "extra fine," and relying on them for general shop use isn't really out of line.

Remember that abrasives are cutting tools. They do their job by removing material almost like tiny chisels. The "chisel" you start with will leave minute ridges and grooves that you must remove with smaller "chisels." Always start with the least coarse abrasive that will do the job. With today's materials, it's not likely that you will generally have to go beyond a "medium" classification, which would encompass grits from about #60 to #100.

Beyond this first grit, if you want a truly professional job, you will find it unwise to make jumps exceeding two

8/0 = 280	3/0 = 120	1½ = 40
7/0 = 240	2/0 = 100	2 = 36
6/0 = 220	0 = 80	2½ = 30
5/0 = 180	½ = 60	3 = 24
4/0 = 150	1 = 50	

Here are the number equivalents of the various grit sizes.

grit sizes. If you go beyond this, you may find that the finer grits will not remove the ridges and furrows left by the initial sanding. The surface might feel smooth to your hand, but there will be crevices that will be revealed when you apply stain. These imperfections will also occur when you have done considerable cross-grain sanding and insufficient with-the-grain sanding. In the extreme, and especially with a belt sander, the flaws will emerge as cross-grain swirls. Do cross-grain work, regardless of the grit of the paper, only when you wish to remove material fast. For the desired smoothness, do the bulk of the work by stroking with the grain.

COATINGS

When abrasive particles are placed in a close-packed formation, the descriptive term is "closed coat." The result is a fast-cutting and durable abrasive surface but one that can clog easily under certain conditions. When abrasive particles are applied with spaces between so that only about 50% to 70% of the backing is covered, the product is called "open coat." This type won't cut as fast

as a closed-coat design simply because there aren't as many abrasive particles. On the other hand, it will not clog as quickly.

Closed coats cut faster, are more durable and do a smoother job. Open coats are best for soft materials, gummy materials and for finish removal chores.

CARE OF ABRASIVES

The cost of abrasive materials can add up if you are too casual with how you use them and neglect some simple maintenance chores. When the paper becomes worn so that it doesn't cut anymore, you have no choice but to discard it. However, a coarse-grit paper, for example, used to the point where it no longer does the job it was designed for can be used further as a finer grit.

Dry cleaning with a brush will slow the accumulation of stubborn waste on an abrasive surface. When the

Frequent "dry cleaning" with a brush will help prevent buildup of grit-clogging waste. Use a circular motion with the belt stationary. A soft brush will do the job when the waste is loose, especially on fine papers.

MATERIAL	FIRST STEP	SECOND STEP	FINAL
oak	$2\frac{1}{2}$-$1\frac{1}{2}$	$\frac{1}{2}$-1/0	2/0-4/0
maple	$2\frac{1}{2}$-1	$\frac{1}{2}$-1/0	2/0-4/0
maple (curly)	$2\frac{1}{2}$-$1\frac{1}{2}$	$\frac{1}{2}$-1/0	2/0-4/0
birch	$2\frac{1}{2}$-1	$\frac{1}{2}$-1/0	2/0-4/0
mahogany	$2\frac{1}{2}$-$1\frac{1}{2}$	$\frac{1}{2}$-1/0	2/0-3/0
walnut	$2\frac{1}{2}$-$1\frac{1}{2}$	$\frac{1}{2}$-1/0	2/0-4/0
fir	$1\frac{1}{2}$-1	$\frac{1}{2}$-1/0	2/0
pine	$1\frac{1}{2}$-1	1/0	2/0
gum	$2\frac{1}{2}$-$1\frac{1}{2}$	$\frac{1}{2}$-1/0	2/0-3/0
willow	2	$\frac{1}{2}$-1/0	2/0
cypress	$2\frac{1}{2}$-$1\frac{1}{2}$	$\frac{1}{2}$-1/0	2/0
plaster			5/0-8/0
hardboard		3/0-4/0	5/0-7/0

Here are grit sizes to choose for various materials. If the material is fairly smooth to begin with, you can skip the first step.

Use a wire brush when the accumulation is stubborn. Generally, a wire brush works best on coarse papers, a softer brush on fine papers.

Washing in lukewarm water with ordinary laundry soap can double the life of an abrasive. Use a piece of wood as a scrubbing board. Rinse in clean water and allow the belt to dry before using. Paint solvent also can be used if abrasive is clogged with pitch and gum.

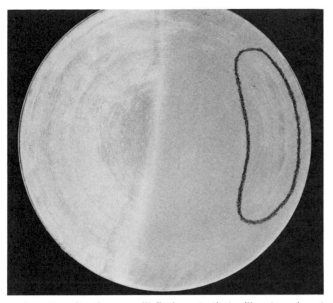

In some situations you'll find spots that will not wash out. Such spots can be the result of uneven mounting of the disc. Despite these areas, there can still be lots of surface left on an abrasive that can be used.

accumulation is powdery and loose, a bristle brush will do. When the accumulation is thick, a wire brush may be used. Work the brush in all directions to re-expose the sharp cutting grains. When you are doing such work on a power tool, don't work with the machine running or you will soon have a "brushless" brush. Instead, rotate the belt sander or the disc sander by hand as you scrub out the wood dust.

Many times you can double the useful life of an abrasive belt by scrubbing it in lukewarm, sudsy water. Rub vigorously with a stiff brush to work waste out of the valleys. Use a cloth to mop off the excess moisture and then place the belt back on the machine to dry. Another method is to stretch the washed belt lightly between two pipes or poles correctly spaced in holes drilled in a board. If the belt shrinks, readjust the machine tension to compensate.

Remove accumulations of pitch that cause slick spots on the belt with a brush that you have soaked in turpentine. Use a circular motion; then stroke in one direction to throw off the solvent and dirt. Quickly pat dry with a cloth before the solvent can penetrate the backing.

18 HAND GRINDERS AND FLEX SHAFTS

From the homecraftsman to the diemaker, from the dentist to the podiatrist, the handful of speed and power known as the hand grinder can be a most helpful power tool. Quite often, it's true talents are unappreciated, probably because its small size creates an image of delicate precision and very light-duty applications. Paradoxically, these qualities in themselves are enough justification for rating the hand grinder as an important shop tool. It can get into places that other tools can't reach. A touch with a hand grinder will often add a crafted look to an otherwise routinely finished project.

But the hand grinder is not a toy; it is not a hobby tool. For one thing, modern versions are much improved in terms of power and durability. For another, there is a wide range of designs available. Not all of them are palm size; those that are recommended for tool and die rooms and for tool post grinding are comparatively husky fellows. Weights of the small ones are listed in ounces, while the big ones are called out in pounds.

In application, the tools should be visualized as high-speed shaping equipment that will drive an endless assortment of abrasive wheels, brushes, buffs, drums, bits, saws, and discs. They will do machining jobs on most any material, as well as drill, cut, smooth, and polish. They can be used to shape or sand wood or metal. They can be used on plastics and will mark steel or glass. Often, they enter areas of sharpening, engraving, and routing. You can drill holes with them that would be rough to do with a conventional drill. Therefore, the term "grinder" does not describe the tool fully. What you can accomplish with the tool depends pretty much on what you lock in the chuck.

The secret of the tool's fast, smooth performance is speed. Speeds can range from 17,000 rpm's to over 30,000 rpm's, and such revolutions are available no matter what you pay for the tool. Prices can range from under $20.00 to over $50.00; generally, the more you pay, the more weight and power you will get. Heavier models will handle larger cutting tools; their collets or chucks will take shank sizes up to $\frac{1}{4}''$. The smaller units will take shank sizes up to about $\frac{1}{8}''$.

Weight, of course, is an important factor in choosing a hand grinder. The big units do heavier jobs than you

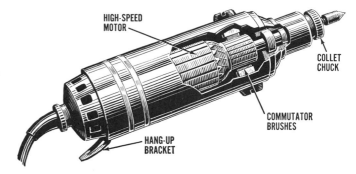

Basic parts of a hand grinder. How you care for the grinder will depend on the design. Some require oiling; some do not. Read the owner's manual carefully.

should attempt with palm-size versions, but they may also be used for delicate touch work.

Because of the variety of accessory holders that are available commercially or that you can make yourself, the grinder does not have to be limited to hand-held use. With some stands, it can often be used in combination with other tools. Team it with a lathe or a drill press, for instance, and you can use it as a precision milling, grinding or routing accessory that can do many jobs normally possible only with much costlier machines.

There are many stands—even drill-press versions—available so the hand grinder can be used as a stationary tool. It may be held vertically, horizontally, tipped at an angle, or even inverted for use as a miniature shaper. By clamping the tool in a rigid position, you can apply the work to the cutter as you would with any stationary tool, and this often guarantees precision that is difficult to duplicate when working freehand.

Cutting tools. The word "cutters" is used in a general sense to encompass all items that you can lock in the chuck of the tool. Generally, any cutter that has a larger than `$\frac{1}{8}''$ shank is meant for bigger, heavier grinders, whereas any cutter that has a $\frac{1}{8}''$ shank or smaller is meant for light-duty grinders.

Cutters come either mounted or unmounted. The mounted ones have the cutter permanently attached to

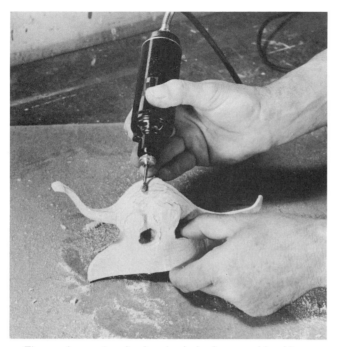

The modern palm-size hand grinder has considerably more power and durability than older models. They may be used freehand, as shown, or in stands that are available in stores or you can make yourself.

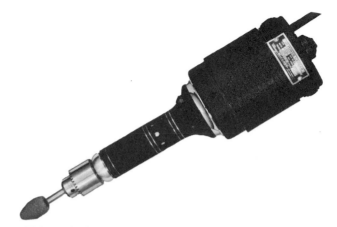

This model has a cartridge spindle that is meant to assure smoother, cooler, more accurate vibration-free operation. Note that it employs a Jacobs' chuck with ¼" capacity. Speed is 18,000 rpm's.

This high-speed, heavy-duty hand grinder takes ⅛" and ¼" collets. It weighs almost three pounds and can reach a speed of 30,000 rpm's.

The heavier units can be used almost like miniature, bench-top ''lathes.'' Here, the work is shaft-mounted and worked on with a hand-held cutter. It's also permissible to grip the grinder in a vise as long as you provide protection for the casing.

Hand grinders can often be bought in kits that include a good storage case, plus an assortment of sanding discs, wire brushes, steel cutters, and buffs. Usually, extra collets are also included.

STANDS FOR HAND GRINDERS

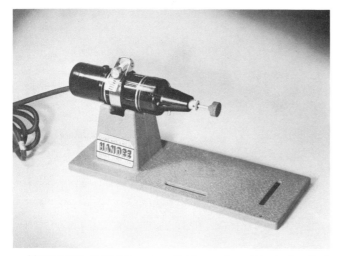

Many types of stands are available, such as this design that grips the grinder in a horizontal position.

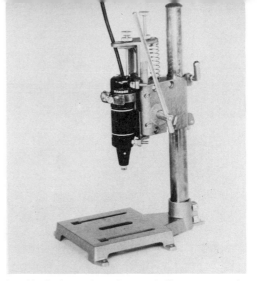

Another kind of stand works much like a conventional drill press. The main adjustment to the work is done by situating the head; feeding is done by using the lever.

This stand provides flexibility so that you can tilt the grinder to an angle that is convenient for the job you are doing.

the shaft. When the cutter is worn, you throw the whole unit away. Incidentally, dentists accept minimum use of their cutters in order to save you discomfort. These partially used cutters can still be used on wood and metal in a home shop; therefore, you might ask your family dentist to save you his discards.

Unmounted cutters are locked on a special fixture that is called a *mandrel*. This is a shaft with a device at one end for gripping the cutter. The lock-on arrangement may resemble a small nut and bolt, a straight or tapered thread, or a flathead screw that you turn into a threaded hole in the end of the shaft. Typical accessories for mounting on mandrels are felt wheels for polishing, small buffs, rubber polishers, and small steel saws.

In most cases, brushes are permanently mounted and are available in various types. Steel wire, brass wire, nylon and bristle are very common. Use the soft brushes for cleaning operations on soft materials and the hard ones on tougher materials or when you wish to produce a decorative brushed effect on metal surfaces. Mild abrasive compounds such as ordinary household cleansers may be used with the brushes.

Use steel saws to cut wood, very soft metals, and plastics. Abrasive discs (also called "saws") are good for cutting or slotting nonferrous and ferrous metals and for many applications on stones used in lapidary work.

Mounted abrasive wheels come in an endless variety and numerous grades and grains. Since they are adequately described and pictured in major manufacturers' accessory catalogs, interested readers can write to companies such as the Dremel Mfg. Co., P.O. Box 518, Racine, Wis. 53401; Chicago Wheel & Mfg. Co., 1101 West Monroe St., Chicago, Ill. 60607; or The Foredom Electric Co., Route 6, Stony Hill, Bethel, Conn. 06801 and ask for detailed listings.

Most small-size grinders use collets to grip the shank of the cutting tool, and it is important to use the correct collet. If you don't, you will not grip the cutting tool securely. For example, a $\frac{1}{8}''$ collet will grip shank sizes from $\frac{3}{32}''$ up to $\frac{1}{8}''$. A $\frac{3}{32}''$ collet will grip shank sizes from $\frac{1}{16}''$ up to $\frac{3}{32}''$. A $\frac{1}{16}''$ collet will grip shank sizes from $\frac{1}{64}''$ up to $\frac{1}{16}''$. There are also adapter chucks for use with collets for gripping very tiny (60/80) drills.

Make a storage chest. The hand grinder (or a machine specifically designed to drive a flex shaft) can be

Accessory bits handle just about any job

CUTTERS FOR CARVING, ROUTING, MILLING, AND ENGRAVING

STEEL AND BRISTLE BRUSHES

GRINDING WHEELS FOR SHAPING AND SHARPENING

SANDING, POLISHING, AND SAW DISKS

DRUM SANDER   MINIATURE DRILL BITS

Typical categories of accessory bits show wide variety of jobs that can be done with the hand grinder.

considered a small workshop in itself. Because the numerous cutting tools and other accessories that go along with grinder use are usually small, easy to damage or lose, it pays to make a special case to house the equipment.

The case shown was designed for a flex-shaft tool, but its interior can easily be organized to accommodate just a hand grinder or both types of tools. The important thing is to lay out all the equipment you have and to design the case specifically for each piece, plus other items you plan to add later. Making the case as a closed box and then slicing off the lid on a table saw is a good way to assure an accurate fit.

You'll note in the accompanying construction drawing that the cutters are stored on shelves that are drilled to receive the tool shanks. This system works very well for mounted cutters. For unmounted ones, drive slim nails up through the bottom of the shelf. Be sure to dull the points on the nails.

The overall size of the case, as shown, is about $7\frac{1}{2}''$ x $17\frac{1}{2}''$ x $22\frac{1}{2}''$. These dimensions can be increased a few inches without making the case unwieldy. Install a handle at the top and a latch to keep it closed; then you can tote it about for any work you must do outside the shop.

Operational hints. Always rely on the speed of the tool to do the work. For example, a tool that is running at 24,000 rpm's and is driving a cutter that has 16 flutes is actually making 384,000 cuts every minute. That kind of cutting speed seldom requires excessive pressure to get the job done. Too many beginners apply too much pressure which almost stalls the tool. Then they lessen the pressure and allow the rpm's to build up again and, unfortunately, go about doing the same thing over again. This is very bad practice as far as work quality is concerned, and it can do considerable harm to the tool. If the tool gets hot or if there is an obvious decrease in speed, it's almost certain that you are trying to force the cut. Choose the right style of cutter and the right cutter shape for the job you must do, use a touch that is just light enough to keep the cutter working, and you will get maximum efficiency and work quality.

Work that is large enough to sit on its own or that can be gripped securely in one hand may be worked on in a freehand manner. Grip the work in one hand, the tool in the other. Establish one rule: avoid pointing the cutter toward your gripping hand. Then if you should slip, you won't cut more than the work.

Small work is best gripped in a vise or clamped to a bench top. A handscrew clamp, with cardboard used when necessary between the work and the clamp jaws, makes a good "vise" for holding pieces.

There is no law that says you must not grip the grinder

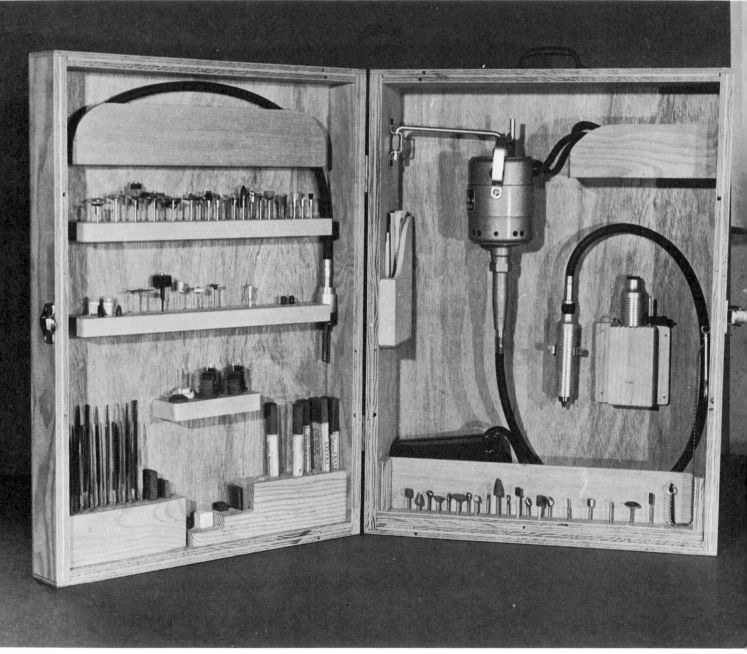

A tote-about chest is a good way to house your hand-grinder workshop. This one is arranged for a motor-flex shaft combination, but you can change the interior design to suit your own equipment.

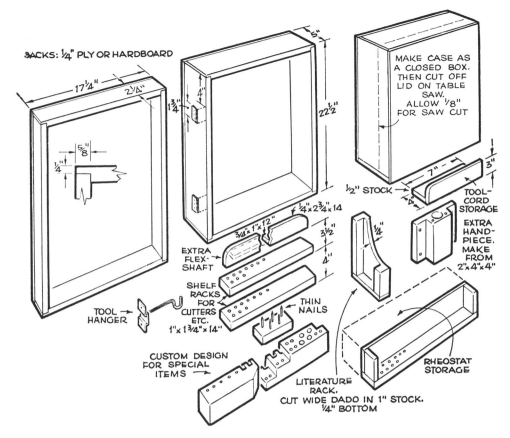

Construction details of the tote-about case. Dimensions can easily be altered to suit your needs.

in two hands. Often, you can work more accurately if you grip the cutting end of the tool between thumb and fingers of the left hand and "palm" the other end of the tool in your right hand.

When working with wood, do the final passes so you are cutting with the grain. You'll find that a minimum of sanding with a fine-grit paper will finish the job quickly. If you wish to get a sculptured effect on small pieces, work with a rotary brush to remove wood from between hard grain areas.

Tips on plastics. Plastics are either *thermosetting* or *thermoplastic*. Bakelite, Marblette, and Plaskon are example trade names of the former. Lucite, Plexiglas, and Acrylite are examples of the latter. Once the first type has set, it will not become pliable again. The second type becomes pliable when correct heat is applied.

Thermoplastics will soften if you generate enough heat with the cutter. The gummy result can quickly clog the tool and even cause a drill to be cemented in the hole you are trying to drill. The answer is to work with light touches and frequent retractions to minimize heat buildup. In general, use coarser fluted cutters than you

would use on wood or metal. Check the cutter frequently for signs of gumming and when it occurs, stop working long enough for things to cool down. Clean the cutters with a small brush. Often, plastic chips that have cooled on the cutter can be flicked off with a fingernail.

As a sharpener. Most any tool in the shop or in the house can be ground or honed by using a hand grinder as long as you fit it with the correct abrasive. Mostly, the hand grinder serves best as a touchup tool or as a honer. The removal of a lot of material, necessary when you are forming a new edge, is best done on a bench grinder.

Many times the success of a sharpening job depends entirely on wheel choice. This is true, for example, when you are cleaning out the gullets of a circular saw blade or redoing the teeth of a chain saw. Wise choice of cutter automatically produces the shape you need. All you do is apply the tool at the correct angle.

As a router. The small hand grinder is not about to rival the big jobs you can do with a regular portable router, but on a small-job basis it can match the big fellow almost function for function. In fact, for many

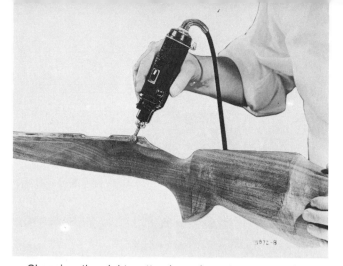

Choosing the right cutter is as important as application techniques. That is why an extensive assortment of cutters is good to have. Don't hesitate to change from one cutter to another when the work shape calls for it.

With a hand grinder, you can work on hard steel or etch glass as easily as you can work on wood. Whatever the job, selection of the right kind of cutter is primary.

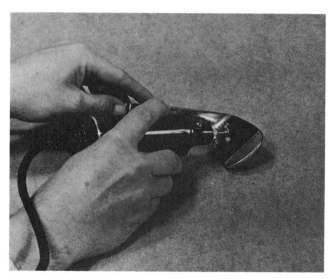

A hard wire brush will do a good job of cleaning dirt from the grooves, such as those on golf-club heads.

In using a hand grinder, keep the cutter moving. Grip the work and the tool to keep vibration at a minimum level.

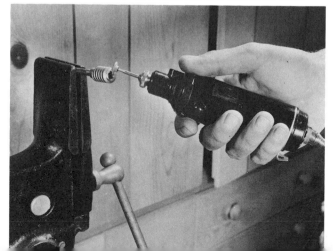

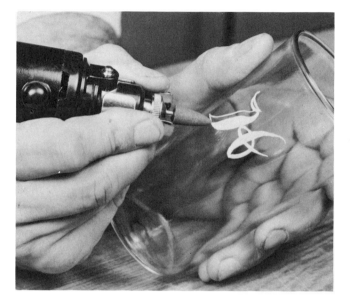

techniques, particularly in light-cut applications such as inlay or marquetry work, the palm-size tool can be more convenient to use while still doing an exemplary job.

With some of the hand grinders (especially the Dremel), accessories are available that are specially designed so the tool can function as a miniature router-shaper that will do some surprising things in a wood-working shop.

Such accessories are light and neat, easy to attach and handle, and are used pretty much like larger, conventional portable router bases. Adjustments are provided for depth of cut, and the accessory may include an edge-guide fence so you can do straight cuts parallel to an edge.

Adjustment of the fence in terms of distance from the cutter runs from zero to about $3\frac{1}{4}''$—not a startling capacity but when it proves limiting, you can remove the edge guide and work against a clamped guide strip as

HOW TO USE A HAND GRINDER AS A ROUTER

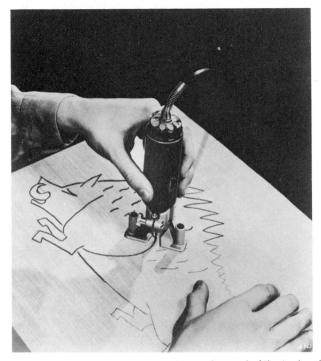

A "shaping table" attached to the cutting end of the tool and combined with a bench stand can be used as shown here to provide accurate control for freehand routing. The table is adjustable for depth of cut.

Shaped edges are also possible, although cutter sizes you can use with a small hand grinder can't compete with the ones that are available for full-size router use. Deep cuts are accomplished by making repeat passes.

To do freehand work and other surface routing where you want the tool to be square to the work surface, remove the edge guide and work with only the baseplate.

Use a single rod for pivot cutting. A length of ¼" drill rod with a hole drilled at one end so a nail can be used as a pivot point will set you up for such work.

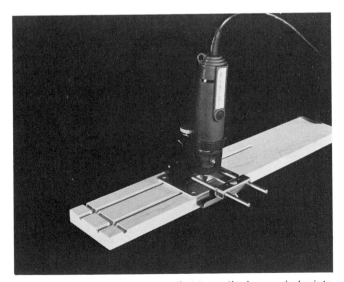

Dremel makes an accessory that turns the hang grinder into an impressive miniature router-shaper. The edge guide sets distance of cut from the edge of the work. Capacity is limited but you can substitute longer rods for the ones provided or work without the edge guide, using a straight-edged guide strip which is clamped to the work.

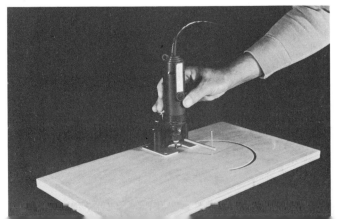

A shaper table will broaden the use of the tool. This simple version can be made in minutes. It provides for an upside-down anchor arrangement for the grinder. A straight piece of wood clamped to the table serves as a fence.

USE ROUTER-SHAPER BASEPLATE AS TEMPLATE

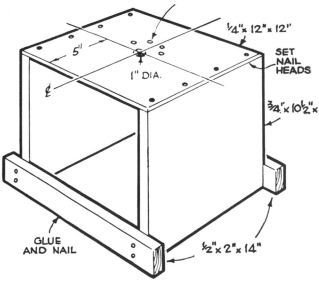

Construction details of the shaper table. The grinder is secured with screws that normally hold the baseplate.

Sharpening jobs also depend primarily on selecting the right type and shape of cutter. Special shapes are available for working on such items as chain saws or circular-saw blades. Here, a cone-shaped grinding bit is used to clean out the gullets of a circular-saw blade.

Bits and points are sized so that you can touch up small cutting tools like router bits.

Don't use a small hand grinder in place of a bench grinder. Instead, use it, as shown here, to do final touches after you have renewed the edge of a tool on a bench grinder.

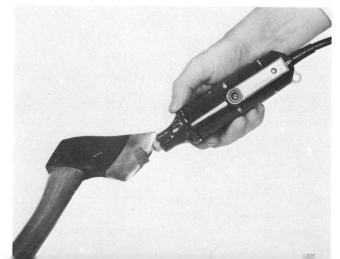

you would with a conventional router. It's also possible to substitute longer rods than those provided with the guide. An extra piece of rod, which you can buy in any hardware store, will come in handy as a pivot for guiding the tool through perfect circular cuts.

The palm-size tool does have limitations. Don't expect to form full-size bead-and-cove or drop-leaf table edges on 1″ stock. It will be possible to do such functions on $\frac{1}{4}$″ or maybe even $\frac{1}{2}$″ stock. Much, beyond the full profile shape of the cutter itself, can be accomplished simply by making repeat passes to deepen the shape achieved with the cutter or by using different cutters on the same edge to create your own form.

Other practical applications for the tool include mortising for hinges and strikes, raising or carving figures for nameplates or house numbers, inletting for escutcheons, and forming decorative or joint-type grooves.

How fast you can feed depends on the hardness of the material. Feed must never be so fast or so heavy that you stall the tool or allow the cutter and the work to get too hot.

Make a shaper table. This simple table you can make in minutes. It provides an upside-down anchor for the grinder which is secured with screws normally used to hold the baseplate. Depth-of-cut adjustments are handled as they are for normal use; a clamped block will serve as a fence. Remember that the table is designed for use with a router-base accessory on the grinder.

Make a swivel jig. With this unusual fixture you can cut many decorative patterns. Since it is designed so the whole bit can be applied to the work, there are no limitations on where you can use it. Cuts can be made on parts before assembly, or you can work on a completed project.

The jig permits the grinder to rotate as well as swivel so you can cut a wide variety of geometric designs. While the jig is not difficult to make, it does require careful work to avoid extra play in either of the actions. The hole in the stand can be formed accurately on a drill press. The indexer disc can be formed in similar fashion but be sure its OD fits well in the stand hole. Actually, it's best to cut the indexer a fraction oversize and then sand it for a perfect fit. The swivel collar is best done on a lathe with the work mounted on a screwcenter. Note that two versions of the collar are given. One has to be a tight fit for the grinder; the other depends on a hose clamp for the grip.

HOW TO MAKE A SWIVEL JIG

You cam make a swivel jig for almost any type of hand grinder. Tool rests and pivots in swivel collar.

Since the grinder rotates as well as swivels, the jig will let you cut an endless variety of geometric designs such as those shown. Note that the tool can be swung through a full arc so that all cuts have a central intersection point, or the cuts can be stopped.

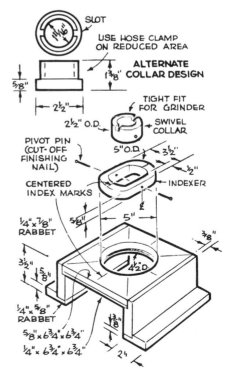

Construction details of the swivel jig. Use hard maple for all parts. Do construction work carefully. You want to avoid play between the collar and the indexer as well as between the indexer and the hole in the platform.

FLEX SHAFTS

With a flexible shaft, you can grip any cutter that is operable in a hand grinder, but you can work as if your fingers were a drill chuck powered by a motor in your shoulder! That is not too unrealistic a picture of what a flexible shaft is. The torque and the rpm of whatever power source you choose nestle in the palm of your hand, and the dexterity in your fingers, wrist, and elbow directs the power exactly where you want it.

Using a flex shaft allows you to be no longer hampered by the rigidity of a solid, straight-line shaft as you are when using cutters in, for example, a drill press, a portable drill, or even a hand grinder.

You can use a flex shaft with the delicacy of a surgeon or the muscle of a steelworker; but to do either efficiently, you must make a wise choice of shaft and motor. The power source for small flex shafts can be existing shop tools such as a drill press, lathe or portable drill. However, many of these tools have a lot more torque than small shafts are designed for.

The right core size. Jobs of delicate precision are accomplished more with speed than with power. On the other hand, heavy sanding or weld grinding require husky torque more than they do speed. In general, small-core shafts are made for high speed (as high as 35,000 rpm's) and a light touch; large-core units are designed for jobs that are done with heavy feed pressure.

The core size is the diameter of the shaft itself, not the casing; however, it's reasonable to assume that the larger the casing, the larger the core.

A large core can run from about $\frac{5}{16}''$ up to $\frac{1}{2}''$. Small-core units can start as fine as $\frac{1}{16}''$. Make $\frac{3}{16}''$ the maximum core for jobs that require flexibility and control more than power. A $\frac{1}{4}''$ or $\frac{5}{16}''$ shaft is fine for light-duty jobs such as polishing, buffing, and grinding. For jobs such as heavy sanding and grinding, a core that is at least $\frac{3}{8}''$ in diameter is needed.

All flex shafts include a core, which turns, and a casing, which doesn't. The casing can be a hoselike affair or a spirally wound steel tube that resembles the type of armored cable often used in electrical work. In good units, the core (no matter whether it is large or small) is made up of spirally wound, directionally alternating layers of steel wire. The "pitch" of the final layer of wire indicates the direction of rotation.

The most common pitch lets you use most motors and shop tools as power sources. But since shaft cores are sometimes made with unusual pitches, check this feature before you equip yourself.

The rotation rule. Literature that comes with the tool—and usually an arrow marked on the casing—will

Range of flex-shaft sizes is indicated by typical light-duty and heavy-duty shafts. The small one relies on light touch and high speed. The big flex shaft will do well under heavy power and heavy feed pressure.

Flexible shafts come in various lengths and different diameters. You can buy them to be powered by existing shop tools or to be used with special flexible-shaft machines like the one below.

The advantage of machine-and-shaft combinations is that they are "tuned" to work together for highest efficiency.

tell you the correct direction of rotation. Failure to comply can result in unwinding the core wires, especially under heavy-torque conditions. It's possible to ignore the rule, but to do it safely requires a technical decision that must be based on loading the unit to no more than half its power rating. Such information may not be available to you and even if it were, the limits would be difficult to establish in a home shop. Therefore, adhere to the one-direction-of-rotation rule.

Shaft ends. The coupling end of larger units is usually designed for locking directly to a motor shaft, but the size of the coupling is not always a good indication of the power requirements. For example, a 72″ x ½″ core shaft bought at Sears will fit ½″ or ⅝″ motor shafts and has a 1 HP capacity rating. A 50″ x ⅜″ core shaft bought at the same place will also fit ½″ or ⅝″ motor shafts, but the capacity rating is only a ½ HP. A full load from the larger motor applied to the smaller shaft, even though it fits on the motor spindle, can damage the unit. Therefore, make it a special point to check the capacity of the shaft in terms of HP it can handle.

In use. The major rule is not to overload. Remember this especially when you drive a small shaft with drill-press or lathe power. The available torque may be far beyond the capacity of the shaft. In other words, let the shaft decide the capacity, not the power source.

The tool-mounting end of many large shafts is a straight, threaded spindle fitted with flanges and a locking nut. This spindle lets you mount any accessory that has a center hole. You can also buy conventional chucks that screw onto the threaded spindle so you can mount shafted tools such as drills and drum sanders.

Use care with grinding wheels, and be sure to protect yourself by adding accessory wheel guards. These safety devices cover most of the wheel and have a handle that lets you grip with firmness. Safety goggles should be worn.

Although a 6″ grinding wheel can be driven by a ½″ core shaft, it's better to stay with 4″ wheels on any of the heavy-duty shafts. When you work with small shafts (for example, a ⅛″ core), the wheel diameter should not exceed 1″. Acceptable speeds are determined by efficiency and safety. A safe speed for a 6″ wheel can range from about 4,000 rpm's to 4,500 rpm's, but this type of determination is not something you need judge for yourself. Maximum rpm's are printed on the flanges of the wheel. Read the instructions and obey them.

Very small shafts. While many of the smaller flexible shafts are actually variable-speed tools, they'll be most valuable when used on a universal-type motor with a speed range up to 15,000 to 20,000 rpm's. This is true

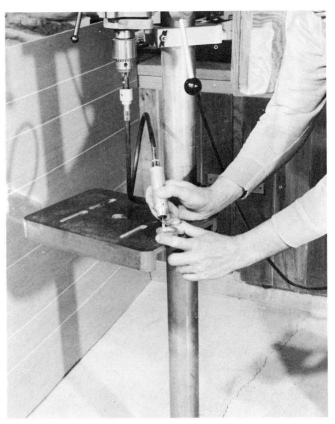

Be careful when powering a flexible shaft with a drill press or a lathe or even a portable drill. Many times, such tools have more torque than the flex shaft was designed to take.

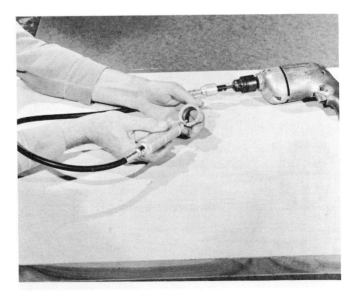

A light touch is always necessary when working with a flexible shaft. If you wish to remove a lot of material quickly, you had better rely on another shop tool.

EQUIPMENT FOR FLEX-SHAFT ENDS

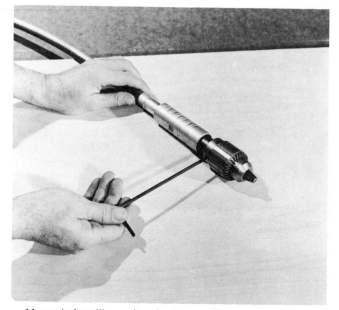

Many shafts will permit a chuck mounting. The chuck may be locked on with a set screw as shown here or it may be designed to screw on.

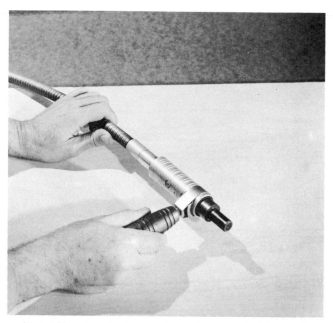

An auxiliary handle to permit two-hand control is excellent to use with a heavy-duty shaft.

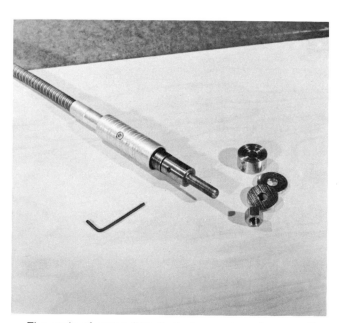

The ends of some flex shafts have arbors for mounting various accessories such as buffs, wire brushes, and grinding wheels. Others have ends designed to accept an adapter so that you can secure items that have a center hole to the adapter with a nut.

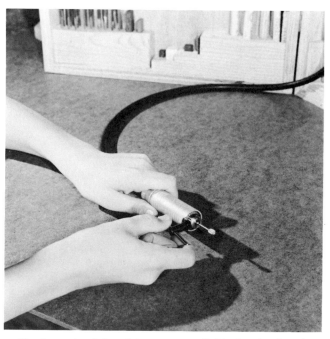

Key-type chuck handpieces are available for the Foredom line of flex shafts. They will grip anything up to $5/32''$ in diameter. Other types have greater capacity but need a variety of collets for full use.

even though there are applications where less speed is more efficient. To give any of these tools a full range of use, you can always work with a rheostat, which is sold as an accessory, for speed control.

Where high speed and a light touch are needed for the job at hand, you may be disappointed if you are running the shaft off a drill press or similar power source. It would be better to buy a complete assembly that includes the shaft and the motor. Some craftsmen even use a motor salvaged from a sewing machine, or some other high-speed universal motor.

Another solution, when you want more speed than the power source can provide, is to buy a special handpiece with a planetary drive which automatically increases the speed at the handpiece to $2\frac{1}{2}$ times the input speed. Thus, for example, if you are driving a shaft at 5,000 rpm's, you'll get 12,500 rpm's at the handpiece. The one shown can be run as high as 35,000 rpm's and can be equipped with collets to take shafts from $\frac{1}{16}''$ to $\frac{1}{4}''$.

With small flex-shaft machines, projects such as carving delicate features, engraving plastics, and drilling hair-size holes can be accomplished.

How to equip yourself. Your interests will, of course, dictate what equipment you choose. For example, if you want to do welding, clean up dents in auto bodies, or apply a satin finish to metals or a sculptured texture to large wood panels, then you want a big, heavy-duty shaft, preferably one driven by its own motor and mounted on a roll-around pedestal (see accompanying plans for making one).

If you are interested in jobs such as carving in various materials, engraving, gunsmithing, model building, jewelery making or polishing, then you should think about a small hand grinder and/or a flex shaft setup, which could be a special power source and flexible shaft tool.

Unique handpiece made by Foredom contains a speed-boosting mechanism that delivers 2½ times the speed of the motor. It will work up to 35,000 rpm's. The handpiece also has a control that lets it slip if it is overloaded.

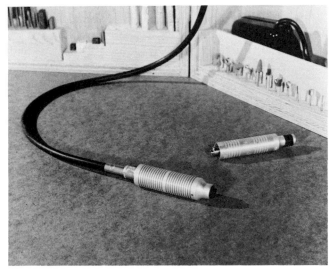

AN ALL-PURPOSE TABLE FOR PORTABLE TOOLS

You can't beat the convenience of portable tools in any work situation where it's better to apply the tool to the job, but the reverse is also true. Quite often it's easier to work more precisely when the tool is stationary and you apply the work to it. With this multi-purpose table, you can convert your portable tools to stationary tools.

Picture the table as a sturdy box with a hinged top. The big 23″ x 23½″ top provides more useful working surface than most 8″ circular saws. It is completely portable; you can set it on a bench or even a pair of saw-horses that are spanned with a sheet of plywood. You can also organize it around a freestanding unit of its own. A system of interchangeable inserts provides for the use of each hand-held power tool.

Most of the construction work can be done with portable tools. Form dadoes with your cutoff saw by setting blade projection to the required depth and make repeat, overlapping passes to achieve the width. A straightedge, clamped to the work, will guide the saw to assure parallel cuts.

For slots, drill a series of overlapping holes on a com-mon center line and then clean up with a file. Internal cutouts are easy to do with a saber saw.

You want to be careful to keep the dadoes in the table top parallel to the table opening and to the table sides. These grooves will be guides for the miter gauge so accuracy of the finished machine relates strongly to the care you use when making it. Since the end result can be a lifetime tool, it pays to use extra time to make it correctly.

Complete all parts for the table saw first; then you can use your new "stationary saw" to speed up the rest of the project. Make a separate insert for each tool you plan to mount, adapting it to accommodate the specific tool. Except for the drill, tools can be easily mounted on the underside of the insert with holes through their base-plates.

Sand all surfaces very smooth and apply several coats of sealer with a rubdown between coats using either very fine sandpaper or steel wool. Stop applying sealer when the surface feels supersmooth to the touch. Then end up with an application of hard paste wax.

Here is the home-made all-purpose table mounted on its own stand. The stand is a commercial unit, but you can easily make your own using 2×4's and plywood.

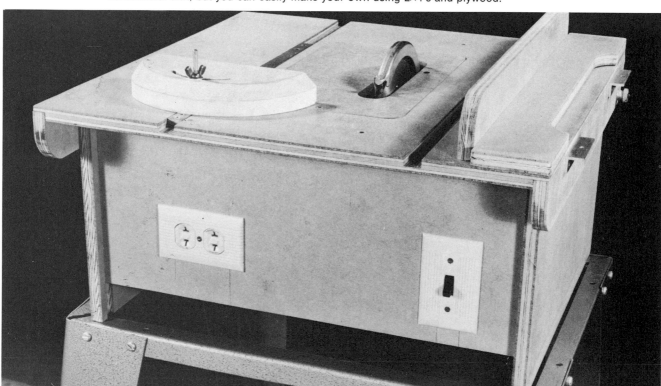

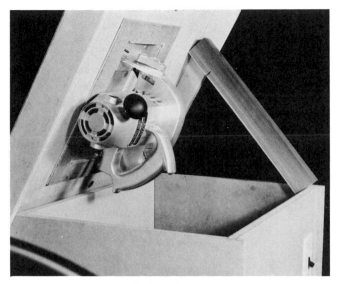

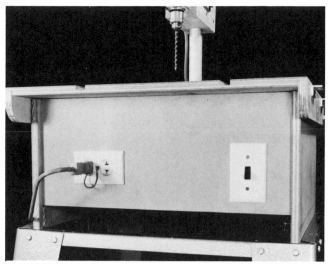

The top of the table pivots on two ¼" bolts for easy mounting of any tool. The stick in the photo is simply a prop to keep the table top up.

The outlet is wired to be controlled by the on-off switch. Tool switches are locked in the "on" position, and the cords are plugged into the outlet. Therefore, you control tool activity with the table switch.

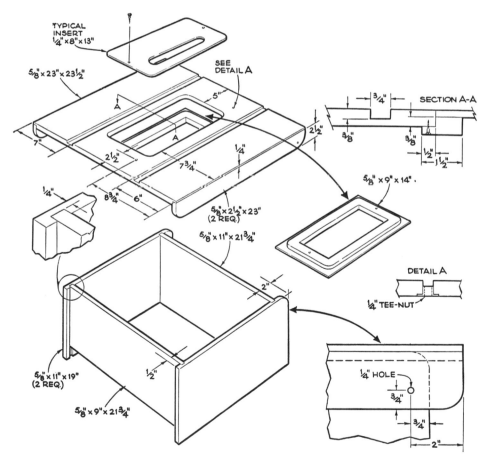

Construction details of the basic table. A hardboard covered plywood is a good choice for material because it takes abuse and will hold up a long time.

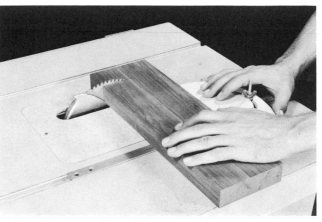

The rip fence is used by setting it parallel to the saw blade and clamping it in place. It becomes a very efficient table saw with a work surface that is larger than those of many of the smaller table saws you can buy.

The miter gauge is used for crosscutting or mitering. If you wish, you can mark the miter-gauge head for various settings. You can even buy a ready-made miter gauge and cut the table slots to suit.

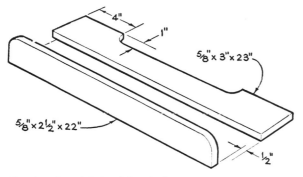

Construction details of the rip fence.

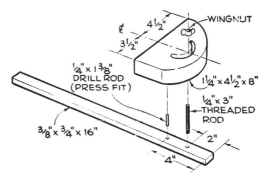

Construction details of the miter gauge.

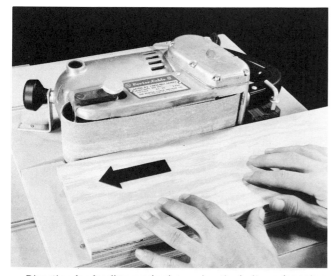

Direction for feeding work when using the belt sander setup is indicated by the arrow. The work should be moved in a direction that is opposite the belt's travel.

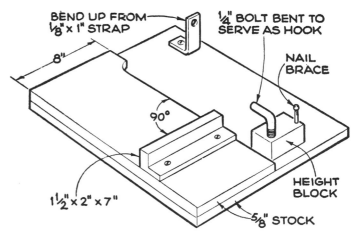

The belt sander has a mounting of its own, but a standard insert can be attached to the underside so the assembly can be fitted easily to the table. Raised work surface follows belt contour for sanding curves. Bend a piece of 1/8" strap steel to the shape shown and drill a hole through the vertical leg to fit the knob-base. You can make the L-shaped holddown from a 1/4" bolt.

The drill press design may have to be modified in some details to fit your drill, but the basic design will work for most models. Shape the front end of the drill mounting block to fit the case of your particular tool. Use a U bolt to hold your drill to the mounting block.

Careful work will assure that the drill bits work parallel to the column, even if you have to use shims between the drill case and the mounting block. Bolts in the linkage should be just tight enough to keep the drill from sliding down due to it's own weight.

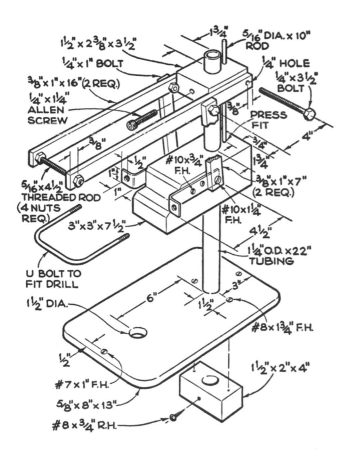

Construction details of the drill press. If you can't find a U-bolt that works correctly for you, you can easily bend one up out of threaded rod. Make the hole in the mounting block so that the column fits in it tightly.

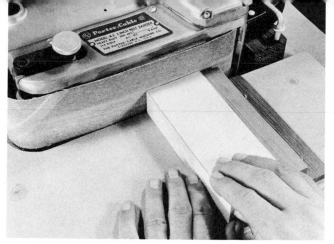

A detachable stop is a valuable addition to the sander setup. Angle between it and the abrasive surface should be 90° so that sanded ends will be square.

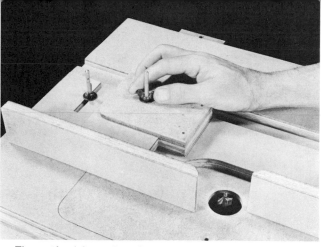

The outfeed fence is adjustable. In a "back" position, it is in line with the infeed fence.

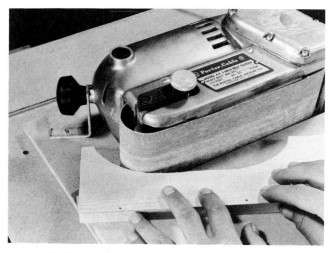

Use the front end of the sander to smooth inside curves.

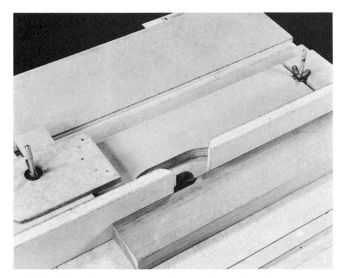

The outfeed fence projects beyond the infeed fence by the depth of the cut to allow for it when the entire edge of the stock is to be removed.

This arrangement for use of the router provides a good shaper setup. The fences are individually adjustable; depth of cut is achieved by working the router's own mechanism, as you would when using it freehand.

Adjust the fence as a unit to set for depth of cut when only a portion of the stock edge is to be removed by the cut.

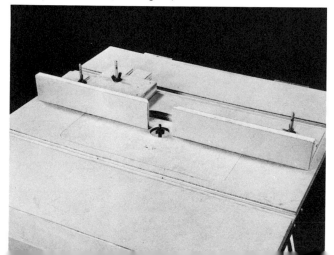

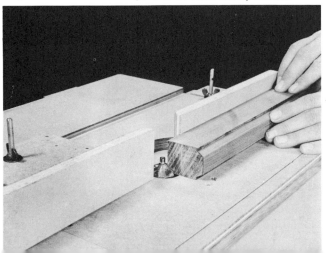

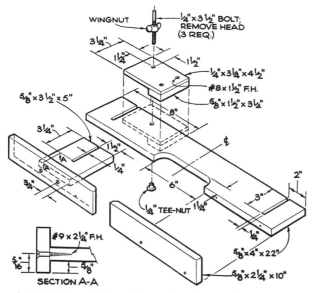

Construction details of the router-shaper setup.

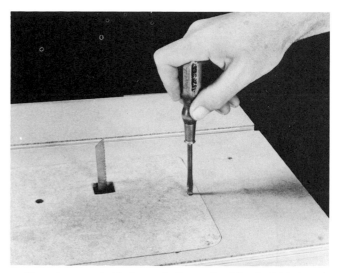

Mounting a portable jigsaw to the underside of a table insert gives you a very efficient stationary saber-sawing setup.

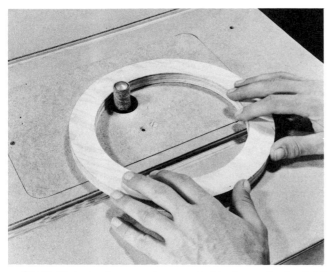

Small drum sanders may be mounted in the router for light sanding jobs; but since the speed of any router is excessive for such work, apply very light pressure. You can experiment with other type cutters, such as burrs and files.

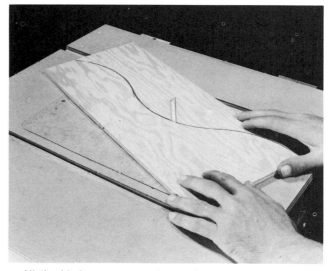

All the blades you normally use in the saber saw can be utilized when the tool is mounted in the table. In this position the blade cuts on the "down" stroke so good side of stock should be facing upwards.

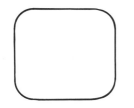

INDEX